الاستنباط من البحر العميق

AL- ISTINBĀTU MIN AL BAHRI AL A'MÌQ

DROPS FROM THE DEEP OCEAN

REFLECTIONS ON THE QUR'AN

Istiqãmah and Tawhid in Ulûhiyyah, Rubûbiyyah and U'bûdiyyah of Allah ﷻ

with a focus on

- ► Contemporary Renderings
- ► Psychological Explorations
- ► Western Discourses
- ► Lexical Analysis

VOLUME 3

Dr. M. Yunus Kumek

Address to the Islamic Religious Scholars & Philosophers

Medina House
publishing

Cover Photo by Y. Kumek, Alexandria, Egypt, January 12, 2019.

Medina House᷍
publishing

www.medinahouse.org
170 Manhattan Ave, Po. Box 63
New York 14215
contact@medinahouse.org

Copyright © 2021 by Medina House᷍ Publishing

ISBN 978-1-950979-27-1

Published in the United States of America.

TABLE OF CONTENTS

VOLUME 3

INTRODUCTION

If there is anything good and beneficial, it is fully from Allah ﷻ. I believe in this fully. If there is anything bad, incorrect, and unpleasant, it is fully from my own nafs. I believe in this fully. My nafs is so raw, rude, and dirty to claim anything good. It constantly takes me to sins, lies, arrogance, harām, and displeasures of Allah ﷻ. Therefore, it will be another lie to claim to itself anything good and beneficial. Especially, this lie is worse than others because it is about the deen of Allah ﷻ. Because of the enormity of this lie, one of the first people to be punished in the ākhirah is a person using the deen to gain fame, position, and other cheap gains as mentioned by the Prophet saw. These people will be the first to be thrown in Jahannam with humiliation. May Allah ﷻ protect me and everyone in this field with the Divine Fadl[1] and Rahmah[2] and have mercy on me and us due to being the followers of Al-Mustafa ﷺ, Al- Habib. That is my and our only hope ﷺ. I myself read the beneficial parts later in these texts to benefit my own raw and rude nafs and I sometimes do not remember who wrote those passages. Being a vehicle is an honor on the path of Allah ﷻ. May Allah ﷻ protect me and us from being the fasiq as the Prophet ﷺ mentions that Allah ﷻ will support this deen with the hand of a fasiq [1] [2].My initial intention in these writings InshAllah was to benefit my own self through the tool of writing. I hope that I still maintain the same intention. I hope the initial intention does not change with other cheap and dirty motivations, or if it does change, it changes to a better one with the Fadl and Rahmah of Allah ﷻ and with the honor of being the follower of Al Mujtaba[3], Al-Murtadha[4], ﷺ Ameen.

---

1. Favor.
2. Mercy.
3. The Elect.
4. The One who is Content.

نبيا و رسولا⁵ ﷺ رضينا بالله ربا و بالإسلام دينا و بمحمد

On a side note, one can ask why sometimes the expression[6] الله اعلم is present and sometimes it is not. In its true reality, in all cases the expression الله اعلم should present. Yet, this should be assumed by the reader. In the cases of the possibly more felt need due to the wrong and misunderstood renderings, the true reality of الله اعلم is emphasized and reminded to the reader, inshAllah.

Yet, in the hadith the first person thrown to Jahannam is to be the person acquiring fame with religious teachings [2] which is petrifying and disabling to all the faculties. When thinking of the shafa'ah[7] of al-Sādiq Al- Amin[8] ﷺ and Fadl and Mercy, and Rahmah of Allah ﷻ, it is the only hope with al-Mu'min ﷻ and the loyal saw who does not forget the dirty ones on that petrifying Day, inshAllah.

---

5. We are pleased with Allah ﷻ as our lord, And Islām as our religion, and Muhammed ﷺ as a prophet and messenger.
6. Allah ﷻ knows the Best.
7. Intercession.
8. The Trustworthy one, The Honest One. ﷺ

WHAT IS THE QURÃN?

It is important to remind ourselves of a few points about the Qurān before we engage ourselves. If we know about the source, the writer, the main content of the text, whether it is fictional or nonfictional, real, original, and authentic, then we can read the text accordingly.

In this case, it is important to know about the existence of different sciences and disciplines emerging around the Qurān.

Recitational Sciences

One of the ways of upholding the Qurān has been through the means of memorization and continuous recitation.

To understand this concept better, one should attend a Qurān competition or watch it on YouTube. In these competitions, young toddlers to children or teenagers to adults are being tested from memory for the correct pronunciation of the letters of the words from the entire text of the Qurān.

In the other words, the judge in the competition recites a few random words from the selection of approximately eighty thousand words, and then the person is required to recite the passages where these words are located correctly and with the correct pronunciation of the letters. This can be amazing, especially for a non-Muslim, but for Muslims this is somewhat common that millions in each generation memorize the Qurān in such a meticulous way with correct pronunciation of the letters.

This discipline is a separate discipline of the Qurān in that there are different specialized schools in correct, full, and engraved memorization (Pakka in Urdu). For example, in these schools, the terms of memorization can vary with just a few mistakes on words on a hundred pages (5 ajza[9]) being called mediocre memorization (Kacha in Urdu). Depending on the school, the students or administrators can let the student go to the next part of the Qurān or they prevent

---

9. Sections.

the student from passing to the next step until those few mistakes in these hundred pages are fixed. The full-time memorization schools can keep the same student from a year to years depending on the student. In these specialized schools, the preferred method of teaching includes having the student stay one or two more years, to engrave the student's memorization further with this already perfect memorization called as dour[10] in Urdu language.

The method of memorization can vary from one culture or country to another. The above descriptive method is based on some of the South Asian (Indo-Pak) cultures [3]. This is only one of the methods of preservation of the Qurãn by millions in each generation since the time of the Prophet ﷺ.

---

10. Revision.

METHODOLOGY (CONTEMPORIZING THE LANGUAGE OF OUR ESTABLISHED USÛL)

One should remember in any of the renderings of the Qurãn one should primarily consider the initial and primary meanings through the methodology of muffasirun. In this methodology, the understanding of riwayah, narrations as explained by Rasulullah saw with their sabab nuzul, and early Salaf of the Sahabah and Tabiu'n precedes the engagements of dirayah, using other analysis in the contexts of intellect, time, and context.

With respect to our Salaf, and the contemporary renderings of literature review, one can update the classical usûl[11] due to the changing times and need. In this new updated methodology, the usûl in derivation of the knowledge and rulings can be والله اعلم:

Primary Usûl

1. The Qurãn
2. The Hadith
3. Primary Ijmã' (Consensus of Early Salaf-Sahabah/Tabi'ûn)
4. Primary Analysis (Qiyãs-Ex: Four Mazhabs: Hanafi, Shãfi, Hanbalì, Malikì)

Secondary Usûl

5. The data from natural and social sciences including culture & context—experts/scholars of natural/social sciences (replacing u'rf in terminology).
6. Secondary Ijmã' (Consensus of Late Pious Scholars)
7. Secondary Analysis

---

11. Fundamentals.

One should remember that the primary usûl overweighs the secondary usûl. The reason of the existence of secondary usûl is to accept the realities of discovered sunnatullah whether we call this sunnatullah as natural or social sciences such as medicine, psychology, anthropology, and others. To give an example for secondary usûl one can consider smoking. First, one can review this case in the lines of primary usûl. Then, one can consider the data from medicine that smoking causes tuberculosis and lung diseases. One can consider late pious scholars if they have valuing system such as makrûh or other categorizations while being aware of this data from medicine. Then, secondary analysis can be made. The results and approaches for secondary analysis Cannot supersede the boundaries and guidelines of primary analysis, primary Ijmā, the hadith and the Qurān.

Among our pious salaf, ijmā or consensus occurred with Guidance, the Fadl[12] and Rahmah[13] of Allah ﷻ handling the same subject matter and coming out with a similar conclusion and forming the ijmā or consensus by different scholars at different times in different regions of the world.

It may be sometimes questionable if each of the pious salaf living at similar times in history or different times in history or generations did have access to the books written by these usuli scholars. In other words, coming to the similar conclusions as called ijmā at similar or different times of history or generations possibly due to not having easy access to the full literature because of the limited tools of communication and publication, these scholars have arrived at similar conclusions with the Guidance, the Fadl, and Rahmah of Allah ﷻ. This is another miracle of the Qurān.

This is another proof of the authenticity of the Qurān with the content and usûl as agreed upon by the salaf. Independent experts at different times in history in different parts of the world reach the same conclusion without having much access to the prior works of the field compared to today.

With today's easily accessible communication tools, one should review the data available in different disciplines with the experts of that field before going to the step of analysis (qiyās). In this updated

---

12. Favor.
13. Mercy,

methodical approach, one should work together with the experts of the field when making analysis. Independent committees working on a subject can establish ijmā or consensus about subject matter. Our accessible communication systems, emerging widely and quickly spreading problems in the matters of the dīn can necessitate this ijmā or consensus methodology during our current times instead of waiting for it to occur over time as has happened in the past. This approach will inshAllah prevent more damages instigated by the Shaytan and their followers.

Including the data as 'urf from natural and social sciences with the experts of the committees in that field before doing the analysis, will fit in better as following the means as a way of showing respect to Allah ﷻ as all the causalities, sciences, and means are created by Allah ﷻ. One can refer to these means as social or natural sciences or 'adatullah or sunnatullah as mentioned in the Qurān. We hope that we follow genuinely and humbly these sunnatullah in order to attract the Fadl and Rahmah of Allah ﷻ on us, Ameen.

When we discuss the disconnection between the academic research and scholarship in practice today, this problem can be valid not only in Islamic sciences but in different fields as well. Today, secular publication curriculums dictated by the state departments especially promote relevance and embodiment of the academic knowledge in practice in order to experience the knowledge. In another perspective, there is an effort to minimize the disconnection between the theory and practice. Yet, the disconnect still exists. The students or seekers of knowledge can still be unmotivated due to this real and existing disconnect.

If we take one example, in academic articles in the fields of social sciences or natural sciences, there is a term, concept, or case that the article revolves around. The whole article tries to support this concept, case, or the term with different perspectives and renderings. When one reviews the Qurān, it is not uncommon to realize in a chapter that there is a key term. Then, this key term is presented in different conjugations of the Arabic language or in different synonyms or other means contextualizing the case and emphasizing this concept in different parts of the surah or even in different parts of the Qurān. The naïve approaches of the uneducated may superficially understand this as mere repetition. Yet, the humble, educated intellectual can correspond these approaches with the new, developing fields of social and natural sciences.

One of the important methodologies of the Qurān teaches us the importance of sabab-I nuzul. This can be translated as contextualization of meanings, theorizations through aqidah (Islamic disciplines of creed), and fiqh (Islamic disciplines of law). The reason especially to emphasize this point is the expectation regarding people of the book as mentioned وَقَالَ الَّذِينَ كَفَرُوا لَوْلَا نُزِّلَ عَلَيْهِ الْقُرْآنُ جُمْلَةً وَاحِدَةً كَذَلِكَ لِنُثَبِّتَ بِهِ فُؤَادَكَ وَرَتَّلْنَاهُ تَرْتِيلًا {الفرقان/32}[14].

One can clearly and amazingly see another miracle of the Qurān with the piece-by-piece revelations, and then rearrangement of these contextualization through as-sababu-nuzûl[15] with their inclusion in surahs and arrangement of these surahs, and final compilation as a book. This is the methodology taught to us by Allah ﷻ.

In today's discipline of social studies, an arguable reality is that everything has a context. From this contextualization, case studies, generalizations, and theories develop to span across space and time. Across the space and time means in this case, across the Arabs, countries, regions, ethnicities, age groups and generations, and centuries. This is a current methodology that our modern scientific academic institution has fully adapted today. Yet, this was there and given to us 1600 years ago by Allah ﷻ.

Yet, in this sense of the methodology, the Qurān breaks the solid boundaries between wahiy, reason, mind, and experience through the methodology of contextualization referred to as sabab nuzûl. In other words, if the Qurān was revealed in a similar way as the Tawrah as tablets as the wahiy, then the mind and experience distinction can be more clearly reflected on the social norms belonging only to those times and spaces of revelation.

Yet, the existence of sabab nuzûl is another proof for the universality, flexibility, adaptability, and contextualization of the Qurān for all times and spaces. There is no book or scripture after the Qurān because there is no need for a new book.

Yet, the Qurān with the as-sababu nuzul[16] builds up all the teachings from real cases with critical thinking, reasoning, experience of mind

---

14. And those who disbelieve say, "Why was the Qurān not revealed to him all at once?" Thus [it is] that We may strengthen thereby your heart. And We have spaced it distinctly.
15. The reason for narration.
16. The reason for narration.

and heart in order to reflect the social norms of relevance in our times and spaces which will be valid until the Day of Judgment, SubhanAllah!

This is amazing! Alhamdulillah!

On another note, as one can start reading the Qurān from Surah Fatiha until the end of Surah Nās, one can clearly realize this continuity in that all the meanings, flow, context, siyaq, sibaq, ayahs, and surahs are bounded together. This is as if it is one nafqah[17]. It is one piece. It is one single time revelation. It is one tablet similar to the Tawrā. It is very difficult to assign these maqta[18] ع (stop signs) differentiating the topics in its true sense. Especially, one can realize this with the notion of baratul-istidlal as a terminology in balagah of the Qurān.

In this context, the words نزّلنا[19] and انزلنا are used in the Qurān indicating a single revelation from Lawhi Mahfuz[20] and the other indicating piece-by-piece revelation of the Qurān with contextualization of human realities.

In other words, contextualization reveals our humanness. As humans, we may have a limited capacity to bear and engage with the Qurān as a whole, entire piece. Allah ﷻ mentions in the Qurān this human reality and their engagement with the Qurān and yet, a person can still have the benefit of the Qurān if he or she reads a few ayahs from the Qurān as mentioned عَلِمَ أَن لَّن تُحْصُوهُ فَتَابَ عَلَيْكُمْ فَاقْرَؤُوا مَا تَيَسَّرَ مِنَ الْقُرْآنِ عَلِمَ أَن سَيَكُونُ مِنكُم مَّرْضَى وَآخَرُونَ يَضْرِبُونَ فِي الْأَرْضِ يَبْتَغُونَ مِن فَضْلِ اللَّهِ وَآخَرُونَ يُقَاتِلُونَ[21] فِي سَبِيلِ اللَّه فَاقْرَؤُوا مَا تَيَسَّرَ مِنْهُ

On the other hand, Allah ﷻ also reminds of the people who are elect but can try to embody the nuzûl of the Qurān as a single piece and they cannot stop reading until they make khatim, finish the Qurān. Rasulullah saw, Osman ra, Imam Abu Hanifah rh, Imam Shafii rh and others as mentioned إِنَّ رَبَّكَ يَعْلَمُ أَنَّكَ تَقُومُ أَدْنَى مِن ثُلُثَيِ اللَّيْلِ وَنِصْفَهُ وَثُلُثَهُ وَطَائِفَةٌ مِّنَ[22]

---

17. One piece.
18. Stop signs.
19. We have sent down.
20. Protected book (i.e. the Qurān).
21. He has known that you [Muslims] will not be able to do it and has turned to you in forgiveness, so recite what is easy [for you] of the Qurān. He has known that there will be among you those who are ill and others traveling throughout the land seeking [something] of the bounty of Allah ﷻ and others fighting for the cause of Allah ﷻ. So recite what is easy from it
22. Indeed, your Lord knows, [O Muhammad ﷺ], that you stand [in prayer] almost two thirds of the night or half of it or a third of it, and [so do] a group of those with you.

الَّذِينَ مَعَكَ. The number of them may not be many but they are associated directly with Rasulullah ﷺ as mentioned with the word مَعَكَ[23].

The full ayah of the above discussion is below as:

إِنَّ رَبَّكَ يَعْلَمُ أَنَّكَ تَقُومُ أَدْنَى مِن ثُلُثَيِ اللَّيْلِ وَنِصْفَهُ وَثُلُثَهُ وَطَائِفَةٌ مِّنَ الَّذِينَ مَعَكَ وَاللَّهُ يُقَدِّرُ اللَّيْلَ وَالنَّهَارَ عَلِمَ أَن لَّن تُحْصُوهُ فَتَابَ عَلَيْكُمْ فَاقْرَؤُوا مَا تَيَسَّرَ مِنَ الْقُرْآنِ عَلِمَ أَن سَيَكُونُ مِنكُم مَّرْضَى وَآخَرُونَ يَضْرِبُونَ فِي الْأَرْضِ يَبْتَغُونَ مِن فَضْلِ اللَّهِ وَآخَرُونَ يُقَاتِلُونَ فِي سَبِيلِ اللَّهِ فَاقْرَؤُوا مَا تَيَسَّرَ مِنْهُ وَأَقِيمُوا الصَّلَاةَ وَآتُوا الزَّكَاةَ وَأَقْرِضُوا اللَّهَ قَرْضًا حَسَنًا وَمَا تُقَدِّمُوا لِأَنفُسِكُم مِّنْ خَيْرٍ تَجِدُوهُ عِندَ اللَّهِ هُوَ خَيْرًا وَأَعْظَمَ أَجْرًا وَاسْتَغْفِرُوا اللَّهَ إِنَّ اللَّهَ غَفُورٌ رَّحِيمٌ[24] {المزمل/20}

One can ask why the Qurān is deemed the greatest miracle of Rasulullah ﷺ?

There are very simple, easy, and straightforward answers for this question.

First, this is the last book of Allah ﷻ. Being the last book requires no need of any other scriptures from Allah ﷻ. If there are no more scriptures from Allah ﷻ, then the Qurān should be preserved, and remain authentic and original until the Day of Judgment. Allah ﷻ promises and gives us the covenant that the Qurān will not change and will be authentic and original until the End of Days. In other words, the preservation of the Qurān is by the Divine Assurance.

One of the reasons for different scriptures being sent by Allah ﷻ is due to the changes and alterations of the original messages in these scriptures. If the Qurān will not be changed and will be authentic, then there is no need for another scripture. The Qurān is fully satisfactory and sufficient.

Second, a miracle as a teaching lasts just a few seconds, a few minutes, hours, or mostly days to bring people back into the realities

---

23. With you.
24. Indeed, your Lord knows, [O Muhammad ﷺ], that you stand [in prayer] almost two thirds of the night or half of it or a third of it, and [so do] a group of those with you. And Allah ﷻ determines [the extent of] the night and the day. He has known that you [Muslims] will not be able to do it and has turned to you in forgiveness, so recite what is easy [for you] of the Qurān. He has known that there will be among you those who are ill and others traveling throughout the land seeking [something] of the bounty of Allah ﷻ and others fighting for the cause of Allah ﷻ. So recite what is easy from it and establish prayer and give zakāh and loan Allah ﷻ a goodly loan. And whatever good you put forward for yourselves—you will find it with Allah ﷻ. It is better and greater in reward. And seek forgiveness of Allah ﷻ. Indeed, Allah ﷻ is Forgiving and Merciful.

of truth. In this sense, miracles from Allah ﷻ can make enormous transformations in people instantly and permanently as one can witness this with magicians going through this change when they encountered the true miracles shown by Musa as mentioned (26 : 46-48) [4].

A Book that is sent from the Creator, original and authentic, and that explains all of our purposes, our selves, knowns and unknowns-then this is a gigantic miracle! When there is a miracle, that does not last for a few seconds, a few minutes or a few days, but lasts a thousand years or until the end of the human journey, then this is in itself an enormous miracle, Rahmah[25], and Fadl[26] from Allah ﷻ.

In other words, if Rasulullah ﷺ is the last messenger of Allah ﷻ until the End of Days, then there should be a teaching or something that would counter this sunnatullah if there is a need. With the Fadl, A'dl[27], and Rahmah of Allah ﷻ, Allah ﷻ gives the Qurān to us as a permanent teacher until the End of Days.

Accessibility of this miracle, and availability of this miracle at all times to everyone is another miracle.

This is all from the Fadl, Tawfiq and Rahmah of Allah ﷻ.

[28]الحمد لله على نعمه الاسلام

---

25. Mercy.
26. Favor.
27. Justice.
28. Praise be to Allah ﷻ for the blessing of Islām.

VOLUME 3

Surah Fatiha

بِسْمِ اللّهِ الرَّحْمَنِ الرَّحِيمِ ²⁹{الفاتحة/1}

الْحَمْدُ لِلّهِ رَبِّ الْعَالَمِينَ ³⁰{الفاتحة/2} الرَّحْمنِ الرَّحِيمِ ³¹{الفاتحة/3} مَلِكِ يَوْمِ الدِّينِ ³²{الفاتحة/4} إِيَّاكَ نَعْبُدُ وإِيَّاكَ نَسْتَعِينُ ³³{الفاتحة/5} اهدِنَا الصِّرَاطَ الْمُسْتَقِيمَ ³⁴{الفاتحة/6} صِرَاطَ الَّذِينَ أَنعَمتَ عَلَيهِمْ غَيرِ الْمَغضُوبِ عَلَيهِمْ وَلَا الضَّالِّينَ ³⁵{الفاتحة/7}

[1-3]

بِسْمِ اللّهِ الرَّحْمَنِ الرَّحِيمِ ³⁶{الفاتحة/1}

الْحَمْدُ لِلّهِ رَبِّ الْعَالَمِينَ ³⁷{الفاتحة/2} الرَّحْمنِ الرَّحِيمِ ³⁸{الفاتحة/3}

After the initial Rahmah as {الفاتحة/1}³⁹ بِسْمِ اللّهِ الرَّحْمَنِ الرَّحِيمِ
Then, the a'zamah⁴⁰ {الفاتحة/2}⁴¹ رَبِّ الْعَالَمِينَ follows. Then, immediately Rahmah follows as {الفاتحة/3}⁴² الرَّحْمنِ الرَّحِيمِ. Because, when one thinks about the A'zamah of Allah as Rabbul A'alamin and مَلِكِ يَوْمِ الدِّينِ⁴³ the person may be crushed in between. Yet, Allah mentions الرَّحْمنِ الرَّحِيمِ, so that as humans of nothingness, we receive the Fadl⁴⁴ and Rahmah⁴⁵ of Allah to exist, to breathe, and to know our Creator and the purpose of our existence.

---

29. In the name of Allah, the Entirely Merciful, the Especially Merciful.
30. [All] praise is [due] to Allah, Lord of the worlds.
31. The Entirely Merciful, the Especially Merciful,
32. Sovereign of the Day of Recompense.
33. It is You we worship and You we ask for help.
34. Guide us to the straight path.
35. The path of those upon whom You have bestowed favor, not of those who have evoked [Your] anger or of those who are astray.
36. [All] praise is [due] to Allah, Lord of the worlds.
37. The Entirely Merciful, the Especially Merciful.
38. The Entirely Merciful, the Especially Merciful.
39. [All] praise is [due] to Allah, Lord of the worlds.
40. Intention.
41. Lord of the worlds.
42. The Entirely Merciful, the Especially Merciful.
43. Sovereign of the Day of Recompense.
44. Favor.
45. Mercy.

2

Surah Baqara

[17]

مَثَلُهُمْ كَمَثَلِ الَّذِي اسْتَوْقَدَ نَاراً فَلَمَّا أَضَاءتْ مَا حَوْلَهُ ذَهَبَ اللّهُ بِنُورِهِمْ وَتَرَكَهُمْ فِي ظُلُمَاتٍ لاَّ يُبْصِرُونَ[46] {البقرة/17}

According to Qatadah (rh) the expression مَثَلُهُمْ كَمَثَلِ الَّذِي اسْتَوْقَدَ نَاراً can indicate La ilaha illa Allah [5].When the munafiqs die, their light that is the effect of La ilaha illa Allah disappear as mentioned with ذَهَبَ اللّهُ بِنُورِهِمْ.

The pronoun هُمْ[47] in the expression بِنُورِهِمْ[48] can allude to the magnitude of their disappointment when their nûr, light, is taken away because when everyone has light and the person is deprived of this ni'mah[49], then the person can be deeper in regret. For example, sometimes there is a power outage. When all the houses have power except this person's house, then he or she can experience more uneasiness. The pronoun هُمْ can indicate these implicit meanings by specifying them in their exclusivity for not benefitting from this widely available nûr of imān available to everyone and yet, they cannot benefit from it, اللهﷺ اعلم[50]

One should remember that in the depictions of the Qurān and hadith, there is no extravagance or exaggeration. In literature, when humans use metaphorical language or parables, they like to exaggerate as much as possible to get attention. Especially, in our current times in the novel writing industry, the writers may not have the concern of being careful about the issues of exaggeration or presenting ungrounded cases because often, the main concern can be completing this book or piece of writing in order to be the best-seller on the market. On the other hand, in Islamic teachings, exaggeration is considered to be lying. Lying is haram and is one of the serious sins.

---

46. Their example is that of one who kindled a fire, but when it illuminated what was around him, Allah ﷺ took away their light and left them in darkness [so] they could not see.
47. Their.
48. Their light.
49. Blessings.
50. Allah ﷺ knows best.

In the expression[51] وَتَرَكَهُمْ فِي ظُلُمَاتٍ لَّا يُبْصِرُونَ[52], both وَتَرَكَهُمْ فِي ظُلُمَاتٍ and لَا يُبْصِرُونَ[53] are complementary to each other and include different possibilities. Because, if they were only in dhulumāt[54], one can ask if they can still see and benefit and get guidance. Then, the answer is "no" with the expression لَا يُبْصِرُونَ. If they cannot see, can they sometimes be in light or guidance? Then, the answer is "no" with the expression وَتَرَكَهُمْ فِي ظُلُمَاتٍ[55].

The word تَرَكَهُمْ[56] can portray the depth of their loneliness. The word[57] فِي in the expression فِي ظُلُمَاتٍ[58] can show that it is as if they are buried in the darkness of a grave, may Allah ﷻ protect us.

In the above example, one can realize that when the Qurān gives examples, it aims at both the logic and emotions. It does not utilize solely logic premises and causality expressions aiming only at the intellect like in the discourses of philosophy, but it also aims at and fulfills the emotions. At the same time, it is not only like a piece of literature aiming at the emotions similar to the styles of novels, but it also aims at and satisfies the intellect. Therefore, people with different levels of education, socio-economic level, gender, ethnic groups, etc., each benefit from the Qurān. An intellectual benefits from the Qurān as well as a layman or a farmer benefits from the Qurān, as mentioned in لَوْ أَنزَلْنَا هَذَا الْقُرْآنَ عَلَى جَبَلٍ لَّرَأَيْتَهُ خَاشِعًا مُّتَصَدِّعًا مِّنْ خَشْيَةِ اللَّهِ وَتِلْكَ الْأَمْثَالُ نَضْرِبُهَا لِلنَّاسِ لَعَلَّهُمْ يَتَفَكَّرُونَ[59] {الحشر/21}.

Sometimes for a layman or learners at different levels at different times in history, places, and contexts, it is difficult to understand the essentials about Allah ﷻ, Uluhiyyah[60], and the realities of the afterlife. Therefore, giving examples can make it easier for everyone to understand.

---

51. And left them in darkness [so] they could not see.
52. And left them in darkness.
53. [So] they could not see.
54. Darkness.
55. And left them in darkness.
56. And {He ﷻ} left them·
57. In.
58. In darkness.
59. If We had sent down this Qurān upon a mountain, you would have seen it humbled and splitting from fear of Allah ﷻ. And these examples We present to the people that perhaps they will give thought.
60. Realm of power.

There are different mental and emotional faculties in a human. One of them is doubt or skepticism. With the coordination of the external elements such as Shaytan and internal elements of nafs, sometimes this notion of doubt can put a curtain on a very clear and explicit reality. In that perspective, the Qurān brings examples to remove skepticism from a person's mind and heart about these very obvious realities.

One should differentiate between the real and image/reflection in similes. In other words, one should remember that in the language of metaphors, examples, or comparisons, one cannot replace the literal with the figurative or the real object with the figurative image. If that differentiation is not made and understood, then one can cause a lot of problems and deviations from the original teachings especially while reviewing and analyzing the scriptures.

Therefore, in English there are words of similarity such as "like and as." If one assumes that they don't exit or skips these little-looking words with big meanings, then the person can make the crucial mistake of replacing the original with something figurative. For example, if someone says, "God is caring and protective like our father," compared to "God is caring and protective, our father." Then, humanization and shirk enter into this presentation clearly, when this very subtle point is missed. Therefore, scholarly (salaf) and canonized (ijmā) approaches are always guidelines to take the person from the drifts of these insignificant-looking, life-threatening points as mentioned وَتِلْكَ الْأَمْثَالُ

نَضْرِبُهَا لِلنَّاسِ وَمَا يَعْقِلُهَا إِلَّا الْعَالِمُونَ [61] {العنكبوت/43}.

In the expression فِي[62] ظُلُمَاتٍ, the word ظُلُمَاتٍ[63] is nakrah. This shows that they did not know this type of dhulumāt, darkness before. In this sense, when something is not known it may have more fear-inducing effects with anxiety and devastation on the person. One can think about a pandemic deadly virus. People don't see it but feel enormously scared and fearful due to its spread. When they can't see it, then it induces more panic and terror. SubhanAllah!, May Allah ﷻ protect us, Ameen!

The expression لَا يُبْصِرُونَ[64] can allude to one of the biggest musibahs, misfortunes, of not seeing it. There is no maful after لَا يُبْصِرُونَ. This can

---

61. And these examples We present to the people, but none will understand them except those of knowledge.
62. In darkness.
63. Darkness.
64. {So} they could not see.

be due to the general problem of their not seeing or understanding. For example, they don't see what is beneficial for them so that they cannot engage themselves. They don't see their friends so they cannot ask for help from them in this darkness. They don't see the dangers so they cannot protect themselves.

One can also analyze the meaning of light as the symbolism of imān. Our perspectives of life through objects, incidents, humans, or engagements come through general feelings and emotions in a person. In this regard, when a person sometimes has the light of imān, the sakina, tranquility, peace, joy, and happiness flow into this person's spiritual faculties and then become represented internally and externally in their emotions and feelings. When there is no imān or no light, then the person becomes immersed in the dark states of kufr within the spiritual states of depression, anxiety, fear, and hopelessness.

When one analyzes this ayah from the perspective of the phenomenon of changing light intensity in a room, this sensation can be the cause of many medical disorders [5] such as migraine, epilepsy, fainting, eye and brain diseases, etc. as mentioned with the current symptomatic diagnosis. In other words, a person's retina can adjust to differentiate some of the objects when staying for some time in a fully dark room. Yet, if the light switch is constantly turned on and off, the neurological motors may not be able to acclimate and focus on the differentiation of the objects but rather preoccupy themselves in order to adapt themselves to this changing light intensity. With these perspectives, one can analyze the grave disturbance of the person as depicted by the illustration in this ayah.

As the light can indicate the imān, the ayah can allude to the *intermittent* exposure of these people with imān. Here, the word intermittent can explain this irregular and on-and-off exposure of theirs to the discourses of the light of imān in their lives. Yet, they followed blindly by imitating their forefathers, cliques, culture, or society without putting forth reason and conscience[65] اعلم الله.

In following their inherited teachings from their forefathers, culture, or society, there can be two perspectives. One is that their forefathers, culture, or society were already misguided, and they continued with this misguidance. For example, أَوْ تَقُولُواْ إِنَّمَا أَشْرَكَ آبَاؤُنَا مِن قَبْلُ وَكُنَّا ذُرِّيَّةً مِّن بَعْدِهِمْ

---

65. Allah ﷻ knows the Best.

لَقَدْ وُعِدْنَا هَذَا نَحْنُ وَآبَاؤُنَا مِن قَبْلُ إِنْ هَذَا ⁶⁶ {الأعراف/174}, or أَفَتُهْلِكُنَا بِمَا فَعَلَ الْمُبْطِلُونَ, or إِلَّا أَسَاطِيرُ الْأَوَّلِينَ ⁶⁷ {النمل/68}. In these cases, they assume their forefathers were in misguidance and they follow their misguided path. So, they want to normalize this in their reasoning. They indulge themselves in mere or blind following without critical thinking.

The other perspective is that their forefathers were in guidance, but they did not follow them. For example, فَخَلَفَ مِن بَعْدِهِمْ خَلْفٌ أَضَاعُوا الصَّلَاةَ وَاتَّبَعُوا الشَّهَوَاتِ فَسَوْفَ يَلْقَوْنَ غَيًّا {مريم/59}. In this case, their forefathers were already in guidance, but they did not follow up on it.

Both cases require critical thinking regarding what they inherit from their forefathers, culture, norms, and society.

It is important to analyze the above cases in relevance to their initial reason of revelation referred to as sabab nuzûl⁶⁸.

There was a group among munāfiq who heard similar teachings from the teachings of Tawrah and Injîl [6]. When the Qurān was revealed with very natural and logical teachings they remembered also the teachings of Tawrah and Injîl. Then, some of their initial forefathers believed but the later ones did not. Or, some believed in the beginning but then, they disbelieved later. This is mentioned as أُوْلَئِكَ الَّذِينَ اشْتَرُوُاْ الضَّلَالَةَ بِالْهُدَى فَمَا رَبِحَت تِّجَارَتُهُمْ وَمَا كَانُواْ مُهْتَدِينَ ⁶⁹ {البقرة/16}. They exchanged guidance for misguidance by their own free choice.

There was another group among them who were expecting the revelation of the Qurān and the coming of the new Prophet saw. After the Qurān was revealed and Rasulullah ﷺ was sent, due to their identity dynamics, they did not want to follow them because the Prophet ﷺ was not from their ethnicity or tribe. Therefore, they opposed him according to Ibn Abbas (RA) and Suddi (RH) [27].

In the examples given in the Qurān, a lot of topics can be presented in one ayah. Although we arrive at immediate meanings, if the same ayah is analyzed for different situations at different times and in different contexts, other meanings can reveal themselves, too.

---

66. Or [lest] you say, "It was only that our fathers associated [others in worship] with Allah ﷻ before, and we were but descendants after them. Then would You destroy us for what the falsifiers have done?"

67. We have been promised this, we and our forefathers, before. This is not but legends of the former peoples."

68. Reason of narration.

69. Those are the ones who have purchased error [in exchange] for guidance, so their transaction has brought no profit, nor were they guided.

One can review this ayah with its initial encounters of revelation during the time of the Prophet in its social, geographical, and contextual norms. For example, consider a person or a few people who are travelling in the desert and may not have guidance or may have lost their way. Then, they can light a fire at night in order to protect themselves from any wild animals or insects. Additionally, it can serve to inform any traveling group in the desert about their existence and their location so that they can find them and help them. Or, it can be to warm themselves up and to see at night in the dark.

These are some literal or external depictions of this case according to the initial encounters with the revelation. One can now try to understand the internal and emotional engagements of these people in the desert depicting and indulging themselves in intense fear, hopelessness, and panic. After this stage, the magnitude and quality of these emotions can now be transformed to another level in order to comprehend the constant psychology of a munāfiq who has the continuous feelings of insecurity, fear, and anxiety.

In another perspective, this ayah can allude to the lower social class of munāfiqeen. One can imagine this in daily small ghetto or street-level interactions among people and the emergence of this group identity among them.

The second group that will be presented in ayahs 19 and 20 can allude to the people who associate themselves with a higher social class among munāfiq. One can see that two different examples can allude to the different groups among munāfiq[70], اعلم الله.

When one analyzes the statement مَثَلُهُمْ كَمَثَلِ الَّذِي اسْتَوْقَدَ نَاراً فَلَمَّا أَضَاءتْ[71] مَا حَوْلَهُ ذَهَبَ اللهُ بِنُورِهِمْ in the ayah, there are two main actions. One is اسْتَوْقَدَ نَاراً[72] by the munāfiqeen and the other is ذَهَبَ اللهُ بِنُورِهِمْ[73] by Allah ﷻ. This can indicate that a person with his or her free choice can choose something and use their inclination to start something as if switching on a button or lighting a fire. This is can be called starting something, or initiation.On the other hand, the execution and the continuity, success, or creation of that inclination, intention, acquirement, or switching it on

---

70. Allah ﷻ knows the Best.
71. Their example is that of one who kindled a fire, but when it illuminated what was around him, Allah ﷻ took away their light
72. Kindled a fire.
73. Allah ﷻ took away their light.

at all depends on the Mashiyyah[74] of Allah ﷻ. In other words, although the person wants to do something, if Allah ﷻ does not want that, then this will not be created and given to this person by Allah ﷻ. If someone tries to start something but it is not successful or does not continue, we may say "there is no barakah[75] in it." In other words, having barakah or blessing or not achieving the accomplishment can possibly indicate Divine Intervention or Mashiyyah. There are exceptions to this notion as in the cases of istidraj meaning that Allah ﷻ sometimes enables people with what they think that they want as a type of test or trial.

At another level, this ayah can indicate two different processes. One is starting up something as mentioned in[76] اسْتَوْقَدَ نَارًا and the other is maintaining or sustaining it as mentioned in[77] ذَهَبَ أللهُ بِنُورِهِمْ. In other words, humans are given the ability to start something with اسْتَوْقَدَ نَارًا with their free choice given to them by Allah ﷻ. Yet, for this start-up process, the human's lifespan is 60-70 years on average. The person does not have the means in his or her creation lifespan to maintain what they started because of their limited time. Therefore, the true Rabb, Care Taker and Maintainer of something, the systems, the universe, and social events and actions over generations through the eras of history is Allah ﷻ as implied with ذَهَبَ أللهُ بِنُورِهِم[78]. Then, one can ask: What makes something successful over the years throughout generations, eras, and history that it becomes sustainable? The answer is the Mashyiyyah[79], the Fadl[80], Rahmah[81] and Tawfiq[82] of Allah ﷻ. When Allah ﷻ wants, then Islam spreads from a desert to all of the world through one person, Rasulullah ﷺ, and now, has nearly two billion followers. When Allah ﷻ has the Mashiyyah, the Qurān is preserved and read by the Muslims and is one of the most read books in human history. When Allah ﷻ gives the tawfiq for a writing or a teaching, then for example, a 12th-century piece, such as Imam Ghazali's writings remain widely studied even today.

---

74. Permission.
75. Blessing.
76. Kindled a fire.
77. Allah ﷻ took away their light.
78. Allah ﷻ took away their light.
79. Permission.
80. Favor.
81. Mercy.
82. Reconcile.

On the other hand, there were a lot of good or evil-seeming start-up initiatives that took place throughout history, but some continued and some faded away as Allah ﷻ showed the Mashiyyah or not as expressed with ذَهَبَ أَلله بِنُورِهِم [83]. A similar expression with the word ذَهَبَ[84] is used in the following ayahs as لَذَهَبَ بِسَمْعِهِمْ وَأَبْصَارِهِمْ إِنَّ الله عَلَى كُلّ شَيْءٍ قَدِيرٌ [85] {البقرة/20}.

It is important to remember that a person must not mix his or her role with what Allah ﷻ decrees. Our goal is to strive for the good to please Allah ﷻ by constantly asking and begging for the Fadl[86], Rahmah[87] and Tawfik[88] of Allah ﷻ about these good-seeming endeavors of ours. It is not our job to decide on the sustainability of our endeavors, but to work towards them by fulfilling these means. Yet, at the same time, constantly asking, begging, and crying to Allah ﷻ that hopefully, we are pleasing Allah ﷻ in our engagements and not displeasing Allah, inshAllah.

اللهم اجعلنا على الصراط الذين انعمت عليهم انعمت عليهم غير المغضوب عليهم و لا الضالين. امين [89].
The expression[90] ذَهَبَ أَلله بِنُورِهِم can also indicate a response against the stance of mutazilah that they give full effect to the reason and causality. One can see that, as in this case, if Allah ﷻ does not want something to happen, then it does not happen. Although the munāfiqeen tried to start up something, it did not continue. Allah ﷻ prevented their evil with the Fadl[91] and Rahmah[92].

The last expression وَتَرَكَهُمْ فِي ظُلُمَاتٍ لاَ يُبْصِرُونَ[93] {البقرة/17} can indicate all of these emotional renderings of fear, anxiety, depression, panic, and distress. At the same time, it can indicate the intellectual and physical renderings of incapacity, inability, ineffectiveness, weakness, and failure.

In another perspective, when one analyzes this ayah one can discover an interesting psychological trait of human beings. When a person is already weak and incapacitated, then at this point, the person makes a

---

83. Allah ﷻ took away their light.
84. Taken away.
85. He could have taken away their hearing and their sight. Indeed, Allah ﷻ is over all things competent.
86. Favor.
87. Mercy.
88. Reconcile.
89. Oh Allah ﷻ make us on the path of those upon whom You have bestowed favor, not of those who have evoked [Your] anger or of those who are astray.
90. Allah ﷻ took away their light.
91. Favor.
92. Mercy.
93.

move to correct his or her position or to get some empowerment. Now, with this move, his or her situation gets worse. This person ultimately feels regret from this attempt. Then, the person becomes indulged in very dark and convoluted disappointments and depression. One can draw out these meanings from the above example of the person traveling with all of these weaknesses and unknowns who then lit a fire but this only increases the depression in the current state of this person.

In the expression مَثَلُهُمْ كَمَثَلِ الَّذِي[94], the sila word الَّذِي[95] is expressed in singular form instead of plural form الَّذِينَ[96] although the munāfiqeen were not one person but more. Yet, this can possibly indicate their disposition with a selfish attitude that each person really was and is concerned about their own selves. Being in a group necessitates sacrifice, having community-mindedness and social or group concerns to maintain the unit. Yet, the munāfiqeen are deprived of these traits as well.

This individualist or selfish approach as mentioned with the sila word الَّذِي instead of the sila word الَّذِينَ can also be due to not being able to identify themselves in darkness as described in the example in the ayah. For example, when a few people want to form a jama'ah[97] to pray in a dark room, if they cannot see each other and if they cannot identify the qibla, then it is very difficult for them to unite and form a jama'ah to turn to the same qibla, direction. Similarly, if the munāfiqeen are in darkness, in reality, they cannot truly unite and form a jama'h for the same goal, yet everyone may be worried about their own selfish interests as mentioned with the singular sila word الَّذِي instead of the plural sila word of الَّذِينَ[98], والله اعلم.

The word[99] مَا حَوْلَهُ can indicate that if or when they start a fitnah, their fitnah can be limited and confined only to their surroundings.

In the expression وَتَرَكَهُمْ فِي ظُلُمَاتٍ[100], the word ظُلُمَاتٍ[101] can indicate that they are in multiple psychological depressive states of fear, anxiety, insecurity, paranoia, suspicion, and distrust. The word تَرَكَهُمْ[102] can

---

94. Their example is that of one who.
95. The one who.
96. Those who.
97. Congregation.
98. Allah ﷻ knows best.
99. What was around him.
100. And left them in darkness.
101. Darkness.
102. Left them.

amplify this effect when they know and realize that no one can help them with these piles of darkness of depressive states.

One can realize that the expression {البقرة/17} لاَّ يُبْصِرُونَ[103] can include the future. In other words, they may not be physically blind nor sustain blindness but real vision or perception necessitates understanding through the heart and mind. To support this stance, the ayah أَفَلَمْ يَسِيرُوا فِي الْأَرْضِ فَتَكُونَ لَهُمْ قُلُوبٌ يَعْقِلُونَ بِهَا أَوْ آذَانٌ يَسْمَعُونَ بِهَا فَإِنَّهَا لَا تَعْمَى الْأَبْصَارُ وَلَكِن تَعْمَى الْقُلُوبُ الَّتِي فِي الصُّدُورِ[104] {الحج/46} can allude to these type of cases.

In the expression مَثَلُهُمْ كَمَثَلِ الَّذِي اسْتَوْقَدَ نَاراً[105] can indicate something similar to turning on light which can have some virtuous meanings. Or, it can also mean to light a fire which can have evil meanings for other cases. Similarly, the genuine teachings of the religion can be hidayah[106] for believers and misguidance for munāfiqeen. In both cases, it is up to the user how they want to use their free will to take a position and execute an action. For example, someone can use the fire to do something virtuous and beneficial. Or, he or she can use it to harm their own self and others. Similarly, a person can benefit from the Qurān and the teachings of the Prophet saw both in this dunya and in the ākhirah. Or, he or she can destroy both his dunya and ākhirah, thinking that he or she is doing something good, as mentioned

خَسِرَ الدُّنْيَا وَالْآخِرَةَ ذَلِكَ هُوَ الْخُسْرَانُ الْمُبِينُ[107] {الحج/11}

الَّذِينَ آتَيْنَاهُمُ الْكِتَابَ يَعْرِفُونَهُ كَمَا يَعْرِفُونَ أَبْنَاءهُمُ الَّذِينَ خَسِرُواْ أَنفُسَهُمْ فَهُمْ لاَ يُؤْمِنُونَ[108] {الأنعام/20}

أُوْلَئِكَ الَّذِينَ خَسِرُواْ أَنفُسَهُمْ وَضَلَّ عَنْهُم مَّا كَانُواْ يَفْتَرُونَ[109] {هود/21} لَا جَرَمَ أَنَّهُمْ فِي الآخِرَةِ هُمُ الأَخْسَرُونَ[110] {هود/22}

---

103. They could not see.
104. So have they not traveled through the earth and have hearts by which to reason and ears by which to hear? For indeed, it is not eyes that are blinded, but blinded are the hearts which are within the breasts.
105. Their example is that of one who kindled a fire.
106. Guidance.
107. He has lost [this] world and the Hereafter. That is what is the manifest loss.
108. Those to whom We have given the Scripture recognize it as they recognize their [own] sons. Those who will lose themselves [in the Hereafter] do not believe.
109. Those are the ones who will have lost themselves, and lost from them is what they used to invent.
110. Assuredly, it is they in the Hereafter who will be the greatest losers.

قُلْ هَلْ نُنَبِّئُكُمْ بِالْأَخْسَرِينَ أَعْمَالًا ¹¹¹ {الكهف/103} الَّذِينَ ضَلَّ سَعْيُهُمْ فِي الْحَيَاةِ الدُّنْيَا وَهُمْ يَحْسَبُونَ أَنَّهُمْ يُحْسِنُونَ صُنْعًا¹¹² {الكهف/104}

The position of a munāfiq is more devastating than the position of a kafir. A munāfiq uses the religion to destroy himself or herself and others. Kafir does not use the religion but uses his or her own ego to destroy oneself and others. Both are losers.

As mentioned before, munāfiqeen lit the fire of fitnah. Yet, Rasulullah ﷺ turns on the light of imān with Islam.

May Allah ﷻ protect us for the sake of surah Al-Asr so that we are not also one of the losers, al-khafirun:

بِسْمِ اللهِ الرَّحْمَنِ الرَّحِيمِ¹¹³

وَالْعَصْرِ ¹¹⁴ {العصر/1} إِنَّ الْإِنْسَانَ لَفِي خُسْرٍ ¹¹⁵{العصر/2} إِلَّا الَّذِينَ آمَنُوا وَعَمِلُوا الصَّالِحَاتِ وَتَوَاصَوْا بِالْحَقِّ وَتَوَاصَوْا بِالصَّبْرِ ¹¹⁶{العصر/3}

Ameen.

[18]

صُمٌّ بُكْمٌ عُمْيٌ فَهُمْ لَا يَرْجِعُونَ ¹¹⁷{البقرة/18}

This ayah summarizes their disposition in a dense form after the previous ayah. This is the depressive, dark, gloomy, and miserable picture of nifāq. Later in the Sûrah, the stance of kafir is presented in a similar way in their kufr as وَمَثَلُ الَّذِينَ كَفَرُواْ كَمَثَلِ الَّذِي يَنْعِقُ بِمَا لَا يَسْمَعُ إِلَّا دُعَاء وَنِدَاء صُمٌّ بُكْمٌ عُمْيٌ فَهُمْ لَا يَعْقِلُونَ ¹¹⁸{البقرة/171}.

---

111. Say, [O Muhammad ﷺ], "Shall we [believers] inform you of the greatest losers as to [their] deeds?
112. [They are] those whose effort is lost in worldly life, while they think that they are doing well in work."
113. In the name of Allah ﷻ, The Entirely Merciful, The Especially Merciful.
114. By time.
115. Indeed, mankind is in loss.
116. Except for those who have believed and done righteous deeds and advised each other to the truth and advised each other to patience.
117. Deaf, dumb and blind—so they will not return [to the right path].
118. The example of those who disbelieve is like that of one who shouts at what hears nothing but calls and cries [i.e., cattle or sheep]—deaf, dumb and blind, so they do not understand.

In both cases of kafir and munāfiq, they have the shared traits and outcomes of صُمٌّ بُكْمٌ عُمْيٌ[119]. Yet, in the case of munāfiqeen, they cannot go back to their original, true, and natural disposition of a sincere, honest, and truthful stance as mentioned with {البقرة/18} لاَ يَرْجِعُونَ[120]. When one analyzes the ayah endings about munāfiqun in Surah Munāfiq, it is interesting to realize these supporting dispositions for their case as, فَهُمْ لاَ يَعْلَمُونَ[124] {المنافقون/8} and لاَ يَفْقَهُونَ[121] {المنافقون/3}, لاَ يُفْقَهُونَ[122] {المنافقون/7}[123].

In the case of kafirs, they have the opportunity of being in the correct, authentic, and original stance by being followers of Rasulullah ﷺ and yet, they don't use their intellect as mentioned with {البقرة/171} لاَ يَعْقِلُونَ[125].

In both cases, they have the opportunity. Everyone receives different forms of data to click on with their free will in themselves for the initial step of recognition and appreciation of Allah ﷻ. This can be called imān. This data can come to the person through different signs from all around in one's surroundings. Today, we can call this natural and social sciences. Secondly, this data can come to the person directly from the Qurān and the Prophet ﷺ in a very clear and unambiguous way. This is the direct revelation from Allah ﷻ for this person about their search and questions. In addition, this data can come to the person through inner feelings and emotions. This can be called conscience, guiding the person if this faculty of a person is not dead.

Now, some people may not be at this level of feeling a need for this type of search. They can be in the mode of heedlessness or "I don't care." Yet, the wisdom of evil-seeming incidents, trials, tests, or difficulties can be considered a wake-up call for this person to realize this need and to move on to their real purpose.

At another level, the difference between a kafir and munāfiq is similar to two cars. One ignites the car and moves on after recognizing the imān and excels in its true application with the teachings of the Qurān and Sunnah. This can be similar to the situation of a kafir then becoming a Muslim. At the time of the Prophet (ﷺ), there were a lot of people who gave a very difficult time to the Prophet and Muslims with

---

119. Deaf, dumb, and blind.
120. The will not return. {to the right path}.
121. So they do not understand.
122. They do not understand.
123. They do not understand.
124. So they do not know.
125. Understand.

their kufr in Makkah. Later, at the time of hudaybiyah, the same people recognized their prior wrong stance and became Muslim [8].

The other can be similar to a car among many other moving cars but this car in particular does not move. The person does not put in any effort to start the car. Due to the relativity effect in physics [9],this person looks at other cars and sees that all are moving and then, thinks that his or her car is moving as well. This is similar to a munāfiq. This person is among Muslims. Yet, he or she does not put in an effort for a true and genuine imān, اعلم الله[126]. Therefore, this person is in the position of مُذَبْذَبِينَ

.بَيْنَ ذَلِكَ لاَ إِلَى هَؤُلاء وَلاَ إِلَى هَؤُلاء وَمَن يُضْلِلِ اللّهُ فَلَن تَجِدَ لَهُ سَبِيلاً [127] {النساء/143}

The opposite of this ayah can indicate that if they used their hearing, seeing, talking, and understanding faculties, then they could have been genuinely guided, . اعلم الله Since they lost all these abilities they have now become hopeless as mentioned فَهُمْ لَا يَرْجِعُونَ[128]. It is interesting that the ayah starts with صُمٌّ[129] instead of other possible qualities of a human being.

Perhaps, if they listened to the internal and external signs that were constantly being sent to them by Allah ﷻ as mentioned with[130] صُمٌّ, then they would not be munāfiq, اعلم الله[131]. Then, they would use their tongue to make tawbah[132] and istighfar but they did not as mentioned بُكْمٌ[133].

Along the same lines, if they used their ability of seeing and took heed of what they saw, developed imān, and maintained this imān as mentioned with عُمْيٌ[134], then they would not be munāfiq, اعلم الله[135]. The opposite case is presented as لَقَدْ كُنتَ فِي غَفْلَةٍ مِّنْ هَذَا فَكَشَفْنَا عَنكَ غِطَاءكَ فَبَصَرُكَ الْيَوْمَ حَدِيدٌ[136] {ق/22}. In the ākhirah, the person has the certainty of seeing and understanding all of the realities. This can be the case for some people in this dunya. Allah ﷻ can remove the veils of some individuals close to Allah ﷻ up to a degree in this dunya before they die as well, الله اعلم.

With all of these actions of their hearing, speaking, and seeing faculties, they could have made tawbah and turned back to Allah ﷻ. Yet, they did not as the last phrase فَهُمْ لَا يَرْجِعُونَ[137] can indicate. Especially, this natural causative outcome is presented with the connector فَ[138].

When one reviews this ayah with the previous ayah, it is always possible to derive different human psychological engagements that are applicable to our time. For example, if a person wants to travel, he or she sets on a journey at night. After a while on the highway in the middle of night, the person may want to talk to someone on the phone so that he is not alone because he is bored and that one can listen to him even though it can be an idle or useless talk. He starts dialing his cell phone but no one answers to chat that late at night, and this can allude to صُمٌّ[139]. In the middle of night, being lonely, he now gives up the hope of talking to someone. After a while of trying to dial on the phone, he loses his energy and motivation even to talk people and now prefers silence. This can allude to بُكْمٌ[140]. After a while of silence, not talking or hearing from anyone, now the person becomes sleepy and starts daydreaming while driving on the highway. He startles and wakes up with fear with the veering of the car to the side of the road and onto the shoulder. After a while again he falls asleep while driving and wakes up startled and this continues. This can allude to عُمْيٌ[141].

After this painful and scary driving, with all the feelings and emotions, then he says to himself, "Maybe I should go back to my home, have a good sleep, and go another time to my destination." But now, he already drove some time, and he does not find the energy in himself and the to go back his home as mentioned فَهُمْ لَا يَرْجِعُونَ[142].

Now, one can really try to embody the emotional and psychological pain of this person. In the middle of night, he does not know where he is. He cannot ask for any help. He is by himself. He does not know the town or the people of this town. He does not have energy or stamina to

---

137. So they will not return.
138. So.
139. Deaf.
140. Dumb.
141. Blind.
142. So they will not return.

go back. SubhanAllah! The Qurān depicts the psychology of a munāfiq as a constant disposition with these feelings in his or her life. What a torture! May Allah ﷻ protect us, Ameen.

One can argue that these are all perspectives of a person. In other words, if a person has a good perspective of life, then he or she can have a good life. If a person has a bad perspective, then accordingly he or she may suffer. That is right, but this perspective is built up in its true sense with imān. In other words, people who don't have true imān can seem to have a good perspective in life up to a point, but then an evil-seeming incident can come hit them and knock them down. The person cannot find the stamina to get back up again. As the Prophet saw mentions, the example of a kafir is an old tree who is not affected and seems tough and sustainable with their principles. Yet, a strong wind can blow against this tree, and knock down the tree, and the tree is dead now. An example of a believer is a young tree who can bend with winds but comes back to its original position at the end.

A true imān builds up the good perspective with stamina in the person with worship, humbleness, and knowledge. When one analyzes the Qurān, the teachings of the Prophet ﷺ, and the teachings of the salaf[143] derived from these two main sources, one can clearly and undoubtedly realize that all of these teachings are building up a true imān in a person so that the person can still maintain a good perspective in life depending on the time, context, and location.

The expression لَا يَرْجِعُونَ[144] can possibly indicate different levels at different perspectives. For example, after being a munāfiq, it can mean that a person cannot go back to the original essence of their fitrah. Or, they cannot go back to their prior beliefs once they know the teachings of Islam and that Islam makes perfect sense yet still, they don't want to accept and follow it due to different motives such as arrogance or identity issues. Or, they cannot go back to the times when they were expecting a messenger from their own group but since it did not happen, these hopes are all gone.

One can compare and review the expressions لَا يَرْجِعُونَ as in the case of this ayah compared to لَن يَرْجِعُونَ[145]. In the case of لَا يَرْجِعُونَ, there can be still some hope for them if they use their free will with their intention

---

143. Pious predecessors.
144. They will not return.
145. They will never return.

and inclination. In the case of يَرْجِعُونَ لن, there is no way or they will never be able to go back. With the Fadl[146] and Rahmah[147] of Allah ﷻ, this expression لن يَرْجِعُونَ is not used in this ayah. Yet, there is still chance for the munāfiqeen to make tawba[148] before they die. In this expression of لَا يَرْجِعُونَ but not presented as لن يَرْجِعُونَ, the importance of a human's free will is emphasized, الله اعلم.

It is interesting to realize one of the intrinsic linguistic qualities in صُمٌّ بُكْمٌ عُمْيٌ فَهُمْ لَا يَرْجِعُونَ {البقرة/18}[149]. Arabic is a language where there are both male and female attachments to each noun. In this case, the plural forms of both female and male are the same for the words[150] صُمٌّ بُكْمٌ عُمْيٌ. This can indicate that there is no difference of gender identity in the personality traits. These traits can be good or bad. In other words, one's value in Islam is according to one's character traits and not according to one's gender. The first and foremost important trait is gratefulness, gratitude, and thankfulness to one's Creator Who is Allah ﷻ. This gratitude in the form of recognition and appreciation can be called imān. The continuation of this trait is established by constant reminder of this required disposition of gratefulness and appreciation to Allah ﷻ by five-times prayers.

[19-20]

أَوْ كَصَيِّبٍ مِّنَ السَّمَاء فِيهِ ظُلُمَاتٌ وَرَعْدٌ وَبَرْقٌ يَجْعَلُونَ أَصْابِعَهُمْ فِي آذَانِهِم مِّنَ الصَّوَاعِقِ حَذَرَ الْمَوْتِ واللّهُ مُحِيطٌ بِالْكَافِرِينَ {البقرة/19}[151] يَكَادُ الْبَرْقُ يَخْطَفُ أَبْصَارَهُمْ كُلَّمَا أَضَاء لَهُم مَّشَوْاْ فِيهِ وَإِذَا أَظْلَمَ عَلَيْهِمْ قَامُواْ وَلَوْ شَاء اللّهُ لَذَهَبَ بِسَمْعِهِمْ وَأَبْصَارِهِمْ إِنَّ اللّه عَلَى كُلِّ شَيْءٍ قَدِيرٌ {البقرة/20}[152]

With the methodology of tafsir (usul), one can analyze the above ayah alongside the previous and following ayahs as well as locate the meanings

---

146. Favor.
147. Mercy.
148. Repentance.
149. They are deaf, dumb, and blind so they will not return {to the right path}.
150. Deaf, dumb, and blind.
151. Or [it is] like a rainstorm from the sky within which is darkness, thunder and lightning. They put their fingers in their ears against the thunderclaps in dread of death. But Allah ﷻ is encompassing of the disbelievers.
152. The lightning almost snatches away their sight. Every time it lights [the way] for them, they walk therein; but when darkness comes over them, they stand [still]. And if Allah ﷻ had willed, He could have taken away their hearing and their sight. Indeed, Allah ﷻ is over all things competent.

by analyzing the entire Qurān as well as the traditions of Hadith and literature of tafsir. At the same time, one can analyze the sentences, phrases, and words in the above ayahs by localizing them.

One can realize that the above ayahs continue on about the inner psychological renderings of munāfiqeen. It is interesting to note that the Qurān makes itnāb, a detailed explanation about their case.

The word[153] صَيِّب can indicate something that afflicts the person. The word musibah is derived from the same word. In its contextual meaning, it can mean something coming or pouring from the sky above down upon the earth. This can indicate rain. In this case, صَيِّب being nakrah can indicate a large amount of rain as if it is pouring rain.

This word also can indicate the source of what is coming. In this case, the word can refer to clouds.

To include these meanings within the context of the ayah, this word is translated in English translations of the Qurān either as rainstorm [1] [2] or cloudburst [3], a sudden rainstorm. This rendering in translations is due to the following expression فِيهِ ظُلُمَاتٌ[154] which can indicate the piles of clouds about to storm. To support this disposition of the translation, the word صَيِّب is mentioned as nakrah. The indication of the vast occupancy of the sky with clouds as nakrah can indicate abundance in quantity.

If one reviews the word صَيِّب implicitly with the meanings of musibah, this can indicate the amount of depression that munāfiqeen go through. In this case, the expression فِيهِ ظُلُمَاتٌ explains these dark depressive states further.

The expression مِّنَ السَّمَاء[155] can indicate ta'keed in directionality. To express this directionality, anything that is above the person can be considered السَّمَاء[156]. This can be relative. For example, for us clouds can be in the السَّمَاء. For the clouds, things in outer space can be السَّمَاء such as the moon being in the السَّمَاء.

At another level, the word السَّمَاء can indicate the notion of respect, awe, and elevation embedded in directionality with our humanly renderings. For example, Allah ﷻ is beyond the directions. Yet, we open our hands towards السَّمَاء when we make dua. This shows respect

---

153. Rainstorm.
154. Within which is darkness.
155. From the sky.
156. The sky.

with the notion of directionality[157], الله اعلم. Similar notion is imbedded when we turn towards the direction of Ka'abah (qiblah). Yet, Allah ❧ is beyond the directions. These can be considered as part of the shia'r to be respected, practiced, and implemented as performed by Rasulullah ﷺ. In this perspective, following Rasulullah ﷺ becomes utmost critical to understand the boundaries of this shia'r so that the person does not swing between the two extremes of ifrād and tafrîd.

On another perspective, when one reviews the ayah وَيَوْمَ تَشَقَّقُ السَّمَاء بِالْغَمَامِ وَنُزِّلَ الْمَلَائِكَةُ تَنزِيلًا [158] {الفرقان/25}, this ayah can indicate another perspective for the word السَّمَاء as mentioned in the ayahs وَجَعَلْنَا السَّمَاء سَقْفًا مَّحْفُوظًا وَهُمْ عَنْ آيَاتِهَا مُعْرِضُونَ [159] {الأنبياء/32} and {الطور/5} وَالسَّقْفِ الْمَرْفُوعِ [160]. In these perspectives, السَّمَاء is a protected ceiling, yet when the time comes in Qiyamah, this ceiling can collapse or be destroyed as mentioned in وَيَوْمَ تَشَقَّقُ السَّمَاء بِالْغَمَامِ [161].

One can review other ayahs of the Qurān about sama as: الَّذِي جَعَلَ لَكُمُ الأَرْضَ فِرَاشاً وَالسَّمَاء بِنَاء وَأَنزَلَ مِنَ السَّمَاء مَاء فَأَخْرَجَ بِهِ مِنَ الثَّمَرَاتِ رِزْقاً لَّكُمْ فَلاَ تَجْعَلُواْ لِلّهِ أَندَاداً وَأَنتُمْ تَعْلَمُونَ [162] {البقرة/22}

هُوَ الَّذِي خَلَقَ لَكُم مَّا فِي الأَرْضِ جَمِيعاً ثُمَّ اسْتَوَى إِلَى السَّمَاء فَسَوَّاهُنَّ سَبْعَ سَمَاوَاتٍ وَهُوَ بِكُلِّ شَيْءٍ عَلِيمٌ [163] {البقرة/29}

One can refer to the tafasir for the different renderings of السَّمَاء[164]. Analyzing the verses of the Qurān only around the word السَّمَاء can be a separate volume of a book especially when one engages with tafāsir, hadith, the updated scientific discoveries, and different sciences in natural sciences, humanities, and social sciences.

If one can pronounce the word رَعْدٌ[165] with its correct makhraj and intoning, one can really feel a roaring sound similar to a thunder mimicking the loudness with the sound of ر with a full mouth, with

---

157. Allah ❧ knows the Best.
158. And [mention] the Day when the heaven will split open with [emerging] clouds, and the angels will be sent down in successive descent.
159. And We made the sky a protected ceiling, but they, from its signs, are turning away.
160. And [by] the ceiling [i.e., heaven] raised high.
161. And [mention] the Day when the heaven will split open with [emerging] clouds.
162. [He] who made for you the earth a bed [spread out] and the sky a ceiling and sent down from the sky, rain and brought forth thereby fruits as provision for you. So do not attribute to Allah ❧ equals while you know [that there is nothing similar to Him].
163. It is He who created for you all of that which is on the earth. Then He directed Himself to the heaven, [His being above all creation], and made them seven heavens, and He is Knowing of all things.
164. The sky.
165. Thunder.

piercing sound effects of غ, and a sharp ending and echoing sounds in the ear of د which is a letter of qalqala as explained in detail in the science of pronunciation called tajwid. As a miracle of the Qurān, the words in the Qurān embody the explained meanings when they are pronounced with the correct makhraj and tajwid of the sciences of pronunciation and intoning.

The word[166] بَرْقٌ can refer to lightning. As it can refer to the light that is appearing in this process, it can also refer the quickness of this event. The name of the carrier of Rasulullah ﷺ during miraj was Buraq [4] which has the same root word with بَرْقٌ.

It is interesting to realize that the words رَعْدٌ وَبَرْقٌ[167] have وَ, harf-atf. This can indicate that the sound and lightning are not in a causality relationship, but they are the occurrence and results of the same event. This process is "the occurrence of a natural electrical discharge of very short duration and high voltage between a cloud and the ground or within a cloud, accompanied by a bright flash and typically also thunder." [5]On another note, when رَعْدٌ is mentioned then بَرْقٌ comes into the mind before it is mentioned. When بَرْقٌ is mentioned then رَعْدٌ comes into the mind before it is mentioned. Both remind of each other.

In the expression[168] فِيهِ ظُلُمَاتٌ وَرَعْدٌ وَبَرْقٌ, it is interesting to note that if there is only ظُلُمَاتٌ[169] without وَرَعْدٌ وَبَرْقٌ[170] then, the person may think that they can acclimate to the darkness. Yet, this changing condition of sound and light with وَرَعْدٌ وَبَرْقٌ eliminates this possibility of acclimation or makes it very difficult.

As the speed of light is much faster than the sound, there is a delay between the flashing light and the sound of thunder. Therefore, if one analyzes the ayah[171] وَرَعْدٌ وَبَرْقٌ يَجْعَلُونَ أَصْابِعَهُمْ فِي آذَانِهِم مِّنَ الصَّوَاعِقِ, after this process is mentioned as explained above with the words رَعْدٌ وَبَرْقٌ[172], then the sound being mentioned later in the ayah as الصَّوَاعِقِ[173] can

---

166. Lightning.
167. Thunder and lightning.
168. Within which is darkness, thunder and lightning.
169. Darkness.
170. And thunder and lightning.
171. Within which is darkness, thunder and lightning. They put their fingers in their ears against the thunderclaps.
172. Thunder and lightning.
173. Thunderclaps.

indicate this delay in the sound waves being slower and it is heard later by humans after their observation of the flashing of lightning, الله اعلم.

One of the miracles of the Qurān is that the explanations of natural events in the Qurān are always compatible with changing and updating scientific discoveries. There are a lot of books written in different fields such as physics, chemistry, biology, and others. Many former expert-written books have become nullified and disposed of due to their contradictory nature revealed by new discoveries in science through the advent of technology. Yet, the Qurān is always compatible with updating scientific discoveries. This is in itself one of the miracles of the Qurān besides many others.

In another perspective of explanations mentioned in the classical tafāsir, all of the incidents and natural events occurring in the universe are governed by an angel or angels [6]. Although we name or refer to them with the laws of physics and other sciences, in their other dimensions, there are angels establishing and monitoring and intervening these events and incidents in the universe. For example, there are angels governing lightening, thunder, and rain. One can view the above occurrences mentioned in the ayah with this perspective as well.

The word يَجْعَلُونَ[174] can indicate the meaning of assigning something. In other words, they assigned their fingers or hands to block their ears from hearing as mentioned يَجْعَلُونَ أَصْابِعَهُمْ فِي آذَانِهِم مِّنَ الصَّوَاعِقِ حَذَرَ الْمَوْتِ[175]. Yet, sometimes people assign or match a duty for something or someone that does not indicate or reveal the real purpose of that thing. In other words, there can be a mismatch and wrong insight of assignment. When Allah ﷻ assigns something or someone, there is always a purpose, hikmah, wisdom, and full and perfect match. One can review the ayahs of the Qurān around this word يَجْعَلُونَ[176] to realize this methodology especially very careful and meticulous distinction in the choice of this word as presented in the Qurān, SubhanAllah. As the name of this book is istinbat, someone can really feel this diving into a deep ocean and taking pearls and diamonds out but still there are infinite and endless amounts of these precious items left in the ocean. As the person dives

---

174. They put.
175. They put their fingers in their ears against the thunderclaps in dread of death.
176. They put.

and gets them, they want to get more and more with positive greed, hunger, and with a constantly increasing appetite, SubhanAllah.

The word الصَّوَاعِقِ[177] is the jam, plural of صاعق. There are cases of punishments and deaths through terrifying and possibly amplified and varied types of sounds mentioned in the Qurān. For example: فَإِنْ أَعْرَضُوا فَقُلْ أَنذَرْتُكُمْ صَاعِقَةً مِّثْلَ صَاعِقَةِ عَادٍ وَثَمُودَ[178] {فصلت/13}, وَأَمَّا ثَمُودُ فَهَدَيْنَاهُمْ فَاسْتَحَبُّوا الْعَمَى عَلَى الْهُدَى فَأَخَذَتْهُمْ صَاعِقَةُ الْعَذَابِ الْهُونِ بِمَا كَانُوا يَكْسِبُونَ[179] {فصلت/17}, فَعَتَوْا عَنْ أَمْرِ رَبِّهِمْ فَأَخَذَتْهُمُ الصَّاعِقَةُ وَهُمْ يَنظُرُونَ[180] {الذاريات/44}. The expression as[181] الصَّوَاعِقِ is[182] مِّنَ الصَّوَاعِقِ حَذَرَ الْمَوْتِ can indicate this reality when the word mentioned. The expression حَذَرَ الْمَوْتِ can specify this fear from death.

In the expression[183] وَاللّهُ مُحِيطٌ بِالْكَافِرِينَ, the word بِالْكَافِرِينَ[184] can indicate any person who covers the realities, the fitrah, the natural disposition, one's tendencies to believe, and one's need for Allah ☀. In this sense, a kafir and a munāfiq can share similar characteristics.

In this expression وَاللّهُ مُحِيطٌ بِالْكَافِرِينَ[185], their qualities are emphasized. In other words, the ayah could have been[186] وَاللّهُ مُحِيطٌ بِهِم. Yet, their qualities are emphasized but not their individual selves. In this perspective, the dislike is not for the person but for the act or the sin.

The connector أَوْ[187] in the beginning of the ayah can show different types of munāfiqeen. It can also be understood as the continuation of the initial descriptions as presented by the 17th and 18th ayahs.

In the analysis of أَوْ showing the different types, when one compares the type of munāfiq in the previous ayahs (17-18) with the type of munāfiq mentioned in these ayahs (19-20), this type can be different than the ones before. In addition, in the expression أَوْ كَصَيِّبٍ[188] the word أَوْ can indicate two types of munāfiqeen. Both types can have some

---

177. Thunderclaps.
178. But if they turn away, then say, "I have warned you of a thunderbolt like the thunderbolt [that struck] A'ad and Thamūd.
179. We guided them, but they preferred blindness over guidance, so the thunderbolt of humiliating punishment seized them for what they used to earn.
180. But they were insolent toward the command of their Lord, so the thunderbolt seized them while they were looking on.
181. Against the thunderclaps in dread of death.
182. Thunderclaps.
183. But Allah ☀ is encompassing of the disbelievers.
184. The disbelievers.
185. But Allah ☀ is encompassing of the disbelievers.
186. But Allah ☀ is encompassing of them.
187. Or.
188. Or {it is} like a rainstorm.

similarities and differences. It can also indicate two groups that are split and are in conflict with each other, Allahu A'lam.

Another possibility is that munāfiqeen can assume each ayah of the Qurān revealed to Rasulullah saw similar to the thunder and lightning on them as mentioned يَكَادُ الْبَرْقُ يَخْطَفُ أَبْصَارَهُمْ [189] and[190] أَوْ كَصَيِّبٍ مِّنَ السَّمَاء. The ayahs of the Qurān have been explaining the real inner motivation of these munāfiqeen and their real intentions. They had been so scared that an ayah would reveal to the Prophet saw and expose them.

The Different Types of Munāfiqeen

The first group of munāfiqeen in {البقرة/18} [191] صُمٌّ بُكْمٌ عُمْيٌ فَهُمْ لاَ يَرْجِعُونَ cannot express themselves as mentioned بُكْمٌ[192]. The second type of munāfiq have some type of ability to differentiate things as mentioned أَوْ كَصَيِّبٍ مِّنَ السَّمَاء فِيهِ ظُلُمَاتٌ وَرَعْدٌ وَبَرْقٌ يَجْعَلُونَ أَصْابِعَهُمْ فِي آذَانِهِم مِّنَ الصَّوَاعِقِ حَذَرَ الْمَوْتِ وَاللّهُ مُحِيطٌ بِالْكَافِرِينَ [193] {البقرة/19}. For example, they can differentiate things related with sound as mentioned يَجْعَلُونَ أَصْابِعَهُمْ فِي آذَانِهِم مِّنَ[194] الصَّوَاعِقِ. They have some ability of sight and hearing.

The first group of munāfiq as mentioned in ayahs 17 and 18 don't know much what is happening around them and they are disconnected with realities as mentioned صُمٌّ بُكْمٌ عُمْيٌ فَهُمْ لَا يَرْجِعُونَ[195]. Therefore, they don't have much fear. The other group detailed in ayahs 19 and 20 have some type of understanding of realities. Therefore, they have some fear, anxiety, and uneasiness as mentioned يَجْعَلُونَ أَصْابِعَهُمْ فِي آذَانِهِم مِّنَ الصَّوَاعِقِ[196] حَذَرَ الْمَوْتِ.

With the above perspectives, the second type of munāfiq has more suffering than the first type of munāfiq due to their cognizance of some knowledge and recognition. For example, if a person drives a car and makes mistakes with passengers in the car, the person sitting in the front seat next to the driver can suffer more when he witnesses all of

---

189. Or [it is] like a rainstorm from the sky.
190. The lightning almost snatches away their sight.
191. Deaf, dumb, and blind, so they will not return {to the right path}.
192. Dumb.
193. Or [it is] like a rainstorm from the sky within which is darkness, thunder and lightning. They put their fingers in their ears against the thunderclaps in dread of death. But Allah ﷻ is encompassing of the disbelievers.
194. They put their fingers in their ears against the thunderclaps.
195. Deaf, dumb and blind—so they will not return [to the right path].
196. They put their fingers in their ears against the thunderclaps in dread of death.

the different possible tragedies and averted accidents and crashes. On the other hand, the ones in the back seat may be sleeping or chatting with each other and not be fully aware of things happening like the one sitting in the front seat.

Similarly, our minds can sometimes be harmful to us if we know something and don't act upon it, compared to the people who don't know and don't have the guilt, regret, ,and self-blame feelings of not acting upon this knowledge. Therefore, some scholars [6] assert that animals involve themselves with certain engagements with less or no psychological or self-reflective pain compared to humans. Yet humans are given by Allah ﷻ the superior ability of self-reflection, self-accountability, regret, remorse, and accordingly asking of forgiveness from Allah ﷻ and from people.

Istiqamah, Positive & Negative Change, and Nifāq

One can be on the istiqamah, on the path of Allah ﷻ, with a positive change. In this positive change, there is always an energy and activism to do good work to please Allah ﷻ. One calls this futuwwah. The fuel of nondepleted energy to always do the a'amalu salih[197], virtuous acts, can stem from futuwwah regardless of one's age.

On another note, one should see this positive change as an asset. A person always looking for opportunities, changing the format, and adapting and updating oneself with the context to achieve the khayr[198] and yet at the same time being careful with the makrûhāt[199] can be boosting vertically and positively in one's relationship with Allah ﷻ. In this regard, change is a good phenomenon. This is encouraged. One can also call this jihad as the struggle of adaptation, change, and still maintaining an increase in one's relationship with Allah ﷻ.

In this perspective, positive change and istiqamah[200] are related. In other words, people can assume linearity or stagnancy or passivism in the word istiqamah. Yet, istiqamah can entail positive change while having incremental or linear increase in one's relationship with Allah ﷻ.

---

197. Righteous deeds.
198. Goodness.
199. Disliked actions.
200. The path of Allah ﷻ·

In this perspective, istiqamah does not entail passive adaptation of a wird or an awrād. It is the effort of keeping one's awrad with constant embodiment of the meanings and recitations and yet at the same time looking for more opportunities of positive change and increase in quality and quantity.

The expression and constant required repetition of the dua in our salah as اهدِنَا الصِّرَاطَ المُستَقِيمَ {الفاتحة/6}[201] صِرَاطَ الَّذِينَ أَنعَمتَ عَلَيهِمْ غَيرِ المَغضُوبِ عَلَيهِمْ وَلاَ الضَّالِّينَ {الفاتحة/7}[202] can indicate this dynamic and positive changing effort of istiqamah compared to its negative or passive assumed interpretations.

Another very striking example is the constant repetition of فَأَتبَعَ سَبَبًا ثُمَّ أَتبَعَ سَبَبًا {الكهف/92}[205], {الكهف/85}[203], and ثُمَّ أَتبَعَ سَبَبًا {الكهف/89}[204]. In this case, Zulqarnayn (as) is adapting constant positive change, means, or reasons in order to achieve and do good deeds. One of the messages for us with this constant repetition of the phrase أَتبَعَ سَبَبًا[206] can be that we should be constantly looking at the means or opportunities with a positive change to please Allah ﷻ. This effort in itself as the real jihad can inshAllah keep the person on the istiqamah of positive and linear increase in one's relationship with Allah ﷻ.

Istiqamah, in this sense requires holding your initial asset and building on it. Istiqamah requires continuity of the positive change. Istiqamah requires predictability about this person's traits such as this person always runs behind the opportunities of doing the good deeds. Istiqamah indicates futuwwah and positive change and upholding and invigorating spiritual enlightenment.

Societies, communities, business ventures, and families require istiqamah. In this regard, istiqamah requires stability, growth, trusted bonds, stable markets, and unified families. With istiqamah societies, communities, business ventures, and families can grow positively and there can be a linear increase.

---

201. Guide us to the straight path.
202. The path of those upon whom You have bestowed favor, not of those who have evoked [Your] anger or of those who are astray.
203. So he followed a way.
204. Then he followed a way.
205. Then he followed a way.
206. Followed a way.

Then, one can ask: What is a negative change and how can it be related with nifãq[207]?

Nifãq is the opposite of istiqamah. Nifãq indicates negative change or negative energy for negative change. Nifãq indicates gloominess or darkness. Nifãq indicates unpredictability. Nifãq indicates not having set values, goals, and aims. Nifãq indicates change not for positive virtuous acts but change built on self or lowly temporal interests or motivations. Therefore, when humanity regardless of religion, gender, ethnicity, and other differences, is happy all together about a virtuous act of achievement that benefits everyone, people of nifãq can be sad and crying for this unification of the common good. Nifãq indicates disunity and chaos in the humanity's shared ethical and moral values.

Chaos, instability, distrust, and volatility caused by nifãq can cause societies, communities, and families to decline in their spiritual and worldly growth. In the families where there is nifãq, the families cannot support each other with sakina, peace, and tranquility. These families, sooner or later, are likely to break up and all of the family members become enemies to each other as if the parents did not take care of these children, as if the spouses did not spend many years together, and as if the children do not carry the same kinship bonds of being from the same mother and father. In these business markets of nifãq[208], businesses cannot grow, and they always are hesitant to make new investments.

Nifãq can desire for unfair exclusivity and privilege. The prime example of this unfair exclusivity or privilege was presented by Shaytan as {ص/76} [209] قَالَ أَنَا خَيْرٌ مِّنْهُ خَلَقْتَنِي مِن نَّارٍ وَخَلَقْتَهُ مِن طِينٍ.

Exclusivity or privilege is not a right and is thereby given on merit. This is a statement in today's civilized society that has become a law. Having a driver's license in New York is a privilege but not a right according to the laws of New York State [14]. It is gained on the basis of merit. The person should embody the struggle, effort, and means to have this privilege.

---

207. Hypocrisy.
208. Hypocrisy.
209. He said, "I am better than him. You created me from fire and created him from clay."

Similarly, Allah ﷻ chooses with the Divine Mashiyyah[210] however and whomever Allah ﷻ wants. Allah ﷻ is Al-Hakîm[211] and Al-A'lîm[212] as mentioned {البقرة/30} [213]قَالَ إِنِّي أَعْلَمُ مَا لاَ تَعْلَمُونَ.

In other words, if one analyzes the ayahs,

وَإِذْ قَالَ رَبُّكَ لِلْمَلاَئِكَةِ إِنِّي جَاعِلٌ فِي الأَرْضِ خَلِيفَةً قَالُواْ أَتَجْعَلُ فِيهَا مَن يُفْسِدُ فِيهَا وَيَسْفِكُ الدِّمَاء وَنَحْنُ نُسَبِّحُ بِحَمْدِكَ وَنُقَدِّسُ لَكَ قَالَ إِنِّي أَعْلَمُ مَا لاَ تَعْلَمُونَ[214] {البقرة/30} وَعَلَّمَ آدَمَ الأَسْمَاء كُلَّهَا ثُمَّ عَرَضَهُمْ عَلَى الْمَلاَئِكَةِ فَقَالَ أَنبِئُونِي بِأَسْمَاء هَؤُلاء إِن كُنتُمْ صَادِقِينَ[215] {البقرة/31} قَالُواْ سُبْحَانَكَ لاَ عِلْمَ لَنَا إِلاَّ مَا عَلَّمْتَنَا إِنَّكَ أَنتَ الْعَلِيمُ الْحَكِيمُ {البقرة/32}[216]

قَالَ يَا آدَمُ أَنبِئْهُم بِأَسْمَآئِهِمْ فَلَمَّا أَنبَأَهُمْ بِأَسْمَآئِهِمْ قَالَ أَلَمْ أَقُل لَّكُمْ إِنِّي أَعْلَمُ غَيْبَ السَّمَاوَاتِ وَالأَرْضِ وَأَعْلَمُ مَا تُبْدُونَ وَمَا كُنتُمْ تَكْتُمُونَ[217] {البقرة/33}

although Allah ﷻ does not need any explanation in the Divine Choice, Mashiyyah[218], Allah ﷻ still explains to us that Allah ﷻ makes ever decision with wisdom, hikmah.

In this regard, with a similar approach, one can analyze the critical expression اللّٰه اصْطَفَى[219] in the below ayahs:

إِنَّ اللّٰه اصْطَفَى آدَمَ وَنُوحًا وَآلَ إِبْرَاهِيمَ وَآلَ عِمْرَانَ عَلَى الْعَالَمِينَ[220] {آل عمران/33}

---

210. Permission {of Allah ﷻ}
211. The Wise.
212. The All-Knower.
213. He [Allah ﷻ] said, "Indeed, I know that which you do not know."
214. And [mention, O Muhammad], when your Lord said to the angels, "Indeed, I will make upon the earth a successive authority." They said, "Will You place upon it one who causes corruption therein and sheds blood, while we declare Your praise and sanctify You?" He [Allah ﷻ] said, "Indeed, I know that which you do not know."
215. And He taught Adam the names—all of them. Then He showed them to the angels and said, "Inform Me of the names of these, if you are truthful."
216. They said " Exalted are you; we have no knowledge except what you have taught us. Indeed, it is You who is the Knowing, The Wise.
217. He said, "O Adam, inform them of their names." And when he had informed them of their names, He said, "Did I not tell you that I know the unseen [aspects] of the heavens and the earth? And I know what you reveal and what you have concealed."
218. Permission {of Allah ﷻ}
219. Allah ﷻ chose.
220. Indeed, Allah chose Adam and Noah and the family of Abraham and the family of I'mrān over the worlds—

وَإِذْ قَالَتِ الْمَلَائِكَةُ يَا مَرْيَمُ إِنَّ اللَّهَ اصْطَفَاكِ وَطَهَّرَكِ وَاصْطَفَاكِ عَلَى نِسَاءِ الْعَالَمِينَ [221]
{آل عمران/42}

قَالَ يَا مُوسَى إِنِّي اصْطَفَيْتُكَ عَلَى النَّاسِ بِرِسَالَاتِي وَبِكَلَامِي فَخُذْ مَا آتَيْتُكَ وَكُن مِّنَ الشَّاكِرِينَ [222] {الأعراف/144}

Yet, when Allah ﷻ gives this honor of istafā[223], then the person should make hamd[224] as mentioned قُلِ الْحَمْدُ لِلَّهِ وَسَلَامٌ عَلَى عِبَادِهِ الَّذِينَ اصْطَفَى آللَّهُ خَيْرٌ أَمَّا يُشْرِكُونَ[225]{النمل/59}although the responsibility can be heavy.

Still, the chosen ones can make mistakes, may Allah ﷻ protect us, as mentioned ثُمَّ أَوْرَثْنَا الْكِتَابَ الَّذِينَ اصْطَفَيْنَا مِنْ عِبَادِنَا فَمِنْهُمْ ظَالِمٌ لِّنَفْسِهِ وَمِنْهُم مُّقْتَصِدٌ وَمِنْهُمْ سَابِقٌ بِالْخَيْرَاتِ بِإِذْنِ اللَّهِ ذَلِكَ هُوَ الْفَضْلُ الْكَبِيرُ[226]{فاطر/32}

Allah ﷻ wills and chooses with the Divine Mashiyyah[227] the individuals for a high purpose with some consideration of their merit but yet with the Divine Fadl[228] and Rahmah[229] of Allah ﷻ. Yet, it can be against the adab[230] with Allah ﷻ to ask for a privilege similar to Shaytan.

Asking for privilege can indicate arrogance most of the time. A privilege given without asking can indicate uneasiness or discomfort in the individual due to its responsibility as happened with Rasulullah ﷺ when he saw first received the wahy[231]. He saw ran to his wife Khadijah (RA). When Musa as received the wahy he initially started running, then all were comforted by Allah ﷻ.

Nifāq can embody the desire to always have more than others in worldly means. Nifāq can desire more privilege than others in worldly

---

221. And [mention] when the angels said, "O Mary, indeed Allah ﷻ has chosen you and purified you and chosen you above the women of the worlds.
222. [Allah ﷻ] said, "O Moses, I have chosen you over the people with My messages and My words [to you]. So take what I have given you and be among the grateful."
223. Choose.
224. Praise.
225. Say, [O Muhammad ﷺ], "Praise be to Allah ﷻ, and peace upon His servants whom He has chosen. Is Allah ﷻ better or what they associate with Him?"
226. Then We caused to inherit the Book those We have chosen of Our servants; and among them is he who wrongs himself [i.e., sins], and among them is he who is moderate, and among them is he who is foremost in good deeds by permission of Allah ﷻ. That [inheritance] is what is the great bounty.
227. Permission {of Allah ﷻ}
228. Favor.
229. Mercy.
230. Respect.
231. Revelation.

means. Therefore, nifāq can require injustice and unfairness in order to satisfy the privileged groups.

In analyzing the types of munāfiqeen, the hadith,[232] ثلاث آية المنافق [إذا حدث كذب ، وإذا وعد أخلف ، وإذا اؤتمن خان [7] [4] can also differentiate and detail these types. In another hadith, Rasulullah ﷺ said another trait as mentioned [233]أَرْبَعٌ مَنْ كُنَّ فِيهِ كَانَ مُنَافِقًا خَالِصًا ، وَمَنْ كَانَتْ فِيهِ خَصْلَةٌ مِنْهُنَّ كَانَتْ فِيهِ خَصْلَةٌ مِنَ النِّفَاقِ حَتَّى يَدَعَهَا : إِذَا اؤْتُمِنَ خَانَ ، وَإِذَا حَدَّثَ كَذَبَ ، وَإِذَا عَاهَدَ غَدَرَ ، [وَإِذَا خَاصَمَ فَجَرَ [7]. In different parts of the Qurān, some of the constant themes mentioned discuss their changing, unpredictable, unstable, and volatile character. They are not established and founded in virtue and character development. They don't have values that they stand for. When they see a benefit or self-interest, they side with that group. This group that they side with can be Muslims or not. It doesn't matter. Their self-interest or benefit determines which group they need to side with. Here is an example of this disposition in the Qurān: مُذَبْذَبِينَ بَيْنَ ذَلِكَ لاَ إِلَى هَؤُلاء وَلاَ إِلَى هَؤُلاء وَمَن يُضْلِلِ اللّهُ فَلَن تَجِدَ لَهُ سَبِيلاً[234] {النساء/143}.

One other common trait is that when they are disconnected from their clique or friends, they see everything in the universe to be scary, terrifying, lonely, and random. There is a big difference of perspectives between a person of imān and a munāfiq. One's perspective with imān or a true believer sees everything as a friend, with structure and working under the command of Allah ﷻ. Therefore, if people seem to be scared of a creation or anything, then this person, the true mu'min[235], reminds the people to calm down. This mu'min or the true believer can even communicate with that evil or scary-looking thing, as the creation of Allah ﷻ, to warn and remind that thing that, "You are a creation of Allah ﷻ, so remember that!"

One can see the prime examples of these engagements in the life of Rasulullah ﷺ. The Prophet ﷺ orders the tree to bend its branches with the permission of Allah [ﷻ], and then the tree bends its branches.

---

232. The signs of a munāfiq are three: When he talks he lies, when he promises he breaks his promise and when he is trusted he breaks the trust.

233. Whoever has all these four traits altogether in oneself, then this person is a definite munāfiq. Whoever has one of these traits, then this person carries one of the signs of nifāq until he or she leaves this trait. When he talks he lies, when he promises he breaks his promise, when he is trusted he breaks the trust, and when he is in argument, he does not observe any limits.

234. Wavering between them, [belonging] neither to these [i.e., the believers] nor to those [i.e., the disbelievers]. And whoever Allah ﷻ leaves astray—never will you find for him a way.

235. Believer.

The Prophet ﷺ orders the mountain Uhud to stop shaking with the permission of Allah ﷻ, and the mountain stops. We refer to the shaking of a mountain as an earthquake or as the possible eruption of a volcano. Yet, the Prophet saw knows the reality beyond our naming or terminologies, and when he saw orders them with this password or passcode, then everything that seems scary or frightening can become friendly.

Even, these occurrences may be against and beyond the laws of physics and natural sciences. The Prophet saw splits the moon, the animals come and talk with the Prophet ﷺ, the wooden pillar in the mosque starts crying. These incidents were all witnessed and reported by hundreds of people. There is not the slightest doubt about their reality and truth. The mu'min connects everything with Allah ﷻ. Saying bismillah at the beginning of everything is a Divine expression expected to remind the person of this absolute reality and truth. Then, everything reveals to the person their true and real meanings and essence beyond their fake delusions.

On the other hand, the munāfiq or a kafir, engages himself or herself with a pseudo, self-induced meaning wasting his or her time with the notions of lollipop effects. Instead, if one takes another perspective, he or she can still enjoy life by facing the realities without being shocked by the realities in life and after death before it is too late.

In their life perspective, munāfiq and kafir views everything as threatening, hostile, and intimidating. They assume that everything works together, liaises, and networks against them. According to their perspective, there is nothing on the earth, even in the universe, that can benefit them. Everything is against them. This psychology is very self-destructive.

When one thinks about the absence of ibadah and imān, everything becomes chaotic, random, scary, purposeless, and dark. Any unknown becomes a terrorizing monster as compared to a guest sent from Rabbul A'lamin. In ibadah, conformity and compliance are referred to as "obedience" in traditional language and brings a complete and perfect structure. Yes, submission, conformity, compliance, and obedience set and establish a complete structure and order in a person's life as Abdullah. With this embodiment of the structure and order, the person can now realize the realities and wisdom, the hikmah[236] for the occurrences, incidents, and systems. A person who embodied and personalized the structure and order in their own life can now realize the structure and order in the universe, galaxies, cells, micro-organisms, and in the personal lives of individuals. With this realization, everything makes sense as if completing a jigsaw puzzle. Everything becomes a friend with the Nûr of imān.

One of the arguments for the endless punishment of a kafir in Jahannam is due to attribution of kufr, purposelessness, and randomness of all the infinite creation of Allah ﷻ. In other words, all the countless creation of Allah ﷻ assert their right and open a lawsuit against this person on the Judgment Day for being accused and slandered with kufr. Therefore, the kafir deems to have an endless punishment in the afterlife due to his or her false accusation and slander against all the creation [6].

On the other hand, a mu'min, a true believer of Allah ﷻ with ikhlas[237] can even hear the dhikr of everything in the universe through the light of imān. Everything becomes his or her friend because they all have a purpose, meaning, and goal in their lives like this person. These purposes, meanings, and goals are SubhanAllah, Alhamdulillah, and Allahuakbar. In other words, everything is constantly recognizing and glorifying Allah ﷻ with the Perfect and Complete Names and Attributes with SubhanAllah; persistently showing thanks and gratitude with Alhamdulillah; and continuously remembering the Greatness of Allah ﷻ that Allah ﷻ is above anyone, everyone, anything, and everything as mentioned with the divine phrase of Allahuakbar. Therefore, Allahuakbar as a phrase is in comparative form rather than superlative form linguistically. This can indicate that as humans we construct constantly and dynamically fears and anxieties with things in life. This phrase constantly tells the person, "Allah ﷻ is more powerful than that thing that you are afraid of. So, don't make shirk. Turn to Allah ﷻ and rely on Allah ﷻ." In other words, the phrase AllahuAkbar reminds the person of the constant need of repetition, dhikr of this phrase as constant fears, anxieties, or implicit shirks can infiltrate the heart and mind of the person.

---

236. Wisdom.
237. Sincerity.

If one analyzes the common themes in both examples given in ayahs 17 and 19-20, one should realize a few important notions. In both cases, they are in anxiety, panic, and fear and there is no hope for them. If one relates two examples, one can also add a connection between them. When they lit a fire, then a storm or rain can extinguish this fire. The point of starting something and maintaining it are two separate engagements as mentioned before.

Another commonality is the notion of ni'mah being a punishment for some people. Light, or rain can be a ni'mah for plants, animals, and living beings. At the same time, a thunder strike or rain in the form of a flood can be a punishment. In one perspective, these can be ni'mah for the ones who deserve them like the believers because they know and appreciate Allah ☙ Who created them. Yet, the same items can be a punishment for the ones like kafir or munāfiq, who may not deserve them due to their unappreciative and ungrateful behavior to Allah ☙. Or, these items created by Allah ☙ do not show their merciful side but rather they show their anger to humans who do not appreciate Allah ☙.

This interpretation can be supported with the ayahs:

وَقَالُوا اتَّخَذَ الرَّحْمَنُ وَلَدًا ²³⁸{مريم/88} لَقَدْ جِئْتُمْ شَيْئًا إِدًّا ²³⁹{مريم/89} تَكَادُ السَّمَاوَاتُ يَتَفَطَّرْنَ مِنْهُ وَتَنشَقُّ الْأَرْضُ وَتَخِرُّ الْجِبَالُ هَدًّا ²⁴⁰{مريم/90} أَن دَعَوْا لِلرَّحْمَنِ وَلَدًا ²⁴¹{مريم/91} وَمَا يَنبَغِي لِلرَّحْمَنِ أَن يَتَّخِذَ وَلَدًا ²⁴²{مريم/92} إِن كُلُّ مَن فِي السَّمَاوَاتِ وَالْأَرْضِ إِلَّا آتِي الرَّحْمَنِ عَبْدًا ²⁴³{مريم/93}.

These ayahs indicate the anger of the skies, the earth, and the mountains due to the false attribution of people about Allah ☙. In other words, all the beings truly know and recognize Allah ☙ except some humans and Jinn. All these beings and creation can show their displeasure and disapproval for their kufr through different means.

In one interpretation, all the beings and creation show anger because when these few don't recognize Allah ☙ truly with their kufr, then they

---

238. And they say, "The Most Merciful has taken [for Himself] a son."
239. You have done an atrocious thing.
240. The heavens almost rupture therefrom and the earth splits open and the mountains collapse in devastation.
241. That they attribute to the Most Merciful a son.
242. And it is not appropriate for the Most Merciful that He should take a son.
243. There is no one in the heavens and earth but that he comes to the Most Merciful as a servant.

attribute randomness, chaos, no purpose, and false accusations for the existence of all these beings in the universe. Yet, everything is creation, servant and worshipper of Allah ﷻ as mentioned إِن كُلُّ مَن فِي السَّمَاوَاتِ وَالْأَرْضِ إِلَّا آتِي الرَّحْمَنِ عَبْدًا[244] {مريم/93}.

To continue with this discussion, the due process of all the uncountable number of creation against the kafir necessitates an uncountable retribution, or uncountable/unlimited time in Jahannam. In other words, uncountable creation of Allah ﷻ claims their right against this kafir because he or she accused this being with some false accusations. Then, due to the Just Name of Allah ﷻ, this person ends up in Jahannam because of their kufr. This is due to not having and embodying لا اله الا الله محمد رسول الله[245]. May Allah ﷻ protect us, Ameen.

In this case, one can analyze

أَوْ كَصَيِّبٍ مِّنَ السَّمَاء فِيهِ ظُلُمَاتٌ وَرَعْدٌ وَبَرْقٌ يَجْعَلُونَ أَصَابِعَهُمْ فِي آذَانِهِم مِّنَ الصَّوَاعِقِ حَذَرَ الْمَوْتِ واللّهُ مُحِيطٌ بِالْكَافِرِينَ[246] {البقرة/19}.

The thunder punishes their ears as mentioned وَرَعْدٌ وَبَرْقٌ يَجْعَلُونَ[247] أَصَابِعَهُمْ فِي آذَانِهِم مِّنَ الصَّوَاعِقِ and can make them deaf. The lightning punishes their eyes as mentioned يَكَادُ الْبَرْقُ يَخْطَفُ أَبْصَارَهُم[248] and can make them blind.

In another interpretation, in the statement فِيهِ أَوْ كَصَيِّبٍ مِّنَ السَّمَاء[249], ظُلُمَاتٌ وَرَعْدٌ وَبَرْقٌ, the word كَصَيِّبٍ[250] can indicate Islam was revealed from Allah ﷻ to all humans. As the rain صَيِّبٍ[251] can give life to plants and other beings, Islam can give life to the ruh, to the souls. The words وَرَعْدٌ[252] وَبَرْقٌ can indicate, the wa'ad and wa'id, the rewards and punishment. The word ظُلُمَاتٌ[253] can indicate different types of kufr and nifāq.

---

244. There is no one in the heavens and earth but that he comes to the Most Merciful as a servant.
245. Theres no god except Allah ﷻ, and Muhammed ﷺ is the messenger of Allah ﷻ.
246. Or [it is] like a rainstorm from the sky within which is darkness, thunder and lightning. They put their fingers in their ears against the thunderclaps in dread of death. But Allah ﷻ is encompassing of the disbelievers.
247. And thunder and lightning. They put their fingers in their ears against the thunderclaps.
248. The lightning almost snatches away their sight.
249. Or [it is] like a rainstorm from the sky within which is darkness, thunder and lightning.
250. [It is] like a rainstorm.
251. Rainstorm.
252. And thunder and lightning.
253. Darkness.

One can realize that the rain is a ni'mah, a blessing from Allah ﷻ. Yet, there is a specific mention that this is a ni'mah or blessing-seeming punishment as mentioned in the expression أَوْ كَصَيِّبٍ مِّنَ السَّمَاء فِيهِ ظُلُمَاتٌ[254]. One can remember the ayah فَلَمَّا رَأَوْهُ عَارِضًا مُّسْتَقْبِلَ أَوْدِيَتِهِمْ قَالُوا هَذَا عَارِضٌ مُّمْطِرُنَا بَلْ هُوَ مَا اسْتَعْجَلْتُم بِهِ رِيحٌ فِيهَا عَذَابٌ أَلِيمٌ {24/الأحقاف}. The people of Ahqaf saw the clouds and they thought that it was a blessing, but it was a punishment as mentioned فِيهَا عَذَابٌ أَلِيمٌ {24/الأحقاف}. This is a similar ayah as presented with[255] فِيهِ ظُلُمَاتٌ in this ayah of discussion. The people of tasawwuf can call this istidraj as well.

In all of the above descriptions, a person who is scared of everything will suffer more from the above depictions and situations. Depending on the personality of the person, the inner and psychological effects of these concepts of fear, anxiety, depression, and uneasiness can be different. A treacherous or fearful person can have amplified effects of these situations. This can be due to one's spiritual state that he or she assumes that everyone and everything is against this person. One can also correlate their inner psychological, mental, and emotional world with the word فِيهِ ظُلُمَاتٌ. They have a fixed perception. They see and understand everything with this perception of فِيهِ ظُلُمَاتٌ. One can think about a person that when he or she is pessimistic, this person interprets all of their life incidents according to this negative, depressive, and doomster perspective.

When one combines external darkness coming with كَصَيِّبٍ[256] مِّنَ السَّمَاء فِيهِ ظُلُمَات and internal darkness present with the pessimistic, negative, depressive, and doomster perspective of the person, then one can possibly better realize why ظُلُمَات[257] is plural. In other words, there are multiple sources of darkness for the munāfiq. Therefore, ظُلُمَات is presented as Jam, plural, والله اعلم[258].

To understand their helplessness, one can try to picture the ayah أَوْ[259] كَصَيِّبٍ مِّنَ السَّمَاء فِيهِ ظُلُمَاتٌ وَرَعْدٌ وَبَرْقٌ يَجْعَلُونَ أَصْابِعَهُمْ فِي آذَانِهِم مِّنَ الصَّوَاعِقِ حَذَرَ الْمَوْتِ. When there is the fear of darkness, thunder, rain with darkness, they try to put their fingers to their ears. Yet, they know that this cannot help them.

---

254. Or [it is] like a rainstorm from the sky within which is darkness.
255. Within which is darkness.
256. Or [it is] like a rainstorm from the sky within which is darkness.
257. Darkness.
258. Allah ﷻ knows best.
259. Or [it is] like a rainstorm from the sky within which is darkness, thunder and lightning. They put their fingers in their ears against the thunderclaps in dread of death.

One can ask if the musibah is specific to a certain group of people or for all people who have similar traits. Then, the expression وَٱللّٰهُ مُحِيطٌ[260] بِٱلْكَافِرِينَ can show that it is any person who has the trait or attribute of ungratefulness to Allah ﷻ.

In the expression كُلَّمَا أَضَاءَ لَهُم مَّشَوْاْ فِيهِ[261] can allude to the opportunistic approach of munāfiqeen. In other words, munāfiqeen look for an opportunity to cause fitnah among people as مَّشَوْاْ فِيهِ[262] can indicate. They just look for a small interval similar to a small or quick lightening interval of a thunder as كُلَّمَا أَضَاءَ لَهُم[263] can indicate. One can realize a similar opportunistic approach of munāfiqeen' effort to act in these short intervals as also mentioned in ٱلَّذِي ٱسْتَوْقَدَ نَاراً فَلَمَّا أَضَاءَتْ مَا حَوْلَهُ[264] ذَهَبَ ٱللّٰهُ بِنُورِهِمْ. In this case, they try to light a fire but it has a short life as Allah ﷻ does not maintain their extended times for fitnah as mentioned ذَهَبَ ٱللّٰهُ بِنُورِهِمْ[265], ٱللّٰه اعلم[266].

In all of these cases of munāfiqeen, one should remember that these ayahs are not only referring to a group of people. On our end, we should try to analyze our own selves about the possible traits of nifāq that we carry. Accordingly, we try to rectify them.

When one reviews the depictions of the psychology of a munāfiq in the above ayahs, in all of these difficult and hopeless situations of a munāfiq, one can ask why the munāfiq does not desire to die. The expression وَلَوْ شَاءَ ٱللّٰهُ لَذَهَبَ بِسَمْعِهِمْ وَأَبْصَارِهِمْ[267] can respond to this possible question. If Allah ﷻ wanted, then their life could be terminated at any time but they live until their destined times, ajal.

When one reviews this ayah, one can realize that clouds, thunder, and lightning are all a'bd, servants of Allah ﷻ although humans can be scared of them. The statement إِنَّ ٱللّٰهَ عَلَى كُلِّ شَيْءٍ قَدِيرٌ {البقرة/20} can show the peaceful states of tawakkul when the person is distressed about the fitnahs of munāfiqeen, and anything that can cause distress in life. Sometimes the person can even get emotions and feel anxious, stressed,

---

260. Allah ﷻ is encompassing of the disbelievers.
261. Every time it lights [the way] for them, they walk therein.
262. They walked therein.
263. Every time it lights {the way} for them.
264. One who kindled a fire, but when it illuminated what was around him, Allah ﷻ took away their light.
265. Allah ﷻ took away their light.
266. Allah ﷻ knows best.
267. And if Allah ﷻ had willed, He could have taken away their hearing and their sight.

fearful, or uneasy. In these cases and all of the time, know that إِنَّ اللهَ عَلَى
كُلِّ شَيْءٍ قَدِيرٌ {البقرة/20} removes all these burdens from the person.

The dua of Rasulullah ﷺ as[268] رَبِّي اللهُ لَا اله الا هو عليه توكلت و هو رب
العرش العظيم is one of the duas to be read regularly to remind of this reality
to the person. Humans are weak. For a few seconds, we can feel good
and happy. Then immediately after, we get these feelings of anxiety, fear,
or uneasiness that are related with unknowns, any expectations placed
upon us, or anything we fear due to the consequences of our actions and
decisions. Therefore, إِنَّ اللهَ عَلَى كُلِّ شَيْءٍ قَدِيرٌ[269] {البقرة/20} reminds us of this
easing point of aqidah[270] and leading the mu'min to ease and tawakkul[271]
but at the same time leading the munāfiq or kafir to fear, hopelessness,
and anxiety.

One of the styles of the Qurān besides many is to use embedded
meanings with the concept of mahthuf[272]. Mahthuf can be translated as
embedded meanings. One of the benefits of this style when used with
a simile is to give power and personal imagination to a depicted case.
In this case, when the ayah mentions أَوْ كَصَيِّبٍ مِّنَ السَّمَاء فِيهِ ظُلُمَاتٌ وَرَعْدٌ[273]
وَبَرْقٌ, there is no full or extended description of this simile due to the
I'jāz, concise or dense style, of the Qurān through the style of mahzthuf.
Yet, the simile describes the inner and psychological engagements of
munāfiqeen like a person who is traveling in the middle of the desert
and this person is exposed to a super heavy rain with darkness, thunder,
and so forth. Instead, there are a few words with dense, embedded
meanings which are ready to be expanded upon with the imagination
of the person.

It is important to pay attention that the word صَيِّبٌ[274] is used instead
of مطر[275]. This can indicate that the rain that they received was not
rahmah, blessing but azthab, punishment.

In the expressions such as أَوْ كَصَيِّبٍ مِّنَ السَّمَاء[276], the word مِّنَ[277] can
show the direction. This can mean that the rain is coming from the sky.

---

268. My lord is Allah ﷻ, there is no go but Him. I trust in him, and He is the Lord pf the Great
Throne.
269. Indeed Allah ﷻ is over all things competent.
270. Belief.
271. Trust.
272. Embedded meanings.
273. Or [it is] like a rainstorm from the sky within which is darkness, thunder and lightning.
274. Rainstorm.
275. Rain.
276. Or {it is} like a rainstorm from the sky.
277. From.

In this case, the word sky includes both the rain and clouds. With the current scientific discoveries, the formation of rain occurs in the clouds. The word cloud defined in Oxford dictionary is [21] "a visible mass of condensed water vapor floating in the atmosphere, typically high above the ground". The word sky in popular usage is "the region of the atmosphere and outer space seen from the earth" [21]. Allah ﷻ presents us the Qurān in such a way that there is no contradiction with scientific discoveries as mentioned أَفَلاَ يَتَدَبَّرُونَ الْقُرْآنَ وَلَوْ كَانَ مِنْ عِندِ غَيْرِ اللهِ لَوَجَدُواْ فِيهِ اخْتِلَافًا كَثِيرًا[278] {النساء/82}.

Yet, at the same time, the style may not be immediately straightforward for the layman as if forcing the people to believe and taking away the free will option from the person. In the Mashiyyah[279] of Allah ﷻ, the person should take a tiny step with their own will with their intention and inclination of niyyah, intention, and mayalan.

However, for the people of knowledge, taqwa, understanding, i'lm (الْعَالِمُونَ)[280] and ulul-al-bāb[281] (أُوْلُوا الْأَلْبَابِ), the Qurān is very clear and straightforward that it increases their certainty, yaqeen as mentioned وَتِلْكَ الْأَمْثَالُ نَضْرِبُهَا لِلنَّاسِ وَمَا يَعْقِلُهَا إِلَّا الْعَالِمُونَ[282] {العنكبوت/43}

أَمَّنْ هُوَ قَانِتٌ آنَاء اللَّيْلِ سَاجِدًا وَقَائِمًا يَحْذَرُ الْآخِرَةَ وَيَرْجُو رَحْمَةَ رَبِّهِ قُلْ هَلْ يَسْتَوِي الَّذِينَ يَعْلَمُونَ وَالَّذِينَ لَا يَعْلَمُونَ إِنَّمَا يَتَذَكَّرُ أُوْلُوا الْأَلْبَابِ[283] {الزمر/9}

أَلَمْ تَرَ أَنَّ اللَّهَ أَنزَلَ مِنَ السَّمَاء مَاء فَسَلَكَهُ يَنَابِيعَ فِي الْأَرْضِ ثُمَّ يُخْرِجُ بِهِ زَرْعًا مُّخْتَلِفًا أَلْوَانُهُ ثُمَّ يَهِيجُ فَتَرَاهُ مُصْفَرًّا ثُمَّ يَجْعَلُهُ حُطَامًا إِنَّ فِي ذَلِكَ لَذِكْرَى لِأُوْلِي الْأَلْبَابِ[284] {الزمر/21}

هُدًى وَذِكْرَى لِأُوْلِي الْأَلْبَابِ[285] {غافر/54}

---

278. Then do they not reflect upon the Qurān? If it had been from [any] other than Allah ﷻ, they would have found within it much contradiction.
279. Permission. {of Allah ﷻ}
280. The ones who study the Deen.
281. The men of understanding.
282. And these examples We present to the people, but none will understand them except those of knowledge.
283. Is one who is devoutly obedient during periods of the night, prostrating and standing [in prayer], fearing the Hereafter and hoping for the mercy of his Lord, [like one who does not]? Say, "Are those who know equal to those who do not know?" Only they will remember [who are] people of understanding.
284. Do you not see that Allah sends down rain from the sky and makes it flow as springs [and rivers] in the earth; then He produces thereby crops of varying colors; then they dry and you see them turned yellow; then He makes them [scattered] debris. Indeed in that is a reminder for those of understanding.
285. As guidance and a reminder for those of understanding.

يُؤْتِي الْحِكْمَةَ مَن يَشَاء وَمَن يُؤْتَ الْحِكْمَةَ فَقَدْ أُوتِيَ خَيْرًا كَثِيرًا وَمَا يَذَّكَّرُ إِلاَّ أُوْلُواْ
الأَلْبَابِ 286 {البقرة/269}

It can also indicate that the rain is showering on the earth as if it is coming from the entire sky and that there is no spot that is left out. This style can amplify the effect of the hopeless situation of the munāfiqeen.

One should remember the very delicate and sometimes complicated rules of Arabic language in the application of different styles of literature especially in the cases of similes, metaphors, and allegories. These can be considered under the science of balagah and I'jaz of the Qurān. Therefore, one should not review and analyze them literally but within the established rules of different styles of the language.

In the expression يَجْعَلُونَ أَصَابِعَهُمْ فِي آذَانِهِم [287], the word أَصَابِعَهُمْ [288] can indicate one's entire fingers. It is meant here that they try to block their ears with their fingertips. In that sense, this expression can portray their panic with the word أَصَابِعَهُمْ, الله اعلم [289].

When one analyzes the two expressions يَجْعَلُونَ أَصَابِعَهُمْ فِي آذَانِهِم [290] in this ayah and صُمٌّ [291] in the previous ayah, in both cases the center of focus is the ears or hearing. In this perspective, since they did not want to use their hearing faculties before for understanding and knowing the truth and Al-Haqq [292], now the same faculties are being punished. The munāfiqeen previously blocked them before from the true and solacing lights of imān. Now, they are blocking them from the terrifying lights of thunder. In this case one can see this cause and effect relationship. So, our actions and dispositions have their effects both in this world and in the afterlife.

Munāfiqeen reaction to all of these may not be because of any concern but due to the concern of dying as mentioned حَذَرَ الْمَوْتِ [293]. In other words, the munāfiqeen love life so much that they don't want to meet with Allah ﷻ.

---

286. He gives wisdom to whom He wills, and whoever has been given wisdom has certainly been given much good. And none will remember except those of understanding.
287. They put their fingers in their ears.
288. Their fingers.
289. Allah ﷻ knows best.
290. They put their fingers in their ears.
291. Deaf.
292. The Truth.
293. In dread of death.

In the expression وَأللّٰهُ مُحِيطٌ بِالْكَافِرِينَ[294], the lafzu Jalal and Mubarak اللّٰه can possibly indicate that their last resort of hope is not there for them. One of the Attributes of Allah ﷻ is Al-Ākhir[295] and Al-Awwal[296]. When the attribute Al-Ākhir is implied with اللّٰه, the lafthu[297] Jalal and Mubarak, it can indicate the loss of the Real and Last and First place of hope, shelter, and refuge Who is Allah ﷻ.

In the expression[298] وَأللّٰهُ مُحِيطٌ بِالْكَافِرِينَ, the word مُحِيطٌ[299] can indicate that whatever munāfiqeen are exposed to through rain, thunder, darkness, and all other agents, they all work under the command of Allah ﷻ. They don't come to them randomly, but they are all representations of مُحِيطٌ.

In addition, the word مُحِيطٌ can indicate a very serious warning to all munāfiqeen and kafirs. This warning can imply an announcement of, "Oh munāfiqeen and kafirs! Wherever you go on the earth, or in space, Allah ﷻ surrounds and overpowers you with I'lm[300] and Qudrah[301]."

In this perspective, the word مُحِيطٌ in the expression مُحِيطٌ وَأللّٰهُ[302] بِالْكَافِرِينَ can be very petrifying in the context of the ayah. When Allah ﷻ surrounds completely and fully as mentioned with the word[303] مُحِيطٌ, then there is no possibility of exit at all. In this sense, one can ask the possible question what could be the meaning of[304] بِالْكَافِرِينَ? Is it an absolute or complete kufr? Or, is it partial kufr? In this case, one can make the possible argument that if a person receives the breezes of hope and rays of help, comfort, or assistance sometimes, then this cannot be an absolute kufr. In the case of an absolute kufr, as the ayah can indicate, the person would be in full depression and spiritual darkness without any hope and any real assistance due to the مُحِيطٌ[305]. Then there is no possibility of exit or hope and comfort, اللّٰه اعلم[306].

---

294. Allah ﷻ is encompassing of the disbelievers.
295. The Last.
296. The first.
297. Word.
298. Allah ﷻ is encompassing of the disbelievers.
299. Encompassing.
300. Knowledge.
301. Power.
302. Allah ﷻ is encompassing of the disbelievers.
303. Encompassing.
304. Of the disbelievers.
305. Encompassing.
306. Allah ﷻ knows best.

If one analyzes the two expressions in ayahs 17 as[307] فَلَمَّا أَضَاءتْ حَوْلَهُ and كُلَّمَا أَضَاء لَهُم مَّا[308] in ayah 20, in both cases there is some type of on-and-off or sporadic light. In both cases or types of nifāq[309], the common word[310] أَضَاء is used. Yet, this light not is sufficient enough to induce imān them similar to a car ignition system that if the alternator or ignition is broken, it may still have some noise or power, yet it is not sufficient to get the car moving.

In the expression وَاللَّهُ مُحِيطٌ بِالْكَافِرِينَ[311], the harf-jar ب can indicate that when the munāfiqeen and kafirs run away from the gadab of Allah ﷻ as mentioned with مُحِيطٌ[312], then they again encounter this gadab as indicated with the harf-jar ب.

Both kafir and munāfiq have common and similar pains, depression, fears, and anxieties. Both of their hearts can feel the spiritual darkness and the pain related with it. The example أَوْ كَصَيِّبٍ مِّنَ السَّمَاء فِيهِ ظُلُمَاتٌ وَرَعْدٌ وَبَرْقٌ[313] can indicate this type of psychological pain and their emotional engagements.

This notion of spiritual darkness is very vividly described in another set of ayahs as:

وَالَّذِينَ كَفَرُوا أَعْمَالُهُمْ كَسَرَابٍ بِقِيعَةٍ يَحْسَبُهُ الظَّمْآنُ مَاء حَتَّى إِذَا جَاءهُ لَمْ يَجِدْهُ شَيْئًا وَوَجَدَ اللَّهَ عِندَهُ فَوَفَّاهُ حِسَابَهُ وَاللَّهُ سَرِيعُ الْحِسَابِ[314]{النور/39} أَوْ كَظُلُمَاتٍ فِي بَحْرٍ لُّجِّيٍّ يَغْشَاهُ مَوْجٌ مِّن فَوْقِهِ مَوْجٌ مِّن فَوْقِهِ سَحَابٌ ظُلُمَاتٌ بَعْضُهَا فَوْقَ بَعْضٍ إِذَا أَخْرَجَ يَدَهُ لَمْ يَكَدْ يَرَاهَا وَمَن لَّمْ يَجْعَلِ اللَّهُ لَهُ نُورًا فَمَا لَهُ مِن نُّورٍ[315] {النور/40} أَلَمْ تَرَ أَنَّ اللَّهَ يُسَبِّحُ لَهُ مَن فِي السَّمَاوَاتِ وَالْأَرْضِ وَالطَّيْرُ صَافَّاتٍ كُلٌّ قَدْ عَلِمَ صَلَاتَهُ وَتَسْبِيحَهُ وَاللَّهُ عَلِيمٌ بِمَا يَفْعَلُونَ[316] {النور/41}

---

307. But when it illuminated what was around him.
308. Every time it lights [the way] for them.
309. Hypocrisy.
310. Encompassing.
311. Allah ﷻ is encompassing of the disbelievers.
312. Encompassing.
313. Or [it is] like a rainstorm from the sky within which is darkness, thunder, and lightning.
314. But those who disbelieved—their deeds are like a mirage in a lowland which a thirsty one thinks is water until, when he comes to it, he finds it is nothing but finds Allah ﷻ before him, and He will pay him in full his due; and Allah ﷻ is swift in account.
315. Or [they are] like darknesses within an unfathomable sea which is covered by waves, upon which are waves, over which are clouds—darknesses, some of them upon others. When one puts out his hand [therein], he can hardly see it. And he to whom Allah ﷻ has not granted light—for him there is no light.
316. Do you not see that Allah ﷻ is exalted by whomever is within the heavens and the earth and [by] the birds with wings spread [in flight]? Each [of them] has known his [means of] prayer and exalting [Him], and Allah ﷻ is Knowing of what they do.

So, this notion of spiritual darkness expressed with the word ظُلُمَاتِ[317] in the ayahs is valid for both munāfiq and kafir. Yet, this depressive and pessimistic state is terminated when the person knows Allah ﷻ through true remembrance of dhikr similar to all of creation as mentioned أَلَمْ[318]

تَرَ أَنَّ اللَّهَ يُسَبِّحُ لَهُ مَن فِي السَّمَاوَاتِ وَالْأَرْضِ وَالطَّيْرُ صَافَّاتٍ كُلٌّ قَدْ عَلِمَ صَلَاتَهُ وَتَسْبِيحَهُ

If we assume a literal incident of أَوْ كَصَيِّبٍ مِّنَ السَّمَاء فِيهِ ظُلُمَاتٌ وَرَعْدٌ[319] وَبَرْقٌ happening, rain with darkness, thunder and lightning, a mu'min knows that they all work under the command of Allah ﷻ. A kafir or munāfiq does not know or truly embody this. Therefore, this knowledge makes a huge difference between two groups in both of their mental and emotional psychological engagements.

This can be similar to the following example. If there is a monster, one gets so scared and runs away because they don't know what this monster would do- kill the person or do destruction. They don't know why or who sent this monster. This randomness, chaos, and uncertainty instills an indescribable fear and pain in the person. This is the example of a munāfiq and kafir. They don't believe in Allah ﷻ and the Prophet ﷺ. They cannot understand and know the true meanings of everything because they disconnect their true and purposeful relationships with Allah ﷻ and Rasulullah ﷺ. Their true purpose of creation and meanings reveal themselves when they are connected with their Owner, Allah ﷻ. This definite, true, authentic, genuine, and actual relationship is explained by the Qurān, all the messengers, and the Prophet ﷺ.

On the other hand, if the person knows this monster-looking animal, the owner of it, and why it came, then this person even can give orders to this animal, reminding it that they also know the owner of it. Then, this monster-looking animal becomes friends with this person. This is the stance of a believer, a mu'min, or a Muslim. A mu'min and a Muslim know that all the evil-seeming incidents and things have a purpose and work under the command of Allah ﷻ. With this stance, the person becomes fearless and even, can give orders to them in the Name of the Creator, the Real Owner, Allah ﷻ as Rasulullah ﷺ did. Rasulullah ﷺ ordered and split the moon (Sûrah Qamar) [4], and ordered the

---

317. Darknesses.
318. Do you not see that Allah ﷻ is exalted by whomever is within the heavens and the earth and [by] the birds with wings spread [in flight]? Each [of them] has known his [means of] prayer and exalting [Him].
319. Or [it is] like a rainstorm from the sky within which is darkness, thunder and lightning.

mountain to stop shaking which we call this shaking an earthquake and the mountain stopped shaking [15].

From another perspective, conscience can be referred to as the true inner feeling helping the person in decision-making to differentiate between right and wrong. The existence of small faded impulses of true conscience in kafir and munāfiq can also put them in different types of spiritual and psychological sufferings and pains. When a person executes an action, if he or she considers a small possibility of being wrong, then, this person can suffer later in their memory renderings and visits to these past events. Therefore, kafir and munāfiq can have another possible source of pain due to their intentional and determined wrong stance.

In the expression[320] وَاللهُ مُحِيطٌ بِالْكَافِرِينَ, one can ask why the word بِالْكَافِرِينَ[321] is used although the discussion is about munāfiqeen. There can be possible reasons for this.

When there are different analogies to explain a topic, sometimes the reader can focus on the details of the analogy rather than the main message in the analogy or example itself. In this regard, using an infrequent key word about the topic can allude to the gist of the problem and refocus the attention on the real problem. In this sense, kufr is the essence of nifāq. The word kufr repeats itself frequently in different parts of the Qurān with different derivations of the word. Yet, the usage of kufr has been an infrequent word in the last few ayahs and has not been used so far. By being used here again, the reader is brought back to the real problem of kufr[322], اللهُ اعلم.

In another perspective, going back to the discussion of أَوْ[323] briefly mentioned above that there are two different groups of munāfiqeen. One is portrayed with the ayahs 17 and 18 and the other is with the ayahs 19 and 20. In the first case of the ayahs 17 and 18, these munāfiqeen have some light but as soon as it occurs it may vanish as mentioned فَلَمَّا[324] أَضَاءَتْ مَا حَوْلَهُ ذَهَبَ اللهُ بِنُورِهِمْ that they did not benefit from this light. Then, their disposition is detailed more clearly as صُمٌّ بُكْمٌ عُمْيٌ فَهُمْ لاَ يَرْجِعُونَ[325] {البقرة/18}.

---

320. Allah ﷻ is encompassing of the disbelievers.
321. Of the disbelievers.
322. Allah ﷻ knows best.
323. Or.
324. But when it illuminated what was around him.
325. Deaf, dumb and blind—so they will not return [to the right path].

In the other case of the ayahs 19 and 20[326], كُلَّمَا أَضَاءَ لَهُم مَّشَوْا فِيهِ وَإِذَا أَظْلَمَ they benefit from this light as mentioned with عَلَيْهِمْ قَامُو[327] مَّشَوْا فِيهِ. Yet, when this light is not present then they benefit their ceases as mentioned وَإِذَا أَظْلَمَ عَلَيْهِمْ قَامُو[328].

In order to emphasize the difference between this group and the prior group, Allah ﷻ mentions if Allah ﷻ wanted, then their case could be similar to the prior ones in that they would not have any light nor any benefit at all as mentioned وَلَوْ شَاءَ أَللَّهُ لَذَهَبَ بِسَمْعِهِمْ وَأَبْصَارِهِمْ[329] similar to the prior case as mentioned صُمٌّ بُكْمٌ عُمْيٌ فَهُمْ لَا يَرْجِعُونَ[330] {البقرة/18}.

Another difference between the above two groups can be related with their social status or education levels. The first group of nifāq can represent the people with no or minimum education level with incognizance as mentioned صُمٌّ بُكْمٌ عُمْيٌ فَهُمْ لَا يَرْجِعُونَ {البقرة/18}. The latter group can be somehow or somewhat called educated and aristocrats of that society. They have some understanding and benefit from this as mentioned with كُلَّمَا أَضَاءَ لَهُم مَّشَوْا فِيهِ[331]. Yet, this light, knowledge, cognizance, perspective, or disposition is not sufficient for them to fully walk on the path as mentioned وَإِذَا أَظْلَمَ عَلَيْهِمْ قَامُوا[332].

If one reviews both set of ayahs, 17th & 18th and 19th & 20th, representing two different examples, one can implicitly deduce the case of a traveling person in both similes. In this perspective, the psychology of a traveling person can be similar to the psychology of a munāfiq. When one reviews the duas of the Prophet ﷺ about traveling [16], these duas are especially addressing and asking protection from the issues of a person traveling in uncertainty, fear, anxiety, unknowns of what can happen to the family left behind, and unexpected engagements of traveling. Similarly, a munāfiq carries these similar dispositions of fear and anxieties due to unknowns and uncertainties lifelong. These times of difficulty can be temporary for a traveling person as the Prophet ﷺ mentions traveling is similar to a sample of small punishment from Jahannam. Yet, for a munāfiq these dispositions can make the person suffer for their entire life and it

---

326. Every time it lights [the way] for them, they walk therein; but when darkness comes over them, they stand [still].
327. They walk therein.
328. But when darkness comes over them, they stand [still].
329. And if Allah had willed, He could have taken away their hearing and their sight.
330. Deaf, dumb and blind—so they will not return [to the right path].
331. Every time it lights [the way] for them, they walk therein.
332. But when darkness comes over them, they stand [still].

can make both this life and the afterlife be suffering and punishment. One should always remember in the types of similes used in the Qurān that there are always possibilities of different meanings and renderings especially when one reviews different possibilities of similes in balagah for example being a compound simile, murakkab or mufarraq.

The verb يَكَادُ[333] can express the proximity of something about to happen. It expresses the closeness of its occurrence. The verb يَكَادُ most of the time is used without اَن with mudari.

When one reviews the phrase يَكَادُ الْبَرْقُ يَخْطَفُ أَبْصَارَهُمْ[334], there is a term used for potentially permanent or temporal blindness due to intense exposure of light. It is called flash blindness [8]. The word يَكَادُ can express this proximity of the full blindness yet there can be a partial or flash blindness. Yet, due to the Rahmah[335] of Allah ﷻ, it did not occur.

On another note, the word يَخْطَفُ[336], is presented in الْخَطْفَةَ خَطِفَ مَنْ إِلاَّ فَأَتْبَعَهُ شِهَابٌ ثَاقِبٌ[337] {الصافات/10}. This can show a quick and fast effect with this word of يَخْطَفُ[338]. It is interesting to note this word يَخْطَفُ is presented especially with the cases of occurrences with light or speed of light. In this case, this word is used in relation to الْبَرْقُ[339], lightning. In the other case, الْخَطْفَةَ خَطِفَ[340] is used in relation to jinn and angels who are known to be in a similar realm. This can be another example besides many to show the perfectness and flawlessness of the Qurān in the word usage, compatibility, and consistency as mentioned الْحَمْدُ لِلَّهِ الَّذِي أَنزَلَ عَلَى عَبْدِهِ الْكِتَابَ وَلَمْ يَجْعَل لَّهُ عِوَجَا[341] {الكهف/1}, Alhamdulillah!

The word أَبْصَارَهُمْ[342] can allude initially to eyes. Yet, basar is also associated with the heart. In other words, there is the seeing and cognitive ability of the heart.

---

333. Almost.
334. The lightning almost snatches away their sight.
335. Mercy.
336. Snatches.
337. Except one who snatches [some words] by theft, but they are pursued by a burning flame, piercing [in brightness].
338. Snatch.
339. Lightning.
340. Snatches [some words] by theft.
341. [All] praise is [due] to Allah ﷻ, who has sent down upon His Servant [Muhammad (ﷺ)] the Book and has not made therein any deviance.
342. Their sight.

In the phrase أَضَاءَ لَهُم كُلَّمَا[343], the word كُلَّمَا[344] can indicate that they don't want to miss any of the light that appears and they are so in need of it. The word كُلَّمَا in the context of this ayah can indicate the repeated occurrences as "every time."

It is interesting to note that this type of light similar to the light of thunder, is not really very useful. It has the immediate dense burst which can cause flash blindness [8]. It lasts such a short time that one can not really adjust themselves between its start and end enough to benefit from it.

In the expression أَضَاءَ لَهُم[345], the harf jar ل can indicate that when a person is exposed to trials and tests, he or she may view everything solely for their benefit or against their interest. This can symbolize the psychology of a person in these situations.

The phrase مَّشَوْأ فِيه[346] can indicate their difficulty in walking or moving in order to take advantage of this light. In other words, another word could have been used instead of مَّشَوْأ فِيه to indicate a meaning of running or moving fast so that they were in a rush to benefit from this light. Yet, a possible reason can be that a person who is in difficulty is expected to hasten to remove their difficulty. Their disability of the lack of the full benefit from this light can be correlated with the type of the light because the simile is given as a thunder light in the ayah. Thunder lights are not used by people to benefit from its light in normal conditions. Or, it can be related to munāfiq's disability due to the lack of their desire to benefit from this light if this light specifies a positive notion related with imān.

In the expression مَّشَوْأ فِيه[347] can show, their walking only occurs at the intervals of lightning. In other words, they don't or can't walk other than within this short, one-second-long time interval.

When one reviews the ayah, ابْصَارَهُمْ[348] is used two times in this ayah. The word عيون is not used. The word basirah can reveal inner malicious renderings of munāfiqeen compared to the word[349] عيون.

---

343. Every time it lights [the way] for them.
344. Every time.
345. It lights {the way}.
346. They walk therein.
347. They walk therein.
348. Their eye sight.
349. Eyes

The وَ in the expression أُوَإِذَا أَظْلَمَ عَلَيْهِمْ قَامُوا[350] can indicate a connection to the case of psychological states of fear with the previous case in munāfiqeen when sharp lightning occurred as they also experienced the fear and depression. In other words, both cases indicated with وَ can be considered mutually as dhulumat[351] or depressive inner states of munāfiqeen in the cases of lightning or darkness being without light.

The إِذَا in the expression وَإِذَا أَظْلَمَ عَلَيْهِمْ قَامُوا can indicate a sudden switch between lightning and darkness. This process itself induces another level of zulumāt leading to an additional psychological state of fear in munāfiqeen.

The word أَظْلَمَ[352] can indicate the magnitude of darkness especially felt after the disappearance of an intense light. These feelings can be so high due to the relative effects of switching a light on and off. It is also interesting to note that the black holes are formed according to the definition in astronomy when a massive star with an intense light collapses into its own gravitational force and disappears [5]. Similarly, this effect can be similar in the psychology of the munāfiqeen in two extremes of light and darkness, الله اعلم[353].

It is interesting to note from the hadith of Rasulullah ﷺ as [الظلم ظلمات يوم القيامة[354]. In the hadith, the darkness is expressed as a convoluted process of a deep, endless case. The definition of black hole alludes literally to this convoluted effect of darkness [5]. In our contemporary language, one can translate and contextualize the above hadith as "oppression is similar to a black hole pulling and sucking his or her owner into its endless darkness."

In the expression وَإِذَا أَظْلَمَ عَلَيْهِمْ[355], the word عَلَيْهِم can indicate that the dhulumāt that munāfiqeen are exposed to, are not random but specifically sent for them. One of the core principles in our aqidah[356] is that there is no randomness or haphazardness in the creation of Allah ﷻ, nor in the encounters of the personal and social events. Everything has a purpose. One can also relate this with the notion of qadar on a small scale and with different Names and Attributes of Allah ﷻ such as Al-

---

350. But when darkness comes over them, they stand [still].
351. Darkness.
352. Darkness comes over.
353. Allah ﷻ knows best.
354. Injustice is injustices in the day of resurrection.
355. But when darkness comes over them.
356. Belief.

A'dl[357], Al-Hakim[358], and Al-Karim[359] at a bigger scale of understandings, meanings, and correlations.

The word عَلَيْهِم[360] can also indicate that the person gets what he or she desires with the A'dl, Justice of Allah ﷻ. This is mentioned in different parts of the Qurãn

مَثَلُ مَا يُنفِقُونَ فِي هَذِهِ الْحَيَاةِ الدُّنْيَا كَمَثَلِ رِيحٍ فِيهَا صِرٌّ أَصَابَتْ حَرْثَ قَوْمٍ ظَلَمُواْ أَنفُسَهُمْ فَأَهْلَكَتْهُ وَمَا ظَلَمَهُمُ اللَّهُ وَلَكِنْ أَنفُسَهُمْ يَظْلِمُونَ[361] {آل عمران/117}

هَلْ يَنظُرُونَ إِلاَّ أَن تَأْتِيَهُمُ الْمَلائِكَةُ أَوْ يَأْتِيَ أَمْرُ رَبِّكَ كَذَلِكَ فَعَلَ الَّذِينَ مِن قَبْلِهِمْ وَمَا ظَلَمَهُمُ اللَّهُ وَلَكِن كَانُواْ أَنفُسَهُمْ يَظْلِمُونَ[362] {النحل/33}

وَمَا ظَلَمْنَاهُمْ وَلَكِن كَانُوا هُمُ الظَّالِمِينَ[363] {الزخرف/76}

One should not think that Allah ﷻ sends them a punishment randomly, yet this result is the result of their own choices and rendering.

In the expression وَإِذَا أَظْلَمَ عَلَيْهِمْ قَامُواْ[364], the word قَامُوا[365] can indicate different possibilities. One possibility can show the immediate or unexpected process of thunder light, switching on and off, and catching them while they were standing there. In this case, the word قَامُوا can be translated as "became motionless while standing."

Another possibility is that when there was no light they panicked and stood up. It is expected that when there is an undesirable situation, a person can be patient, sit still, and wait until the situation gets better. The word قَامُوا in this case can show their panicky attitude by standing up prematurely when there was no light.

Another possibility can be related with their unfamiliarity of truly worshipping Allah ﷻ by going back and establishing a true and sincere

---

357. The Just.
358. The wise.
359. The generous.
360. Over them.
361. The example of what they spend in this worldly life is like that of a wind containing frost which strikes the harvest of a people who have wronged themselves [i.e., sinned] and destroys it. And Allah ﷻ has not wronged them, but they wrong themselves.
362. Do they [i.e., the disbelievers] await except that the angels should come to them or there comes the command of your Lord? Thus did those before them do before them. And Allah ﷻ wronged them not, but they had been wronging themselves.
363. And We did not wrong them, but it was they who were the wrongdoers.
364. But when darkness comes over them, they stand [still].
365. They stand {still}.

connection with Allah ﷻ during the times of difficulty. For example, قَالَ لَقَدْ ظَلَمَكَ بِسُؤَالِ نَعْجَتِكَ إِلَى نِعَاجِهِ وَإِنَّ كَثِيرًا مِّنْ الْخُلَطَاء لَيَبْغِي بَعْضُهُمْ عَلَى بَعْضٍ إِلَّا الَّذِينَ آمَنُوا وَعَمِلُوا الصَّالِحَاتِ وَقَلِيلٌ مَّا هُمْ وَظَنَّ دَاوُودُ أَنَّمَا فَتَنَّاهُ فَاسْتَغْفَرَ رَبَّهُ وَخَرَّ رَاكِعًا وَأَنَابَ ([366] سجدة مستحبة)(ص/24}, In this ayah when Dawud as faced a trial, test, and difficulty, he as immediately made istigfar as mentioned فَاسْتَغْفَرَ رَبَّهُ, and went into the positions of ruku' and sujud as this is an ayah of sajdah as mentioned with the words وَخَرَّ رَاكِعًا وَأَنَابَ. Conversely, the munāfiqeen during times of difficulty got even more agitated and stood up as mentioned with قَامُوا instead of making istigfar and coming back to Allah ﷻ. One can realize that the two actions of قَامُوا and رَاكِعًا in the above analysis are totally opposite of each other. The dispositions, expectations, and outcomes of kufr and imān are totally opposite of each other.

On a side note, the word خَرَّ[367] in the expression وَخَرَّ رَاكِعًا وَأَنَابَ[368] can show this innate natural disposition of a person embodied in asking forgiveness, making istigfar at all times and especially during times of challenges. Rasulullah ﷺ mentions the closest point of a person to Allah ﷻ is the place of sujud [2]. The person runs to Allah ﷻ to be closer and asks for help in these situations and in all situations.

On the other hand, the word قَامُوا[369] can indicate the embodied disposition of panic, fear, stress, and disconnecting further by standing up. This person of kufr or nifāq gets further away and distanced from Allah ﷻ.

After mentioning the sababs, the causes such as thunder, lightning, or others, then the expression[370] وَلَوْ شَاء اللّٰه لَذَهَبَ بِسَمْعِهِمْ وَأَبْصَارِهِمْ, the Mai'shah Ilāhiya[371], the Divine Will, is mentioned. In other words, all those are sabab[372], simple causes. Yet, the a'tf, connector, و can symbolize

366. [David] said, "He has certainly wronged you in demanding your ewe [in addition] to his ewes. And indeed, many associates oppress one another, except for those who believe and do righteous deeds—and few are they." And David became certain that We had tried him, and he asked forgiveness of his Lord and fell down bowing [in prostration] and turned in repentance [to Allah ﷻ].

367. Fell down.

368. And fell down bowing [in prostration] and turned in repentance [to Allah ﷻ].

369. They stand {still}.

370. And if Allah had willed, He could have taken away their hearing and their sight.

371. Divine will.

372. Simple cause.

the a'dalah[373] and hikmah[374] of Allah ﷻ that Allah ﷻ implements and executes with Justice and Wisdom. In other words, there are a lot of evil-seeming incidents that are happening all around us. If we do not observe them from the perspectives of hikmah, wisdom, and understanding, and look for the real realities behind these evil-seeming incidents then, life can seem miserable due to wrong interpretations of their evil-seeming nature. On the contrary, with the understanding of true imān, life can become similar to watching a fiction movie, understanding the mysterious realities and wisdom behind them arranged and set by Allah ﷻ.

In the expression وَلَوْ شَاءَ اللّٰهُ لَذَهَبَ بِسَمْعِهِمْ وَأَبْصَارِهِمْ[375], the word لَوْ can indicate that Mai'shah Ilahiya[376] is not dependent on causes or sabab[377].

Allah ﷻ is beyond time. Therefore, one of the renderings of the Qurān to indicate this notion is that sometimes verbs are indicated in the past tense, madi. In other words, time is a concept with the classifications of past, present, and future for humans. Yet, for Allah ﷻ, everything is the same in their relationship with time in the Divine I'lm[378], Qada[379] and Qadar[380] of Allah ﷻ. One of the ways to express this reality is in madi, past tense form. As a side topic to discussion, Allah ﷻ has attributes of Al-Awwal[381] and Al-Akhir[382]. In a similar approximation, Rasulullah ﷺ advised the usage of the word "dahr" in proper relation to Allah ﷻ when some people used this word improperly [15]. This same word is mentioned in the first ayah of surah al-Insān [4] .

The word شَاء is the connector between the cause and effect in the incidents. In other words, the causes are means for the Ma'ishah[383] of Allah ﷻ, for the evil-seeming incidents that disrespectful people like us ought not to blame Allah ﷻ in our thoughts and speeches. In other words, the adab with Allah ﷻ requires constant cleansing of thoughts

---

373. Justice.
374. Wisdom.
375. And if Allah had willed, He could have taken away their hearing and their sight.
376. Divine Will.
377. Simple cause.
378. Knowledge.
379. Fate.
380. Destiny.
381. The First.
382. The last.
383. Divine will.

before they transform into the actions of words or bodily engagements. Then, this establishes the steps for the true love of Allah ﷻ.

Similarly, the adab[384] with Rasulullah ﷺ requires constant cleansing of thoughts before they turn into the actions of words or other renderings. Then, this establishes the steps for the true love of Rasulullah ﷺ.

Sometimes, having a thought without adab does not cause a harm if it is caught immediately and terminated immediately with istigfar. Then, these thoughts don't fester and they disappear. The person can get immense reward for this. The adab with Allah ﷻ and Rasulullah ﷺ requires perceiving everything as beautiful, appropriate, perfect, and meaningful. This is the reality. It is not a self-induced perspective.

Therefore, the adab requires the disposition to be such as: "Oh Allah! I may not truly understand the hikmah behind this evil-seeming incident but I know You are the Rabbul Alamin, and everything that comes from You is beautiful, meaningful, and purposeful. Please make this a source of opportunity for increase of Your Blessings on me. Allow it to increase my closeness to You, Ya Allah! and make my life easy with a'fiyah[385] in this dunya and ākhirah!, Ameen."

The people without adab can seem to even be religious but if they don't have this understanding then, this disease sooner or later will reveal itself and cause them to lose all of their efforts. Shaytan is a prime example of this. Angels are the opposite. Humans are mixed between the angelic and satanic levels.

Shaytan did not understand and lost the adab by questioning without adab, and showing displeasure to the Mai'shah[386] of Allah ﷻ about the creation of humans. Angels kept their adab by trying to understand the hikmah of the creation of humans and fully submitted to the Mai'shah of Allah ﷻ. As humans were the trial and test for both, then humans adapted by going between the two extremes.

Rasulullah ﷺ has reached the highest pinnacle of submission to the Ma'ishah of Allah ﷻ as even he ﷺ surpassed the angels. Musa as and others can be at other pinnacles.

Conversely, there are humans at the lowest potholes due to having no adab and even they surpassed the Shaytan. The munāfiqeen at all times and especially the ones with Rasulullah ﷺ can surpass the

---

384. Respect.
385. Health.
386. Divine Will.

Shaytan, being with Rasulullah ﷺ and yet, not having adab and true imān. Similarly, the people with Musa as in their engagements of قَالُواْ ادْعُ لَنَا رَبَّكَ يُبَيِّن لَّنَا مَا هِيَ قَالَ إِنَّهُ يَقُولُ إِنَّهَا بَقَرَةٌ لاَّ فَارِضٌ وَلاَ بِكْرٌ عَوَانٌ بَيْنَ ذَلِكَ فَافْعَلُواْ مَا تُؤْمَرُونَ {البقرة/68}[387], [388]ادْعُ لَنَا, the way of questioning with their words قَالَ رَبِّ فَأَنظِرْنِي إِلَى يَوْمِ يُبْعَثُونَ can be compared with what Shaytan said رَبَّكَ {ص/79}[389]. One says رَبَّكَ[390] and the other says رَبِّ[391]. This can be another representation of the extremes in two different opposites, الله اعلم[392]. May Allah ﷻ make us die as true Muslims with true imān, Ameen.

As one reviews in the parts of the above ayahs as وَاللّهُ مُحِيطٌ[393], إِنَّ اللّه عَلَى كُلِّ شَيْءٍ قَدِيرٌ[395]and, بِالْكَافِرِينَ,وَلَوْ شَاء اللّهُ لَذَهَبَ بِسَمْعِهِمْ[394] وَأَبْصَارِهِمْ one can realize that lafthu Mubarak[396], أللّه, is explicitly mentioned. This can be due to the need of a person to constantly understand, realize, and focus on the reality that everything happens with the Ma'ishah[397] of Allah ﷻ and not due to the simple, apparent causes.

If one analyzes the phrase وَلَوْ شَاء أللّه[398], the verb[399] شَاء does not have a specific maful, object but it is left general. This can indicate that Maisha[400] and iradah[401] of Allah ﷻ, Divine Will and Willpower are not affected by the causes. For example, in physics there is an action and reaction force relationship. If something has an effect on another thing, then that something gets affected as well. It is bi-directional. In this case, as indicated in the ayah, having no maful can indicate this absence of effect on Maisha of Allah ﷻ. This effect is unidirectional.

---

387. They said, "Call upon your Lord to make clear to us what it is." [Moses] said, "[Allah ﷻ] says, 'It is a cow which is neither old nor virgin, but median between that,' so do what you are commanded."
388. Call upon your lord.
389. He said, "My Lord, then reprieve me until the Day they are resurrected."
390. Your Lord.
391. Lord.
392. Allah ﷻ knows best.
393. Allah ﷻ is encompassing of the disbelievers.
394. And if Allah ﷻ had willed, He could have taken away their hearing and their sight.
395. Indeed, Allah ﷻ is over all things competent.
396. Blessed word.
397. Divine Will.
398. And if Allah ﷻ had willed.
399. Willed.
400. Divine will.
401. Will power.

When the word ذَهَبَ[402] is used with بـ as in the expression ذَهَبَ[403] بِسَمْعِهِمْ, then it can have the meaning of taking something away. If one analyzes the word لَذَهَبَ in the expression وَلَوْ شَاءَ أللَّهُ لَذَهَبَ بِسَمْعِهِمْ وَأَبْصَارِ هِمْ[404], this word can indicate that Allah ﷻ does not neglect the evil renderings but gives respite and delay. In other words, Allah ﷻ does not immediately punish people due to their evil renderings as mentioned وَلَوْ يُؤَاخِذُ اللَّهُ النَّاسَ بِمَا كَسَبُوا مَا تَرَكَ عَلَى ظَهْرِهَا مِن دَابَّةٍ وَلَـٰكِن يُؤَخِّرُهُمْ إِلَىٰ أَجَلٍ مُّسَمًّى فَإِذَا جَاءَ أَجَلُهُمْ فَإِنَّ اللَّهَ كَانَ بِعِبَادِهِ بَصِيرًا[405] {فاطر/٤٥}. There are different Names of Allah ﷻ such as As-Sabûr[406] and Al-Halîm[407]. One can understand this respite and delay with these Names and Attributes of Allah ﷻ.

From another perspective, this word لَذَهَبَ[408] in the expression[409] وَلَوْ شَاءَ اللَّهُ لَذَهَبَ بِسَمْعِهِمْ وَأَبْصَارِهِمْ, can indicate that people's evil renderings are not lost but preserved and restored. Either it is erased or terminated if the person makes tawbah[410] or if not, it can be left for accountability. For example, if a person sees boiling water then he or she may think that the water is disappearing. Yet, a person who knows simple chemistry or physics understands that the water changes its phase from liquid form into gas form and it is still there. Similarly, when Allah ﷻ gives respite for people's evil renderings, it does not mean that Allah ﷻ does not interfere or there are swerved constructions of a passive God especially as wrongfully understood in some of the Western perceptions.

When one analyzes the words بِسَمْعِهِمْ وَأَبْصَارِ هِمْ[411], the focus point here is not the physical ear and eyes represented by the organs, but rather the abilities and emotions that are associated with hearing and seeing. Abilities and emotions are all gifts given by Allah ﷻ. They are not there as a natural cause. They are not present due to various causes. The person should not take them for granted. If Allah ﷻ wanted, all those abilities and emotions can be taken away.

---

402. Taken away.
403. Taken away their hearing.
404. And if Allah ﷻ had willed he could have taken away their hearing and their eye sight.
405. And if Allah ﷻ were to impose blame on the people for what they have earned, He would not leave upon it [i.e., the earth] any creature. But He defers them for a specified term. And when their time comes, then indeed Allah ﷻ has ever been, of His servants, Seeing.
406. The Patient.
407. The Forbearer.
408. Would have taken away.
409. And if Allah ﷻ had willed he could have taken away their hearing and their eye sight.
410. Repentance.
411. Their hearing and their eyesight.

Also, the words بِسَمْعِهِمْ[412] is presented as singular and[413] أَبْصَارِهِم is presented as plural. This can indicate that seeing can include many incidents or objects at a time. However, hearing can involve only one incident at a time.

The expression إِنَّ اللَّه عَلَى كُلّ شَيْءٍ قَدِيرٌ[414] can indicate that sometimes our own problems and wrong construction of our ideas about Allah ﷻ cause doubts, fears, and uneasiness. Yet, it is our problem. For example, this occurs when people face some of the problems caused by munāfiqeen or others. Or, when we encounter a problem in our life, then we immediately dive into looking into means asking for help or solace from them. If the person establishes a method of always going back to Allah ﷻ with[415] إِنَّ اللَّه عَلَى كُلّ شَيْءٍ قَدِير , then this person will be in no or minimum uneasy states of heart and mind.

In the statement إِنَّ اللَّه عَلَى كُلّ شَيْءٍ قَدِيرٌ, the lafzu Mubarak[416] اللَّه is explicitly mentioned instead of other Names or[417] هو to indicate the importance of attribution directly to Uluhiyyah[418] to Allah ﷻ. When Allah ﷻ creates everything from nothing, then Allah ﷻ does not leave his creation by themselves in uncertain states or without supervision in chaos and darkness. Yet, Allah ﷻ shows constant guidance and signs. Allah ﷻ is active and interferes with wisdom, hikmah[419].

In the sentence[420] إِنَّ اللَّه عَلَى كُلّ شَيْءٍ قَدِيرٌ, the word كُلّ[421] can indicate that all of the occurrences and everything depends on the Mashiyyah and enablement of Allah ﷻ. The word شَيْءٍ[422] can signify that when something is created by Allah ﷻ, that can be named شَيْء. Or, it can mean anything possible or impossible, existent or non-existent. Yet, the continuation and sustenance of this thing, شَيْء, needs and depends always on the Creator, Allah ﷻ, Rabbul A'lAmeen, the Sustainer and Nourisher of everything.

---

412. Their hearing.
413. Their eyesight,
414. Indeed, Allah ﷻ is over all things competent.
415. Indeed, Allah ﷻ is over all things competent.
416. Blessed word.
417. Him.
418. Realm of power.
419. Blessings.
420. Indeed, Allah ﷻ is over all things competent.
421. All.
422. Things.

There is a substantial discussion among the scholars about the word شَيْءٍ[423] in its relationship with 'aqidah[424], kalām[425], and how and for who this word can be used [9].

In the statement of إِنَّ اللَّهَ عَلَى كُلِّ شَيْءٍ قَدِيرٌ[426], the word قَدِير[427] can be translated as Allah ﷻ can do anything and everything whatever and however Allah ﷻ wants.

In the testimonial إِنَّ اللَّهَ عَلَى كُلِّ شَيْءٍ قَدِيرٌ, the word قَدِيرٌ is used instead of قادِر[428].

The word قادِر can indicate strength to do something. It is in the form of ismu-fai'l. In this regard, this word can be used for humans as well. The strength with this word indicates a one-way, limited strength.

On the other hand, the word قَدِير[429] can indicate both ways of potential strength. In this potentiality, Allah ﷻ can execute the action or not. In other words, the word قَدِير can entail the Mashiyyah, the Divine Will. For example, if a person gets a shot to prevent a potential disease, then in this process, there is a weak microbe injected into the immune system of the person. The person has the strength, قادِر, to give the shot to another person. If the person decides to take back this injected microbe from the person, he or she can't do it. It is a one-way process.

On the other hand, Allah ﷻ can give sickness to a person and yet at the same time, Allah ﷻ can give shifaa, heal or cure this person. Therefore, Allah ﷻ is قَدِير and has both ways of Full Strength and Control. Therefore, we use this word قَدِير only for Allah ﷻ. Allah ﷻ has the strength to do anything, and everything in any way with reversible effects. The created beings have limited strength. Their limitations can present themselves in the quality, quantity, and reversibility of these applications.

One can witness this effect when Ibrahim as challenged Namrud with his claim of strength as mentioned:

أَلَمْ تَرَ إِلَى الَّذِي حَاجَّ إِبْرَاهِيمَ فِي رَبِّهِ أَنْ آتَاهُ اللَّهُ الْمُلْكَ إِذْ قَالَ إِبْرَاهِيمُ رَبِّيَ الَّذِي يُحْيِي وَيُمِيتُ قَالَ أَنَا أُحْيِي وَأُمِيتُ قَالَ إِبْرَاهِيمُ فَإِنَّ اللَّهَ يَأْتِي بِالشَّمْسِ مِنَ الْمَشْرِقِ فَأْتِ

---

423. Things.
424. Belief.
425. Word.
426. Indeed, Allah ﷻ is over all things competent.
427. Competent.
428. The All-Capable.
429. Competent.

In .بِهَا مِنَ الْمَغْرِبِ فَبُهِتَ الَّذِي كَفَرَ وَاللّٰهُ لاَ يَهْدِي الْقَوْمَ الظَّالِمِينَ 430{البقرة/258} this case, Ibrahim as exactly challenged Namrud with this case of reversibility of a phenomenon. Namrud claimed a strength similar to the indications of the word قَدِير 431 by saying قَالَ أَنَا أُحْيِي وَأُمِيتُ 432. Then, Ibrahim as refuted this claim by asking فَإِنَّ اللّٰهَ يَأْتِي بِالشَّمْسِ 433 مِنَ الْمَشْرِقِ فَأْتِ بِهَا مِنَ الْمَغْرِبِ. Namrud simply and clearly lost this argument as mentioned434 فَبُهِتَ الَّذِي كَفَر.

In addition, the word435 قَدِير can indicate and emphasize the continuation. In other words, Allah ﷻ is always Active, interferes, and all the Names and Attributes of Allah ﷻ are constantly manifested in the creation. The word قَدِير can also indicate the unlimited vast authority, control, and dominion of Allah ﷻ. Yet, at the same time, this control, authority, and dominion directly belongs to Allah ﷻ, as Zatiyyah. It does not and cannot bear or tolerate change. At the same time, this dominion, control, and authority are necessary. It cannot tolerate any deficiency or imperfection. The Names such as Al-Razzaq436, Al-Gaffar437, Al-Muhyi438, and Al-Mumit439 can be the reflections of this Dominion, Control, and Authority of Allah ﷻ.

When we analyze the ayah إِنَّ اللّٰهَ عَلَى كُلِّ شَيْءٍ قَدِيرٌ 440, the word قَدِيرٌ can indicate as mentioned the Qudrah441 of Allah ﷻ to do anything and everything. The word قَادِر 442 can indicate the Quwwah443 of Allah ﷻ when the Qudrah of Allah ﷻ is in qada.

---

430. Have you not considered the one who argued with Abraham about his Lord [merely] because Allah ﷻ had given him kingship? When Abraham said, "My Lord is the one who gives life and causes death," he said, "I give life and cause death." Abraham said, "Indeed, Allah ﷻ brings up the sun from the east, so bring it up from the west." So the disbeliever was overwhelmed [by astonishment], and Allah ﷻ does not guide the wrongdoing people.
431. Competent.
432. He said, "I give life and cause death."
433. "Indeed, Allah ﷻ brings up the sun from the east, so bring it up from the west."
434. So the disbeliever was overwhelmed [by astonishment].
435. Competent.
436. The Sustainer.
437. The All-Forgiving.
438. The Giver of Life.
439. The Bringer of Death; The Destroyer.
440. Indeed Allah ﷻ is over all things competent.
441. The will {of Allah ﷻ }
442. The All-Capable.
443. The power.

If we analyze for example {الذاريات/58}[444] إِنَّ اللَّهَ هُوَ الرَّزَّاقُ ذُو الْقُوَّةِ الْمَتِينُ,
it is the Quwwah of Allah ﷻ that is emphasized with الْمَتِينُ[445] to indicate
the Divine Mashiyyah[446] and Qudrah[447] of Allah ﷻ.

On the other hand, if we analyze the expression[448] و لا حول الاَّ بالله
لا قوَّة as mentioned in the hadith [7] بالله لا حول و لا قوَّة الاَّas, the limited
potentiality of mashiyyah for humans is indicated with the word hawla,
حول as compared to the Infinite Divine Mashiyyah expressed with
Qudrah. The word قوَّة is used for Allah ﷻ and humans. Yet, to differentiate
this usage, الْمَتِينُ[449] is used to indicate the Divine Mashiyyah and Infinite
Qudrah of Allah ﷻ. At the same time, human's enablement of anything
as the reflection of Names and Attributes of Allah ﷻ is executed only
with the enablement of Allah ﷻ as mentioned[450] بالله الاَّ لا قوَّة.

In this ayah, one can see with the expression وَلَوْ شَاءَ اللَّهُ لَذَهَبَ بِسَمْعِهِمْ
{البقرة/20}[451] وَأَبْصَارِهِمْ إِنَّ اللَّهَ عَلَى كُلِّ شَيْءٍ قَدِيرٌ that if Allah ﷻ wanted, then
وَلَوْ شَاءَ أللَّهُ لَذَهَبَ بِسَمْعِهِمْ وَأَبْصَارِهِمْ[452]. This can indicate the Qudrah[453] of Allah
ﷻ as detailed in the above discussion.

According to the some of the scholars, ayahs 17th to 22nd is the
continuation of the same type of munãfiqeen. Or, they can possibly
explain different types of munãfiqeen.

On another note, each ayah of the Qurãn can have a specific
addressee. Yet, at the same time, each ayah of the Qurãn can cover
different meanings for everyone including the Muslims, kafirs,
munãfiqeen, and other groups.

In this regard, with possible implied meanings of the ayahs from
the 17th to the 20th, they can also possibly imply the fluctuating spiritual
states of a Muslim. Most of the time, we don't know what is halal and
what is haram. Sometimes, if we know them, we don't implement them.
Yet, when we implement the light—Nûr of the Qurãn and Sunnah—we
make some progress. When we stop doing this and spend most of our

---

444. Indeed, it is Allah ﷻ who is the [continual] Provider, the firm possessor of strength.
445. The Firm Possessor of Strength.
446. Permission.
447. The will {of Allah ﷻ }
448. There is no might and power except from Allah ﷻ.
449. The Firm Possessor of Strength.
450. There is no power except by Allah ﷻ·
451. And if Allah ﷻ had willed, He could have taken away their hearing and their sight.
Indeed, Allah ﷻ is over all things competent.
452. And if Allah ﷻ had willed, He could have taken away their hearing and their sight.
453. The might of Allah ﷻ.

time involving ourselves with and setting our main framework of life on what others say, the norms and cultures of the society and time, then we drench ourselves in constant darkness of spiritual pain, fear, anxiety, worries, and sadness due to the absence of the Nûr—light of the pillars of the Qurān and Sunnah. May Allah ﷻ protect us, Ameen.

From another perspective, these can be analyzed within the perspectives of psychology and sociology.

One can analyze these cases as a group phenomenon. Within the principles of sociology, one can analyze these cases with the procedures of claims-making and other parameters leading to policy-making through the perspectives of macro-sociological approaches. At another level, one can analyze the cases between the subjects and social problem workers with detailed analysis of individualized behaviors through the perspectives of micro-sociological approaches [10].

The perspectives of micro-sociological approaches can lead to the psychological analysis of these individuals. One can analyze these cases as cases of the individual rather than analyzing them as a group.

In this case, Rasulullah ﷺ is the first person addressing these social problems as a group phenomenon as a sociological case, and also as an individual phenomenon as a psychological case.

As a sociological case, there are different campaigns that these people engage themselves in as a group that these ayahs can allude to.

In today's six-stage social problem process [10], these groups identify the first three steps of this process as initial claims making, media coverage, and public reaction. Yet, Allah ﷻ did not give them the ability to make policies at the time of Rasulullah ﷺ. The campaigns that today's media coverage and public reaction entail were moreso small groups of people challenging the newly established, fresh society at the time of Rasulullah ﷺ.

According to these small groups who were not successful in policy making, they may have asserted that there was no progress being made in social problems due to expecting a full solution to each problem (perfectibility); and the case of proportion being that when big problems disappear, then relatively small problems can seem bigger (proportion) [10].

Yet, there was huge progress in addressing the social problems according to the objective and fair measurement tools of sociology in that society in a short amount of time. The Qurān in the application of the sunnah, swiftly, smoothly, softly, and effectively implemented these changes. The problems related to individual rights and equality, property rights, gender rights and equality, domestic violence and all other sociological problems were present much more abundantly (compared to today) before Islam in the pre-Arab society with tribal laws gauged by power and superiority of lineage.

Rasulullah ﷺ established the new guidelines of the society with contextualization with each sabab-ul-nuzûl[454], case by case. Accordingly, Divine Guidelines were established with the changing needs and contexts of people. In other words, in these guidelines or as one can refer to them as policies as in sociology, humans were reminded of this importance of adaptation or change through the processes of nāsikh, context, sabab-ul-nuzul[455], different chains of narration of hadith contextualizing to each person. Lastly, the ayah implied this perfect and peak level of these guidelines in 23 years with the ayah of "اليوم أكملت لكم دينكم[456]".

Yet, Allah ﷻ, the Qurān, Rasulullah ﷺ, the hadith have all emphasized the importance of scholars and scholarship. One of the main reasons this role was critical was due to their presenting the main teachings of the Qurān and Sunnah of Rasulullah ﷺ according to the changing needs of time, people, culture, and context.

Then, the examples of Imams Abu Hanifah rh, Shafii (rh), Malik (rh), Ahmad (rh) have established transgenerational guidelines in legal rulings, fiqh from the Qurān and Hadith due to flows of different need-based cases immediately in early periods after the demise of the Rasulullah saw.

Imams Maturudi (rh) and Ashari (rh) established transgenerational guidelines in aqidah structuralized from the Quran and Hadith due to flows of different discussions of intellect in early periods immediately in early periods after the demise of the Rasulullah ﷺ.

As the religion has been growing with both aqidah, belief, and amal[457], fiqh, the essence of engagement with the religion has seemed to be affected with Greek philosophy in the 10th and 11th centuries. Due to this need, Allah ﷻ enabled Imam Ghazali (rh) to establish the

---

454. The reason for narration.
455. Reason for narration.
456. Today I have completed your religion.
457. Actions.

transgenerational guidelines in the format of the essence of the religion both through the discourses of mind-intellect and heart-tasawwuf.

Currently, we are moving into a time when the faculties of intellect or mind and the faculties of heart or experience are trying to be put together. In other words, the value of both are accepted as important. Yet, we need to extend our scholarship to make this already available unification of both the heart and mind available to the Muslims who have been upset due to their religious education implying the disagreement between heart and mind. At the same time, we need to extend our scholarship to make this unification of the heart and mind available and accessible in the language, culture, and context of people who are not Muslims.

When a person analyzes these ayahs within the discipline of psychology referred to as ilmu-nafs in traditional literature, the evil crime renderings of a person are expected to induce guilt in the person. The person can remove these feelings to a positive gain by asking for forgiveness from the people and from Allah ﷻ. Yet, if the person does not want to face oneself with self-accountability of inner conversations with qualms, compunctions, demur, misgiving or scruples, then the feelings leading to the psychological diseases such as a persecution complex can develop. Persecution complex is an obsessive feeling or fear that one is the object of collective hostility or ill treatment on the part of others [5].

One should analyze these fields such as psychology with their terms and findings within the framework of the Qurān and Sunnah as it is an immediate and first reference point. The problems of submitting oneself fully to the discipline of psychology can be another problem among some Muslims.

In other words, psychology and psychotherapy assume certain premises as made by the lead people in this field such as Sigmund Freud and others. All the hours, days, weeks, or years of psychotherapy sessions can be conducted to lead the person to this premise as originally established by the founders of this field. Yet, this premise in its explicit term can be contradicting to the simple and apparent teachings of the Qurān and Sunnah. As the person is convinced and ultimately embodies this contradictory premise at the end of all these sessions, then the person starts having an identity crisis with their religion. Then, the person is forced to make a choice between dual identities which can be very painful. Or, the person can struggle all of one's life in order to harmonize these perspectives. Or, the person can ignore and assume that this problem does not exist. Or, decide there is no contradiction and he or she tries to move on by consciously not thinking about the conflicting perspectives.

There are reported cases of these conflicts either among new Muslims or Muslim-born individuals especially in non-Muslim countries and some in Muslim countries who have the common scarcity of grounded, genuine Islamic knowledge through the Qurān and Sunnah [20]. This conflict could be mitigated using a traditional, legitimate approach of grounding the individuals first with sciences and embodiment of the Qurān and the Sunnah, and then engaging them with the unfiltered, natural and social sciences. Yes, our filtration of the clean knowledge comes with our reference point to Rabbul Alalamin. In other words, wahiy as the Qurān and Hadith shows us the guidelines of what to learn and how to learn. After this content knowledge and with its usul as established for thousands of years it can be called filtering for the clean and purposeful, beneficial, and relevant knowledge. After this, one can make analysis in the arena of unfiltered literature.

In other words, the current available knowledge in natural and social sciences does not have any concern about or methodology to deal with their conflicting nature with wahiy. I believe that in the reality of the true science, the genuine natural and social sciences findings do not conflict with the teachings of the wahiy. Yet, as humans are advancing in every field, today's findings and analysis can be contradictory to tomorrow's new findings. Yet, today we assume that these findings are final and when they are accepted by some, then they are considered backwards. Similarly, a case of today's natural or social sciences may seem contradictory today with the wahiy. Yet, tomorrow this finding may be wrong and tomorrow's new finding can be in full harmony with wahiy.

Yes, ilmu-nafs, psychology or psychotherapy, has been a traditional discipline in Islam. Allah ﷻ mentions in the Qurān وَلَا تَكُونُوا كَالَّذِينَ نَسُوا اللَّهَ فَأَنسَاهُمْ أَنفُسَهُمْ أُولَٰئِكَ هُمُ الْفَاسِقُونَ ﴿الحشر/19﴾ [458]. Knowing and discovering oneself within the guidelines of the Qurān and sunnah can transform, uphold, and boost the person to a spiritual positive vertical axis.

---

458. And be not like those who forgot Allah ﷻ, so He made them forget themselves. Those are the defiantly disobedient.

At the same time, it is important to recognize, learn, and benefit from the widespread terminologies as spread by different fields such as psychology. The popularized teachings of Buddhism in its relationship to psychology can show the value of this dual interaction. Yet, Islamic teachings of ilmu-nafs[459] especially through the practice and teachings of tasawwuf (Sufism) for thousands of years have not been as recognized, appreciated, and adopted in fields such as psychology as another avenue of helping people who are in need regardless of their religious association.

[21-22]

يَا أَيُّهَا النَّاسُ اعْبُدُوا رَبَّكُمُ الَّذِي خَلَقَكُمْ وَالَّذِينَ مِن قَبْلِكُمْ لَعَلَّكُمْ تَتَّقُونَ [460] {البقرة/21} الَّذِي جَعَلَ لَكُمُ الأَرْضَ فِرَاشاً وَالسَّمَاء بِنَاء وَأَنزَلَ مِنَ السَّمَاء مَاء فَأَخْرَجَ بِهِ مِنَ الثَّمَرَاتِ رِزْقاً لَّكُمْ فَلاَ تَجْعَلُوا لِلّهِ أَندَاداً وَأَنتُمْ تَعْلَمُونَ [461] {البقرة/22}

Ibadah, worship is the essence in order to embody imān and the true tawhid. Ibadādah are all the teachings of Allah ﷻ through the Qurān and the sunnah of Rasulullah ﷺ. These teachings include all the categorizations as methodically established through the legal schools. Some of these detailed categorizations are fardh, wajib, sunnah, mustahab, mubāh, makrûh, and haram. Halal is a general term used to denote all permissible items and haram is a term popularly used to denote impermissible items or engagements as set by Allah ﷻ. In its general meaning, ibadah means to implement the fardh, wajib, sunnah, mustahab and to be within the limits of halal. At the same time, ibādah means not to engage with haram and to avoid makruh items as much as possible.

Ibadah supports, establishes, and solidifies the pillars of imān. The faculties of mind, heart, emotions, and experience are substantiated about the teachings of imān, tawhid, and marifatullah[462] through the

---

459. Psychology.
460. O mankind, worship your Lord, who created you and those before you, that you may become righteous
461. [He] who made for you the earth a bed [spread out] and the sky a ceiling and sent down from the sky, rain and brought forth thereby fruits as provision for you. So do not attribute to Allah ﷻ equals while you know [that there is nothing similar to Him].
462. Knowledge of Allah ﷻ.

establishment and continuation of ibadah as practiced by the Prophet saw.

Ibadah establishes peace and happiness in this world and in the afterlife. Ibadah helps support one's worldly engagements with structure, order, discipline, and barakah. Ibadah helps by improving one's self-development.

Ibadah is a connection and a bridge between the creation and the Creator. The person performs acts that are prescribed by Allah ﷻ in order to connect to Allah ﷻ. These acts are not humanly made or discovered but directly instructed by the prophets and Rasulullah ﷺ.

Ibadah is not only the salah, sawm, or zakah. Ibadah is all the guidelines encompassing the categorizations of fardh, sunnah, mustahab and at the same time avoiding the haram and makruh. When a person implements any mundane-looking episode such as going to the bathroom with the duas of the Prophet ﷺ, then this normal engagement transforms itself into an ibadah by remembering Allah ﷻ as taught by the duas of the Prophet ﷺ.

In this sense, ibadah takes place throughout all of the day and all of the night. This makes our religion one of full conscious implementation with awareness 24 hours a day. In this perspective, ihsān is the expected state and goal. The level of ihsan is not a mere thought or emotional state but ihsan is embodied with this complete conscious and constant embodiment of ibadah during different daily engagements as epitomized by the Habib, al-Mustafa, Rasulullah ﷺ.

The purpose of ibadah is to direct the thoughts and emotions and to focus on Rabbul A'lamin. As we are distracted daily, hourly, and by the minute, the ibadah establishes this collection of oneself with their body, thoughts, and emotions and leads them to focus on Rabbul A'lamin. These renderings are some of the hikmahs, wisdoms of ibadah.

Yet, ibadah requires that logic and reason to be followed after humbleness and humility requirements of submission and conformity. Yes, ibadah is submission, compliance, and accepting that which the person does not know, and one is weak and is in need in their relationship with Rabbul Alamin.

One should remember that there is a very fine line in this submission. This is only for Rabbul Alamin as is required by the ibadah. Therefore, if a person performs this submission to another being other than Rabbul A'lamin then, this person is in full loss. May Allah ﷻ protect us, Amin.

In ibadah, conformity and compliance referred to as "obedience" in traditional language brings a complete and perfect structure. Yes, submission, conformity, compliance, and obedience sets and establishes a complete structure and order in a person's life as Abdullah. With this embodiment of the structure and order, the person can now realize the realities and wisdom, the hikmah for the occurrences, incidents, and systems. A person who embodied and personalized the structure and order in their own life can now realize the structure and order in the universe, galaxies, cells, micro-organisms, and in the personal lives of individuals. With this realization, everything makes sense as if completing a jigsaw puzzle. Everything becomes a friend with the Nûr of imān.

When one thinks about the absence of ibadah and imān, everything becomes chaotic, random, scary, purposeless, and dark. Any unknown becomes a terrorizing monster as compared to a guest sent from Rabbul A'lamin.

One of the arguments for the endless punishment of a kafir in Jahannam is due to attribution of kufr, purposelessness and randomness to all the infinite creation of Allah ﷻ. In other words, all the countless creations of Allah ﷻ assert their rights and open a lawsuit against this person on Judgment Day for being accused and slandered with kufr, purposeless, randomness, aimlessness, and lies. Even though we may not understand, this slander is a huge defamation, discrimination, abuse, and offense to a tiny atom, electron, or proton. The countless creations now assert their rights against this kafir. Therefore, the kafir is deemed to have an endless punishment in the afterlife due to his or her false accusation and slander against all of the creation [6].

The prevalence of hikmah[463] is encountered through constantly and regularly engaging oneself with everything in the galaxies, atoms, and universes. In other words, the art, style, beauty, elegance, splendor, taste, sophistication, and impressiveness shining in all of the creation and incidents with different motifs, designs, and patterns prevails the hikmah, the wisdom of realities.

---

463. Wisdom.

One can perceive from the above discussions of ibādah[464] how it leads to structure and order, and order and structure leads to the hikmah, the opening of the wisdom of realities.

The human being is the center of all creation. All the laws of physics, chemistry, systems, natural and social sciences are related back to the human beings as they are the central focal point. Yet, it is expected from the humans to uphold these laws, natural and social sciences as established by Allah ﷻ so that humans serve their purpose of creation. Yet, if they don't serve this purpose, it can be similar to working against the teeth of cog machinery and causing oneself to hurt. Serving this purpose of humans can only be achieved through ibādah.

When a person makes ibādah, by practicing what is permissible, approved of, and aiming for the pleasure of Allah ﷻ and avoiding the impermissible and aiming to avoid the displeasure of Allah ﷻ, the person establishes self-discipline and structure. This person can have different responsibilities in the society, in the family, and in different institutions. With this trait of ibādah, the person can be wholly successful and serving the community, family, society while fulfilling his responsibility satisfactorily in different institutions. If this person with this embodiment of ibādah is not present, all these gains and servitude would be absent.

Yes, true servitude to humanity comes first with true servitude to Allah ﷻ. When the person embodies this true trait of servitude to Allah ﷻ, called ibādah, then, the person can serve all of humanity and creation as the reflection of this true servitude. During his or her service, this person constantly gets motivated and encouraged not only because of witnessing spiritually and bodily happy and healthy families, individuals, or societies after their service; but he or she is more truly motivated to please Allah ﷻ and make investments for their afterlife.

The people deprived of this true ibādah, and imān in Allah ﷻ can still receive partial satisfaction for their service due to witnessing satisfied individuals. Yet, there are a lot of individuals who do not get much recognition from people after their service. Due to not witnessing satisfied people, there are people who begin viewing humans as evil creatures. This is all due to a wrong main intention and motivation of servitude.

---

464. Worship.

Yet, a mu'min always aims for the highest in their transactions. All the happy and satisfied individuals can be the immediate results, but the main intention is to please Allah ﷻ by serving the people. A believer does not care for or expect the satisfaction or applause of people after their service. They keep it as secret as possible to emphasize their sincerity in that they only engage in these activities to please Allah ﷻ and they only expect their rewards from Allah ﷻ.

When a person performs an ibādah such as fasting or salah, this person realizes and knows that at the same time there are billions doing the same with this person. This realization and knowledge make him or her connect to the billions with a positive group identity named or referred to as Muslims.

In another perspective, the person gets assured of their belonging that they all together establish connection with Allah ﷻ. This way of connection and disposition of the person is not something personal but it is authentic and approved and originally instructed by Allah ﷻ since the creation of the first human. This knowledge and practice with ibādah give more assurance and encouragement to the person. Especially, this can be an uplift for the person during their times of struggle, need, and weakness.

In this regard, Muslim is not a simple group identity of today. It has been the true, original, humble, and appreciative stance of all the people since the time of Adam as. Therefore, Adam as, Nuh as, Ibrahim as, Musa as, Isa as, and, Rasulullah ﷺ, Muhammad ﷺ were all Muslims. Ibadah makes us connect to all of them, including all of the prophets and messengers of Allah ﷻ and their true followers.

Ibadah is the only true vehicle that can make the person travel in their spiritual journey in order to reach to the level of al-insan al-kamil[465].

The human being has a tiny physical body compared to the bodies in the galaxies and universes. He or she is very weak, always in need, and in destitution. Yet, compared to the animals, the human being has an elevated soul. He or she has a lot of potential and skills. She or he has endless inclinations, desires, and ideas. In this perspective, ibadah is the only, but only, true vehicle that can help the person reach their endless

---

465. Complete person.

desires, inclinations, and ideas by connecting him or herself to the One Who is Al-Baqi, the Infinite, Rabbul A'lamin.

In other words, Allah ﷻ enabled humans in their creation with these endless needs and inclinations in order for them to realize and connect to the Infinite, Al-Baqi[466], Ar-Rahman[467], Ar-Rahim[468], Al-Latif[469], Al-Khabir[470], Al-A'lim[471], Al-Hannan[472], Al-Mannan[473], Al-Kareem[474], and to all the other Names and Attributes of Rabbul A'lamin, Allah ﷻ. This connection point is called iman. The journeying after this connection point is called ibadah. Through lifelong continuous ibadah[475], the connection point gets stronger, similar to the cell phone or wireless symbols of connection displayed on these gadgets.

Sometimes the desire of the soul for expansion through feelings, spiritual and mindful journeys can cause the person to store up negative energy in the form of depression, anxiety, uneasiness and worry. Yet, if this desire of the soul for expansion is channeled correctly through ibadah, then the soul is fed its food and becomes content, happy, and satisfied.

In other words, the soul and heart's desire to expand is a signal of hunger and starvation. If they are not fed through ibadah, then the soul and heart may die due to hunger or from poisonous food fed by the material or worldly means of ostentation, arrogance, and vanity.

Yes, ibadah is the embodiment of humbleness and humility as the beautiful and clean, halal and zabîha food of the soul and the heart. Ibadah accompanied by the expensive, organic, and pure food of crying through tears has a very high value for Allah ﷻ.

The tears flow, the heart pumps, and the eyes become wet due to the inability of feelings to contain our lack of our appreciation for Allah ﷻ. This state and disposition of the heart and mind can elevate the person vertically in their relationship with Allah ﷻ through ibadah.

---

466. The infinite.
467. The Compassionate.
468. The Most Merciful.
469. The Kind.
470. The All-Aware.
471. The All-Knowing.
472.
473. The Defender.
474. The Generous.
475. Worship.

Ibadah is not only the salah, fasting, or zakāh. Following the sunnahs of Rasulullah ﷺ with the intention of following the beloved is ibadah in every minute or in all small-seeming incidents.

Yes, the heart constantly cries and asks for expansion through ibadah. Soul constantly desires for Allah ﷻ through ibadah. Each of our sighs can become ibadah with the intention of following the beloved saw. We follow the beloved because the Beloved, Allah ﷻ loves the beloved, Rasulullah saw. If we meet at the same point where Allah ﷻ's love is directed to through ibadah, inshAllah, we can also become beloved by the Beloved ﷻ. May Allah ﷻ help us and enable us through love of ibadah and in following Rasulullah ﷺ in all of the sunnahs, Ameen.

The life is short. Ibadah makes this short life meaningful with expansion to the infinity by connecting to the Al-Baqi[476], the Infinite. If one does not want to die with death, then he or she should connect to Allah ﷻ through ibadah.

Allah ﷻ gave us so many avenues and different ways of connecting through different ibadah. Besides the required, fardh ibadahs, if a person increases the connection through nafawil, they can pray, fast, read the Qurān, give charity, or do the good work as part of the ibadah and following the sunnah of Rasulullah ﷺ.

Ibadah is a tool to expand the skills and abilities of the person.

Ibadah helps the person to understand their own selves better. Sometimes, our own selves can become so complicated with different emotions, thoughts, physical, social, kinship, and professional engagements. Ibadah helps the person to identify their own selves in detailing their engagements with the identification of their purpose and meanings. One can understand ibadah in this case as the strongest tool of focus and concentration.

Ibadah is the vehicle for the person to achieve their goals. When the person better knows oneself and fully connects to Allah ﷻ with reliance and tawakkul[477], then the person is given what they aim for with the Grace, Fadl and Rahmah of Allah ﷻ.

Ibadah is the facilitator to expand the thoughts, feelings, and experiences of a human. Yet, at the same time, ibadah is the organizer to structure these feelings, experiences, and thoughts. Ibadah filters their

---

476. The Infinite.
477. Trust.

remnants with realization and istigfar and keeps their useful ones on the path of Allah ﷻ.

As we are constantly exposed to a flux of interactions with people and our surroundings, a sensitive soul and heart constantly gets affected by these interactions. Each interaction can be similar to a pill or a medicine that can have an immediate effect. Or, their effects can be felt after an hour, day, week, month, year, or even after years. In these interactions, the effects of sins can have different durations as well as the effect of positive, boosting experiences which can be called openings in the fields of tasawwuf.

Sometimes, if these interactions are poison, then ibadah can be the antidote. It helps the person first realize the problem in these engagements. Then, it makes the person to go back to Allah ﷻ with regret and repentance. Then, the antidote is present. These poisonous effects can be removed from the heart and mind with the Fadl, and Rahmah of Allah ﷻ. اللهم اجعلنا منهم[478] For example, as an ibadah, when the person is praying and reading the Qurān, the Qurān can talk to the person and make him or her realize their problems. As soon as this realization happens, if the person bursts into tears with regret in front of Allah ﷻ, then, inshAllah, the poisonous effects of these sins are terminated from the heart and mind with the Fadl[479] and Rahmah[480] of Allah ﷻ. اللهم اجعلنا منهم.

Sometimes, the ibadah can lead to the positive, boosting experiences which can be called openings in the fields of tasawwuf. In these cases, it is expected that the person is in a fully appreciative state of hamd[481] and shukr[482]. As Rasulullah ﷺ was constantly journeying vertically in these openings, he saw his name embodied as "Muhammad", as the embodiment of gratitude or appreciation for Allah ﷻ. As in the hadith mentioned by Aisha (ra), Rasulullah ﷺ was engaging in the ibadah, tahajjud, at night with tears. When asked by Aisha (ra) why are there so many tears with full engagement of ibadah at nights although the Rasulullah ﷺ has been under warranty by Allah ﷻ, he ﷺ made this famous diamond statement[483] "افلم أكون عبدا شكورا؟" "Shouldn't I be the

---

478. Oh Allah ﷻ, make us from them.
479. Favor.
480. Mercy.
481. Praise.
482. Gratitude.
483. Should I not be a grateful servant.

Adorer of Allah ﷻ constantly being in gratitude and appreciation for all the showering ni'mahs[484]?"

In the above renderings, one can see the two perspectives of ibadah.

Ibadah is the tool that structures one's gauges of internal drive forces that take commands from the free will of the person. In traditional texts, these internal driving forces or faculties can also be referred to as the forces of anger (ghadab) and lust (shah-wah). For example, a person may want to get up and break his or her cycle of sleep to pray tahajjud. The person may want to do this. Yet, if the internal gauge and driving force of the person is not strong, the person may not be able to break the cycle of sleep to pray although he or she may desire to get up and pray. Ibadah in different forms helps the person to execute free will in a positive, virtuous, structured, and disciplined way. It helps the person to control and direct these personal, internal driving forces.One can see the similar benefits of ibadah in our current social problems related to drugs, alcohol, and other types of addictions. The people don't want to be in this cycle. Yet, they don't have the sufficient internal driving force to break these cycles. Ibadah can also help in these cases as current modern AA or addiction services highly recommend spirituality as a way of possible exits from these addictions [21] as well.

Our hearts, minds, and emotions are constantly polluted with different dirt during the day. Sometimes a bad hearing, witnessing an abuse or evil with the eyes, smelling a bad smell, eating something not pure or clean or overeating, and sleeping too much in the heedlessness of darkness can be the causes of this dirt on the heart, mind, and emotions. Sometimes a word of praise, appaluse, an affirmation, or the number of the "likes" of people on the phone, internet, or Facebook can lead the person to have poison intakes into the heart, mind, and emotions. Rasulullah ﷺ in this context mentions the breaking of the neck as the breaking of the core pillar of the physical body corresponding to the breaking of the heart as the pillar of the spiritual body.

Yet, with all this dirt, filth, poison, and toxic materials pouring into the heart, mind, and emotions, the ibādah contains the bleach, medicine, and antidote that has the tools to help the heart, mind, and emotions go through a process of removing all the dirt. Yet, it does not

---

484. Blessings

have any chemical or side effect reaction. It only brings the breezes of calmness, tranquility, and serenity referred to as sakina from Allah ﷻ.

As our hearts and minds need constant cleaning, this constant process of self-dealing through ibadah can take the person to reach to the approximations of maturity. One can call this a level of كمال, completeness.

The relationship between the Creator, Allah ﷻ, and the creation, the person, is called ibādah. The approximations to the level of كمال, completeness is achieved through the process of ibādah. In other words, the perfection of a human كمال, completeness in his or her creation outcome and purpose is achieved through connecting to the All Perfect One in the Divine Attributes, Allah ﷻ. The expression of this linking, connection, attribution, and relation is called ibādah.

Therefore, one can understand the ayah [485] وَمَا خَلَقْتُ الْجِنَّ وَالْإِنسَ إِلَّا لِيَعْبُدُونِ {الذاريات/56} that Allah ﷻ created humans and jinn so they can strive to achieve to the approximations of the levels of كمال, completeness, through the process of ibādah. One can consider the discussions of perfectness, كمال about angels. Their[486] كمال can be analyzed around their zeal and indulgence with ibādah as well.

In this perspective, seeing ibādah as something lowly especially in non-religious but in both Western and Muslim societies is a very reductionist approach of the naïve, ignorant, and the inexperienced.

The essence of ibādah is ikhlas, sincerity. Ikhlas, sincerity, in ibādah is performing the ibādah simply because it is the order from Rabbul Alamin. The real purpose of the ibādah is not doing or performing them due to their benefits. Allah ﷻ as the Rabbul Alamin makes everything required with their full and perfect, calming, and essential benefits for us. Yet, the reason or purpose of the ibadah in its initial stage of intention and purpose is to perform it because it is the order and instruction from the Rabbul A'lamin.

Sometimes, we mix these two perspectives. For the novice or beginner, it is okay and normal to be obsessed with the benefits of ibādah in the initial stage. The medical benefits, the benefits related to the discipline, structure, order, calmness, tranquility, sakina[487] and spiritual expansion, and many other countless benefits are there. Even,

---

485. And I did not create the jinn and mankind except to worship Me.
486. Completeness.
487. Tranquility.

the benefits related with the afterlife of getting a mansion, good luxurious life, food, drink and many others are there. Yet, as the person establishes themselves, the ikhlas, sincerity, and real purpose and intention of the ibadah is and should be because they are the order from Rabbul Alamin.

In this perspective, one can analyze the ayah as mentioned by Yusuf as {يوسف/101} [488] تَوَفَّنِي مُسْلِمًا وَأَلْحِقْنِي بِالصَّالِحِينَ. Why does Yusuf as mention the desire of ending his life as a Muslim? Here, Muslim is the attitude and disposition of submission to the command of Allah ﷻ as ikhlas, sincerity.

To summarize, the essence and the soul of the ibādah is sincerity. Sincerity is required to do the ibādah because it is the command of Allah ﷻ. A person can prefer to do a certain form of ibādah. Yet, this preference should not be the goal and purpose of that ibādah. The purpose should be due to ibādah being the command and order of Allah ﷻ.

In a practical example, someone can say, "I like to pray, make salah more in nawafil than fasting in nafāwil. I do both salah and fasting because Allah ﷻ is pleased with these ibādah and they are the order and command of Allah ﷻ."

Sometimes, we mix the means and the ends when we involve ourselves with an action. The reason is that when we make an intention to do an action there are things, side effects, or by-products that can come along the way while being in the constant effort of reaching towards the goal.

When a person tries to make an action to please Allah ﷻ as the goal and as the main purpose, the person can encounter different side effects or by-products as they involve themselves with this action.

Some of these by-products can be pleasure, benefit, recognition, fame, position, the concerns of gaining reputation and being applauded, admired and praised. Yet, after a while, if the person does not constantly daily, hourly, and even sometimes by the second refresh their imān or real intention, then these side effects can become their end goal. This can a show an implicit switch of the initial intention and aim to the pseudo and bogus ones.

In other words, when a person becomes so apt and concerned about these by-products then they become the goal. In the works of the religion, this could be very daunting and dangerous. A person starts

---

488. Cause me to die a Muslim and join me with the righteous."

good but loses later. Allah ❀ puts benefits into the ibādah. Allah ❀ supports the person in the works of the religion by opening people's hearts, recognition, and acceptance. Yet, if the person normalizes this expectation of getting a benefit or being accepted by people, then the person can lose the end goal.

Allah ❀ is so generous, the Most Generous, Ar-Rahman[489] and Ar-Rahim[490]. In the cases of 99.9 %, Allah ❀ gives immediate pleasures, benefits and results in these engagements of ibadah[491] or true service for the religion of Allah ❀. Yet, this less than 0....1% of the time, when there is no pleasure, result, benefit or if there is difficulty, the person immediately, disconnects and becomes ungrateful in their relationship with Allah ❀. The absence of benefit, pleasure or results can serve as reminders for us to check the internal disposition of the person if the he or she is engaging with these acts for the real and expected reason or due to getting the by-products. Yet, a lot of people unfortunately fail in these reminders, may Allah ❀ protect us, Ameen. This psychology of the human is repeatedly mentioned in the Qurān to emphasize this reality as for example[492] وَإِذَا مَسَّ الإنسَانَ الضُّرُّ دَعَانَا لِجَنبِهِ أَوْ قَاعِدًا أَوْ قَآئِمًا فَلَمَّا كَشَفْنَا عَنْهُ ضُرَّهُ مَرَّ كَأَن لَّمْ يَدْعُنَا إِلَى ضُرٍّ مَّسَّهُ كَذَلِكَ زُيِّنَ لِلْمُسْرِفِينَ مَا كَانُواْ يَعْمَلُونَ {يونس/12} The person should be in the state of the heart and mind that he or she should not care if their message is accepted or not. Their heart and mind should not be affected by the people's approval of the message or rejection of the message. Their heart and mind should not be affected by getting a benefit or not from an ibādah.

There are a lot of Qurān reciters that may get discouraged to recite the Qurān due to their voice not being liked by others. There are a lot on the opposite side who may like to recite the Qurān because people like to listen to this person. Both are dangerous dispositions. Dawûd as did not desire the publicity but wanted to the engage with the book of Allah ❀. Then, the mountains and birds came to listen to him. His publicity and fame was protected by their mention in the Qurān and scriptures.

In all these points, one can clearly and simply deduce if Allah ❀ is pleased, then anything can happen. If Allah ❀ is not pleased then there

489. The Compassionate.
490. The Most Merciful.
491. Worship.
492. And when affliction touches man, he calls upon Us, whether lying on his side or sitting or standing; but when We remove from him his affliction, he continues [in disobedience] as if he had never called upon Us to [remove] an affliction that touched him. Thus is made pleasing to the transgressors that which they have been doing.

is no real value even if people make this person so famous. Even, in this case, more importantly, the person can lose their afterlife as mentioned by the first three people to be thrown to Jahannam in the hadith [2]. This is very scary. May Allah ﷻ protect us from this end, help us maintain our real goal and intention of pleasing Allah ﷻ until we die with the Fadl[493] and Rahmah[494] of Allah ﷻ, Ameen. It is very difficult.

In other words, doing things with the intention to please Allah ﷻ with ikhlas and sincerity is important and the key. Ikhlās, sincerity, as defined before is doing something because Allah ﷻ orders it. Following the sunnah with this intention is the key. Rasulullah ﷺ brings and acts on actions which are pleasing to Allah ﷻ. Following Rasulullah ﷺ with this intention is ikhlas, sincerity.

There were a lot of prophets and messengers of Allah ﷻ who had only a few or no possible followers. Yet, they were given the rank of prophets and messengers by Allah ﷻ. So, the ranks given by Allah ﷻ are not according to our gains or achievements even in the works of the religion.

To remind this to our beloved and selected Prophet ﷺ, there is a positive and praising reminder as mentioned in the Qurān "لعلك باخع نفسك على آثارهم ان لم يومنوا بهذا الحديث اسفا[495]". Yet, this is a positive praise for the Prophet. Yet, for our levels, there is this danger of negative greed due to the attachments to the poisonous by-products.

Although there is a correlation most of the time between the result and the engagement as mentioned with "الا الذين امنوا و عملوا الصالحات[496]" or[497] "و اما من ثقلت موازينه", yet this correlation of a'mālu-salih[498] and or[499] "ثقلت موازينه" relies on the actions where the real should not be lost that the person is engaging in all in order to please Allah ﷻ. As the Prophet ﷺ, says" there is a piece in the body. If it gets ruined, all of the body gets ruined [2]" can allude to this fact. At the same time, the hadith of Aisha ra about muhsinun, "They do good things, but they have the hesitancy

---

493. Favor.
494. Mercy.
495. Then perhaps you would kill yourself through grief over them, [O Muhammad ﷺ], if they do not believe in this message, [and] out of sorrow.
496. Except those who believed and did righteous deeds.
497. Then as for one whose scales are heavy [with good deeds],
498. Righteous deeds.
499. Who's scales are heavy {with good deeds}.

of being accepted by Allah ﷻ" Rasulullah ﷺ defines them as the real people of ihsan. [500]اللهم اجعلنا منهم.

Sometimes, to remind oneself of this real intention and purpose, the person can go into seclusion, or do I'tikāf, or fast. In all of these ibādah, the self-engagement of the person is expected to remind the person of their real goal. Sometimes, when the person minimizes the external side effects they can re-focus on the real goal and intention. In these types of ibādah, the person tries to maximize disconnect from the possible by-product causing effects so that they can try to focus on their real journey of the one and only goal in life which is to please and connect to Allah ﷻ with imān, islam, and ihsan. The goal is to connect to Allah ﷻ with intention and action of the true ibādah. These can all be in the realm of the ikhlās, sincerity. Refocusing on the essence of the ibādah, which is with ikhlās, is the end result of these types of engagements.

In the engagements of philosophers in their practice of mental seclusion for focus or in the engagements of other groups such as in eastern religions utilizing seclusion or fasting and self-discipline, they can experience some of the by-products and side effects of these engagements. Yet, since they don't follow the guidelines given to us as the biggest gift from the Qurān and sunnah, they get lost and run behind the pseudo-goals, vanishing sooner or later on the journey.

The sincere ones like Aristotle at the times of fitrah, the era of spiritual chaos, before Islam could prove the Oneness and Uniqueness of Allah ﷻ with a methodology.

When one initially reads the expression يَا أَيُّهَا النَّاسُ اعْبُدُواْ رَبَّكُمُ[501], a question may arise as to why we need to worship. Humans constantly question everything. Especially, during our current times, this type of attitude is encouraged with the notions of critical thinking in the curricula of secondary and higher education.

The answer comes immediately explaining the reason and Who to worship as الَّذِي خَلَقَكُمْ وَالَّذِينَ مِن قَبْلِكُمْ لَعَلَّكُمْ تَتَّقُونَ[502]. When one analyzes the portion الَّذِي خَلَقَكُمْ[503] that in itself is sufficient reason for someone to worship. When the person is created by Allah ﷻ from nothing and

---

500. Oh Allah ﷻ, make us from them.
501. O mankind, worship your lord.
502. Who created you and those before you,
503. Who created you.

brought into existence, that in itself is the biggest ni'mah[504]. When the person understands this, the form of thanking, gratitude, and appreciation is expressed in a form called ibadah.

From another perspective, the person should know Who their Creator is as mentioned الَّذِي خَلَقَكُمْ وَالَّذِينَ مِن قَبْلِكُمْ[505]. Then, this requires knowledge of tawhid, the Same, One, and Unique Creator, Allah ﷻ.

In addition, Allah ﷻ is Ar-Rahmān[506] and Ar-Rahīm[507], so generous and merciful. As humans are selfish, they always want to engage with something if there is benefit. Immediately, in this ayah the benefit of worship is mentioned as لَعَلَّكُمْ تَتَّقُونَ[508]. In other words, Allah ﷻ immediately presents the benefit of ibādah although the first expression of الَّذِي خَلَقَكُمْ[509] is sufficient reason for a person to worship and make ibādah to Allah ﷻ.

Tawhid in Uluhiyyah[510], Rububiyyah,[511] and 'Ubudiyyah[512] of Allah ﷻ

Tawhid in Uluhiyyah

The verse {الأنبياء/22} لَوْ كَانَ فِيهِمَا آلِهَةٌ إِلَّا اللَّهُ لَفَسَدَتَا فَسُبْحَانَ اللَّهِ رَبِّ الْعَرْشِ عَمَّا يَصِفُونَ[513] is sufficient proof of why there should be tawhid in Uluhiyyah[514]. In other words, this verse simply and in a very straightforward way explains that Uluhiyyah necessitates tawhid logically. Deity necessitates oneness. Multiplicity in deity brings chaos. This is a very clear and simple logical disposition. It is a necessary requirement that the Creator should be One. Allah ﷻ is One.

Multiplicity in deity brings destruction of the structure and order in micro and macro systems. These destructions or terminations occur in human anatomical and physiological systems as well as in galaxies, stars, planets, and beyond. The finely detailed, perfect and complex

---

504. Blessings.
505. Who created you and those before you.
506. The Compassionate.
507. The Most Merciful.
508. That you may be righteous.
509. Who created you.
510. Realm of divineness.
511. Lordship.
512. Servanthood.
513. Had there been within them [i.e., the heavens and earth] gods besides Allah ﷻ, they both would have been ruined. So exalted is Allah ﷻ, Lord of the Throne, above what they describe.
514. Realm of power.

systems, structures, and order cannot tolerate any type of, even a second of, confusion or chaos in multiplicity due to the multiplicity of deity.

We witness this in our human social lives which require multiplicity. The existence of social problems mainly stems from this multiplicity. Yet, for humans it is normal because we need each other in a social life. Social life requires multiplicity. Yet, multiplicity brings chaos in the form of social problems as mentioned in ظَهَرَ الْفَسَادُ فِي الْبَرِّ وَالْبَحْرِ بِمَا كَسَبَتْ أَيْدِي النَّاسِ لِيُذِيقَهُم بَعْضَ الَّذِي عَمِلُوا لَعَلَّهُمْ يَرْجِعُونَ 515{الروم/41}.

Allah ﷻ is As-Samad[516]. Everyone and everything needs Allah ﷻ. Allah ﷻ does not need anyone. Allah ﷻ is Al-Ahad, One. There is no multiplicity in deity. Allah ﷻ is Unique in this perspective. No one has this attribute and quality except Allah[517] و لم يكن له كفوا احد ,ﷻ. There is no one equal to Allah ﷻ in Oneness and Uniqueness.

In this regard, multiplicity requires relation, copulation, connection, kinship, tie, link, association, partnership, consanguinity, family ties, origin, descent, lineage, heredity, childhood, paternity, maternity, parentage, and ancestry. In this regard, Allah ﷻ is One and Unique and does not have any parents, father, or mother, and does not have any of the above multiplicity related cases of partnership as mentioned[518] "لم يلد و لم يولد."

In each of the above cases, one proposition requires another proposition. For example:

Oneness (Al-Ahad[519]) requires being free of need (As-Samad[520]) unlike humans who require multiplicity in social life and due to their needs. The one who is free of need can fulfill all the needs of others as As-Samad also requires. The One Who is One has no dependency, (As-Samad), and requires no dependency in lineage, origin, descent, ancestry, and association as mentioned

al-Ahad		as-Samad		Lam Yalid wa Lam Yulad		Wa Lam Yakun Lahu Kufuwan Ahad
• Oneness • NO multiplcility		• Free of need, yet everything depends and needs Allah (ﷻ)		• NO partnership, lineage, parentage		• Allah ﷻ is Unique, One,.

---

515. Corruption has appeared throughout the land and sea by [reason of] what the hands of people have earned so He [i.e., Allah] may let them taste part of [the consequence of] what they have done that perhaps they will return [to righteousness].

516. The Everlasting.

517. Nor is there to Him ﷻ any equivalent.

518. He ﷻ neither begets nor is born.

519. The Unique.

520. The Everlasting.

with[521] لم يلد و لم يولد. The One Who has these attributes requires to be Unique and there is no other partnership.

One can also look at this from the other direction, as

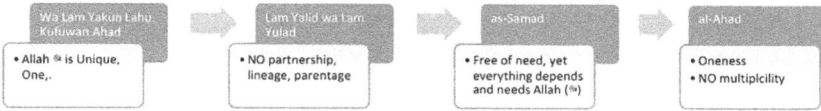

Wa Lam Yakun Lahu Kufuwan Ahad		Lam Yalid wa Lam Yulad		as-Samad		al-Ahad
• Allah ✺ is Unique, One,.		• NO partnership, lineage, parentage		• Free of need, yet everything depends and needs Allah (✺)		• Oneness • NO multiplcility

This will be still valid and in the same proposition. The result will be that Allah ✺ is One, Unique. Everyone and everything needs Allah ✺ and Allah ✺ does not need anyone.

One can also realize that one of the key phrases in this critical Surah is Al-Ahad. The name of the Sûrah is very short. With its shortness, it is a very critical surah in the Qurãn. Yet, Al-Ahad is repeated twice, although the Surah is short and very critical.

This can show more focus and takid on this Name and Attribute of Allah ✺, Al-Ahad. One can understand the essence of tawhid to be in knowing and accepting Al-Ahad. It is interesting to see the embodiment of this Name of Allah ✺ in Sahaba in their dhikr as "Al-Ahadu". They were repeating this Name and Attribute of Allah ✺ against multiplicity, shirk, and partnership of deities practiced by the people of Mecca.

From this perspective, if this critical Name and Attribute of Allah ✺ is put at the central point of this surah as:

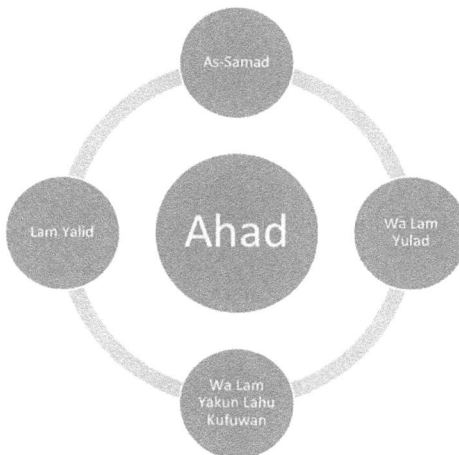

---

521. He ✺ neither begets nor is born.

The above presentation in English can be

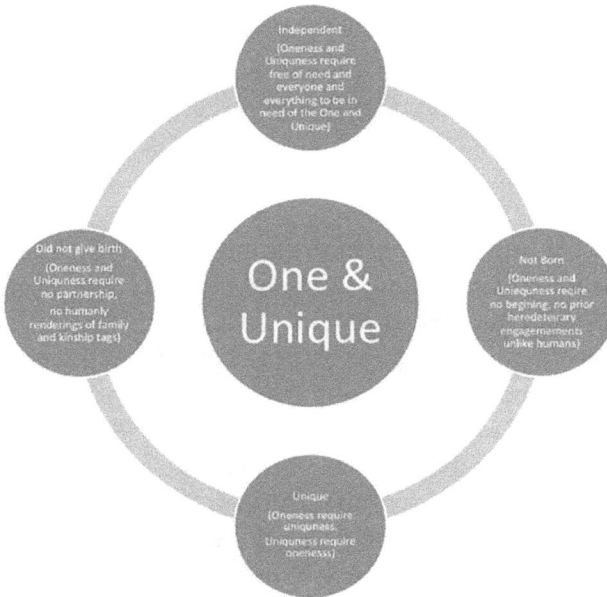

In this regard, one can see that Al-Ahad[522] can be approximated to be translated as the One and Unique as the ayah[523] "و لم يكن له كفوا احد" emphasizes this Uniquenessembedded the expression of the Oneness of Allah ﷻ.

Yet, in our human renderings of language, and in our human renderings of multiplicity of being born from parents and giving birth to children, we witness this constant partnership and pair relation in all of the creation of Allah ﷻ. Therefore, we may sometimes use the wrong language regarding the Uluhiyyah[524]. As long as we don't mean it, inshAllah, Allah ﷻ can forgive us, as Allah ﷻ knows our limits and Allah ﷻ is the Most Merciful, the Most Forgiving.

Therefore, if the person may not be able to make all these logical deductions, Allah ﷻ teaches us to believe and to follow what is already given. In other words, the expressions of Qul[525], huwa[526], and Allahu,

---

522. The Unique.
523. Nor is there to Him ﷻ any equivalent.
524. Realm of power.
525. Say.
526. He ﷻ

until we attain Ahad[527]. As a mercy and Fadl[528] of Allah ﷻ, Allah ﷻ puts the protective layers on imān in order for us to follow with adab and respect what is told until we reach to the level of Ahad.

In this perspective, the expressions of Qul[529], Huwa, and Allahu can all entail Rahmah[530] covered farness, (buu'd) so that we can follow and believe but not follow into the humanizations of deity until with practice, 'ibādah, humbleness, sincerity, and knowledge, we can reach the real yaqîn of Al-Ahad[531]. This Rahmah of Allah ﷻ can be :

Qul	➡	Huwa	➡	Allahu	➡	Ahad

The problem occurs when the person takes a clear stance in their disposition of Uluhiyyah[532] with multiplicity. Then, this becomes an enormous slander to all of creation. All of creation requires tawhid for their purpose, meaning, and livelihood. This becomes an enormously ungrateful, unappreciative, inconsiderate disposition to Allah ﷻ, to hold partners in multiplicity.

The surah of ikhlās entails the Names and Attributes of Allah ﷻ related with the Uluhiyyah.

In this regard, the Name and Attribute, As-Samad[533] can be one of them.

Change and limitation are deficiencies and they imply need. Need implies being dependent on others. Limitation implies temporality. This applies to all of creation. Creation has multiplicity.

Constancy, consistency, independence, and continuity implies permanency, perpetuality, and eternity. Eternity implies endlessness. Permanency implies no beginning. This is all only for the Creator. As-Samad can have these meanings.

---

527. One.
528. Favor.
529. Say.
530. Mercy.
531. The One.
532. Realm of Power.
533. The Everlasting.

As-Samad implies distinctiveness and exclusivity. Distinctiveness implies uniqueness. Uniqueness implies Oneness. The Creator is One and Unique.

Allah ﷻ is Al-Wahid, One. Allah ﷻ is Unique, Al-Ahad. Allah ﷻ is not part of the Change, but is Permanent, Perfect, and Infinite, As-Samad.

As-Samad[534] and Al-Ahad[535] imply other Names and Attributes of Allah ﷻ related with Uluhiyyah[536]. These can be Al-Baqi[537], Al-Badî'[538], Al-Khaliq[539], Al-Mumît[540], Al-Muhyi[541], Al-Wajibul Wujud[542], Al-Qayyum[543], Al-A'liyy[544], Al-A'zeem[545] and others. Therefore, surah ikhlās[546] has this distinct position of reflecting the Uluhiyyah[547] of Allah ﷻ.

Multiplicity implies creation. Being a creation implies need. Need implies fears, anxieties, uneasiness, stress, worries, restlessness, concerns, nervousness, and discomfort. Fears, anxieties, uneasiness, stress, worries, restlessness, concerns, nervousness, and discomfort imply dependency. Dependency on someone or something implies fulfillment of the needs, comfort of the hearts and minds, relief of the fears, anxieties, uneasiness, stress, worries, restlessness, concerns, nervousness, and discomfort by a caregiver who either has the same needs in different levels or by a Care Giver Who is Independent from all of these needs.

A caregiver who has similar needs in different levels as compared to the person who receives the care can be any human who is considerate to help others with their problems. A Care Giver Who is Independent from all of these needs is the Rabb as the attribute of Allah ﷻ.

---

534. The infinite.
535. The Unique.
536. Realm of Power.
537. The Immutable.
538. The Originator; The Incomparable.
539. The Creator.
540. The Bringer of Death; The Destroyer.
541. The Giver of life.
542. An Obligation to Exist.
543. The Sustainer of All.
544. The Sublimely Exalted.
545. The Magnificent.
546. Sincerity.
547. Realm of Power.

Caregiving implies the rububiyah[548]. Tarbiyah[549] of humans for other humans is limited. Most of the time human caregiving is a disposition of kinship support or social support to uplift the patience and stamina of a person while that person is experiencing that need.

The True, Full, and Perfect Rububiyah[550] implies the Rabb as the attribute of Allah ﷻ that Allah ﷻ created all of creation to have different needs so that they can realize and appreciate their Real Rabb.

Rabbul Alamin fully and perfectly fulfills all of the needs of all of the creation as compared to the peripheral or pseudo-tarbiya[551] of humans for others. Yet, Allah ﷻ orders and gives rewards to the ones who have the concern and make the effort to help others.

Allah ﷻ wants humans to reflect these Names and Attributes of Allah ﷻ related with Rububiyyah[552]. On the other hand, Allah ﷻ prohibits humans to reflect the Names and Attributes of Allah ﷻ related with Uluhiyyah.

The Names and Attributes of Allah ﷻ related with Uluhiyyah indicate Uniqueness and Oneness. This is a lie for humans if they make any minute claim. Yet, the Real and True ilāh[553] is Allah ﷻ. When this is not realized then, people mostly make explicit shirk related with the Uluhiyyah of Allah ﷻ as mentioned with فَلاَ تَجْعَلُواْ لِلّهِ أَندَاداً وَأَنتُمْ تَعْلَمُونَ {البقرة/22}[554] and {الإخلاص/4} وَلَمْ يَكُن لَّهُ كُفُوًا أَحَدٌ[555].

The Names and Attributes of Allah ﷻ related with Rububiyyah indicate encouragement for humans to reflect these Names and Attributes. The hadith mentioning that Allah ﷻ created humans in the Divine image [2] [15] can imply the reflections of the Names and Attributes of Allah ﷻ in Rububiyyah.

Yet, the Real and True Rabb is Allah ﷻ. When this is not realized then, people make mostly make implicit shirk related with the Rububiyyah of

---

548. Lordship.
549. Education.
550. Lordship.
551. Education.
552. Lordship.
553. God.
554. So do not attribute to Allah ﷻ equals while you know [that there is nothing similar to Him].
555. Nor is there to Him ﷻ any equivalent.

وَلَمْ and as mentioned with {البقرة/22}⁵⁵⁶ وَلاَ تَجْعَلُواْ لِلّهِ أَندَاداً وَأَنتُمْ تَعْلَمُونَ. In other surah as mentioned as well: يَكُن لَّهُ كُفُواً أَحَدٌ⁵⁵⁷{الإخلاص/4}

قُلْ يَا أَهْلَ الْكِتَابِ تَعَالَوْاْ إِلَى كَلَمَةٍ سَوَاء بَيْنَنَا وَبَيْنَكُمْ أَلاَّ نَعْبُدَ إِلاَّ اللّهَ وَلاَ نُشْرِكَ بِهِ شَيْئاً وَلاَ يَتَّخِذَ بَعْضُنَا بَعْضاً أَرْبَاباً مِّن دُونِ اللّهِ فَإِن تَوَلَّوْاْ فَقُولُواْ اشْهَدُواْ بِأَنَّا مُسْلِمُونَ⁵⁵⁸{آل عمران/64}

وَلاَ يَأْمُرَكُمْ أَن تَتَّخِذُواْ الْمَلاَئِكَةَ وَالنِّبِيِّيْنَ أَرْبَاباً أَيَأْمُرُكُم بِالْكُفْرِ بَعْدَ إِذْ أَنتُم مُّسْلِمُونَ⁵⁵⁹{آل عمران/80}

اتَّخَذُواْ أَحْبَارَهُمْ وَرُهْبَانَهُمْ أَرْبَاباً مِّن دُونِ اللّهِ وَالْمَسِيحَ ابْنَ مَرْيَمَ وَمَا أُمِرُواْ إِلاَّ لِيَعْبُدُواْ إِلَهاً وَاحِداً لاَّ إِلَهَ إِلاَّ هُوَ سُبْحَانَهُ عَمَّا يُشْرِكُونَ⁵⁶⁰{التوبة/31}

يَا صَاحِبَيِ السِّجْنِ أَأَرْبَابٌ مُّتَفَرِّقُونَ خَيْرٌ أَمِ اللّهُ الْوَاحِدُ الْقَهَّارُ⁵⁶¹{يوسف/39}

It is required for a person to be thankful, show gratitude, appreciation, and gratefulness to everyone who does something good for us. One should not mix this disposition with the disposition of showing the most gratitude, appreciation, and gratefulness to Allah. Allah created us. Then, Allah gives our constant sustenance as mentioned إِنَّ اللَّهَ هُوَ الرَّزَّاقُ ذُو الْقُوَّةِ الْمَتِينُ⁵⁶²{الذاريات/58}. In other words, this ayah implies the A'dl, Just, Name of Allah that if Allah created the person, then Allah gives them their sustenance fully as the Rabb.

If parents are involved in the delivery of a child as the means of the creation of Allah, they may have an innate feeling and natural (fitri) impulse of feeding their children. Similarly, as Allah is beyond the

---

556. So do not attribute to Allah equals while you know [that there is nothing similar to Him].
557. Nor is there to Him any equivalent.
558. Say, "O People of the Scripture, come to a word that is equitable between us and you— that we will not worship except Allah and not associate anything with Him and not take one another as lords instead of Allah." But if they turn away, then say, "Bear witness that we are Muslims [submitting to Him]."
559. Nor could he order you to take the angels and prophets as lords. Would he order you to disbelief after you had been Muslims?
560. They have taken their scholars and monks as lords besides Allah, and [also] the Messiah, the son of Mary. And they were not commanded except to worship one God; there is no deity except Him. Exalted is He above whatever they associate with Him.
561. O [my] two companions of prison, are separate lords better or Allah, the One, the Prevailing?
562. Indeed, it is Allah who is the [continual] Provider, the firm possessor of strength.

human renderings, Allah ﷻ fulfills their sustenance as mentioned إِنَّ[563] اللَّهَ هُوَ الرَّزَّاقُ. In this ayah, there can be an implication for the required fulfillment of their sustenance (rizq) by Allah ﷻ with attributes of Allah ﷻ of Adl, Justice and ذُو الْقُوَّةِ الْمَتِينُ[564].

This sometimes overlooked notion is mentioned in اللَّهُ الَّذِي خَلَقَكُمْ ثُمَّ رَزَقَكُمْ ثُمَّ يُمِيتُكُمْ ثُمَّ يُحْيِيكُمْ هَلْ مِن شُرَكَائِكُم مَّن يَفْعَلُ مِن ذَلِكُم مِّن شَيْءٍ سُبْحَانَهُ وَتَعَالَى عَمَّا يُشْرِكُونَ[565] {الروم/40} because most of the time people accept that Allah ﷻ created the person and can at any time take their life. Yet, in their lifespan, when they have different means of sustenance, then people tend to make shirk. Therefore, this ayah and others clearly remind us of this failure as humans.

Yet, Allah ﷻ orders us to be thankful to the means who were the reasons to provide this sustenance such as our parents and remind us that the Real Ar-Razzaq[566] is Allah ﷻ as mentioned قُلْ تَعَالَوْاْ أَتْلُ مَا حَرَّمَ رَبُّكُمْ عَلَيْكُمْ أَلاَّ تُشْرِكُواْ بِهِ شَيْئًا وَبِالْوَالِدَيْنِ إِحْسَانًا وَلاَ تَقْتُلُواْ أَوْلادَكُم مِّنْ إمْلاقٍ نَّحْنُ نَرْزُقُكُمْ وَإِيَّاهُمْ وَلاَ تَقْرَبُواْ الْفَوَاحِشَ مَا ظَهَرَ مِنْهَا وَمَا بَطَنَ وَلاَ تَقْتُلُواْ النَّفْسَ الَّتِي حَرَّمَ اللّهُ إِلاَّ بِالْحَقِّ ذَلِكُمْ وَصَّاكُم بِهِ لَعَلَّكُمْ تَعْقِلُونَ[567] {الأنعام/151}.

The attribute of Allah ﷻ as the Rabb implies other Names and Attributes of Allah ﷻ related with Rububiyyah[568]. These can be Ar-Rahman[569], Ar-Raheem[570], Al-Karim[571], Al-Latif[572], Al-Wahhāb[573], Ar-Razzaq[574] and others. Therefore, the ending surahs of An-Nas and Al-Falaq can hold this distinct position of reflecting the Rububiyyah[575] of Allah ﷻ with the repetition of Rabb in these surahs.

---

563. Indeed Allah is the sustainer.
564. The One with Strong Strength.
565. Allah ﷻ is the one who created you, then provided for you, then will cause you to die, and then will give you life. Are there any of your "partners" who does anything of that? Exalted is He and high above what they associate with Him.
566. The Sustainer.
567. Say, "Come, I will recite what your Lord has prohibited to you. [He commands] that you not associate anything with Him, and to parents, good treatment, and do not kill your children out of poverty; We will provide for you and them. And do not approach immoralities—what is apparent of them and what is concealed. And do not kill the soul which Allah ﷻ has forbidden [to be killed] except by [legal] right. This has He instructed you that you may use reason."
568. Lordship.
569. The Compassionate.
570. The Most Merciful.
571. The Generous.
572. The Kind.
573. The Bestower.
574. The Sustainer.
575. Lordship.

The ayah mentioning the purpose of the creation of humans as

وَعَلَّمَ آدَمَ الأَسْمَاء كُلَّهَا ثُمَّ عَرَضَهُمْ عَلَى الْمَلاَئِكَةِ فَقَالَ أَنبِئُونِي بِأَسْمَاء هَؤُلاء إِن كُنتُمْ صَادِقِينَ 576{البقرة/31} قَالُواْ سُبْحَانَكَ لاَ عِلْمَ لَنَا إِلاَّ مَا عَلَّمْتَنَا إِنَّكَ أَنتَ الْعَلِيمُ الْحَكِيمُ 577{البقرة/32} قَالَ يَا آدَمُ أَنبِئْهُم بِأَسْمَآئِهِمْ فَلَمَّا أَنبَأَهُمْ بِأَسْمَآئِهِمْ قَالَ أَلَمْ أَقُل لَّكُمْ إِنِّي أَعْلَمُ غَيْبَ السَّمَاوَاتِ وَالأَرْضِ وَأَعْلَمُ مَا تُبْدُونَ وَمَا كُنتُمْ تَكْتُمُونَ 578{البقرة/33}

This can imply that the purpose of humans in existence is to learn the Names of Allah ﷻ with Uluhiyyah[579] and Rububiyyah[580] as the marifatullah[581]. Then, apply and reflect the Names and Attributes of Allah ﷻ related with Rububiyyah in their limited life of family, social, and kinship-related engagements in order to help each other. At the same time, constantly make tasbih and tanzîh with SubhanAllah, سبحان ربي الاعلى [583], سبحان ربي العظيم [582], and other similar ones to remind ourselves that Allah ﷻ is beyond our human constructions and imaginations as mentioned {الإخلاص/4} وَلَمْ يَكُن لَّهُ كُفُوًا أَحَدٌ [584].

In this regard, the Uluhiyyah[585] of Allah ﷻ can require submission with humbleness and humility acts of worship such as salah, hajj, and fasting of recognizing our Creator. The Rububiyyah[586] of Allah ﷻ can require genuine concern for others with zakah, امر بالمعروف[587] and نهى عن المنكر [588] and other types of helping each other as outlined in the Qurān and Sunnah.

---

576. And He taught Adam the names—all of them. Then He showed them to the angels and said, "Inform Me of the names of these, if you are truthful."
577. They said, "Exalted are You; we have no knowledge except what You have taught us. Indeed, it is You who is the Knowing, the Wise."
578. He said, "O Adam, inform them of their names." And when he had informed them of their names, He said, "Did I not tell you that I know the unseen [aspects] of the heavens and the earth? And I know what you reveal and what you have concealed."
579. Realm of Power.
580. Lordship.
581. Knowledge of Allah ﷻ.
582. Glory be to My Magnificent Lord.
583. Glory be to my Supreme Lord.
584. Nor is there to him ﷻ any Equivalent.
585. Realm of Power.
586. Lordship.
587. Command good.
588. Forbid the evil.

Tawhid in Rububiyya[589]

When one analyzes the ayah يَا أَيُّهَا النَّاسُ اعْبُدُواْ رَبَّكُمُ الَّذِي خَلَقَكُمْ وَالَّذِينَ مِن قَبْلِكُمْ لَعَلَّكُمْ تَتَّقُونَ[590] {البقرة/21} one can realize the emphasis of the true tawhid so that the person can embody the true Uluhiyyah[591] as mentioned with الَّذِي خَلَقَكُمْ وَالَّذِينَ مِن قَبْلِكُمْ[592] and Rububiyyah[593] of Allah 🌸 as mentioned with رَبَّكُمُ[594] and then, truly apply and embody ubudiyyah[595], 'ibadah as mentioned with يَا أَيُّهَا النَّاسُ اعْبُدُواْ. When the person embodies the true Uluhiyyah, Rububiyyah, and 'Ubudiyyah of Allah 🌸, then the person can embody taqwa as mentioned in this ayah يَا أَيُّهَا النَّاسُ اعْبُدُواْ رَبَّكُمُ الَّذِي[596] خَلَقَكُمْ وَالَّذِينَ مِن قَبْلِكُمْ لَعَلَّكُمْ تَتَّقُونَ {البقرة/21}.

When one reviews the Qurān, there is a lot of emphasis to truly understand and embody the true Uluhiyyah[597] of Allah 🌸. There is a lot of emphasis to truly understand and embody the true Rububiyyah[598] of Allah 🌸. Then, accordingly, the problems and glitches are presented in the ubuddiyyah[599] of people as there are problems in the embodiment of the people in the true Uluhiyyah and Rububiyyah of Allah 🌸.

The examples of this are numerous in the Qurān. One can also view the same approach in the rendering below similarly. The true rububiyyah and uluhiyyah require the true ubudiyyah or ibadah to Allah 🌸 as represented below.

---

589. Lordship.
590. O Mankind, worship your Lord who created you and those before you.
591. Realm of Power.
592. Who created you and those before you.
593. Lordship.
594. Your Lord.
595. Worship.
596. O Mankind, worship your Lord who created you and those before you.
597. Realm of power.
598. Lordship.
599. Worship.

One can experience one's own need and weakness in one's humanness, observe and realize the structure and order in the universe and find one's Sustainer, Care-Giver, the Rabb, Allah ﷻ. This can be called the Rububiyyah[600] of Allah ﷻ. This is sufficient enough to worship and establish ubudiyyah[601] to Allah ﷻ. They submit themselves to Allah ﷻ by engaging themselves constantly with investigation of renderings of Care-Giver and Sustainer Attributes of Allah ﷻ.

On a side note, the creation reflects the Names and Attributes of Allah ﷻ at a very peripheral level. One can witness caretaking, rububiyyah, of the creation for other parts of the creation. From this perspective, certain Names and Attributes of Allah ﷻ related with the Rububiyyah of Allah ﷻ can be reflected in the creation. This reflection can be similar to shadows compared to the real. Or, it can be similar to an image compared to the real.

Yet, the Names and Attributes of Allah ﷻ related with Uluhiyyah[602] of Allah ﷻ only but only belong to Allah ﷻ. The hadith [22] mentions this very critical point with a metaphorical language to underline this life-threatening point that Allah ﷻ mentions al-kibriyaau is the izhar of Allah ﷻ. Whoever tries to claim any reflection of this Attribute and Name of Allah ﷻ, then this person is destroyed [22].

In explicit cases of shirk with Uluhiyyah[603], the examples can be not many as in the cases of Fira'wn or Namrood. Then, both claim owners were destroyed through non-reversible means due to these claims with Uluhiyyah. These claims can be witnessed more among the aristocrats representing power, wealth, and position. The types of claims related to the shirk against Uluhiyyah can be more obvious and clearer as compared to the shirk claims against Rububiyyah of Allah ﷻ.

The shirk against Rububiyyah of Allah ﷻ can be more common and at all levels of people. This type of shirk may not be as explicit. One needs to make an effort to discover this in their self-recognition with the struggle of the cleaning of their heart and mind through reflection, critical thinking, tafakur with clear and sincere intention. One of the famous shirks in this category is riya as mentioned by Rasulullah 1] ﷺ].

---

600. Lordship.
601. Servanthood.
602. Realm of Power.
603. Realm of Power.

Yet, both shirks in Uluhiyyah[604] and Rububiyyah[605], implicitly or explicitly, can implicate or lead to one another.

In the reflection of the Names of Allah ﷻ related with Rububiyyah of Allah ﷻ, the creation has these reflections as a positive, virtuous quality as long as people know that Allah ﷻ is the Real Source of Rububiyyah and they don't make shirk in this disposition.

A parent taking care of his or her children can be an example. This taking care or rububiyyah can be virtuous as long as there is no shirk. The supporting disposition can be the ayah وَأَمَّا الْغُلَامُ فَكَانَ أَبَوَاهُ مُؤْمِنَيْنِ فَخَشِينَا أَن يُرْهِقَهُمَا طُغْيَانًا وَكُفْرًا {الكهف/80}[606] فَأَرَدْنَا أَن يُبْدِلَهُمَا رَبُّهُمَا خَيْرًا مِّنْهُ زَكَاةً وَأَقْرَبَ رُحْمًا[607]{الكهف/81}

Or, the ayah mentions this problem of shirk when the parents fall into shirk in their caretaking process of their children as: هُوَ الَّذِي خَلَقَكُم مِّن نَّفْسٍ وَاحِدَةٍ وَجَعَلَ مِنْهَا زَوْجَهَا لِيَسْكُنَ إِلَيْهَا فَلَمَّا تَغَشَّاهَا حَمَلَتْ حَمْلاً خَفِيفًا فَمَرَّتْ بِهِ فَلَمَّا أَثْقَلَت دَّعَوَا اللّهَ رَبَّهُمَا لَئِنْ آتَيْتَنَا صَالِحاً لَّنَكُونَنَّ مِنَ الشَّاكِرِينَ {الأعراف/189}[608] فَلَمَّا آتَاهُمَا صَالِحاً جَعَلاَ لَهُ شُرَكَاء فِيمَا آتَاهُمَا فَتَعَالَى اللّهُ عَمَّا يُشْرِكُونَ {الأعراف/190}[609] أَيُشْرِكُونَ مَا لاَ يَخْلُقُ شَيْئاً وَهُمْ يُخْلَقُونَ[610] {الأعراف/191}

The rain coming from the sky helping the earth to grow its plants can be another example of the virtue of caretaking one another reflecting on the creation. In this sense, the position of skies can be considered to be caretaking of the earth. Although this can be the rububiyyah-caretaking between the skies and the Earth—they all know their limits as the creation of Allah ﷻ as mentioned ثُمَّ اسْتَوَى إِلَى السَّمَاء وَهِيَ دُخَانٌ فَقَالَ لَهَا وَلِلْأَرْضِ اِئْتِيَا طَوْعًا أَوْ كَرْهًا قَالَتَا أَتَيْنَا طَائِعِينَ[611] {فصلت/11}.

---

604. Realm of Power.
605. Lordship.
606. And as for the boy, his parents were believers, and we feared that he would overburden them by transgression and disbelief.
607. So we intended that their Lord should substitute for them one better than him in purity and nearer to mercy.
608. It is He who created you from one soul and created from it its mate that he might dwell in security with her. And when he [i.e., man] covers her, she carries a light burden [i.e., a pregnancy] and continues therein. And when it becomes heavy, they both invoke Allah ﷻ, their Lord, "If You should give us a good [child], we will surely be among the grateful."
609. But when He gives them a good [child], they ascribe partners to Him concerning that which He has given them. Exalted is Allah ﷻ above what they associate with Him.
610. Do they associate with Him those who create nothing and they are [themselves] created?
611. Then He directed Himself to the heaven while it was smoke and said to it and to the earth, "Come [into being], willingly or by compulsion." They said, "We have come willingly."

In all these engagements of fulfilling responsibility, we are expected to fulfill and help by not forgetting who we are as the creation of Allah ﷻ. We don't claim anything for ourselves but we are thankful and grateful to be the creation of Allah ﷻ and that Allah ﷻ enables us to do something good. All the reflection of Names and Attributes of Allah ﷻ on humans as a virtuous act requires knowing, and accepting the Real Rab, Allah ﷻ. It requires not doing any implicit or explicit shirk with Rububiyyah[612] and Uluhiyyah[613] of Allah ﷻ.

In other words, taking care of others, doing virtuous acts, helping and supporting each other as humans to fulfill our needs and helping others address social problems and doing service to humanity all require in their full sense and reality to recognize the Real Rabb, Allah ﷻ. It requires adab as the creation because the creation is only mimicking or reflecting the shadows of the Real Source, Allah ﷻ in their engagements of good and virtuous acts, morality, and social justice as mentioned قَالَ

.أَمَّا مَن ظَلَمَ فَسَوْفَ نُعَذِّبُهُ ثُمَّ يُرَدُّ إِلَى رَبِّهِ فَيُعَذِّبُهُ عَذَابًا نُّكْرًا [614]{الكهف/87}

This real recognition and not making the shirk leads the person to the next step. This is doing all the virtuous acts, helping others, and trying to solve social problems such as hunger or others not for self-satisfaction or because it is a virtue in the society, but to show gratitude, appreciation, and thankfulness to the Real Rabb, Allah ﷻ as mentioned.

وَيُطْعِمُونَ الطَّعَامَ عَلَى حُبِّهِ مِسْكِينًا وَيَتِيمًا وَأَسِيرًا [615]{الإنسان/8} إِنَّمَا نُطْعِمُكُمْ لِوَجْهِ اللَّه

{الإنسان/9}[616] لَا نُرِيدُ مِنكُمْ جَزَاءً وَلَا شُكُورًا. Yes, the person does all of those engagements to please Allah ﷻ. Allah ﷻ orders these virtuous acts and helping people in their needs.

Some of the contemporary arguments can include the cases of the people who take the positions of atheism or agnosticism, yet they are involved with good and virtuous acts. This is still possible because Allah ﷻ is Just, al-Adl. Due to their engagements, Allah ﷻ can provide them some outcomes for their engagements.

Yet, real Muslims are good business traders of their intentions. They want to make a very high profit in their transaction of intentions.

---

612. Lordship.
613. Realm of Power.
614. He said, "As for one who wrongs, we will punish him. Then he will be returned to his Lord, and He will punish him with a terrible punishment [i.e., Hellfire].
615. And they give food in spite of love for it to the needy, the orphan, and the captive.
616. [Saying], "We feed you only for the countenance [i.e., approval] of Allah ﷻ. We wish not from you reward or gratitude.

When they engage themselves, it is not because it is virtuous or self-satisfying or an applauded norm in the society, but they do it in order to please Allah ﷻ. One should remember Allah ﷻ always orders the good, virtuous, and moral and is not pleased with the evil and oppression as mentioned إِنَّ اللَّهَ يَأْمُرُ بِالْعَدْلِ وَالإِحْسَانِ وَإِيتَاء ذِي الْقُرْبَى وَيَنْهَى عَنِ الْفَحْشَاء وَالْمُنكَرِ

وَالْبَغْيِ يَعِظُكُمْ لَعَلَّكُمْ تَذَكَّرُونَ [617] {النحل/90}.

and

وَإِذَا فَعَلُواْ فَاحِشَةً قَالُواْ وَجَدْنَا عَلَيْهَا آبَاءنَا وَاللَّهُ أَمَرَنَا بِهَا قُلْ إِنَّ اللَّهَ لاَ يَأْمُرُ بِالْفَحْشَاء أَتَقُولُونَ عَلَى اللَّهِ مَا لاَ تَعْلَمُونَ [618] {الأعراف/28} قُلْ أَمَرَ رَبِّي بِالْقِسْطِ وَأَقِيمُواْ وُجُوهَكُمْ عِندَ كُلِّ مَسْجِدٍ وَادْعُوهُ مُخْلِصِينَ لَهُ الدِّينَ كَمَا بَدَأَكُمْ تَعُودُونَ [619] {الأعراف/29}

By making the intention of pleasing Allah ﷻ in their engagement with the virtuous and the prevention of evil, the real Muslims receive the pleasure of Allah ﷻ- self-satisfaction, content, happiness, and peace both in this world and in the afterlife. They don't care about the applause or recognition of the humans as most of the humans don't properly recognize, appreciate and, show gratitude for people's efforts. Yet, they do it solely for Allah ﷻ. As one of the Names of Allah ﷻ is the As-Shakur[620], the Appreciator. Allah ﷻ appreciates in such a way that Allah ﷻ gives immediate peace, blessings, barakah[621], and happiness in this world and more is expected inshAllah in the afterlife.

On a side note, I think it would be fair to recognize the efforts of the humanitarian services of the Christian world. There have been narratives from different groups of Christianity that they do it to please Allah ﷻ. One of the hikmahs[622] intimates that the spread of Christianity and the large number of Christians can possibly be related to Allah ﷻ

---

617. Indeed, Allah ﷻ orders justice and good conduct and giving to relatives and forbids immorality and bad conduct and oppression. He admonishes you that perhaps you will be reminded.
618. And when they commit an immorality, they say, "We found our fathers doing it, and Allah ﷻ has ordered us to do it." Say, "Indeed, Allah does not order immorality. Do you say about Allah ﷻ that which you do not know?"
619. Say, [O Muhammad ﷺ], "My Lord has ordered justice and that you direct yourselves [to the Qiblah] at every place [or time] of prostration, and invoke Him, sincere to Him in religion." Just as He originated you, you will return [to life].
620. The Most Appreciative.
621. Blessings.
622. Wisdom.

giving them the outcome of their effort due to their sincere engagements or efforts to please Allah ﷻ with the Divine Mashiyyah[623], الله اعلم[624].

In this regard, if they update their approach about Uluhiyyah[625] of Allah ﷻ, then they can be role models for everyone. As a further side note, the fluidity or breaking of boundaries between the Christians and Muslims before the End of Times with the Second Coming of Isa [15] and in the language of the hadith [15] [2] the sun rising from the West can show this update, الله اعلم. The level of boundaries or differences can be different and positively change to the authentic in Uluhiyyah[626], Rububiyyah[627] and Ubudiyyah[628] of Allah ﷻ inshAllah. Then, there are not many group boundaries inshAllah.

A zoologist observing the structure and system among ants or bees, an anatomist observing the complicated, perfect structure and system in the human body, and an aerospace engineer trying to mimic the highest, most efficient, and fully optimized design in the birds can all extrapolate the Rububiyyah[629] of Allah ﷻ. As the Rabb, Allah ﷻ establishes, maintains, and sustains all different systems, universes, structures, and order. In other words, the perfect structure, balance, and order observed and experienced in life is due to Rabbul A'lamin as mentioned بِهِ الَّذِي جَعَلَ لَكُمُ الأَرْضَ فِرَاشاً وَالسَّمَاء بِنَاء وَأَنزَلَ مِنَ السَّمَاء مَاء فَأَخْرَجَ مِنَ الثَّمَرَاتِ رِزْقاً لَّكُمْ فَلاَ تَجْعَلُواْ لِلّهِ أَندَاداً وَأَنتُمْ تَعْلَمُونَ[630] {البقرة/22}.

All the established natural sciences, humanities, and social sciences in their methods of experimentation and observations with their correct and true deductions of the laws, theories, and results can show the Rububiyyah[631] of Allah ﷻ. The concepts of measurability, sustainability, reproducibility, consistency, and generalizability in scientific methods are all parts of the structure, balance, and order of Rububiyyah of Allah ﷻ.

---

623. Permission.
624. Allah ﷻ knows best.
625. Realm of power.
626. Realm of Power.
627. Lordship.
628. Servanthood.
629. Realm of power.
630. [He] who made for you the earth a bed [spread out] and the sky a ceiling and sent down from the sky, rain and brought forth thereby fruits as provision for you. So do not attribute to Allah ﷻ equals while you know [that there is nothing similar to Him].
631. Lordship.

The reproducibility, consistency, and generalizability of results can show the perfection, thoroughness, flawlessness, balance, and nobility in the structure and order established by the Rububiyyah of Allah ﷻ. Humans can call this the laws of physics. Although it is logical that we can appreciate and applaud the person who discovered this law such as Newton or Einstein, we don't exalt them. It is logical and expected that we exalt the One, Allah ﷻ Who establishes this structure, order, and perfection for us with today's scientific discoveries in physics and other fields.

When we look at the terms in categorization or valuation in the scientific world, we hear the words assumption, supposition, theory, and law. Scientific law has the highest value of this valuation. Law is "a statement of fact, deduced from observation, to the effect that a particular natural or scientific phenomenon always occurs if certain conditions are present, for example *the second law of thermodynamics.*" [5]. In this perspective, the notion of "constants" in physics such as gravitational constants (g) or Planck's constant (h) can be examples of these clear examples of generalizability formed as a numerical (ratio) constant and now referred to as law. In summary, the teachings of physics, biology, chemistry, math, geometry, social sciences, and others can show this perfect structure in humans, nature, animals, plants, earth, space, galaxies, micro and macro systems. They all show Allah ﷻ, or the Rububiyah of Allah ﷻ.

On another note, the applicability of the laws removes doubts and self-induced fears. For example, the general rule is if a person studies, he or she can pass an exam. If a person works hard, this person can be successful in his or her work. In this sense of social sciences and humanities along with others such as business administration and economics study, these rules and theories are revealed in the complex, social, and professional fields.

One can also note that the term used in the Qurān, "sunnatullah" and in some of the scholarly writings, the term of "adatullah" can refer to the laws discovered in different natural and social sciences today. In other words, Allah ﷻ establishes all of the structure and order through what we call scientific laws or theories. According to some explanations [13], the maintenance or governance of these laws through angels is not contrary to the reality of sunnatullah. Allah ﷻ does not need anyone or anything in any of these assignments. Yet, the angels can witness this sunnatullah, the structure and order in the creation and with the ma'rifah[632] of Allah ﷻ and they can indulge themselves with the dhikr of Allah ﷻ constantly.

In other words, angels don't have the veil of blockage or friction against the astonishments in the ma'rifah of Allah ﷻ. Their constant food and nourishment is through the full embodiment of dhikr with full astonishments of angelic states. Yet, humans due to their intrinsic friction of nafs try to aim and be in these angelic states with their human realities. The term "friction" is a technical term in physics. In Newtonian physics [23], there should be a minimum amount of force to overcome the friction or inertia. In this perspective, once one applies this minimum force, then the object can move. In our terms, humans can take steps against their nafs to reach some of these angelic states. As Allah ﷻ is Just, al-Adl, Allah ﷻ gives humans the opportunity even to surpass beyond the angelic status. Humans have an intrinsic friction of negative or raw nafs (ammarah). Angels don't have this spiritual friction.

In this perspective, rules or social theories sometimes outlined as hikmahs in the tradition are accessible to people who may not be called religious or Muslims. As Allah ﷻ is Just, al-Adil, Allah ﷻ enables everyone to experience the outcomes and results when they follow the structure, laws, and theories as established by Allah ﷻ. Yet, at the end of life and in their lifespan, a person's accountability in front of Allah ﷻ is according to their intention. The intention forms the imān, the belief of the person. If the person does not have imān, he or she can still receive the results of their work, study, and effort due to following the structure or order established by different natural sciences, humanities, and social sciences. A person of imān may not get the results of their work, study, and effort if they don't follow the structure and order established by these sciences. Yet, for the people of imān, Allah ﷻ can give barakah for their effort of studying, working, and if they have the intention of pleasing Allah ﷻ. In this regard, a person of imān can achieve a result with a small effort with the Fadl[633] and Rahmah[634] and Tawfiq of Allah ﷻ referred to as Barakah as compared to the person of kufr who spends all their life trying to achieve the same result. Yet, the disposition of the person of imān should be asking with humbleness and humility for

---

632. Knowledge.
633. Favor.
634. Mercy.

the Khayr outcomes from the tawfiq of Allah ﷻ and at the same time fulfilling the necessary scientific steps to achieve the results. If it is not given to the person, continue to say Alhamdulillah and understand that this can be the khayr for the person, and Allah ﷻ knows the best.

On the other hand, the results or achievements of the world should not mean anything to the people of imān. As long as they have the imān and are struggling in the betterment of their own selves with ibadah, and at the same time not transgressing the rights of others through physical, verbal, and other types of harm, they can be considered the most happy and content in this life. Even though they may appear to be in poverty, have social problems and conflicts, they still consider themselves to be very fortunate in their relationship of the true recognition of Allah ﷻ. This fine perspective can sometimes mislead non-Muslims and some Muslims if they do not understand this very delicate line of real value. In other words, a person externally judges and interprets the conditions of the people of imān as destitution. Then, they extrapolate further the reason for their poverty or destitution is due to Islam.

In these cases, there are two major mistakes. One is that this person in apparent seeming difficulty can be more content and happier than the "liberated" individuals living in luxury. Second is that Islam encourages people to work and follow the rules, theories, and scientific laws as established by Allah ﷻ as a way to show respect to Allah ﷻ. In other words, fulfilling these means or scientific discoveries of natural and social sciences can become a form of dua or prayer if the person has the right intention. There are a lot of ayahs and hadiths that explain the causality relationships as created by Allah ﷻ and they are required to be followed. The hadith of tying the camel [16] and the case of Zulqarnayn follow the reasons and causes (Sûrah Kafh-Cave) [4] and can be some examples of this encouragement of following the means showing respect and full submission to Allah ﷻ. Today's highly pronounced and easily accessible shared social conflicts can be solved by studying and discovering new approaches or laws in social sciences and humanities as set by Allah ﷻ.

The exception of the laws, the necessary condition of applicability, the deadlines of everything such as the destined death (ajal) of a human, the End of the Earth as called Yawmul Qiyamah and others show the human reality of limitation or the creation reality of limitation. To embody this concept by all, there is the reality of everything being terminated and re-creation as mentioned:

يَوْمَ هُم بَارِزُونَ لَا يَخْفَى عَلَى اللَّهِ مِنْهُمْ شَيْءٌ لِّمَنِ الْمُلْكُ الْيَوْمَ لِلَّهِ الْوَاحِدِ الْقَهَّارِ 635
{غافر/16}

كُلُّ مَنْ عَلَيْهَا فَانٍ 636 {الرحمن/26} وَيَبْقَى وَجْهُ رَبِّكَ ذُو الْجَلَالِ وَالْإِكْرَامِ
637{الرحمن/27}

On another note, in our current lives or encounters, the reminder of exceptions to the laws are shown in what we refer to in our human language as "miracles." When there is something extra-ordinary, beyond the observed laws of physics and social sciences, then we call them miracles. Yet, they are reminders for us that Allah ﷻ is watching, interferes, and can interfere at any time, and make the expected outcomes of laws or theories not applicable. In other words, the rare occurrences of these incidents can be due to the freedom of free will of a person with their expected results which bears accountability.

Yet, at the same time, rare occurrences of them in a disturbing way can also show that there is a purpose in one's life and that it is not purposeless.

From another perspective, the constant observance of structure and order in the universe through different discoveries of natural sciences, humanities, and social sciences can also show that there is a purpose, determination, and wisdom in life. In other words, all of the laws of physics, biology, chemistry, math, humanities, and social sciences show what Allah ﷻ wants from humans in their purpose and goal in life as mentioned وَمَا خَلَقْنَا السَّمَاوَاتِ وَالْأَرْضَ وَمَا بَيْنَهُمَا لَاعِبِينَ 638 {الدخان/38} مَا خَلَقْنَاهُمَا إِلَّا بِالْحَقِّ وَلَكِنَّ أَكْثَرَهُمْ لَا يَعْلَمُونَ 639{الدخان/39}

In this perspective, the structure and order observed and discovered in sciences help the person increase their imān incrementally. The exceptions and limiting conditions of these scientific laws and occurrences of miracles observed help the person increase their imān as a boost or geometrically.

The concept of applicability of the law or even constants in certain conditions can show the limitations of these mistakenly exalted or

---

635. The Day they come forth nothing concerning them will be concealed from Allah ﷻ. To whom belongs [all] sovereignty this Day? To Allah ﷻ, the One, the Prevailing.
636. Everyone upon it [i.e., the earth] will perish.
637. And there will remain the Face of your Lord, Owner of Majesty and Honor.
638. And We did not create the heavens and earth and that between them in play.
639. We did not create them except in truth, but most of them do not know.

idolized scientific laws. In other words, Allah ﷻ reminds the person that everything has a limitation except the Unlimited, Al-Baqi[640], Allah ﷻ. One of the delusions of humans is that they make shirk and make partners with Allah ﷻ when they see something immediate and pseudo-exalted by a culture, society, or scientific communities. For the people of Allah ﷻ, even when they are engaged with power, discoveries, and achievements, they remind the people of this unchanging fact that Allah ﷻ is the Real Doer so that they don't make shirk against Allah ﷻ. This is mentioned in the case of Zulqarnayn as the embodiment of achievement of power- that there is a perfect, flawless output. Yet, he reminds that everything perfect and all achievement is from the Rahmah[641] of Allah ﷻ. Yet, all the pseudo-perfections can be destroyed so that people don't make shirk with them but only embody the reality of لا اله الا الله.

فَمَا اسْطَاعُوا أَن يَظْهَرُوهُ وَمَا اسْتَطَاعُوا لَهُ نَقْبًا[642] {الكهف/97}

قَالَ هَذَا رَحْمَةٌ مِّن رَّبِّي فَإِذَا جَاء وَعْدُ رَبِّي جَعَلَهُ دَكَّاء وَكَانَ وَعْدُ رَبِّي حَقًّا[643] {الكهف/98}

Human's current scientific discoveries can be a drop in the ocean of the remaining laws, theories, or systems that are established by the Infinite Rububiyyah[644] of Allah ﷻ. Yet, the real scientists increase their humbleness and humility in front of the amazing Rububiyyah of Allah ﷻ as they discover more and more. The pseudo-scientists become more arrogant and do not appreciate Allah ﷻ. May Allah ﷻ make us from the real ones but not from the pseudo ones, Ameen.

At another level, a person's need, weakness, and constant necessities in life necessitates for him or her to turn to the One Who can take care of all problems, needs, necessities, and relieve them from their worries, anxieties, depressions, fears and anything stemming from their weaknesses. This natural disposition of a human being also guides the

---

640. The Everlasting.
641. Mercy.
642. So they [i.e., Gog and Magog] were unable to pass over it, nor were they able [to effect] in it any penetration.
643. [Dhul-Qarnayn] said, "This is a mercy from my Lord; but when the promise of my Lord comes [i.e., approaches], He will make it level, and ever is the promise of my Lord true."
644. Lordship.

person to find the Rabb, the Care-Giver and the Fulfiller of all needs, Who is Rabbul A'lAlamin Who is Allah ﷺ.

It is interesting to note that even though the person can realize this about the Rububiyyah[645] of Allah ﷺ, he or she may still have tendencies towards and problems of making shirk as mentioned فَلاَ تَجْعَلُواْ لِلّهِ أَندَاداً وَأَنتُمْ تَعْلَمُونَ. Therefore, the person needs to constantly remember and embody the true Rububiyyah of Allah ﷺ without any shirk as they constantly read surah fatiha in their prayers as " الحمد لله رب العالمين[646]."

On another perspective, one can only focus on the reality that he or she is created by Allah ﷺ. That is sufficient enough to worship and establish ubudiyyah[647] to Allah ﷺ. They submit themselves without the need of further investigation or rendering.

The true uluhiyyah[648] and rububiyyah can be called tawhid. This true belief can require the true u'budiyyah or ibadah to Allah ﷺ as represented below.

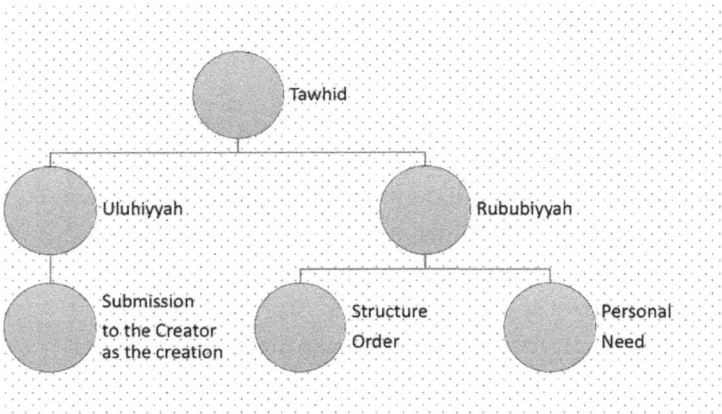

---

645. Lordship.
646. All praise is due to Allah ﷺ, the lord of both worlds.
647. Servanthood.
648. Realm of Power.

Or, in another representation, the true tawhid requires the embodiment of tawhid in all Uluhiyyah[649], Rububiyyah[650] and Ubudiyyah[651] as represented below.

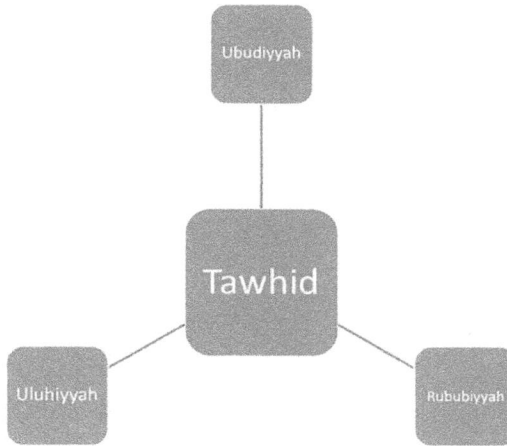

In another perspective, Uluhiyyah[652] is the building of knowledge about Allah ﷻ with the knowledge that is given by the Qurān and hadîth. In this sense, the person is at the level of humble submission as this is required from a person as a finite creation. The person does not try to journey on the waves of the mind regarding the knowledge of the Names and Attributes of Allah ﷻ, or about the cases regarding qadar[653] and others. Yet, the person takes firmly as their pillars the primary guidelines as presented in the Qurān and hadith.

In the approximations of understanding the Rububiyyah[654] of Allah ﷻ, the structure, balance, and order of the universe, nature, the human body, or observable entities, people's minds are forced to engage with the Rububiyyah of Allah ﷻ. In this case, the person may not even be aware of the Qurān and hadith, yet, the mind embedded in each human forces the person to cognize, think, and rationalize about the structure, balance, and order in the micro and macro systems.

---

649. Realm of Power.
650. Lordship.
651. Servanthood.
652. Realm of Power.
653. Power.
654. Lordship.

In addition, the need and weakness of humans in their humanness forces people to engage with the Rububiyyah of Allah ﷻ. In other words, humans have the need to take refuge or shelter in something from their fears, the unknowns, anxieties, and stress.

With the above perspectives, one can view the true approximations of the Uluhiyyah[655] of Allah ﷻ and that these approximative understandings should be given and followed as presented similar to below:

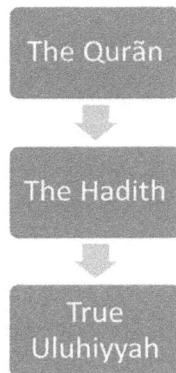

The Qurān

↓

The Hadith

↓

True Uluhiyyah

In the case of Rububiyyah[656], as human mind and experience will force the person, then this can cause the person to think even though they may be unaware of the Qurān and hadith initially as presented below:

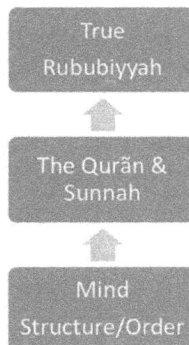

True Rububiyyah

↑

The Qurān & Sunnah

↑

Mind Structure/Order

---

655. Realm of Power.
656. Lordship.

In all of these cases, with the true Uluhiyyah[657] and Rububiyyah[658] struggles of embodiment of the person, the person incessantly seeks how to thank and appreciate Allah ﷻ. Then, this disposition of the struggle of the adornment, appreciation, and thankfulness is called "ibadah" as shown and instructed by the Qurān and sunnah of Rasulullah ﷺ.

One can analyze the surah Fatiha with these themes of Uluhiyyah, Rububiyyah, and 'Ubudiyyah[659] of Allah ﷻ.

In the expression {22/البقرة}[660] فَلَا تَجْعَلُواْ لِلّهِ أَندَاداً وَأَنتُمْ تَعْلَمُونَ, sometimes a person's wrong assumptions about Allah ﷻ can cause a person to commit shirk. Although the person may sometimes know Allah ﷻ truly, yet still he or she may be involved in shirk. Therefore, the scholars have a discussion about when the person involves oneself in a disposition that displeases Allah ﷻ, then the state of imān can leave the person. Although this is a discussion, one may agree or disagree, and even though the person of imān can involve oneself with a sin, then the most important thing is to run to Allah ﷻ and to ask forgiveness from Allah ﷻ.

Tawhid in 'Ubudiyyah[661]

According to tafsîr of ibn Abbas (ra), the order of اعْبُدُواْ is an order of invitation to tawhid [7]. In other words, 'ibadah[662] is the outcome of one's disposition when they try to embody the tawhid in both Uluhiyyah[663] and Rububiyyah of Allah ﷻ. Then. the person can achieve the true tawhid in 'ibadah for Allah ﷻ.

It is interesting to note that the expression of a direct addressee in the Qurān first comes with يَا أَيُّهَا النَّاسُ[664]. This expression is not only for believers but for all of humanity as mentioned يَا أَيُّهَا النَّاسُ. Although surah Baqarah first starts with the dispositions of the believers, kuffar, and munāfiqun, the first case of explicit addressee appears in the Qurān in the form of يَا أَيُّهَا النَّاسُ for all humanity. This can be another besides

---

657. Realm of power.
658. Lordship.
659. Servanthood.
660. So do not attribute to Allah ﷻ equals while you know [that there is nothing similar to Him].
661. Oneness of divineness.
662. Worship.
663. Realm of Power.
664. O mankind.

many other clear proofs that Allah ﷻ sent the Qurān for all of humanity unlike the prior scriptures.

It is interesting to note that the order of 'ibadah or ubudiyyah truly for Allah ﷻ is ordered for all of humanity with the expression[665] يَا أَيُّهَا النَّاسُ اعْبُدُواْ رَبَّكُم. One may ask why the first order for all humanity is not to believe in the Qurān in the sequence of the surahs? Or, why is it not to purify the belief in both Rububiyyah and Uluhiyyah of Allah ﷻ? There can be different possibilities as Allah ﷻ knows the true and best meanings, [666]الله اعلم.

One of the possibilities is that humans can be more aware of their immediate engagements in terms of how they spend most of their time. In other words, humans can be more aware of their visible and observable actions as compared to their invisible and abstract thoughts or ideas. It is a level and self-awareness to monitor one's thoughts, ideas, and intentions as compared to monitoring the actions. Therefore, in worldly, observable, material life, both secular and religious laws are based on actions which may deem reward or punishment.

In other words, actions are generally extrapolated from one's intentions. In this regard, 'ibadah has a meaning that the person spends his or her life working towards something that is more concerning to them. This utmost concern can be due to fear, adornment, or overpowering effects.

In this sense, if the person is always worried and overpowered by financial well-being, then this person struggles and spends all his or her time, effort, and life towards this purpose and this can be his or her 'ibadah. If the person is always worried and overpowered by the concerns of health, then this person struggles and spends all their time, effort, and life towards this purpose and this can be their 'ibadah. If the person is always worried and overpowered by the concerns of not dying and living as long as possible, then this person struggles and spends all their time, effort, and life towards this purpose and this can be their 'ibadah. If the person is always worried and overpowered by the concerns of always having fun, then this person struggles and spends all their time, effort, and life towards this purpose and this can be their 'ibadah. If the person is always worried and overpowered by the concerns of always having

---

665. O mankind, worship your lord who created you
666. Allah ﷻ knows best.

fun, financial well-being, health, not dying, and with others, then this person struggles and spends all their time, effort, and life towards these purposes and these can be their 'ibadah with multiplicities.

If the person is always worried and overpowered by the concerns of always looking for avenues, time and effort-wise to increase their relationship with Allah ﷻ, to please but not displease Allah ﷻ and eagerly meet with Allah ﷻ, then this person struggles and spends all their time, effort, and life towards this purpose and this can be their 'ibadah.

So, ibadah in its general meaning can entail all the observable, apparent, and life-long engagements of the person in life.

In its true sense, 'ibadah for Allah ﷻ should be a life-long engagement and not only five-times prayers. The concern of the person reflecting on the actions makes this a tradition of life-long engagements.

The ayah in this sense explains explicitly this clear disposition as:

{الذاريات/56}667 وَمَا خَلَقْتُ الْجِنَّ وَالْإِنسَ إِلَّا لِيَعْبُدُونِ

{الشرح/8} 669فَإِذَا فَرَغْتَ فَانصَبْ 668{الشرح/7} وَإِلَى رَبِّكَ فَارْغَبْ

On another note, the Qurān mentions the specific cases of ahlu-kitab in the problem of u'budiyyah as:

وَمَا أُمِرُوا إِلَّا لِيَعْبُدُوا اللَّهَ مُخْلِصِينَ لَهُ الدِّينَ حُنَفَاءَ وَيُقِيمُوا الصَّلَاةَ وَيُؤْتُوا الزَّكَاةَ وَذَلِكَ دِينُ الْقَيِّمَةِ 670{البينة/5}

Regarding the above ayah, the essence of oneness in i'badah is reminded with the expression لِيَعْبُدُوا آللَّهَ مُخْلِصِينَ لَهُ الدِّينَ حُنَفَاءَ671 which is opposite to its problematic approaches of multiplicity as implied by the trinity. Although the concepts of prayers and charity are present in Christianity and Judaism, the required plug-in or updates are essential

---

667. And I did not create the jinn and mankind except to worship Me.
668. So when you have finished [your duties], then stand up [for worship].
669. And to your Lord direct [your] longing.
670. And they were not commanded except to worship Allah ﷻ, [being] sincere to Him in religion, inclining to truth, and to establish prayer and to give zakāh. And that is the correct religion.
671. Except to worship Allah ﷻ, [being] sincere to Him in religion, inclining to truth.

to have tawhid as mentioned لِيَعْبُدُوا اَللَّه مُخْلِصِينَ لَهُ الدِّينَ حُنَفَاء وَيُقِيمُوا الصَّلاَةَ[672]
وَيُؤْتُوا الزَّكَاةَ.

In this regard, the expression دِينُ الْقَيِّمَةِ[673] can allude to this
unchanging teaching of Allah ﷻ since the beginning of the creation
for all humans through all the prophets, messengers, and scriptures as
sent by Allah ﷻ. The word الْقَيِّمَةِ[674] can indicate this continuity in this
unchanging teaching. Therefore, if one wants to identify similarities and
commonalities among the religions, tawhid is the one tenet that can
establish this commonality as mentioned here إِلَّا لِيَعْبُدُوا اللَّه مُخْلِصِينَ لَهُ الدِّينَ
حُنَفَاء[675] or as mentioned or as mentioned in: قُلْ يَا أَهْلَ الْكِتَابِ تَعَالَوْاْ إِلَى كَلَمَةٍ
سَوَاء بَيْنَنَا وَبَيْنَكُمْ أَلاَّ نَعْبُدَ إِلاَّ اللَّهَ وَلاَ نُشْرِكَ بِهِ شَيْئًا وَلاَ يَتَّخِذَ بَعْضُنَا بَعْضاً أَرْبَابًا مِّن دُونِ اللَّهِ
فَإِن تَوَلَّوْاْ فَقُولُواْ اشْهَدُواْ بِأَنَّا مُسْلِمُونَ[676] {آل عمران/64}.

Therefore, today's language of religious engagement used by
different institutionalized religions such as Judaism, Christianity,
Islam, Buddhism, Hinduism, and non-institutionalized religions
such as spirituality, mysticism, and others can come together using a
similar shared language of tawhid through different tools experienced
in dedication, open-mindedness, devotion, and practice. In this regard,
they can have a similar and common language about the One and
Unique Creator- Allah ﷻ as God, Elohim, Adonai, the One, and other
beautiful and perfect Names and Attributes of Allah ﷻ.

In this regard, tawhid has been the only unification or string theory
for the true and genuine reality that can unify us and minimize our
conflicts.

'Ibadah is the external engagement of the person with internal
faculties. In this sense, the language of words of external and internal can
become misleading if the person takes it literally. This could be similar

---

672. Except to worship Allah ﷻ, [being] sincere to Him in religion, inclining to truth, and to
establish prayer and to give zakāh.
673. The correct religion.
674. Correct.
675. Except to worship Allah ﷻ, [being] sincere to Him in religion, inclining to truth.
676. Say, "O People of the Scripture, come to a word that is equitable between us and you—
that we will not worship except Allah ﷻ and not associate anything with Him and not take one
another as lords instead of Allah ﷻ." But if they turn away, then say, "Bear witness that we are
Muslims [submitting to Him]."

to the cases of qadar[677] and qada[678], 'ilm[679] and 'amal[680], or knowing and applying the acquired knowledge and experience.

'Ibadah becomes the fruit and output of one's aqidah[681]. The disposition and identity of one assigning oneself to tawhid in Allah ﷻ is represented by 'ibadah.

Different Names and Attributes of Allah ﷻ in Tawhid

One can understand the knowledge about the tawhid in Uluhiyyah[682] as the authentic, true knowledge that is bestowed on us through the Qurān and Sunnah. In this sense, we humbly submit, follow, and accept. The key term, Islām, can be critical in this case in that we must submit ourselves humbly to the truth as Muslims.

One can make an analogy of this in the methodology of natural and social sciences and humanities as inductive reasoning. Inductive reasoning is characterized by the extrapolation of general laws to particular cases [5]. It is the methodology of understanding by having general laws or principles as the primary approach to understanding. In sociology, one may call this macro-analysis of policy making. In education, one may call this a top-down approach as opposed to the grounded theory. When something becomes a scientific word, no one questions its validity, but people follow this law. They use this law to understand another phenomenon.

On the other hand, it can be possible to view the knowledge about the tawhid in Rububiyah[683] as the authentic, true knowledge that is bestowed on us through our daily and constant experience and conscience. In this case, one may try to get a meaning to construct, build, and build until one dies. The key term jihad, struggle can be critical in this case to remember. Jihad is the constant struggle, until one dies, to correctly connect the pieces to have the yaqin, certainty in the tawhid through Rububiyyah of Allah ﷻ. In this sense, the word imān can be critical in that one struggles and tries to establish the yaqîn in Islam

---

677. Destiny.
678. Fate.
679. Knowledge.
680. Actions.
681. Belief.
682. Realm of power.
683. Lordship.

through experiential knowledge and witnessing of knowledge until one dies.

One can make an analogy of this in the methodology of social and natural sciences and in the humanities as is similar to deductive reasoning. Deductive reasoning is characterized by the extrapolation of particular cases to arrive at general laws[5]. It is the methodology of understanding each piece and experience constantly and relentlessly. In sociology, one may call this micro-analysis of policy making. In education, one may call this grounded theory. In anthropology or philosophy, one may call this phenomenology. The engagements of mysticism, experiential and experimental knowledge, can all be under the category of this approach. One can reach to the true tawhid with Rububiyyah of Allah ﷻ.

Therefore, the staging of Islam to Imān can be related to tawhid in Uluhiyyah[684] and Rububiyyah[685] of Allah ﷻ.

In a true religion, both inductive and deductive reasonings, scriptural knowledge bestowed on us, and our experiential and mind-related constant struggle until we die, should be expected to triangulate to the same fact and reality. In other words, all engagements of tawhid in Uluhiyyah and Rububiyyah of Allah ﷻ show the same result of true tawhid about Allah ﷻ.

The Name of Allah ﷻ as Al-Ahad[686] can indicate the Tawhid in Uluhiyyah of Allah ﷻ.

One can also realize that one of the key phrases in this critical Surah of Ikhlās is Al-Ahad. With its shortness, it is a very critical surah in the Qurān. Yet, Al-Ahad is repeated twice although the Surah is short and very critical. As we focus on this surah, Allah ﷻ informs us Who Allah ﷻ is especially in the statement:

Qul ➡ Huwa ➡ Allahu ➡ Ahad

In our human renderings of language, and in our human renderings of multiplicity of being born from parents and giving birth to children,

---

684. Realm of power.
685. Lordship.
686. The Unique.

we witness this constant partnership, pair relationships, and dependency in all creations of Allah ﷻ, then we may sometimes use wrong language about the Uluhiyyah[687]. As long as we don't mean it, inshAllah, Allah ﷻ can forgive us, as Allah ﷻ knows our limits and Allah ﷻ is the Most Merciful, the Most Forgiving.

Therefore, if the person may not be able to make all these logical deductions, Allah ﷻ teaches us to believe and to follow what is already given. In other words, the expressions of Qul[688], huwa[689], and Allahu can possibly instill the farness (b'uud) in this Rahmah[690] of Allah ﷻ for our benefit until we reach to the reality of Ahad with yaqîn. As a mercy and Fadl[691] of Allah ﷻ, Allah ﷻ puts these possible protective layers on imān in order for us to follow the steps of adab and respect and submit ourselves to what is told to us by Allah ﷻ in the Qurān and Hadith until we reach to the level of Ahad.

In this perspective, the expressions of Qul, Huwa, and Allahu can all entail Rahmah-covered farness, (buu'd) so that we can follow and believe but not follow into the humanizations of deity until with practice, 'ibadah, humbleness, sincerity, and knowledge we can reach to the real yaqîn of al-Ahad. This is again from the Rahmah and Fadl of Allah ﷻ. In other words, b'uud or farness possibly indicated in this statement can remind us of our limits as humans in approximating our minds and even experience-related engagements. Therefore, humbleness and humility with adab is always the key, especially regarding Uluhiyyah of Allah ﷻ. Rasulullah ﷺ was the epitome of this trait among all humans as well as in all other spiritual, moral, and ethical traits. Therefore, Rasulullah ﷺ has the highest rank among all humans in his relationship saw as the Habib saw, the loved one by Allah ﷻ. The more the person embodies this adab with Allah ﷻ, the more the person becomes loved by Allah ﷻ, inshAllah.

Adab requires knowing one's limits in one's emotional, verbal, mental, and all other engagements in the relationship with Allah ﷻ. Then, the essence of this adab requires one to be projected in other parts

---

687. Realm of power.
688. Say.
689. He {is}.
690. Mercy.
691. Favor.

such as the Qurān, Rasulullah ﷺ, parents, teachers, and shi'ar of Islam as the reflection of this essential adab with Allah ﷻ.

As Rasulullah ﷺ was the epitome of adab in his journey of mi'raj, Rasulullah ﷺ reached the closest point to Allah ﷻ. Here, we are not talking about a space or time-related point but more within the meaning of level and rank. Another epitome of adab has been Jibril as. It is mentioned that if Jibril as passed certain veils, he could be burnt [6].

In another perspective, as the person is bestowed more and more in bounties, the critical part is that the person similarly is expected to increase their adab with Allah ﷻ. Or, as in the case of Shaytan, does the person lose self-control and pass the limits of adab with Allah ﷻ and fall down from a very high place?

> *May Allah ﷻ protect us, Ameen.*
> *May Allah ﷻ not make us lose the adab with Allah ﷻ, Ameen.*
> *May Allah ﷻ not leave us with our own egoistic selves, Ameen.*

Not everyone is intellectual. The Just, Al-Adl, Name of Allah ﷻ necessitates that the religion be accessible to all levels of learners. In this case, the surah of Ikhlās[692] can be fully sufficient for everyone and especially for the ones who just want to submit themselves to the true and authentic knowledge of Allah ﷻ. There was a sahabah who used to read this surah over and over in his prayers and he mentioned that he loved this surah much [15]. In this perspective, the Name of Al-Ahad[693], and the surah of Ikhlās is sufficient in value, as mentioned by the Prophet ﷺ as one-third of the Qurān [15].

On the other hand if we review the Qurān, many parts of the Qurān engage the person, especially with the Rububiyyah[694] of Allah ﷻ.

When the person analyzes these lifelong experiences, and their true, humble, and open-minded results, these experiences should gauge the person to the true tawhîd of Allah ﷻ with Rububiyyah of Allah ﷻ. This reality is valid if the person is a Muslim or not.

If the person is a Muslim, it will be easier to verify their experience of mind and heart with the authentic bestowed n'imahs[695] of the Qurān

---

692. Sincerity.
693. The Unique.
694. Lordship.
695. Blessings.

and Hadith. Yet, they can still make mistakes due to the overwhelming immediate and short-term effects of these experiences. Humans tend to live in the present time. They hasten to blame the evil-seeming encounters of life. They don't prepare for the long-term and for the afterlife as mentioned in the Qurān [4].

If the person is not a Muslim, he or she may engage themselves with more explicit shirk or errors by attributing this system and structure to other things. Possibly, therefore, the Qurān especially addresses this potential problem in many places within the wrong practices of people and guides them to the tawhid in Rububiyyah[696] of Allah ﷻ.

One may view this as the main problem. In other words, both Muslims and non-Muslims may take either implicit or explicit positions in *shirk*, partnership which impedes their journey of embodying the true tawhid in Rububiyyah of Allah ﷻ.

One of the names of Allah ﷻ that is emphasized with true Rububiyyah of Allah ﷻ is al-Wahid. This Name of Allah ﷻ can include all of the individual experiences of humans' minds and hearts witnessings, observations, and constant experimentations in this world all showing the same result of the One, al-Wahid, Allah ﷻ. All individual experiences in their pieces should bear witness to and in summation can show the Oneness of Allah ﷻ as al-Wahid. This is mentioned with this critical relation between Rububiyyah (Rabb) and al-Wahid in يَا صَاحِبَيِ السِّجْنِ أَأَرْبَابٌ مُّتَفَرِّقُونَ خَيْرٌ أَمِ اللَّهُ الْوَاحِدُ الْقَهَّارُ [697] {يوسف/39}

Therefore, due to problems of distractions due to the multiplicity of these cases and not being able to truly see the true tawhid, One and Unique Allah ﷻ, the Qurān mentions, proves, and eliminates all of the other alternatives with Al-Wahid[698] and Al-Qahhār[699], as in the above ayah and in this ayah very explicitly as: قُل اللَّهُ (قُلْ مَن رَّبُّ السَّمَاوَاتِ وَالأَرْضِ قُلْ أَفَاتَّخَذْتُم مِّن دُونِهِ أَوْلِيَاء لاَ يَمْلِكُونَ لِأَنفُسِهِمْ نَفْعًا وَلاَ ضَرًّا قُلْ هَلْ يَسْتَوِي الأَعْمَى وَالْبَصِيرُ

---

696. Lordship.
697. O [my] two companions of prison, are separate lords better or Allah ﷻ, the One, the Prevailing?
698. The Unique.
699. The Prevailing.

أَمْ هَلْ تَسْتَوِي الظُّلُمَاتُ وَالنُّورُ أَمْ جَعَلُوا لِلَّهِ شُرَكَاءَ خَلَقُوا كَخَلْقِهِ فَتَشَابَهَ الْخَلْقُ عَلَيْهِمْ قُلِ اللَّهُ
خَالِقُ كُلِّ شَيْءٍ وَهُوَ الْوَاحِدُ الْقَهَّارُ ⁷⁰⁰ {الرعد/16}

In this ayah, الْقَهَّارُ⁷⁰¹ is also a very critical Name of Allah ﷻ to further
explain the problem of multiplicity in people's wrong renderings of
Rububiyyah⁷⁰². The Attribute of Allah الْقَهَّارُ ﷻ can allow anything and
everything to happen at any time without any resistance from the
Mashiyyah⁷⁰³ of Allah ﷻ. In other words, the multiplicity of deities as
mentioned with the word arbab is a pseudo and false assumption of
people that they would attribute some power to these deities. In other
words, these assumptions are all groundless, false, and generated by the
human mind and emotional deviations.

Yet, Allah ﷻ is the only and the highest and the true authority in
implementation of power without any resistance as the Attribute الْقَهَّارُ
can entail.

Lastly, after the above ayahs, the Qurān mentions, proves, and
eliminates further in order to establish full certainty with yaqîn, with
the Names and Attributes of Allah ﷻ as Al-Wahid⁷⁰⁴ and Al-Qahhār⁷⁰⁵.
In this case, there is not even a possibility of these pseudo, false, and
self-generated human deviations as a discussion. There is no discussion
of multiplicity nor of the existence of any creation as mentioned: يَوْمَ هُم
بَارِزُونَ لَا يَخْفَى عَلَى اللَّهِ مِنْهُمْ شَيْءٌ لِمَنِ الْمُلْكُ الْيَوْمَ لِلَّهِ الْوَاحِدِ الْقَهَّارِ ⁷⁰⁶ {غافر/16}

In classical literary analysis of these two words, the word ahad⁷⁰⁷ can
mean the oneness in uniqueness, quality, and indivisibility as compared
to the word wahid⁷⁰⁸ which can mean oneness in number, in quantity, and
in all of the individual pieces showing this same oneness. For example,
Zayd is one, unique human-being as an example of ahad. On the other

---

700. Say, "Who is Lord of the heavens and earth?" Say, "Allah." Say, "Have you then taken
besides Him allies not possessing [even] for themselves any benefit or any harm?" Say, "Is the
blind equivalent to the seeing? Or is darkness equivalent to light? Or have they attributed to
Allah partners who created like His creation so that the creation [of each] seemed similar to
them?"583 Say, "Allah is the Creator of all things, and He is the One, the Prevailing."
701. The Prevailing.
702. Lordship.
703. Permission.
704. The Unique.
705. The Prevailing.
706. The Day they come forth nothing concerning them will be concealed from Allah. To
whom belongs [all] sovereignty this Day? To Allah, the One, the Prevailing.
707. Unique.
708. The One.

hand, all people, such as Zayd, A'mr, etc. are all one species of human as wahid.In this perspective of analysis of these Names of Allah ☙, all individual experiences in their pieces should bear witness to al-Ahad, the One and Unique, and their collectivity should show the Oneness of Allah ☙, as Al-Wahid as well. Allah ☙ is Ahad, Unique. Allah ☙ is Wahid, One. Uniqueness necessitates oneness.

Lollipop Effects

Claims of self or nature-related existence

If a person takes the smallest observable or measurable particle, let's say it is an atom. Each atom has a different number of electrons, protons, and neutrons. The identity of each element is determined by the number of different atoms. Each element formed by a different number of atoms can have different qualities.

It is statistically impossible for the electrons, protons, or neutrons forming each atom to come together and form an element by themselves. This element will form with different combinations into DNA, RNA, protein, or an organism. Then, this organism will have life. Then, within all the micro- and macro-systems, there will be a structure or balance. This is illogical, absurd, irrational, unfounded, inconsistent, and impossible.

If we assume the above at micro or angstrom levels (10^{-6} to 10^{-9}), then one can jump up to the macroscopic levels where the units of measurement are at the the speed level of light (10^{8}). In all of these systems, regardless of their size, there is a perfect structure, order, running systems, maintenance, rules, and guidelines.

As a simple example, one can witness in our social life, if there is a small unit or a corner store, people assign duties to prevent chaos. As the organization become more complex as a corporation, then the rules, with a hierarchy, structure, and order can become more detailed in order to run this corporation to minimize the problems.

Similarly, how can a person assume no hierarchy, or no authority in the universe, with perfect, fine, and detailed running of super complex systems both at microscopic and macroscopic levels? This is illogical, absurd, irrational, unfounded, inconsistent, and impossible.

On another note, one can witness the reality of wars, destructions, and chaos in human history, when there is the case of at least two or more people running for authority and leadership. They fight each other to get this authority. How can a person expect this same, simple fact for the universes with more complicated systems which cannot tolerate any type of chaos, lest it be destroyed! This is mentioned in the surah Mu'minun as:

مَا اتَّخَذَ اللهُ مِن وَلَدٍ وَمَا كَانَ مَعَهُ مِنْ إِلَهٍ إِذًا لَّذَهَبَ كُلُّ إِلَهٍ بِمَا خَلَقَ وَلَعَلَا بَعْضُهُمْ عَلَى بَعْضٍ سُبْحَانَ اللهِ عَمَّا يَصِفُونَ 709{المؤمنون/91} عَالِمُ الْغَيْبِ وَالشَّهَادَةِ فَتَعَالَى عَمَّا يُشْرِكُونَ 710{المؤمنون/92}

Our human minds sometimes hide behind impossible possibilities far from logic in order to not face realities. The extrapolation of the discourses of evolution is another avenue that people in the scientific communities hide behind with wrong assumptions and interpretations in some scientific discoveries. In other words, Allah ﷻ can create different species in different forms. Their shapes, heights, and looks can change. Allah ﷻ mentions that Allah ﷻ has created living things from the water. All have a context. Interpretations and extrapolations of a possible truth with generalized and statistically impossible renderings are not deemed to be scientific.

On another note, meaning, value, and goal in our short life requires structure, order, and nobility. Purposelessness, meaninglessness, or having no value invites chaos, destruction, pessimism, and lowliness. Connecting everything in the universe with the randomness of statistically impossible outcomes is accusing them of lowliness. Yet, everything in the universe except some humans know their position in the universe.

A person enters a house which has beautiful and detailed artistic and technological motifs, appliances, and features. While looking for the owner of this house, this person sees a smart TV, a smart refrigerator, and an oven in the kitchen. This person looks at the colorful marble stone with its natural designs on the kitchen countertops. Then, she looks at the

---

709. Allah has not taken any son, nor has there ever been with Him any deity. [If there had been], then each deity would have taken what it created, and some of them would have sought to overcome others. Exalted is Allah above what they describe [concerning Him].
710. [He is] Knower of the unseen and the witnessed, so high is He above what they associate [with Him].

natural oak wood flooring. The flooring color and its touch instills in her a full array of different feelings. This person wants to touch the natural wood with her bare foot. Then, she realizes that there are different types of lighting with different artistic designs of light fixtures. When this person turns on certain light fixtures, they give yellow light. The yellow light reflected on all the designs and artistic rendering of the kitchen makes the person take different pleasures from this beautiful combination of complex and artistic designs with a gushing of emotions in her heart. When this person turns off the yellow light and turns on the white light, this person now sees everything differently with different emotional renderings and perplexities. In all of these mystifications and puzzlements, she develops a very high admiration for the house owner. Then, she says to herself, "The house owner has the ability to establish this structure and order. This house owner should have very high skills of beauty, artistic, and intelligent design."Another person enters the same house and he is amazed with everything similar to the previous person. Yet, this person gets stuck in this amazement and would not be able to move on to the next step. Then, he idolizes these items in the name of science as laws generating these appliances, smart TV, fridge, and light fixtures.

In the above analogy, the first person is the person of imān. She is not stuck on the beautiful and complex systems which necessitate structure and order. She moves on to the next step of finding the Establisher of all of this perfect design and system. The second person is the lost wanderer sometimes referred to by the term fisq. Since, this person doesn't have a clear perspective, meaning, and goal, he or she may get stuck on immediate incidents and not see the realities beyond them. When a person does not have a meaning or goal in life, in reality that person doesn't even know his or her own self. The following ayah can allude to this notion of being a lost wanderer with the translation of the word fasiq[711] as:

$$\text{وَ لَا تَكُونُوا كَالَّذِينَ نَسُوا اللَّهَ فَأَنسَاهُمْ أَنفُسَهُمْ أُوْلَئِكَ هُمُ الْفَاسِقُونَ}^{712}\{الحشر/19\}$$

When people use the word nature, its function is similar to today's publishing companies. It generates and publishes.

---

711. Disobedient.
712. And be not like those who forgot Allah, so He made them forget themselves. Those are the defiantly disobedient.

The Obsession with Impossible Statistical Arguments

One can ask: Why are some people obsessed with getting behind arguments that are statistically impossible? When humans don't want to take the step of imān with their free will even though everything may be clear, simple, and straightforward in front of them, then they need to follow something that will calm their denial. Yes, it is up to the person to decide with their free will either to believe and say [713]"امنت بالله and other pillars." Or, they run behind the impossible possibilities try to calm their inner screAmeeng that tells this person "go back to Allah ."

Yet, at the end there is no compulsion in religion as mentioned in the Qurān, with all the clear ayahs, signs, and indications, the person needs to make a choice using free will. The whole secret of free will, responsibility, and amanah is to *make a choice*. Allah mentions in the Qurān that if Allah wanted, everyone would believe in Allah . Yet, the expected goal for humans is that they themselves will make this choice with their intention, free will, and wil clearly verbalize their stance. One can review the explicit verbalizations of individuals in the Qurān to indicate their stance. For example:

إِنِّي وَجَّهْتُ وَجْهِيَ لِلَّذِي فَطَرَ السَّمَاوَاتِ وَالأَرْضَ حَنِيفًا وَمَا أَنَا مِنَ الْمُشْرِكِينَ[714]
{الأنعام/79}

Even, in some cases, Allah instructs us to verbalize what we should say as:

قُلْ هَذِهِ سَبِيلِي أَدْعُو إِلَى اللَّهِ عَلَى بَصِيرَةٍ أَنَا وَمَنِ اتَّبَعَنِي وَسُبْحَانَ اللَّهِ وَمَا أَنَا مِنَ الْمُشْرِكِينَ[715]{يوسف/108}

وَمَنْ أَحْسَنُ قَوْلًا مِّمَّن دَعَا إِلَى اللَّهِ وَعَمِلَ صَالِحًا وَقَالَ إِنَّنِي مِنَ الْمُسْلِمِينَ[716]{فصلت/33}

At another level, some people possibly do not methodologically follow the epistemology of logic. They follow one step after another.

---

713. I believe in Allah .
714. Indeed, I have turned my face [i.e., self] toward He who created the heavens and the earth, inclining toward truth, and I am not of those who associate others with Allah."
715. Say, "This is my way; I invite to Allah with insight, I and those who follow me. And exalted is Allah; and I am not of those who associate others with Him."
716. And who is better in speech than one who invites to Allah and does righteousness and says, "Indeed, I am of the Muslims."

They use the premises and prepositions of logic and philosophy. They start off using some evidence correctly. Then, in between, or at the end of their statements or arguments, they end up either arriving at a wrong conclusion within the epistemology of following these steps, or they insert unwarranted assumptions in order to fill the gaps in the argument and conclude the narrative. An example of this can be found in the popularized clashes between the scientific communities/defenders of evolution theory and the Western religious authorities.

Within the context of Islam, the Qurān, and the Sunnah, one can find the verses about the creation from water. Then, there is a change. In the context of evolution theory, the doer of the action is always hidden or named "nature." Some of the teachings of this theory are compatible with the teachings in the Qurān and sunnah. One can reconcile these two perspectives and then clearly present the conclusions with a choice of either "a simple logic, accessible and straightforward", Initial Cause, Allah ﷻ; or, very complicated, statistical impossibilities of using some other language such as "nature, laws, universe, etc…" in order to minimize the religious terms.

One of the underlying logical problems occurs when a person assumes something that is unlikely and statistically impossible to happen will without any proof still happen. Then, the person runs behind the doubts, impossible possibilities, and self-depressive states of uncertainty with darkness of anxiety, fear, chaos, stress and insecurity. Yet, the person of imān, can start the journey by taking the initial step of Islam. Then, as he or she goes further, the certainty or yaqîn is expected to increase. This can be referred to as positive states of certainty leading the person to confidence, happiness, falāh, peace, and calmness in this world and in the next. The emerging cases of skepticism, agnostic approaches, and others can be some examples. Critical thinking is important with fine, positive, and constructive approaches. Skeptical approaches leading to negative, depressive states of uncertainty can be self-destructive to all unanswered questions.

Another level of problem occurring in the popular culture is happening in these clashes between the scientific communities/ defenders of evolution theory and Western religious authorities. There are people who have somehow already alienated themselves with their religion. Then, they go full-heartedly and sometimes blindly behind these popularized and scientifically stamped discourses in the replacement of their religion. Then, it becomes backwards if the person does not agree with some of the up-trending popular stances promoted by some scientific communities of journals, articles, and associations.

In this case, mostly, the people who follow these popular up-trends can be the general public who somehow identify themselves as "modern", "cool", "open-minded", or "educated." Yet, their knowledge about the essence of these clashes can lack scholarly depth. They may have more peripheral knowledge. At that level, they can view something impossible as possible without methodological thinking and critical analysis. In these cases, "to follow" the up-trending and normalize this peripheral knowledge in themselves can become natural. This type can be observed more in the states of heedlessness due to the lack of awareness of the reality of these clashes.

One of the key points of the above arguments is the intention and purpose of engagement with this knowledge. If one genuinely tries to search as a matter of life or death or with a vital purpose, then the person will not risk or even entertain the impossible statistical arguments relating to their afterlife, purpose, meaning, and goal in life. They will believe in Allah ﷻ and search and increase their knowledge for tawhid through the teachings of the Qurān and sunnah. On the other hand, if a person views this question as a matter of regular commodity without giving much importance to it, especially within the genuine search of purpose, meaning, and goal in this life and in the afterlife, then they will follow what others say. They will be on the periphery of this search dragged by the popular and cool trending approaches of their time and society.

At another level, in the cases of scholarly stance, the person can see the clear distinction of the impossible. Yet, they may not make the simple, logical, straightforward, and accessible choice of imān but rather make the choice of being in doubt with statistical impossibilities. In these cases, either the preventing factors can be related to some spiritual diseases of group identity or self-identity due to arrogance, jealousy, fear, and others. Or, if they die without making a clear choice while searching the positive states of meaning, purpose, and goal in life, they may be in the category of a'raf as mentioned in the Qurān, [717]الله اعلم.

_____

717. Allah ﷻ knows best.

In the other case of public stance of heedlessness or of following the popular culture, they are not aware of their real state. They don't fully know why they follow.

Or, in some cases, like Aristotle [23], they use the mind and premises of the logic with very delicate accuracy and conclude with an approximation of true Uluhiyyah[718]. Yet, since there is no reported Divine Guidance (wahiy) similar to the Qurān and Sunnah, they may not practically include the language and understandings related with tawhid and ubudiyah of Allah 🌸.

In Islamic epistemology, knowing human limitation is a virtue and required condition in the approximated knowledge related with the Transcendent Infinite Reality, Allah 🌸. In other words, knowing and understanding something fully, especially with mind, can mean surrounding that being intellectually. Yet, limited cannot surround the Unlimited. Humans should know their limits of adab in their knowledge and relations with Allah 🌸, Al-Baqi, the Unlimited. The true knowledge and experience with human limitations can only be approximated with the guidelines of the Qurān, Sunnah, mind, and experience.

Sometimes, a person can be investigating or researching the truth or a phenomenon. In their research, they may find a pseudo, side product. Then, with different constructions or approaches, they may try to justify this pseudo-effect or side product as the reality or truth of this phenomenon.

This case is very common in the experimentations of natural sciences such as physics. When a physicist is acquiring data from a sample, it may be difficult to understand and then interpret what could be considered as "noise"- unwanted, pseudo-effects as compared to the real goal of this experiment.

In the personal journeys of relation with Allah 🌸, there is the case of humans who cannot truly attach themselves to Tawhid, unique, One Creator, Allah 🌸 due to this multiplicity of background noises with varieties. A good scientist or physicist can differentiate these noises from a genuine signal or sign with different wavelengths and frequencies. Similarly, Allah 🌸 gives every human the abilities and skills of mind and experience. With a genuine thirst of searching for the results or answers similar to performing scientific research, Allah 🌸 guides the person to

---

718. Realm of power.

find the real signal, the Qurãn and Rasulullah ﷺ as long as the person maintains humbleness with the motivation and struggle to find and research about it. In this regard, gaining knowledge and learning is also one of the critical elements in order to understand what is genuine and what are pseudo-noises as compared to genuine and authentic signs.

A particle or an atom has a billion different possibilities of doing something. It becomes part of an element, system, human, animal, planet, space, or galaxy. Then, this atom becomes part of the application of a scientific law. The existence of this scientific law in the universe depends now on the critical motion, effect, or contribution of this particle in this system. Among billions of possibilities, the adventure of this tiny atom in its motion, choice, existence, and role. How can it take this role? Then, one can think of billions of atoms with these roles and different purposes being assigned to different tasks. How can they be assigned? After this assignment, in this complexity of billions and more, how can this system be maintained?

The answer is easy and straightforward. This answer is accessible to all levels of learners. The answer is not only for the elite intellectuals in universities with artificially generated titles of recognition in these communities. It is not like the case of impossible statistical arguments that one uses to soothe or trick oneself with, and it is not like the impossibilities of popular terms of skepticism or others.

Allah ﷻ is the One who creates this atom and all others. Allah ﷻ is the One Who orders them to form a structure. Allah ﷻ is the One Who maintains this structure. Allah ﷻ is the One Who establishes the rules as scientific laws as the sunnatullah. Allah ﷻ is the One Who can give at any time the order to these atoms or elements to act in the way that Allah ﷻ orders them contrary to their present duties. Fire not burning Ibrahim as is one example Sûrah Al-Anbiyã; 21:69] [4] of these atoms or elements not acting according to the natural laws but a clear sign that they work under the command of Allah ﷻ however they are ordered to do so. All other miracles are other examples.

When an atom works under the command of Allah ﷻ individually, it still works under the command of Allah ﷻ when this atom becomes part of a system, galaxy, human body, plant, or an animal. This atom does not work for or take orders from the scientific laws or natural laws. Natural or scientific laws are our abstraction and the language of our social constructs to identify these principles in the universe as created and maintained by Allah ﷻ.

The Word "Nature" as a Social Construct

Let us view the word "nature" and how it was popularized and constructed, especially in the last two centuries. This was a replacement of the language for God, especially in the Western world, as one of reactions of the alienation from the religion. Then, as a socially constructed phenomena, the word nature has been used in scientific journals to connect people with an entity which was not clearly defined.

When they were asked, "Do you mean 'God'?" Then, the immediate or defensive response can be, "No, we believe in science." Then, when asked, "What do you mean by nature?" They may reply, "All the scientific laws." Then, if the conversation follows as, "Why do you give a hierarchy as a collective body of laws called nature?" They may reply, "Because there is a governing body." They may be asked, "Then, can you refer this governing being as God?" Then, they would insist and say, "No, we want to call it nature."

When I was teaching at Harvard Divinity school, there was a student. She mentioned that she had a discussion with another person who identified herself as an "atheist." At the end of their ongoing conversations, her friend agreed to use or pray to a term called "mother universe" [24]. These can all be social or personal language related constructs. Yet, one really needs to go back, find, and detect the alienating reasons in the language referrals and reconstruct them with the tanzîh[719] of subhanAllah.

One can note that, the term used in the Qurān, "sunnatullah, and in some of the scholarly writings, the term of "adatullah" can refer to the laws discovered in different natural and social sciences today. In other words, Allah ﷻ can establish all the structure and order through different means such as what we refer to as scientific laws or theories, or nature as popularized today.

Sometimes, our social constructs due to political, cultural, and other reasons can replace a word and people may not realize what they

---

719. Dislike.

really mean when they use it. It can be a reaction, as mentioned, to the religion in this case.

Allah ﷻ has infinite beautiful and perfect names. In Islam, as long as one can find Allah ﷻ with one beautiful name, that is still accepted as long as they understand that the Creator, Allah ﷻ is One and Unique as[720] لَا اله الا الله. It is expected that the person can detail their knowledge without any implicit and explicit partnership, shirk with Allah ﷻ in their connection.

In this regard, a human lifespan can have these cases of multiplicity due to one's lack of knowledge of one's own self in detailing one's own knowledge as mentioned [721] وَلَا تَكُونُوا كَالَّذِينَ نَسُوا اللَّهَ فَأَنسَاهُمْ أَنفُسَهُمْ أُوْلَئِكَ هُمُ الْفَاسِقُونَ {الحشر/19}. The case of using a socially constructed word such as nature is one of these examples. Yet, as the person learns more through mind, heart, and experience related education, then it is expected that that person can embody لَا اله الا الله, that there is unity, One, Allah ﷻ.

At a very clear stance, Allah ﷻ mentions these humans' false social constructs by addressing in the Qurān with a very simple but straightforward question as: أَمْ لَكُمْ كِتَابٌ فِيهِ تَدْرُسُونَ [722] {القلم/37}, is there a book or scripture from "nature," "scientific laws" or other social constructs telling you to follow them or what you follow as mentioned إِنَّ لَكُمْ فِيهِ لَمَا تَخَيَّرُونَ [723] {القلم/38}.

If nature, social, cultural, political, or any identity constructs you have, have sent you a proof or a book, just bring them and let's see if there even is anything as mentioned أَمْ لَكُمْ سُلْطَانٌ مُبِينٌ [724] {الصافات/156} فَأْتُوا بِكِتَابِكُمْ إِن كُنتُمْ صَادِقِينَ [725] {الصافات/157}. This is a very straightforward and simple challenge and the answer is "No, there is no deity who makes this claim except that Allah ﷻ clearly, strongly, and in a very straightforward way mentions that Allah ﷻ is the Creator, Rabbul Alamin and the Qurān and Rasulullah ﷺ have been sent by Allah ﷻ.

In other words, Allah ﷻ as the Rabbul A'lamin sends a book and scripture as mentioned ذَلِكَ بِأَنَّ اللَّهَ نَزَّلَ الْكِتَابَ بِالْحَقِّ وَإِنَّ الَّذِينَ اخْتَلَفُوا فِي الْكِتَابِ

---

720. Theres no god except Allah ﷻ.
721. And be not like those who forgot Allah, so He made them forget themselves. Those are the defiantly disobedient.
722. Or do you have a scripture in which you learn.
723. That indeed for you is whatever you choose?
724. Or do you have a clear authority?
725. Then produce your scripture, if you should be truthful.

لَفِي شِقَاقٍ بَعِيدٍ 726{البقرة/176}. This Book, the Qurān clearly and strongly states without any social construct that this is from the Creator of all universes so that we can place our social constructs in a framework as mentioned إِنَّا أَنزَلْنَا إِلَيْكَ الْكِتَابَ بِالْحَقِّ لِتَحْكُمَ بَيْنَ النَّاسِ بِمَا أَرَاكَ اللَّهُ وَلاَ تَكُن لِّلْخَائِنِينَ خَصِيمًا 727{النساء/105}. Yet, people follow things as shirk that have no clear sign or indication as mentioned أَمْ لَكُمْ أَيْمَانٌ عَلَيْنَا بَالِغَةٌ إِلَى يَوْمِ الْقِيَامَةِ إِنَّ لَكُمْ لَمَا تَحْكُمُونَ 728{القلم/39} سَلْهُم أَيُّهُم بِذَلِكَ زَعِيمٌ 729{القلم/40} أَمْ لَهُمْ شُرَكَاء فَلْيَأْتُوا بِشُرَكَائِهِمْ إِن كَانُوا صَادِقِينَ 730{القلم/41}

If we have a mirror that we hold towards the objects, it will reflect an image of the object. The object in the mirror is formed due to properties of amalgam derived from a mixture of mercury on a glass surface [5]. Yet, we cannot say that mercury, or amalgam, or glass creates the image. Allah ﷻ gives these properties to these elements.

On the other hand, if we don't move the mirror towards different objects, there is a mirror, but it is not functional. It is just staying there and waiting to be explored. Yet, a person comes and takes an action on it by holding it towards the objects. Then, then there is an image. In these perspectives, these natural laws or chemical properties do not have mind, intelligence, willpower, and a goal to do something. They are all the creation of Allah ﷻ waiting to be explored as different signs of Allah ﷻ. The person can ascertain a meaning and use critical thinking for their own purpose, meaning, and goal in life in order to increase their imān and attachment with Allah ﷻ with yaqîn, certainty.

At another scale, if a person watches the stars in the sky on a summer night, there is a sense of amazement, astonishment, awe, wonder, and admiration. To express these inner feelings of joy or admiration, a person who knows and certainly believes in Allah ﷻ may say, "Wow, SubhanAllah! What a perfect creation that Allah ﷻ created, this marvelous, beautiful, perfect structure and order! Alhamdulillah! Thank you, Allah! You give me the ability to recognize, and feel

---

726. That is [deserved by them] because Allah has sent down the Book in truth. And indeed, those who differ over the Book are in extreme dissension.

727. Indeed, We have revealed to you, [O Muhammad ﷺ], the Book in truth so you may judge between the people by that which Allah has shown you. And do not be for the deceitful an advocate.

728. Or do you have oaths [binding] upon Us, extending until the Day of Resurrection, that indeed for you is whatever you judge?

729. Ask them which of them, for that [claim], is responsible.

730. Or do they have partners? Then let them bring their partners, if they should be truthful.

joy and pleasure from all this wonderful, fabulous, and remarkable system structure! Thank You, thank You, thank You, Alhamdulillah, Alhamdulillah, Alhamdulillah!"

On the other hand, the person who may tend to identify himself or herself as an atheist or with similar or more popular identifiers may say in the same scenario of watching the stars on a clear summer night, may say, "Wow! Look at the stars! It is such a nice, amazing, beautiful, perfect structure and order! Look at the scientific laws of physics! It is so amazing! Thank you, science!"

In the above case, the person gets amazed by the perfect structure and order. He or she assumes or animates "science" in order to express his or her gratitude and thankfulness. The laws itself are concepts labeled as "science" in our social constructs.

In a more popular culture, people in the above categories may say, "It is so amazing! Thank you, nature!" Or, "Thank you, mother nature!" Or, "Thank you, universe nature!" (in more intellectual circles).Let's analyze the above cases and try to identify the similarities and differences.

In all cases, when a person finds a perfect structure and order, first they get amazed and astonished. This amazement gives them joy, pleasure, and admiration. This overwhelming admiration and adoration rushes to one's mouth and tongue to verbalize them. Up to this point, everyone shares the same or similar points of amazement of inner boosting feelings regardless of if they are religious or not. One can remember this notion in the separation of state and church. In other words, people may call up to here "secular."

Then, in this verbalization, everyone tries to locate where to give credit, respect, admiration, adoration-to something or someone.

The ones who are alienated from religion tend to cover (kafara-kufr) the reality with some alternative labels of science, scientific laws, nature, mother nature…etc. The ones who know the reality simply and directly utter the name of Allah (☺), God, or the Creator from the deep parts of their heart with full certainty, conviction, and full confidence. They use the expressions, dhikrs such as SubhanAllah, Alhamdulillah, Allahuakbar, or La ilaha illa Allah to verbalize this amazement. In addition, they embody this amazement, adoration, and admiration by salah, daily five-times prayers of bodily movements, and verbal dhikrs showing their constant amazement and adoration, gratitude, and appreciation to Allah ﷻ. In this sense, this is called 'ibadah[731]. The word 'abd has the meaning of adoring and admiring something and following and submitting yourself. In this regards, 'abdullah has this natural disposition of a person who has this amazement, admiration, gratitude, and love and therefore, these moving, internal feelings of embodied adoration fuel up the person's body and tongue with dhikr, five-times prayers and recitation of the Qurān to appreciate and increase their amazement with joy, peace, and happiness in this world and in the afterlife.

On the other hand, the other ones who label themselves as atheist or with similar labels have a hard time finding a good word and using it. They try to avoid saying God because they first identified themselves as 'atheists'. Therefore, they don't want to say something which would contradict with their own selves and how they identify themselves. They try to update and use different expressions over their lifespans for years or generations unless they simply accept and face their own selves before they die.

Instead of doing this, it will be much easier on their souls, hearts, and minds to say Allah. Then, they can go back to the problems of why they were alienated from God due to their wrong constructions. Then, they can re-build their relationship with Allah ﷻ with authentic, positive, and non-alienating realities inshAllah with the Tawfiq, Fadl[732] and Rahmah[733] of Allah ﷻ.

Another example of this can be a small child observing a parade performed by a group of people. The people in this performance or parade walk exactly the same way, at the same time, and with the same hand, arm, and leg movements. A child observing the structure and order in this performance can assume an invisible rope is making everyone move at the same pace and in the same shapes forming an array of geometric structures. Yet, a very ordinary person knows that the people in the parade work under the command of a parade leader. They were first trained by the leader and the parade leader is still there to maintain the structure and order.

---

731. Worship.
732. Favor.
733. Mercy.

Similarly, Allah ﷻ creates and trains the beings such as electrons, atoms, and other beings with the scientific training laws. Yet, Allah ﷻ still maintains this structure.

In a similar sense, one can view nature as the art of Allah ﷻ. This art is not lifeless or motionless like an art piece hanging on the wall. Yet, it has a perfect structure and order with life, service, and eco-system. This art of nature is painted with the scientific or natural laws and is called sunnatullah. The word 'paint' is also used in this context in the Qurān with the word ص صِبْغَةَ[734] as :

صِبْغَةَ اللَّهِ وَمَنْ أَحْسَنُ مِنَ اللَّهِ صِبْغَةً وَنَحْنُ لَهُ عَابِدُونَ[735] {البَقرة/138}

It is interesting to view how this ayah fits exactly with the discussion above when Allah ﷻ establishes a structure of art referred to as nature, scientific laws, or social sciences. Then this art with complex perfect structure and order is the painting of Allah ﷻ. Who can be a better Designer, Artist in this art of nature, as the Master, Originator, Producer, and the Creator than Allah ﷻ? This exact question is in similar renderings as وَمَنْ أَحْسَنُ مِنَ اللهِ صِبْغَةً[736]. Then, one knows and fully realizes Allah ﷻ with full adoration, and then that person becomes the adorer, 'abd as in Arabic language, of Allah ﷻ as[737] وَنَحْنُ لَهُ عَابِدُونَ.

The Qurān Only as a Sufficient Proof: Rububiyyah[738] & Uluhiyyah[739] of Allah ﷻ

If the person cannot read these clear signs of Allah ﷻ in the universe, then one should review the ayahs of the Qurān. All the ayahs of the Qurān encourage the person towards critical thinking as being capable of showing the proofs of all the clear signs in the universe.

One of the vivid and emerging themes in the Qurān in many ayahs is the proof of Rububiyyah of Allah ﷻ in the universe and is a very clear, simple, straightforward, and accessible proof for everyone.

---

734. The religion of Allah ﷻ.
735. [And say, "Ours is] the religion of Allah. And who is better than Allah in [ordaining] religion? And we are worshippers of Him."
736. And who is better than Allah in [ordaining] religion?
737. And we are worshippers of Him."
738. Lordship.
739. Realm of Power.

This accessibility can range from a child to a farmer to a professor. In other words, this sign is one of the clear and available indications of comprehension for all levels of learners regardless of their age, education level, background, and language.

"Why" for Religion and "How" for Science

For example, if we analyze kinship relationships, why does a mother carry the feeling of caring for her child? Why do we feel bad when we see someone in pain? Why do lions or tigers as some of the wildest animals in depiction take care of their babies? Why do the birds take care of their babies? Why does a chicken sacrifice herself to protect her baby from a wolf or fox? Why does a perfect structure exist in a simple, microscopic solid crystal that leads to today's computer technology? Why is there a perfect structure in the orbits of the sun, the moon, and the earth with their perfect velocity that establishes equilibrium/balance with centripetal/centrifugal forces?

All of the above questions and many more are extrapolated from the Qurān with the answer that all is with the Rububiyyah of Allah ﷻ. The Rabb, Allah ﷻ as the Real Care-Taker or Care Giver, the Maintainer, and the Sustainer establishes the means through different vehicles whether people realize it or not.

On the other hand, science looks at the 'how' of the above questions instead of 'why'. For example, how does a mother carry the feeling of caring for her child? How do we feel bad when we see someone in pain? How do lions or tigers as some of the wildest animals in depiction take care of their babies? How do the birds take care of their babies? How does a chicken sacrifice herself to protect her baby from a wolf or fox? How does a perfect structure exist in a simple, microscopic solid crystal that leads to today's computer technology? How is there a perfect structure in the orbits of the sun, the moon, and the earth with their perfect velocity that establishes equilibrium/balance?

The answers to all of the above questions can be rationalized, interpreted, and explained with different natural and social sciences such as physics, biology, chemistry, psychology, sociology, and anthropology. Yet, these are all the means or laws or theories established by Allah ﷻ in order to show the Rububiyyah of Allah ﷻ clearly, simply, and with accessibility for all levels of learners.

In the above perspectives, the questions of "how" should lead to the questions of "why." In other words, the person should not be stuck in the means while trying to reach to the ends.

In other words, the purpose, goal, and meaning are the questions that are given by the religion. In Islam, one can also refer to this as *intention* as a formalized teaching. Execution of the actions to reach a purpose, goal, meaning, or intention comes as *secondary* to the questions of 'how' being answered and scientific knowledge deals with them.

In this regard, the purpose, goal, and meaning is primary. Analyzing, understanding, and looking at the process can be secondary. That *does not mean* that the secondary or science is not important. It is as important as the initial step purpose, goal, and meaning. Once the person takes the initial step of intention, imãn, purpose, goal and meaning, then the latter steps of execution of this through science, actions, and means will support and substantiate this initial step.

Or, if there is a mismatch of intention and action, imãn and amal, purpose and science, then these two will affect each other, either working in harmony of hopeful states of imãn, or in chaos of depressive states of kufr.

Purpose is the motivating factor for doing an action. In today's scientific educational terms, one can also call this as "relevancy" [25] .

Intention is the motivating factor for doing an action.

Imãn is the motivating factor for doing an 'amal.

Imãn is the motivating factor for making the discoveries of science. This is done in order to increase one's imãn and to fully attach oneself with yaqîn, certainty to marifatullah. In each scientific discovery and in theoretical sciences, one can witness and boost one's purpose and meaning in imãn yaqîn to Allah ﷻ, in imãn with yaqin to the afterlife, and in imãn with yaqîn to the other pillars. One of the qualities of a true believer is {البقرة/4} 740 وَبِالآخِرَةِ هُمْ يُوقِنُونَ. In this case, yaqîn, certainty in the afterlife is not an option but a required case for a true believer,741 اللهم اجعلنا منهم آمين.

Islam is the motivating factor for scientific inventions. Applied sciences such as engineering, medicine, business, and social sciences look for the relevancy to help humans and all of creation.

---

740. And who believe in what has been revealed to you, [O Muhammad ﷺ], and what was revealed before you, and of the Hereafter they are certain [in faith].
741. Oh Allah ﷻ, make us from them.

The institutions of waqf, advances in astronomy, physics, medicine, social sciences and other disciplines in the golden ages of Islam had this initial purpose, goal, and intention. Yet, a person or a researcher outside Islam when analyzing this case, can merely focus on the scientific outcomes, and not the purpose or intention motivating these factors.

In these regards, increasing the imān through scientific discoveries and applying relevant technology to help humans and all of creation are within the fold of Islam. For the ones who don't look or assume these engagements are within the fold of this true framework of Imān and Islam, they can use the scientific discoveries and applied sciences to discriminate, abuse, gain power, and make it exclusive and not inclusive for all of humanity.

Some people may not realize this order of theoretical sciences and applied sciences. Sometimes looking at the existing given products in nature urges the person to analyze this structure and order and to go back to their initial intention and purpose in life.

For the people who are heedless, they may not care about the structure or order but it may always be the case of selfish or interest-based relationships. In these cases, it can be important to show them the benefit of what they constantly get for something so that they at least go back to their intention, goal, and purpose and appreciate what they have.

In the descriptions of the ayahs of the Qurān, Allah ﷻ mentions different benefits of the perfection and balance of this structure and order with the Rububiyah[742] of Allah ﷻ.

Yes, as we talk constantly and incessantly about this structure and order in the universe, one can ask: Why it is important? Or why it is important for me? The answer is very clear, yet we sometimes assume it or oversee it without clearly stating and locating our own selves with the answer.

If one asks, "Why is the structure and order in the universe important for me?" Then, the answer is, "Because I benefit from all the structure and order. If there is no structure or order, everything is chaos; everything is in destruction. There is no existence and there is no me. I don't exist. For me to exist, live, and maintain, I need a body, anatomical systems in my body such as respiratory system, nervous system, circulatory system,

---

742.

excretion system, and others. I need external environment or setting, residence, earth, and universe to place my body in so that I can exist and live. If there is no structure and order in my body, then my existence in a perfect environment or earth may not mean much because I need to first maintain my body. Conversely, if I have a perfect body, then chaos in my external setting such as earth may not mean much because I may not exist due to the chaos."

In simpler terms, the person is in need of perfect structure and order in order to exist and live. In other words, the person benefits fully from the perfection and structure in their own creation and in the universe. This is all from the Rububiyyah of Allah ﷻ.

On another note, the name of the perfect structure and order that we witness can be called nature. The rules, principles, and scientific laws in nature can show us this perfect structure and order in detail. When there is a constitution in a country, it may be so inclusive, non-discriminatory, and establishing of security and peace, that we may be amazed with this perfect structure and order in these guidelines. Yet, they are constructed and established principles by humans.

People who live in this country benefit from this security, peace, and safety as established by this constitution bringing structure and order in the society. They benefit from this "privilege" regardless of realizing this benefit or not. People may even migrate to this country for this outcome and for the benefit of this safety, protection, peace, and security in this country due to its constitution bringing order and structure.

Similarly, in order to allude to the reality that humans constantly benefit from this structure and order, one can analyze the below ayahs in Surah ar-Rahman. This surah contains one of the Great Names and Attributes of Allah ﷻ as ar-Rahman. According to the interpretations of the meanings of ar-Rahman, this is the Name of Allah ﷻ that indicates that regardless of being a believer or not, Allah ﷻ gives sustenance, and gives them benefit from what Allah ﷻ created in the universe with great benefits. In other words, regardless of their acknowledgment of the Giver, Allah ﷻ still grants them benefit:

الرَّحْمَنُ 743{الرحمن/1} عَلَّمَ الْقُرْآنَ 744{الرحمن/2} خَلَقَ الْإِنسَانَ 745{الرحمن/3} عَلَّمَهُ الْبَيَانَ 746{الرحمن/4} الشَّمْسُ وَالْقَمَرُ بِحُسْبَانٍ 747{الرحمن/5} وَالنَّجْمُ وَالشَّجَرُ يَسْجُدَانِ 748{الرحمن/6} وَالسَّمَاء رَفَعَهَا وَوَضَعَ الْمِيزَانَ 749{الرحمن/7} أَلَّا تَطْغَوْا فِي الْمِيزَانِ 750{الرحمن/8} وَأَقِيمُوا الْوَزْنَ بِالْقِسْطِ وَلَا تُخْسِرُوا الْمِيزَانَ 751{الرحمن/9} وَالْأَرْضَ وَضَعَهَا لِلْأَنَامِ 752{الرحمن/10} فِيهَا فَاكِهَةٌ وَالنَّخْلُ ذَاتُ الْأَكْمَامِ 753{الرحمن/11} وَالْحَبُّ ذُو الْعَصْفِ وَالرَّيْحَانُ 754{الرحمن/12} فَبِأَيِّ آلَاء رَبِّكُمَا تُكَذِّبَانِ 755{الرحمن/13}

One can realize 31 times the repetition of this expression " فَبِأَيِّ آلَاء رَبِّكُمَا تُكَذِّبَانِ 756{الرحمن/13} " in this surah. This teaching method can instill in the person the realization of this benefit that the person receives incessantly from the structure and order that Allah ﷻ created. In other words, this ayah constantly asks the person, "If you benefit from this structure, order, and ni'mahs[757], then why do you deny?"

If one analyzes this repeated ayah, "Rabb" is used for Allah ﷻ to emphasize the Rububiyyah[758] of Allah ﷻ. Yet, we don't realize this constant benefit we receive that is required for our existence and survival. We don't realize the benefit in this structure and order established by our Rabb, Allah ﷻ.

On a side note, one can find possible relationship with the Name of Allah الرَّحْمَنُ[759] ﷻ and Rabb, Rububiyyah of Allah ﷻ. Allah ﷻ as our Rabb and Ar-Rahman allows everyone to benefit from this structure and order in this dunya as mentioned: الْحَمْدُ للَّهِ رَبِّ الْعَالَمِينَ 760{الفاتحة/2} الرَّحْمَنِ

---

743. The Most Merciful.
744. Taught the Qurān,
745. Created man.
746. [And] taught him eloquence.
747. The sun and the moon [move] by precise calculation,
748. And the stars and trees prostrate.
749. And the heaven He raised and imposed the balance.
750. That you not transgress within the balance.
751. And establish weight in justice and do not make deficient the balance.
752. And the earth He laid [out] for the creatures.
753. Therein is fruit and palm trees having sheaths [of dates].
754. And grain having husks and scented plants.
755. So which of the favors of your Lord would you deny?
756. So which of the favors of your Lord would you deny?
757. Blessings.
758. Lordship.
759. The Merciful.
760. [All] praise is [due] to Allah, Lord of the worlds.

رَبِّ الْعَالَمِينَ[763] {الفاتحة/2}[762] الرَّحِيمِ.[761] In this case, the expression[762] {الفاتحة/2}[763] الرَّحْمنِ following each other consecutively can allude to this general benefit of everyone from this structure and order as established by Allah ﷻ.

On the other hand, the specific benefit of this and more from this structure and order in the ākhirah can be observed only by the people of imān in الرَّحْمنِ الرَّحِيمِ[764] {الفاتحة/3} مَلِكِ يَوْمِ الدِّينِ[765] {الفاتحة/4} إِيَّاكَ نَعْبُدُ وإِيَّاكَ نَسْتَعِينُ[766] {الفاتحة/5} اهدِنَا الصِّرَاطَ الْمُسْتَقِيمَ[767] {الفاتحة/6} صِرَاطَ الَّذِينَ أَنعَمتَ عَلَيهِمْ غَيرِ الْمَغضُوبِ عَلَيهِمْ وَلاَ الضَّالِّينَ[768] {الفاتحة/7}. In other words, the Name of Allah ﷻ as الرَّحِيمِ for khass, is mentioned in the afterlife with the ayah as مَلِكِ يَوْمِ الدِّينِ[769] {الفاتحة/4} and it is for the people of imān as mentioned in إِيَّاكَ نَعْبُدُ وإِيَّاكَ نَسْتَعِينُ[770] {الفاتحة/5} اهدِنَا الصِّرَاطَ الْمُسْتَقِيمَ[771] {الفاتحة/6} صِرَاطَ الَّذِينَ أَنعَمتَ عَلَيهِمْ غَيرِ الْمَغضُوبِ عَلَيهِمْ وَلاَ الضَّالِّينَ[772] {الفاتحة/7}.

To support this stance, another explicit ayah is قُلْ مَنْ حَرَّمَ زِينَةَ اللَّهِ الَّتِيَ أَخْرَجَ لِعِبَادِهِ وَالْطَّيِّبَاتِ مِنَ الرِّزْقِ قُلْ هِي لِلَّذِينَ آمَنُواْ فِي الْحَيَاةِ الدُّنْيَا خَالِصَةً يَوْمَ الْقِيَامَةِ كَذَلِكَ نُفَصِّلُ الآيَاتِ لِقَوْمٍ يَعْلَمُونَ[773] {الأعراف/32}. As mentioned in this ayah, when one recognizes something as n'imah from Allah ﷻ in this dunya, then they are called the people of imān as mentioned لِلَّذِينَ آمَنُواْ فِي الْحَيَاةِ الدُّنْيَا[774].

In other words, this recognition, or appreciation can be called imān. One can possibly realize why we need to say 'Alhamdulillah' at least '33' times after each prayer minimally five times a day. The verbal embodiment of this recognition is "Alhamdulillah". Therefore, the first

---

761. The Entirely Merciful, the Especially Merciful.
762. The Entirely Merciful.
763. Lord of both worlds.
764. The Especially Merciful.
765. Sovereign of the day of Recompense.
766. It is you we worship and you we ask for help.
767. Guide us to the straight path.
768. The path of those upon whom You have bestowed favor, not of those who have evoked [Your] anger or of those who are astray.
769. Sovereign of the day of Recompense.
770. It is you we worship and you we ask for help.
771. Guide us to the straight path.
772. The path of those upon whom You have bestowed favor, not of those who have evoked [Your] anger or of those who are astray.
773. Say, "Who has forbidden the adornment of [i.e., from] Allah which He has produced for His servants and the good [lawful] things of provision?" Say, "They are for those who believe during worldly life [but] exclusively for them on the Day of Resurrection." Thus do We detail the verses for a people who know.
774. Who believe during worldly life.

word in the Qurān after بسم الله الرحمن الرحيم[775] is "Alhamdulillah" as mentioned {الفاتحة/2}[776] الْحَمْدُ لِلَّهِ رَبِّ الْعَالَمِينَ. The gist of imān is recognition and appreciation of Allah ﷻ as mentioned with Alhamdulillah.

Yet, in this dunya, regardless of this recognition or appreciation or not, everyone receives and benefits from this perfect structure and order created by Allah ﷻ as mentioned زِينَةَ اللهِ[777]. The people of kufr in reality benefit from this structure and order due to the existence of people of imān being among them as mentioned لِلَّذِينَ آمَنُوا فِي الْحَيَاةِ الدُّنْيَا[778]. When there are no people of imān left in this dunya, this benefit of structure and order is taken from them as Yawmul Qiyamah occurs. Rasulullah ﷺ mentions that all of the people of imān will die before the destruction of this structure and order of the universe referred to as Yawmul Qiyamah [2]. In order words, there is no purpose for the existence of this perfect structure and order for humans and jinn if there is no one left in existence who recognizes and appreciates this structure and order as a n'imah[779] from Allah ﷻ.

In the afterlife, the people of imān and kufr are separated as mentioned in

Surah Zumar وَسِيقَ الَّذِينَ اتَّقَوْا رَبَّهُمْ and وَسِيقَ الَّذِينَ كَفَرُوا إِلَى جَهَنَّمَ زُمَرًا[780][781] إِلَى الْجَنَّةِ زُمَرًا. Now, these n'imah with more structure, order, and beauty are given only to the people of imān as they recognized before and they will continue to recognize with "Alhamdulillah" as mentioned:

وَقَالُوا الْحَمْدُ لِلَّهِ الَّذِي صَدَقَنَا وَعْدَهُ وَأَوْرَثَنَا الْأَرْضَ نَتَبَوَّأُ مِنَ الْجَنَّةِ حَيْثُ نَشَاءُ فَنِعْمَ أَجْرُ الْعَامِلِينَ[782]{الزمر/74}

وَتَرَى الْمَلَائِكَةَ حَافِّينَ مِنْ حَوْلِ الْعَرْشِ يُسَبِّحُونَ بِحَمْدِ رَبِّهِمْ وَقُضِيَ بَيْنَهُم بِالْحَقِّ وَقِيلَ الْحَمْدُ لِلَّهِ رَبِّ الْعَالَمِينَ[783]{الزمر/75}

---

775. In the name of Allah, the compassionate, the most merciful,
776. [All] praise is [due] to Allah, Lord of the worlds.
777. The decoration of Allah ﷻ.
778. for those who believe during worldly life
779. Blessings.
780. And those who disbelieved will be driven to Hell in groups.
781. But those who feared their Lord will be driven to Paradise in groups.
782. And they will say, "Praise to Allah, who has fulfilled for us His promise and made us inherit the earth [so] we may settle in Paradise wherever we will. And excellent is there ward of [righteous] workers."
783. And you will see the angels surrounding the Throne, exalting [Allah] with praise of their Lord. And it will be judged between them in truth, and it will be said, "[All] praise to Allah, Lord of the worlds."

In the above ayahs, one can see the emphasis of hamd in the afterlife to show the continuation of this recognition and appreciation from this world and into the afterlife as وَقِيلَ الْحَمْدُ لِلَّهِ رَبِّ الْعَالَمِينَ [785], or وَقَالُوا الْحَمْدُ لِلَّهِ [784].

In other words, when one constantly witnesses this interaction of purpose/intention & action, imān & 'amāl, theoretical sciences & applied sciences, and imān & Islam, then the person can be amazed in the states of ihsān. In this amazement, or adoration of Allah ﷻ, the person becomes the real 'abd of Allah ﷻ. The word 'abd can linguistically be translated as "someone who submits to another due to their deep love, adoration, and respect for that person."

The embodiment of 'abd comes through 'ibadah. Dhikrs of bismillah, subhanAllah, alhamdulillah, Allahuakbar, Astagfirullah, La ilaha illa Allah, and others are expected to be the regularized and condensed forms of this verbal embodiment of being the honored 'abd of Allah ﷻ as 'abdullah. Five-times prayers, salah with nawāfill, fasting, zakāh, doing good, and avoiding and stopping evil are all expected to be the regularized and condensed forms of these verbal and bodily embodiments.

In this regard, it is another ni'mah[786] that Allah ﷻ teaches us how to show adoration, ubudiyyah[787] and ibadah[788] to our Creator, Rabbul Alamin. As Allah ﷻ is Al-Hannan[789], Al-Mannan[790], Al-Karîm[791], an Al-Wahhàb[792], even in these 'ibādah Allah ﷻ gives immediate benefits when we engage ourselves and more benefits and rewards after death. In reality, the immediate benefits and afterlife benefits do not need to be there, because we are doing our 'ibādah to express our adoration, love, and respect that we are alive, existing, and constantly under the showers of benefits of structure and order in the universe as created by Allah ﷻ.

Yet, if a person knows someone, you may not do anything for that person, but naturally as a human being you can just ask about, check on, and remember him or her. This minute act makes this person so

---

784. And they said "all praise is due to Allah ﷻ.
785. it will be said, "[All] praise to Allah ﷻ, Lord of the worlds."
786. Blessings.
787. Lordship.
788. Blessings.
789. The Compassionate.
790. The Benefactor.
791. The Generous.
792. The Bestower.

happy that this person constantly sends gifts to this person. You know that you really did not do much but this person appreciates it above and beyond. Allah ﷻ is the source of all humanly appreciations. Allah ﷻ has the Infinite Appreciation as al-Shakur, the Real-Appreciator.

When a person shows this natural and expected step of remembering their Creator, Rabbul 'AlAamin, Allah ﷻ, then al-Shakur gives huge benefits immediately, later, and int he afterlife. The person becomes someone living in Jannah both in this dunya and in the afterlife.

Now, after all of this, the person realizes these realities of how much it makes Allah ﷻ pleased and happy by only recognizing and remembering Allah ﷻ as One and Only with La ilaha illa Allah. Then, remembering Allah ﷻ in five-times prayers and on other occasions as instructed by the Qurān and the sunnah of Rasulullah ﷺ, and comparing them with the huge, immediate benefits here, later, and in the afterlife, then the person starts crying and reading the ayah[793] "و قدر الله حق قدر هما ذكرناك حق ذكرك[794] ما شكرناك حق شكرك[795] ما حمدناك حق حمدك[796] ما عبدناك حق عبادك[797] ما سبحناك حق سبحك [798]

The person thinks about all of these and remembers how much Allah ﷻ is pleased and becomes happy when being remembered:

with even one لا اله الا الله

with even one سبحان الله

with even one الحمد الله

with even one الله اكبر

with even one سبحان الله و بحمده سبحان الله العظيم with even one استغفر الله and others. The person cries and cries, cries due to this deep adoration for Allah ﷻ as being the 'abd, and has embarrassment of himself or herself due to not pleasing and making Allah ﷻ happy as it ought to be, and not to be in heedlessness of selfish engagements.

One day, when Rasulullah ﷺ was crying at night, Aisha (Radiyallahu A'anha) asks him, ﷺ "Why are you crying so much and exerting yourself so much in 'ibadah, yet you are protected as the prophet of Allah ﷻ?"

---

793. And God's destiny is worthy of destiny.
794. We did not remember you the way you are supposed to be remembered.
795. We did not thank you right in the way you are supposed to be thanked..
796. We did not praised you in the way you are supposed to be praised.
797. We did not worship you in the way you are supposed to be worshipped.
798. We did not glorify you in the way you are supposed to be glorified.

Rasulullah ﷺ answers, " افلم أكون عبدا شكورا[799] ". Meaning that Oh A'isha, Allah ﷻ gave so much, Should I not be a thankful servant. "اللهم اجعلنا من الشاكرين. اللهم احفظنا من ان نكون من الغافلين. اللهم اجعلنا من المرضين[800].

Initial Cause & Uluhiyyah of Allah ﷻ

When the ayah mentions الَّذِي خَلَقَكُمْ وَالَّذِينَ مِن قَبْلِكُمْ[801], this and similar ayahs in the Qurān allude to the Uluhiyyah[802] of Allah ﷻ. If we assume a pool of possibilities of existence for creation, Allah ﷻ creates us and brings us into existence. In this regard of the first creation of each species, there is a clear and direct link to the Creator, Allah ﷻ. This clarity of first creation can be called[803] "كن فيكون" in general as the sunnatullah as mentioned in the Qurān, Tawrāh, and the Gospels, "Adam as" for humans or the "big bang" theory according to the scientists. This initial cause and first creation directly and straightforwardly connects without any means to the Uluhiyyah[804] of Allah ﷻ. After the creation of the first species, there is a process or a reproduction process through the sunnatullah, laws, sciences that maintains this structure and order with Rububiyyah[805] of Allah ﷻ. Yet, one can still witness the Uluhiyyah of Allah ﷻ constantly as well.

In another perspective, when analyzes the 17th to 22nd ayahs, the gāib, third prounoun, is used to describe the case. In the 22nd ayah, the ayah starts with يَا أَيُّهَا النَّاسُ اعْبُدُواْ رَبَّكُمُ[806] with a mukhatab pronoun. This can be referred to as taltif (iltifah) in balagah.

One can ponder about the hikmah[807] of the usage of talatif. When a person talks about another in a good or a bad way, the person thinks about this case and person. Over time, the person can have a desire to meet with this person if this person is highly praised and a virtuous person especially as has been previously explained about him or her.

---

799. Should I not be a thankful servant.
800. Oh Allah ﷻ, make us among the ones who are thankful. Oh Allah ﷻ protect us from heedlessness. Oh Allah ﷻ, make us among the ones you are pleased with.
801. He who created you, and those before you.
802. Realm of Power.
803. Be and it is.
804. Realm of Power.
805. Lordship.
806. O mankind, worship your lord.
807. Wisdom.

Similarly, Allah ﷻ gives all humans the opportunity and high status of being directly addressed by Rabbul Alamin ﷻ. This is can be called Tanazzulat of Rabbul AlAmeen ﷻ.

In this regard, being directly addressed by Allah ﷻ is a high status, the ultimate and highest joy and happiness in this world and in the afterlife. If the person can be set back about not performing the 'ibadah of Allah ﷻ, the direct addressing of Allah ﷻ to humans gives them the highest boost and encouragement to humans to perform their 'ibadah for Allah ﷻ for their own benefit.

The direct address to humans by Allah ﷻ in the ayah يَا أَيُّهَا النَّاسُ اعْبُدُواْ رَبَّكُمُ الَّذِي خَلَقَكُمْ وَالَّذِينَ مِن قَبْلِكُمْ لَعَلَّكُمْ تَتَّقُونَ 808 {البقرة/21} is one of the examples besides many that there is no mediation or middle person between the Creator and creation as a general rule. Islamic teachings with the Qurān and sunnah were directing the engagement of problem solving to Allah ﷻ without any intermediators as all the true judgment calls were to be made by Allah ﷻ.

In other words, the practice of the sacrament of reconciliation or penance as Christians structuralized today in their religion has not been practiced among Muslims. There were some cases that were present with the Prophet ﷺ that much required dispositions of Islam to know and implement well. Yet, people did not know much about the practices and implementations of the creed. Therefore, Rasulullah (saw) took some direct stance of giving directions. The ayahs of the Qurān representing different cases were revealed in pieces depending on the instance referred to as the sabab nuzul. In this regard, this practice was not there much after the Prophet saw in Islamic jurisprudence and practice.

The cases of shafah are a different topic and true. Yet, this case is not similar in terms of its structure and practice to the Christian world today. In other words, the general rule is that the person has a direct relationship with Allah ﷻ. The person can always establish a better connection with Allah ﷻ by following the steps of the role models such as Rasulullah ﷺ. This disposition of following first by heart, love of Rasulullah ﷺ and practicing the sunnah of Rasulullah ﷺ can grant inshAllah easier access to the pleasure of Allah ﷻ as compared to the person trying to establish the means by himself or herself.

---

808. O mankind, worship your Lord, who created you and those before you, that you may become righteous.

Following the role models such as Rasulullah ﷺ means that, "Oh Allah! You sent us the Prophet ﷺ to show us how You can be pleased by us. Even though I may not truly understand and embody his teachings ﷺ, I am making the effort and struggle of following Rasulullah ﷺ because You sent him to us to be followed. So, I am following him ﷺ."

In the expression يَا أَيُّهَا النَّاسُ اعْبُدُواْ رَبَّكُمُ الَّذِي خَلَقَكُمْ وَالَّذِينَ [809], there is the direct address to all humans. This message is for all groups of people such as mu'min, kafir, or munāfiqeen as mentioned with يَا أَيُّهَا النَّاسُ [810]. At the same time, this address is beyond the limits of time and generations. In other words, this message is for all generations of people- past, present, and future.

One can ask: How can the order of اعْبُدُواْ [811] entail all different groups such as mu'min, kafir, and munāfiqeen?

For the elect of mu'mins (ashabul muqarrabin) the order اعْبُدُواْ can indicate istiqamah, patience, and continuity in 'ibādah.

For the mediocre mu'mins (ashabul yameen) the order اعْبُدُواْ can indicate an increase in the quality and quantity of the 'ibādah.

For the kafir, the order اعْبُدُواْ can indicate tawhid in ubudiyyah requiring the true imān.

For the munāfiq, the order اعْبُدُواْ can indicate ikhlās, sincerity in 'ibādah.

The word اعْبُدُواْ can indicate making 'ibādah together in jama'ah especially when it is combined with يَا أَيُّهَا النَّاسُ [812].

The expression يَا أَيُّهَا النَّاسُ اعْبُدُواْ رَبَّكُمُ [813] can indicate in a very straightforward way that Allah ﷻ raised the person and gave tarbiya as indicated with رَبَّكُمُ [814]. Therefore, the person should make 'ibadah to Allah ﷻ.

In its reflection or similar to the shadow compared to the essence, parents raise the children with their limited capacity to take care of their needs. Therefore, Allah ﷻ orders us to conform to the parents after submitting oneself to Rabbul A'lamin. In this parent and children relationship, parents engage themselves in doing so much for this child, and after this, the child becomes disrespectful, arrogant, and utters

---

809. O mankind, worship your lord who, who created you and those.
810. O mankind.
811. Worship.
812. O mankind.
813. O mankind worship your lord.
814. Your lord.

words to their parents that can implicitly and explicitly indicate, "I don't care about you! You didn't do anything for me!" similar to قَالَ وَالَّذِي[815] لِوَالِدَيْهِ أُفٍّ لَّكُمَا (Ahqaf 17). This can be very harsh and devastating for the parents.

Allah ☙ is beyond all of the examples and human renderings. Yet, one can have some idea, that although Allah ☙ creates the person from nothing, raises this person fully in his body with all of the organs perfectly working, and while there is a place called Earth with all of the necessary oxygen, food, water, beauty, and other needs of humans provided by Allah ☙ still, the person does not recognize Allah ☙ and similarly utters the words, "I don't care! No one did anything for me!" Yet, Allah ☙ continues to give this person respite and still provides for this person's needs. Allah ☙ only expects recognition and appreciation as one calls this imān and shows this appreciation as the 'ibadah.

Tawhid through Other Perspectives

Internal-Nafsi Proofs

When one analyzes the ayahs يَا أَيُّهَا النَّاسُ اعْبُدُواْ رَبَّكُمُ الَّذِي خَلَقَكُمْ وَالَّذِينَ مِن قَبْلِكُمْ لَعَلَّكُمْ تَتَّقُونَ {البقرة/21}[816] الَّذِي جَعَلَ لَكُمُ الأَرْضَ فِرَاشاً وَالسَّمَاء بِنَاء وَأَنزَلَ مِنَ السَّمَاء مَاء وَفِي, or فَأَخْرَجَ بِهِ مِنَ الثَّمَرَاتِ رِزْقاً لَّكُمْ فَلاَ تَجْعَلُواْ لِلّهِ أَندَاداً وَأَنتُمْ تَعْلَمُونَ {البقرة/22}[817] الأَرْضِ آيَاتٌ لِّلْمُوقِنِينَ {الذاريات/20}[818] وَفِي أَنفُسِكُمْ أَفَلَا تُبْصِرُونَ {الذاريات/21}[819] وَفِي السَّمَاء رِزْقُكُمْ وَمَا تُوعَدُونَ {الذاريات/22}[820] then, one can also witness different classifications, perspectives, or proofs of the true Tawhid and imān for Allah ☙.

In the first part, for the existence of the Creator, there can be three main signs as indicated in these ayahs. These can be internal, nafsi proofs, external, universe-nature related proofs, and methodological, usûli proofs.

---

815. But one who says to his parents, "Uff" to you.
816. O mankind, worship your Lord, who created you and those before you, that you may become righteous.
817. [He] who made for you the earth a bed [spread out] and the sky a ceiling and sent down from the sky, rain and brought forth thereby fruits as provision for you. So do not attribute to Allah ☙ equals while you know [that there is nothing similar to Him].
818. And on the earth are signs for the certain [in faith].
819. And in yourselves. Then will you not see?
820. And in the heaven is your provision and whatever you are promised.

The signs related with the internal, nafsi, that the person knows and experiences the Existence of Rabbul A'lamin as mentioned يَا أَيُّهَا النَّاسُ[821] اعْبُدُواْ رَبَّكُمُ الَّذِي خَلَقَكُمْ as mentioned in this ayah. Or, as this is mentioned وَفِي الْأَرْضِ آيَاتٌ لِّلْمُوقِنِينَ {الذاريات/20}[822] وَفِي أَنفُسِكُمْ أَفَلاَ تُبْصِرُونَ[823]

The person knows from their nafs the Existence of the Rabbul A'lamin. Nafs can also be referred to as conscience, sixth sense, experience, integrity or morality, sense of right or wrong, moral sense, inner voice, ethics, values, standards, principles, compunction, scruples, or qualms [5]. Especially, when one reviews the meanings of compunction, scruples, or qualms although they may have slight variations, they can all indicate this inner push called nafs for the Real Reality of Rabbul Alamin [11]. Their definitions can be as follows [5]:

> To have qualms is to have an uneasy feeling that you have acted or are about to act against your better judgment (she had qualms about changing insurance companies). Misgivings are even stronger, implying a disturbed state of mind because you're no longer confident that what you're doing is right (his misgivings about letting his 80-year-old mother drive herself home turned out to be justified). Compunction implies a momentary pang of conscience because what you are doing or are about to do is unfair, improper, or wrong (they showed no compunction in carrying out their devious plans). Scruples suggest a more highly developed conscience or sense of honor; it implies that you have principles, and that you would be deeply disturbed if you thought you were betraying them (her scruples would not allow her to participate in what she considered antifeminist activities). Demur connotes hesitation to the point of delay, but the delay is usually caused by objections or indecision rather than a sense of conscience (they accepted his decision without demur) [5].

This sign or proof about Wajibul Wujud[824] from their own nafs is the closest to the person. Therefore, the first sign or proof with its proximity to the person is mentioned first in the order of the ayah as يَا أَيُّهَا النَّاسُ[825]

---

821. O mankind, worship your lord who created you.
822. And on the earth are signs for the certain [in faith].
823. And in yourselves. Then will you not see?
824. Obligation to exist.
825. O mankind worship your lord who created you.

اعْبُدُواْ رَبَّكُمُ الَّذِي خَلَقَكُمْ. Yet, for some people, if they are not immune or if they are open to their own nafsi voices, then the external proofs can proceed as mentioned [826]وَفِي الْأَرْضِ آيَاتٌ لِّلْمُوقِنِينَ {الذاريات/20} وَفِي أَنفُسِكُمْ أَفَلاَ [827]تُبْصِرُونَ{الذاريات/21} وَفِي السَّمَاء رِزْقُكُمْ وَمَا تُوعَدُونَ [828]{الذاريات/22}

These proofs are so abundant at every second and in every place. One should remove the curtains of gaflah, the thick veils covering one's heart, mind, eyes, ears, and senses.

External, Universe-Nature Related Proofs

The ayah الَّذِي جَعَلَ لَكُمُ الْأَرْضَ فِرَاشاً وَالسَّمَاء بِنَاء وَأَنزَلَ مِنَ السَّمَاء مَاء فَأَخْرَجَ بِهِ مِنَ الثَّمَرَاتِ رِزْقاً لَّكُمْ فَلاَ تَجْعَلُواْ لِلّهِ أَندَاداً وَأَنتُمْ تَعْلَمُونَ [829]{البقرة/22} can indicate anything to be the external signs outside the body of the person. These proofs are so abundant at every second and in every place. One should remove the curtains of gaflah[830], the thick veils covering one's heart, mind, eyes, ears, and senses.

These signs and realities being discovered more today with scientific laws and theories show a perfect structure, balance, order, and purpose in the universe. They unanimously necessitate for the Wajibul Wujud, Allah ﷻ. They collectively make dhikr for, remembering , and glorifying Allah ﷻ.

Then, from these external signs, there is an indication that the closest sign for humans is the earth, nature, and environment that we use as our habitat as mentioned [831]الَّذِي جَعَلَ لَكُمُ الأَرْضَ فِرَاشاً. The order of these signs in these ayahs presents itself first as the the person (nafs), then earth (nature), and then, the skies (universe, space, galaxies).

The word جَعَلَ[832] is explained in other ayahs with its critical meanings. One can realize that the word جَعَلَ tells us of the secondary nature of responsibility and quality assigned to the creation after their initial creation. In other words, the word جَعَلَ indicates that although the earth is circular and has all the complex rotations and spinning around of its

---

826. And on the earth are signs for the certain [in faith].
827. And in yourselves. Then will you not see?
828. And in the heaven is your provision and whatever you are promised.
829. [He] who made for you the earth a bed [spread out] and the sky a ceiling and sent down from the sky, rain and brought forth thereby fruits as provision for you. So do not attribute to Allah equals while you know [that there is nothing similar to Him].
830. Heedlessness.
831. [He] who made for you the earth a bed [spread out].
832. Made.

orbits and axis around the sun, Allah ﷻ has made the earth a place of inertia, motionlessness, sakina[833], quiet, and immobility so that humans in their creation can use it as a habitat.

This possibility out of all complex impossibilities should force the person to have imān, make sajdah, and show appreciation and gratitude to Rabbul A'lamin.

In other words, if the earth was flat as previously assumed for thousands of years before the advent of science, people may have thought of more possibilities with the temptations of Shaytan to be heedless and cover their tiny understandings about the Real Reality of the Creator. This is the technical word for kafir as a side note.

Similarly, the word جَعَلَ[834] is used for the skies as well. This complexity assigned to their purpose and structure for the sky is assigned to humans as well as mentioned: تَبَارَكَ الَّذِي جَعَلَ فِي السَّمَاء بُرُوجًا وَجَعَلَ فِيهَا سِرَاجًا وَقَمَرًا مُّنِيرًا[835] {الفرقان/61}

Yet, Allah ﷻ shows us that this complex structure and order of the earth, universe, galaxies with their complex motions, geometrical shapes, internal and external atmospheric changes, and all others realized by the scientific discoveries...that these complexities with their order and structure only, but only, show the Real Doer, Allah ﷻ.

In other words, the word جَعَلَ shows us all of this direct assignment to all of these systems and structures. It is not anything else- any scientific law, any human-generated or socially constructed word such as "nature." It is Allah ﷻ Who creates all of these systems from nothing and maintains and upholds their complicated structure with beauty and perfection. Perhaps, we humans can realize and appreciate Allah ﷻ through our covered gloomy and greasy deep heedlessness, ghaflah[836].

If a person does not believe in Allah ﷻ, it is normal to have fears of chaos, destruction, anarchy, turmoil, and disorder in the systems of galaxies, stars, sun, planets, earth, meteors, and natural and social life in the world. When a person realizes this complex structure and order in the universe, if they don't fully believe in Allah ﷻ with full tawhid,

---

833. Tranquility.
834. Made.
835. Blessed is He who has placed in the sky great stars and placed therein a [burning] lamp and luminous moon.
836. Heedlessness.

then they can normally view that everything is connected to each other similar to a thin string. When this string is affected or broken, then there will be destruction of all universes, galaxies, planets, and earth. The scientific extrapolations of these pessimistic approaches without imān can be also viewed within chaos theory in mathematics or the butterfly effect in popularized cultures [5].

These pessimistic and gloomy approaches assume that there is no One Who is in charge of all of these complex systems. Then, with these cool teachings of popularized science trends, there is the constant instillment of fear, pessimism, hopelessness, and purposelessness in life and in the afterlife. Especially, these popular or cool waves have very devastating effects among the youth and for all age groups of learners with all different religious traditions. [27].

Yes, there is the effect of chaos as instigated by humans as mentioned ظَهَرَ الْفَسَادُ فِي الْبَرِّ وَالْبَحْرِ بِمَا كَسَبَتْ أَيْدِي النَّاسِ لِيُذِيقَهُم بَعْضَ الَّذِي عَمِلُوا لَعَلَّهُمْ يَرْجِعُونَ {الروم/41}[837]. In this sense, the definition of the butterfly effect such as "(with reference to chaos theory) the phenomenon whereby a minute, localized change in a complex system can have large effects elsewhere [5] has a purpose.

Yet, a person of true imān with the true and sincere tawhid always knows and reminds oneself and others that everything happens with the Mashiyyah[838], allowance of Allah ﷻ. Everything is under the control of Rabbul A'lamin. Allah ﷻ is the Creator, One, Unique and Alive and maintains and upholds this complex structure, order, and constantly interferes as mentioned

وَلَوْلاَ دَفْعُ اللهِ النَّاسَ بَعْضَهُمْ بِبَعْضٍ لَّفَسَدَتِ الأَرْضُ وَلَكِنَّ اللهَ ذُو فَضْلٍ عَلَى الْعَالَمِينَ {البقرة/251}[839]

and

---

837. Corruption has appeared throughout the land and sea by [reason of] what the hands of people have earned so He [i.e., Allah] may let them taste part of [the consequence of] what they have done that perhaps they will return [to righteousness].
838. Permission.
839. And if it were not for Allah checking [some] people by means of others, the earth would have been corrupted, but Allah is full of bounty to the worlds.

اللّٰهُ لاَ إِلَهَ إِلاَّ هُوَ الْحَيُّ الْقَيُّومُ لاَ تَأْخُذُهُ سِنَةٌ وَلاَ نَوْمٌ لَّهُ مَا فِي السَّمَاوَاتِ وَمَا فِي الأَرْضِ مَن ذَا الَّذِي يَشْفَعُ عِنْدَهُ إِلاَّ بِإِذْنِهِ يَعْلَمُ مَا بَيْنَ أَيْدِيهِمْ وَمَا خَلْفَهُمْ وَلاَ يُحِيطُونَ بِشَيْءٍ مِّنْ عِلْمِهِ إِلاَّ بِمَا شَاء وَسِعَ كُرْسِيُّهُ السَّمَاوَاتِ وَالأَرْضَ وَلاَ يَؤُودُهُ حِفْظُهُمَا وَهُوَ الْعَلِيُّ الْعَظِيمُ 840{البقرة/255}

Yes, reading Ayatul Kursi constantly is one of the examples of a reminder for ourselves of this reality so that the person can be immune against these diseases of fear. This fear of being constantly scared of everything is very common and fluid in the air, similar to a flu virus. It is very widespread and anyone can get it in different quantities. It may come and go. The constant vitamin and flu shot against this virus of fear can be the recitation of Ayatul Kursi.

For a kafir, overwhelming fears can pile up and store negative potential energy. Yet, the person can always remove these with a true imān and tawhid before it becomes too late. When it is too late, it may one day kill the person similar to the swine flu.

An average mu'min can have these effects of fear depending on their level of imān similar to a transient flu. It can come and go. It can be temporary.

A higher level of elect mu'min, a true awliya of Allah ﷻ, has an imān and tawakkul to Allah ﷻ. He or she is a fearless person except regarding the fear of displeasing Allah ﷻ. This is called taqwa. Therefore, the real purpose of our existence is not these useless engagements of fear. The uneasiness of not appreciating, being ungrateful, and displeasing Allah ﷻ should be our main and fruitful worries as mentioned in this ayah as:

يَا أَيُّهَا النَّاسُ اعْبُدُواْ رَبَّكُمُ الَّذِي خَلَقَكُمْ وَالَّذِينَ مِن قَبْلِكُمْ لَعَلَّكُمْ تَتَّقُونَ 841{البقرة/21}

Embedded Need & Taqwa

Humans are created by Allah ﷻ with different needs such as food, air, spouse, social relations, kinship relations, the need for being taken care of, and other needs. For some of these needs, the person finds most of

---

840. Allah—there is no deity except Him, the Ever-Living, the Sustainer of [all] existence. Neither drowsiness overtakes Him nor sleep. To Him belongs whatever is in the heavens and whatever is on the earth. Who is it that can intercede with Him except by His permission? He knows what is [presently] before them and what will be after them, and they encompass not a thing of His knowledge except for what He wills. His Kursi extends over the heavens and the earth, and their preservation tires Him not. And He is the Most High, the Most Great.
841. O mankind, worship your Lord, who created you and those before you, that you may become righteous.

them available in their habitat when they are born and as they grow. For some of their needs they realize as they grow from childhood that they need others such as parents, family members, spouse, friends, and professional engagements in order to fulfil their needs. In their life of maturity, some people attach to these means as though their livelihood depends on them.

One of the critical needs that is embedded in a human being is to believe in (imān) and worship (ibadah).

Most of the time, the person spends his or her life by herself or himself either when walking, sitting, sleeping in the bed, driving, etc. Especially, in these moments, these embedded needs for imān and ibadah can reveal themselves and scream from different spiritual faculties of the person. If the person does not gauge themselves to the correct avenues in order to fulfill their needs, then these spiritual screams or inner declarations can turn into uneasiness, fear, concern, unhappiness, dissatisfaction, and agitation.

Most people can try to soothe these inner voices of screaming with symptomatic approaches similar to taking Tylenol or Ibuprofen. In other words, the person now gauges oneself with engagements such as socializing, eating, watching TV, or listening to music in order to calm and forget about these internal disturbances.

Yet, this is a need similar to the other needs of humans. Feeding ourselves the correct sustenance for this need is similar to other needs and even more important and critical.

Most of our other needs are already fulfilled without much effort.

This embedded need of these inner calls or screams can only be fulfilled by true imān and ibadah as mentioned الَّذِينَ آمَنُواْ وَتَطْمَئِنُّ قُلُوبُهُم بِذِكْرِ اللّهِ أَلاَ بِذِكْرِ اللّهِ تَطْمَئِنُّ الْقُلُوبُ {28/الرعد}842. The purpose of all of our creation is based on fulfilling this need for our own selves as mentioned وَمَا خَلَقْتُ الْجِنَّ وَالْإِنسَ إِلَّا لِيَعْبُدُونِ {56/الذاريات}843.

It is expected to make a little bit of effort with our free will to realize this need and to take the step to fulfill it with the correct, most pure, and perfect sustenance.

---

842. Those who have believed and whose hearts are assured by the remembrance of Allah. Unquestionably, by the remembrance of Allah hearts are assured."
843. And I did not create the jinn and mankind except to worship Me.

This is the whole purpose of our creation. With most of our time, we are expected to engage ourselves to fulfill this need as mentioned فَإِذَا فَرَغْتَ فَانصَبْ ﴿الشرح/7﴾ [844] وَإِلَىٰ رَبِّكَ فَارْغَب ﴿الشرح/8﴾ [845]

Our heart needs it. Our mind needs it. Our immune system needs it. Our happiness depends on it. Our fears can go away. Our anxieties can vanish. Our uneasiness can disappear. Our agitation and worry can transform into satisfaction and calmness. We can smile then and help others who have any type of needs.

The source of all needs stems from the lack of imān and ibādah. Imān and ibādah establish and make physical and spiritual homeostasis in the spiritual and bodily faculties of the person. This balance leads to a strong and powerful and happy individual, happy in life and helping others as achieved and maintained by imān and 'ibādah.

This achievement with imān and 'ibādah can be called taqwa. The expression لَعَلَّكُمْ تَتَّقُونَ ﴿البقرة/21﴾ [846] can allude to this person. The word لَعَلَّكُمْ [847] can indicate this free will of the person that he or she needs to make this little effort of recognition and acting on it in order to aim for the true imān and 'ibādah and maintain it.

In other words, if there is a seed similar to an embedded need in ourselves, then we are expected to grow this seed to a tree of taqwa as the expression لَعَلَّكُمْ تَتَّقُونَ [848] can indicate. The seed is already planted. We are expected to make a little bit of effort by giving water, exposing it to the sunlight, removing the weeds, and trimming the branches as this tree grows. Then, it can even give fruits to benefit others as well.

In the above parable, taqwa is the effort of the manifestation of these potential abilities and skills rooted and existing in the original creation of the person by Allah ﷻ. Taqwa is the proven effort of the person in our current world (a'lami shadah) as its potentiality was rooted in the realms of the souls (alami arwah). Taqwa is the execution of a program with one click after being already downloaded in our original operating system (os). Yet, in all of these examples, there is a common theme that the person needs to make a little bit of an effort. The goal of worship is taqwa.

---

844. So when you have finished [your duties], then stand up [for worship].
845. And to your Lord direct [your] longing.
846. That you may become righteous.
847. That you may become.
848. That you may become righteous.

Change-Process Related Proofs

In the case of both internal and external proofs, one can possibly observe and witness either their own selves or they can observe the systems on the earth, in nature, in the skies, or in space for the tawhid in the belief of Allah ﷻ. This observation as mentioned [849] أَفَلَا تُبْصِرُونَ in the Ayahs وَفِي الْأَرْضِ آيَاتٌ لِّلْمُوقِنِينَ[850]{الذاريات/20} وَفِي أَنفُسِكُمْ أَفَلَا تُبْصِرُونَ {الذاريات/21}[851] وَفِي السَّمَاء رِزْقُكُمْ وَمَا تُوعَدُونَ[852]{الذاريات/22} can be immediately accessible to all levels of learners.

With a little bit of effort in critical thinking and observation of the change, activities, and process as also indicated with أَفَلَا تُبْصِرُونَ[853], one can witness, fulfill, and satisfy one's imān with certainty, yaqīn of tawhid through the change-process related proofs through constant dynamic change in spiritual, physical and experiential internal-nafsi engagements.

An example of this change is indicated in many places in the Qurān. For example:

اللَّهُ الَّذِي خَلَقَكُم مِّن ضَعْفٍ ثُمَّ جَعَلَ مِن بَعْدِ ضَعْفٍ قُوَّةً ثُمَّ جَعَلَ مِن بَعْدِ قُوَّةٍ ضَعْفًا وَشَيْبَةً يَخْلُقُ مَا يَشَاء وَهُوَ الْعَلِيمُ الْقَدِيرُ[854]{الروم/54} Or,

وَفِي الْأَرْضِ آيَاتٌ لِّلْمُوقِنِينَ[855]{الذاريات/20} وَفِي أَنفُسِكُمْ أَفَلَا تُبْصِرُونَ {الذاريات/21}[856]

With a little bit of effort in critical thinking and observation of the operation, method, engineering, and applied sciences as also indicated with أَفَلَا تُبْصِرُونَ[857]in the above ayah, one can witness, fulfill, and satisfy one's imān with certainty, yaqîn of tawhid as mentioned فَانظُرْ إِلَى آثَارِ

---

849. Then will you not see?
850. And on the earth are signs for the certain [in faith].
851. And in yourselves. Then will you not see?
852. And in the heaven is your provision and whatever you are promised.
853. Then do you not see.
854. Allah is the one who created you from weakness, then made after weakness strength, then made after strength weakness and white hair. He creates what He wills, and He is the Knowing, the Competent.
855. And on the earth are signs for the certain [in faith].
856. And in yourselves. Then will you not see?
857. Then will you not see.

رَحْمَتِ اللهِ كَيْفَ يُحْيِي الْأَرْضَ بَعْدَ مَوْتِهَا إِنَّ ذَلِكَ لَمُحْيِي الْمَوْتَى وَهُوَ عَلَى كُلِّ شَيْءٍ قَدِيرٌ[858]
{الروم/50} through the change-process related proofs through external
universe-nature related occurrences.

An example of this change is indicated in many places in the Qurān.
Here is an example of this process in this ayah as وَأَنْزَلَ مِنَ السَّمَاءِ مَاءً[859]
فَأَخْرَجَ بِهِ مِنَ الثَّمَرَاتِ رِزْقاً لَكُمْ. In all of these dynamic changes and processes
one is expected to observe, critically think, and deduce meanings. One
can refer to this knowledge that structures this observation, critical
thinking, and deduction of the meanings as science.

In other words, all of the different branches of both theoretical
and applied sciences are trying to formalize these events in nature, the
universe, environments and societies. They are to be studied as another
alternative proof to show the clarity of tawhid and the true, full faculties
of imān in Allah ﷻ.

An example of this change, process, or science as a proof and sign is
indicated in many places in the Qurān. The process of change as a clear
sign and proof is emphasized, for example, with the word وَمِنْ آيَاتِهِ[860] in:

وَمِنْ آيَاتِهِ أَنَّكَ تَرَى الْأَرْضَ خَاشِعَةً فَإِذَا أَنْزَلْنَا عَلَيْهَا الْمَاءَ اهْتَزَّتْ وَرَبَتْ إِنَّ الَّذِي
أَحْيَاهَا لَمُحْيِي الْمَوْتَى إِنَّهُ عَلَى كُلِّ شَيْءٍ قَدِيرٌ[861] {فصلت/39}

Critical thinking of this process or science is emphasized, for
example, with the word وَلَعَلَّكُمْ تَعْقِلُونَ[862] as mentioned in هُوَ الَّذِي خَلَقَكُمْ مِّن
تُرَابٍ ثُمَّ مِن نُّطْفَةٍ ثُمَّ مِنْ عَلَقَةٍ ثُمَّ يُخْرِجُكُمْ طِفْلاً ثُمَّ لِتَبْلُغُوا أَشُدَّكُمْ ثُمَّ لِتَكُونُوا شُيُوخًا وَمِنكُم مَّن
يُتَوَفَّى مِن قَبْلُ وَلِتَبْلُغُوا أَجَلاً مُّسَمًّى وَلَعَلَّكُمْ تَعْقِلُونَ[863] {غافر/67}

These change-process related proofs can entail critical thinking,
knowledge, and scholarship as indicated in different branches of
sciences. Yet, the person can reach to the level of Khashyah of Allah

---

858. So observe the effects of the mercy of Allah—how He gives life to the earth after
its lifelessness. Indeed, that [same one] will give life to the dead, and He is over all things
competent.
859. And sent down from the sky, rain and brought forth thereby fruits as provision for you.
860. And from his signs.
861. And of His signs is that you see the earth stilled, but when We send down upon it rain, it
quivers and grows. Indeed, He who has given it life is the Giver of Life to the dead. Indeed, He
is over all things competent.
862. That you may become righteous.
863. It is He who created you from dust, then from a sperm-drop, then from a clinging clot;
then He brings you out as a child; then [He develops you] that you reach your [time of]
maturity, then [further] that you become elders. And among you is he who is taken in death
before [that], so that you reach a specified term; and perhaps you will use reason.

❧ when they realize these proofs with their specialties as mentioned { أَلَمْ تَرَ أَنَّ اللَّهَ أَنْزَلَ مِنَ السَّمَاءِ مَاءً [864]إِنَّمَا يَخْشَى اللَّهَ مِنْ عِبَادِهِ الْعُلَمَاء in the ayah فَأَخْرَجْنَا بِهِ ثَمَرَاتٍ مُخْتَلِفًا أَلْوَانُهَا وَمِنَ الْجِبَالِ جُدَدٌ بِيضٌ وَحُمْرٌ مُخْتَلِفٌ أَلْوَانُهَا وَغَرَابِيبُ سُودٌ [865]{فاطر/27} وَمِنَ النَّاسِ وَالدَّوَابِّ وَالْأَنْعَامِ مُخْتَلِفٌ أَلْوَانُهُ كَذَلِكَ إِنَّمَا يَخْشَى اللَّهَ مِنْ عِبَادِهِ الْعُلَمَاءُ إِنَّ اللَّهَ عَزِيزٌ غَفُورٌ [866]{فاطر/28}.

Yet, this change can indicate the process of perfection in the art, design, creation, system, and structure of Allah ❧ as mentioned وَتَرَى الْجِبَالَ تَحْسَبُهَا جَامِدَةً وَهِيَ تَمُرُّ مَرَّ السَّحَابِ صُنْعَ اللَّهِ الَّذِي أَتْقَنَ كُلَّ شَيْءٍ إِنَّهُ خَبِيرٌ بِمَا تَفْعَلُونَ [867]{النمل/88}

Yet, this change can indicate and should lead to constantly taking heed and to ihsan for Allah ❧ but yet the heedlessness, gaflah, continues as mentioned أَلَمْ تَرَ إِلَى رَبِّكَ كَيْفَ مَدَّ الظِّلَّ وَلَوْ شَاءَ لَجَعَلَهُ سَاكِنًا ثُمَّ جَعَلْنَا الشَّمْسَ عَلَيْهِ دَلِيلًا [868]{الفرقان/45} ثُمَّ قَبَضْنَاهُ إِلَيْنَا قَبْضًا يَسِيرًا [869]{الفرقان/46} وَهُوَ الَّذِي جَعَلَ لَكُمُ اللَّيْلَ لِبَاسًا وَالنَّوْمَ سُبَاتًا وَجَعَلَ النَّهَارَ نُشُورًا [870]{الفرقان/47} وَهُوَ الَّذِي أَرْسَلَ الرِّيَاحَ بُشْرًا بَيْنَ يَدَيْ رَحْمَتِهِ وَأَنْزَلْنَا مِنَ السَّمَاءِ مَاءً طَهُورًا [871]{الفرقان/48} لِنُحْيِيَ بِهِ بَلْدَةً مَيْتًا وَنُسْقِيَهُ مِمَّا خَلَقْنَا أَنْعَامًا وَأَنَاسِيَّ كَثِيرًا [872]{الفرقان/49} وَلَقَدْ صَرَّفْنَاهُ بَيْنَهُمْ لِيَذَّكَّرُوا فَأَبَى أَكْثَرُ النَّاسِ إِلَّا كُفُورًا [873]{الفرقان/50}

These proofs are so abundant at every second and in every place. One should remove the curtains of ghaflah, the thick veils covering one's heart, mind, eyes, ears, and senses.

May Allah ❧ protect us from being in ghaflah, Ameen.

---

864. Only those fear Allah, from among His servants, who have knowledge.

865. Do you not see that Allah sends down rain from the sky, and We produce thereby fruits of varying colors? And in the mountains are tracts, white and red of varying shades and [some] extremely black.

866. And among people and moving creatures and grazing livestock are various colors similarly. Only those fear Allah, from among His servants, who have knowledge. Indeed, Allah is Exalted in Might and Forgiving.

867. And you see the mountains, thinking them rigid, while they will pass as the passing of clouds. [It is] the work of Allah, who perfected all things. Indeed, He is Acquainted with that which you do.

868. Have you not considered your Lord- how he extends the shadow, and if he willed, he could have made it stationary. Then we made the sun for it an indication.

869. Then We hold it in hand for a brief grasp.

870. And it is He who has made the night for you as clothing and sleep [a means for] rest and has made the day a resurrection.

871. And it is He who sends the winds as good tidings before His mercy [i.e., rainfall], and We send down from the sky pure water.

872. That We may bring to life thereby a dead land and give it as drink to those We created of numerous livestock and men.

873. And We have certainly distributed it among them that they might be reminded, but most of the people refuse except disbelief.

Methodological-Usuli Proofs

When one analyzes the ayah يَا أَيُّهَا النَّاسُ اعْبُدُواْ رَبَّكُمُ الَّذِي خَلَقَكُمْ وَالَّذِينَ مِن قَبْلِكُمْ لَعَلَّكُمْ تَتَّقُونَ[874]{البقرة/21} one can realize the implied usul or methodology with the expression خَلَقَكُمْ وَالَّذِينَ مِن قَبْلِكُمْ[875].

Humans tend to extrapolate meanings by establishing patterns leading to methodologies, scientific laws, or theories based on the mind and intellect.

Allah ﷻ encourages them to use these methodologies in extrapolation of different current observed or past assumed incidents. The expression خَلَقَكُمْ وَالَّذِينَ مِن قَبْلِكُمْ[876] sets this perspective of usûli or methodical perspective about Who Allah ﷻ is.

There are a lot of human assertions of these usûli cases about the afterlife with wrong methodological approaches that are presented accurately in the Qurãn. In these cases, Allah ﷻ shows, counters, and present their arguments in an established methodology addressing the proofs related to the afterlife and regarding the unobserved incidents of humans' five senses.

Yes, true and authentic logical methodology can travel in the venues of unobserved incidents of humans' five senses. The Qurãn in many places encourages the person to establish this correct usûl or methodology through the intellect in order to instill yaqîn, certainty in the person about the unseen such as the afterlife.

All the proofs as a single unit show the tawhid, Oneness and Uniqueness of Allah ﷻ as Al-Ahad[877]. At the same time, all the proofs together show the Oneness and Uniqueness of Allah ﷻ as Al-Wahid[878].

In the ayah وَأَنزَلَ مِنَ السَّمَاء مَاء فَأَخْرَجَ بِهِ مِنَ الثَّمَرَاتِ رِزْقاً لَّكُمْ فَلاَ تَجْعَلُواْ لِلّهِ أَندَاداً وَأَنتُمْ تَعْلَمُونَ[879]{البقرة/22} the expression رِزْقاً لَّكُمْ[880] can indicate that the right of 'ibadah is only due and belongs only to Allah ﷻ. 'Ibadah is shukr, thanking. Thanking stems from a n'imah, sustenance that the person receives from. Therefore, it is required to thank, make shukr and

---

874. O mankind, worship your lord who created you and those before you, that you may be righteous.
875. Who created you and those before you.
876. Who created you and those before you.
877. The Unique.
878. The One.
879. And sent down from the sky, rain and brought forth thereby fruits as provision for you. So do not attribute to Allah equals while you know [that there is nothing similar to Him].
880. A provision for you.

'ibadah to the One Who gives all the n'imahs[881] as the expression رِزْقاً لَّكُمْ can indicate.

All the ni'mahs coming from the earth are subjugated for the usage of humans in their creation. Therefore, humans appreciate and submit themselves to the One, Allah ﷻ Who made everything on the earth for the service of humans.

The part of the ayah فَلاَ تَجْعَلُواْ لِلَّهِ أَندَاداً وَأَنتُمْ تَعْلَمُونَ [882]{البقرة/22} is related with all other parts of the ayah and to the previous ayah and as a usûl, methodology with all other parts of the Qurān.

This ayah can indicate that when the person worships Allah ﷻ as the Rabb, then he or she should not make shirk. He or she should not take any implicit or explicit partners, things, people, emotions, or others knowingly or unknowingly.

The only true and real Rabb is Allah ﷻ Who creates the person and all others, takes care of all their needs in this life, during death and after death. Allah ﷻ is the One Who prepares the earth, nature, skies, and all of the habitats for humans. Allah ﷻ is the One Who has established the skies similar to a ceiling for the person. Allah ﷻ is the One constantly and continuously sends all of the means of sustenance such as rain, sunlight, the means of vegetation, air, and all others for all humans and other beings. All of the sustenance belongs to Allah ﷻ and is given to us by Allah ﷻ.

Therefore, all of the true gratitude, appreciation, thanking, gratefulness in the form and representation of 'ibādah, worship is only but only for Allah ﷻ. This representation or form referred to as 'ibādah is shown to us as yet another bounty, sustenance, and gift for us by Allah ﷻ in the Qurān and in the Sunnah of Rasulullah ﷺ. Knowing how to thank Allah ﷻ in the form of 'ibādah so that Allah ﷻ is pleased and needs another show of thanks. Applying and practicing this 'ibādah needs another show of thanks due to the enablement of doing it.

Therefore, the person should be in constant gratitude, thankfulness, shukr[883] and hamd[884] disposition to Allah ﷻ. This is the reality. It is not an exaggeration. Ihsan is not a superfluous and exaggerated state of a person but it is the normal and expected position of a person.

---

881. Blessings.
882. So do not attribute to Allah equals while you know [that there is nothing similar to Him]..
883. Gratitude.
884. Praise.

The embodiment of hamd is Muhammad ﷺ, Rasulullah ﷺ and all other prophets, messengers, and the ones striving on the path according to their levels.

The states of hamd and ihsan are very closely related. The true maqam of hamd is the fruit of maqam of ihsan. For some, the maqam of ihsan comes first, and then the maqam of hamd. In other words, the person first needs to embody the full presence of Allah ﷻ constantly. Then, he or she can be in the constant state of hamd due this constant and continuous state of full presence with the embodiment of full presence (khudur) of Allah ﷻ.

[106]

مَا نَنسَخْ مِنْ آيَةٍ أَوْ نُنسِهَا نَأْتِ بِخَيْرٍ مِّنْهَا أَوْ مِثْلِهَا أَلَمْ تَعْلَمْ أَنَّ اللَّهَ عَلَىٰ كُلِّ شَيْءٍ قَدِيرٌ[885]
{البقرة/106}

The existence of ayahs nasqh shows and reminds us of one of the human realities of change. In other words, there are a lot of content, format, and style features of the Qurān directing and showing us the human realities as also mentioned in {الأنبياء/10}[886] لَقَدْ أَنزَلْنَا إِلَيْكُمْ كِتَابًا فِيهِ ذِكْرُكُمْ أَفَلَا تَعْقِلُونَ. In other words, Allah ﷻ teaches us our own realities with the Qurān. In popular language, the Qurān is the manual of a human being. Humans and jinn are expected to read the Qurān in order to understand this machine-looking being with more complicated faculties of emotions, experiences, memories, concerns, worries, attachments, and reasonings.

Therefore, if a person takes a simple machine in order to understand its proper usage, without its manual, he or she may spend hours and still may not fully figure out it's usage. On the other hand, if there is a person who makes a little bit effort of reading the manual, that person can slowly but surely make the incremental steps of understanding and utilizing this machine. If there are any issues, one can constantly go back to the manual to figure out the problems with their solutions.

Similarly, the Qurān and the sunnah are a full, complete, and comprehensive manual for the person. The person constantly engages with the Qurān and sunnah to understand their own real selves,

---

885. We do not abrogate a verse or cause it to be forgotten except that We bring forth [one] better than it or similar to it. Do you not know that Allah is over all things competent?
886. We have certainly sent down to you a Book [i.e., the Qurān] in which is your mention. Then will you not reason?

purpose, and goal in this short lifespan. If the person acts in the illusional dispositions of self-sufficiency, the person for sure wastes all of this short life with the delusions of self-experiential discoveries. All of these discoveries have authentic and true value as long as they are evaluated with the principles and guidelines of the Qurān and sunnah.

In this perspective, during the lifespan of a person, there are a lot of changes as mentioned جَعَلَ ثُمَّ قُوَّةٍ بَعْدِ مِن جَعَلَ ثُمَّ ضَعْفٍ مِّن خَلَقَكُم الَّذِي اللَّهُ .مِن بَعْدِ قُوَّةٍ ضَعْفًا وَشَيْبَةً يَخْلُقُ مَا يَشَاء وَهُوَ الْعَلِيمُ الْقَدِيرُ [887] {الروم/54}

In the history of humans, there are a lot of changes over time in the dynamics of groups, communities, and generations with possible different social, cultural, and norm-related identities. This can possibly be realized in the word آخَرِينَ[888] for example in آخَرِينَ قُرُونًا بَعْدِهِم مِّن أَنشَأْنَا ثُمَّ {المؤمنون/42}[889]. Therefore, Allah ﷻ sent different prophets at different times to different cultures and understandings as mentioned with the expression وَعَادًا وَثَمُودَ وَأَصْحَابَ الرَّسِّ وَقُرُونًا بَيْنَ ذَلِكَ كَثِيرًا in وَقُرُونًا بَيْنَ ذَلِكَ كَثِيرًا {الفرقان/38}[890].

With this notion of human reality, Allah ﷻ teaches us with the style of nasqh that the asl, essence of the deen does not change. Yet, in delivery methods or in the parts, presentation, and format, the furu', details compared to the essence can change according to the audience of different people, age groups, gender, time, culture, and society. Therefore, the concept of mujaddid[891], the reviver in tradition can project itself into this understanding. Mujaddid does not change the a'sil, the essence but presents the existing teachings of the Qurān and the sunnah with a new format and style of addressing the language, problems, context, and culture of their time.

As an example, one can ask: Why didn't Islam immediately abolish slavery? This can be that a system that is the core of life takes time to change. If one analyzes the ayahs of the Qurān, there is full encouragement to free the slaves constantly in all different engagements.

---

887. Allah is the one who created you from weakness, then made after weakness strength, then made after strength weakness and white hair. He creates what He wills, and He is the Knowing, the Competent.
888. After them.
889. Then We produced after them other generations.
890. And [We destroyed] 'Aad and Thamûd and the companions of the well and many generations between them.
891. Re-newer.

Therefore, if one extrapolates these meanings, one can see the intended Qurānic purpose of change, Allahu A'lam.

[269]

يُؤتِي الْحِكْمَةَ مَن يَشَاء وَمَن يُؤْتَ الْحِكْمَةَ فَقَدْ أُوتِيَ خَيْرًا كَثِيرًا وَمَا يَذَّكَّرُ إلاَّ أُوْلُواْ الأَلْبَابِ 892{البقرة/269}

Suddi (rh) mentioned that the word الْحِكْمَة[893] can indicate nubuwwah. Ibn Abbas (ra) and Qatadah (rh) mentioned that this word hikmah is the ilmul-knowledge of the Qurān. The person knows what nasuqh-mansuqh, muhkam-mutashabih, first-last, halal-haram and the similar or different knowledge of methodology about the Qurān. Dahhāq (rh) mentioned that al-hikmah is the Qurān and the understanding of the Qurān. Mujāhid (rh) mentioned that is the Qurān with all related sciences and fiqh.

Another meaning for the word الْحِكْمَة[894] is following the sunnah [6] of Rasulullah ﷺ In other words, following the correct applications of the teaching is the key to opening different avenues of khayr and good as mentioned فَقَدْ أُوتِيَ خَيْرًا كَثِيرٌ[895].

Sometimes, we want to implement something. We have the tools, content, and means. Yet, due to the method of application, the initiative becomes fruitless, unsuccessful, and blocks possible potential khayr and good due to our wrong method of application. The case of[896] فَقَدْ أُوتِيَ خَيْرًا كَثِيرٌ comes and opens itself when the person properly follows the methods of hikmah.

In this sense, one of the things that makes the teachers great starting from all the anbiya, and at the zenith, Rasulullah ﷺ and their followers as the awliyaullah is that they all have the qualities of hikmah in teaching, communicating, and delivery methods of their message. They become successful with a lot of khayr as mentioned فَقَدْ أُوتِيَ خَيْرًا كَثِيرٌ.

On the other hand, people like us tend to rush, don't have any patience, break hearts and minds, and make people uncomfortable and

---

892. He gives wisdom to whom He wills, and whoever has been given wisdom has certainly been given much good. And none will remember except those of understanding.
893. Wisdom.
894. Wisdom.
895. Has certainly been given much good.
896. He has certainly been given much good.

irritated by our methods of teaching, communication, and delivery of the content. We fail and they pass.

May Allah ﷻ give us the hikmah and give the ability to implement it, Ameen.

4

Surah Al-Imran

[7]

هُوَ الَّذِيَ أَنزَلَ عَلَيْكَ الْكِتَابَ مِنْهُ آيَاتٌ مُّحْكَمَاتٌ هُنَّ أُمُّ الْكِتَابِ وَأُخَرُ مُتَشَابِهَاتٌ فَأَمَّا الَّذِينَ فِي قُلُوبِهِمْ زَيْغٌ فَيَتَّبِعُونَ مَا تَشَابَهَ مِنْهُ ابْتِغَاء الْفِتْنَةِ وَابْتِغَاء تَأْوِيلِهِ وَمَا يَعْلَمُ تَأْوِيلَهُ إِلاَّ اللهُ وَالرَّاسِخُونَ فِي الْعِلْمِ يَقُولُونَ آمَنَّا بِهِ كُلٌّ مِّنْ عِندِ رَبِّنَا وَمَا يَذَّكَّرُ إِلاَّ أُوْلُواْ الأَلْبَابِ

{آل عمران/7}[897]

It is interesting to note that Allah ﷻ makes the teachings of the religion آيَاتٌ مُّحْكَمَاتٌ[898] and these clear, straightforward, and easy teachings form the pillars of the religion as mentioned هُنَّ أُمُّ الْكِتَابِ[899]. Yet, some people do not follow the clear guidelines but run behind the complex, multifaceted, compound, and convoluted meanings as mentioned وَأُخَرُ مُتَشَابِهَاتٌ[900]. Here the word مُتَشَابِهَاتٌ[901] is translated as the complex, multifaceted, compound, and convoluted meanings which requires scholarly and exegetical approaches and understandings.

Yet,[902] آيَاتٌ مُّحْكَمَاتٌ can indicate straightforward, easy and clear meanings. For example, Oneness and Uniqueness of Allah ﷻ as mentioned[903] "هو الله احد," can be some of the muhkam and explicit teachings. There are a lot of explicit آيَاتٌ مُّحْكَمَاتٌ verses and teachings in the Hadith.

---

897. It is He who has sent down to you, [O Muhammad ﷺ], the Book; in it are verses [that are] precise—they are the foundation of the Book—and others unspecific. As for those in whose hearts is deviation [from truth], they will follow that of it which is unspecific, seeking discord and seeking an interpretation [suitable to them]. And no one knows its [true] interpretation except Allah ﷻ. But those firm in knowledge say, "We believe in it. All [of it] is from our Lord." And no one will be reminded except those of understanding,
898. Verses [that are] precise.
899. They are the foundation of the Book.
900. And others unspecific.
901. Unspecific.
902. Verses [that are] precise.
903. He, Allah ﷻ is one.

This shows that Allah ﷻ makes the core teachings available and accessible for all levels of learners. In other words, the core teachings of the religion such as Tawhid, Ākhirah, or other ones are for everyone, not only for intellectuals or scholars. In another words, a religion is expected to conform to the needs of all levels of learners and not only intellectuals or scholars. This can be implied with the statement [904]هُوَ الَّذِيَ أَنْزَلَ عَلَيْكَ الْكِتَابَ مِنْهُ آيَاتٌ مُّحْكَمَاتٌ هُنَّ أُمُّ الْكِتَابِ.

Then, one can ask the question: Why do the people in popular culture try to go after the complex and multifaceted meanings of the Qurān without following these clear teachings?

Most of the time, as humans we have the spiritual sickness of being "different" or "cool." This sickness can underlie a bigger, cancerous tumor of arrogance, superiority, and vanity.

In other words, by not following the clear teachings, people try to follow "mystics" or "mysticism" as referred to in the popular culture nowadays. Yet, these could be the possible signs of spiritual diseases as mentioned [905]فَأَمَّا الَّذِينَ فِى قُلُوبِهِمْ زَيْغٌ فَيَتَّبِعُونَ مَا تَشَابَهَ مِنْهُ if the person does not really have this sincere and genuine intention.

Another reason can be due to the assumption that if the layman understands the complex meanings, then they can understand the religion better. This statement can be true if the person understands and practices the core pillars first. Then, studying them can come later with genuine scholarship and practice as mentioned [906]وَمَا يَعْلَمُ تَأْوِيلَهُ إِلَّا أَ اللَّهَ وَالرَّاسِخُونَ فِى الْعِلْمِ. The person can subsequently learn some meanings in order to apply in their lives. Knowledge should not be studied in order to be "cool" or "different." This could be very dangerous for the person.

The real people of knowledge, scholarship, and practice, approach the genuine teachings of the religion with humbleness and submission in all stages of learning as mentioned [907]وَالرَّاسِخُونَ فِى الْعِلْمِ يَقُولُونَ آمَنَّا بِهِ كُلٌّ مِّنْ عِندِ رَبِّنَا.

---

904. It is He who has sent down to you, [O Muhammad ﷺ], the Book; in it are verses [that are] precise—they are the foundation of the Book.
905. As for those in whose hearts is deviation [from truth], they will follow that of it which is unspecific.
906. And no one knows its [true] interpretation except Allah ﷻ. But those firm in knowledge.
907. But those firm in knowledge say, "We believe in it. All [of it] is from our Lord."

[151]

سَنُلْقِي فِي قُلُوبِ الَّذِينَ كَفَرُواْ الرُّعْبَ بِمَا أَشْرَكُواْ بِاللّهِ مَا لَمْ يُنَزِّلْ بِهِ سُلْطَانًا وَمَأْوَاهُمُ
النَّارُ وَبِئْسَ مَثْوَى الظَّالِمِينَ 908 {آل عمران/151}

It is interesting to analyze the above ayah with meanings of "لا اله الا الله." When a person makes shirk in their relationship with Allah ﷻ, there is always fear, uneasiness, anxiety, worry, agitation, depression, and stress as the meaning of the word الرُّعْبَ909 can indicate. In this sense, in the expression of "لا اله الا الله," the word "ilāha910" is not only a symbolic or material idol. It can be any engagement of the person implicitly or explicitly, that leads the person to the undesired states of fear, uneasiness, anxiety, worry, agitation, depression, and stress. When a person truly embodies "لا اله الا الله," "lā" can indicate this negation or removal of fear, uneasiness, anxiety, worry, agitation, depression, and stress overpowering the person. Anything overpowering the person other than Allah ﷻ can be "ilāha". The person reminds oneself with a strong, complete, and full discharge of all fears, uneasiness, anxiety, worry, agitation, depression, and stress. Then, the charge and filling of the heart and mind only and exclusively with Allah ﷻ comes with "لا اله الا الله." This is a constant and required process that is embodied in five-daily prayers. It is also embodied with all the dhikrs such as SubhanAllah, Alhamdulillah, AllahuAkbar, La ilaha illa Allah, and Astagfirullah.

One can remember that the tafsìr of this ayah especially reported by Suddi (rh) [29] in the case of Abu Sufyan making a plan against Muslims, yet Allah ﷻ prevented this by placing fear, sadness and agitation in their hearts.

---

908. We will cast terror into the hearts of those who disbelieve for what they have associated with Allah ﷻ of which He had not sent down [any] authority. And their refuge will be the Fire, and wretched is the residence of the wrongdoers.
909. Terror.
910. God.

5

Surah Nisa

[75]

وَمَا لَكُمْ لاَ تُقَاتِلُونَ فِي سَبِيلِ اللهِ وَالْمُسْتَضْعَفِينَ مِنَ الرِّجَالِ وَالنِّسَاء وَالْوِلْدَانِ الَّذِينَ يَقُولُونَ رَبَّنَا أَخْرِجْنَا مِنْ هَذِهِ الْقَرْيَةِ الظَّالِمِ أَهْلُهَا وَاجْعَل لَّنَا مِن لَّدُنكَ وَلِيًّا وَاجْعَل لَّنَا مِن لَّدُنكَ نَصِيرًا 911{النساء/75}

إِلاَّ الْمُسْتَضْعَفِينَ مِنَ الرِّجَالِ وَالنِّسَاء وَالْوِلْدَانِ لاَ يَسْتَطِيعُونَ حِيلَةً وَلاَ يَهْتَدُونَ سَبِيلاً 912{النساء/98}

وَيَسْتَفْتُونَكَ فِي النِّسَاء قُلِ اللهُ يُفْتِيكُمْ فِيهِنَّ وَمَا يُتْلَى عَلَيْكُمْ فِي الْكِتَابِ فِي يَتَامَى النِّسَاء اللاَّتِي لاَ تُؤْتُونَهُنَّ مَا كُتِبَ لَهُنَّ وَتَرْغَبُونَ أَن تَنكِحُوهُنَّ وَالْمُسْتَضْعَفِينَ مِنَ الْوِلْدَانِ وَأَن تَقُومُواْ لِلْيَتَامَى بِالْقِسْطِ وَمَا تَفْعَلُواْ مِنْ خَيْرٍ فَإِنَّ اللَّهَ كَانَ بِهِ عَلِيمًا 913{النساء/127}

It is interesting to analyze the above ayahs around the word الْوِلْدَانِ[914]. One can realize that the above ayahs are in surah nisa and the word الْوِلْدَانِ is mentioned together with the word النِّسَاء[915]. This can indicate the need for the mother as compared to the father in the upbringing of a child or a toddler in this life. One should analyze the above ayahs in the cases of divorce with the legal rulings of fiqh about child custody.

However, when the perspective is related to having الْوِلْدَانِ as a source of joy, happiness, and coolness of eye, then one can realize the attribution can be to both parents- father and mother- especially in Jannah as وَيَطُوفُ

---

911. And what is [the matter] with you that you fight not in the cause of Allah and [for] the oppressed among men, women, and children who say, "Our Lord, take us out of this city of oppressive people and appoint for us from Yourself a protector and appoint for us from Yourself a helper"?

912. Except for the oppressed among men, women, and children who cannot devise a plan nor are they directed to a way.

913. And they request from you, [O Muhammad ﷺ], a [legal] ruling concerning women. Say, "Allah gives you a ruling about them and [about] what has been recited to you in the Book concerning the orphan girls to whom you do not give what is decreed for them—and [yet] you desire to marry them—and concerning the oppressed among children and that you maintain for orphans [their rights] in justice." And whatever you do of good—indeed, Allah is ever Knowing of it.

914. Children.

915. Women.

يَطُوفُ عَلَيْهِمْ وِلْدَانٌ or عَلَيْهِمْ وِلْدَانٌ مُخَلَّدُونَ إِذَا رَأَيْتَهُمْ حَسِبْتَهُمْ لُؤْلُؤًا مَّنثُورًا916{الإنسان/19}
مُخَلَّدُونَ917{الواقعة/17}, الله اعلم918.

The same الْوِلْدَان who can be a source of happiness in this dunya and in the ākhirah, can be in so much agitation due to the heaviness of the Day of Judgement or the Day of Qiyāmah, as mentioned إِن فَكَيْفَ تَتَّقُونَ كَفَرْتُمْ يَوْمًا يَجْعَلُ الْوِلْدَانَ شِيبًا919{المزمل/17}, May Allah ﷻ protect us, Ameen.

[108]

يَسْتَخْفُونَ مِنَ النَّاسِ وَلاَ يَسْتَخْفُونَ مِنَ اللهِ وَهُوَ مَعَهُمْ إِذْ يُبَيِّتُونَ مَا لاَ يَرْضَى مِنَ الْقَوْلِ وَكَانَ اللّهُ بِمَا يَعْمَلُونَ مُحِيطًا920{النساء/108}

Sometimes a group of words (qawl) as mentioned in this ayah as مِن مَّا لَهُم بِهِ مِنْ عِلْمٍ وَلاَ لآبَائِهِمْ كَبُرَتْ الْقَوْلِ921 or a word (kalimah) as mentioned in كَلِمَةً تَخْرُجُ مِنْ أَفْوَاهِهِمْ إِن يَقُولُونَ إِلَّا كَذِبًا922{الكهف/5} can lead to the displeasure of Allah ﷻ as mentioned with the expressions مَا لَا يَرْضَى923 in this ayah and كَبُرَتْ924 in surah Kahf. Therefore, ahlullah try to first control their thoughts. Then, they try to verbalize all their verbal utterances with this reality. In this case, it is possibly in the category of مَا لاَ يَرْضَى مِنَ الْقَوْلِ925 or كَبُرَتْ كَلِمَةً تَخْرُجُ مِنْ أَفْوَاهِهِمْ. This is not an exaggeration. This is a normal and natural state that a person is expected to be in. اللهم اجعلنا منهم. امين926.

Verbalizing the words and uttering them should be constantly monitored before they become realities of our lives. Once they are uttered they become realities. In this perspective, we do not use the word "creation" for humans. However, we form or contribute to the formation of these words to be in reality with our limited, tiny free will. These formations or utterances can be either good or bad.

---

916. There will circulate among them young boys made eternal. When you see them, you would think them [as beautiful as] scattered pearls.
917. There will circulate among them young boys made eternal.
918. Allah ﷻ knows best.
919. Then how can you fear, if you disbelieve, a Day that will make the children white-haired?
920. They conceal [their evil intentions and deeds] from the people, but they cannot conceal [them] from Allah, and He is with them [in His knowledge] when they spend the night in such as He does not accept of speech. And ever is Allah, of what they do, encompassing.
921. Of speech.
922. They have no knowledge of it, nor had their fathers. Grave is the word that comes out of their mouths; they speak not except a lie.
923. He does not accept of speech.
924. Grave {is the word}.
925. Grave is the word that comes out of their mouths.
926. Oh Allah ﷻ, make us from among them.

The best and highest of these formed words are the words of dhikrs. SubhanAllah, Alhamdulillah, Allahuakbar, Astagfiruallah, La ilaha illa Allah, La hawla wa la quwwata illa billah, subhanAllahu wa bihamdihi subhanAllahu al-Azim are some examples of them.

Once they are uttered from the person's mouth. They are formed. They are in our realities. As the hadith mentions, these words go so high in their value, close to the Arsh of Allah ☝ with buzzing sounds circling as the angels, malaikah try to decode these highly valued dhikrs and they then try to extrapolate them from the earth in order to identify the sender of those phrases [2]. A supporting rendering is also mentioned in the Qurān as مَن كَانَ يُرِيدُ الْعِزَّةَ فَلِلَّهِ الْعِزَّةُ جَمِيعًا إِلَيْهِ يَصْعَدُ الْكَلِمُ الطَّيِّبُ وَالْعَمَلُ الصَّالِحُ يَرْفَعُهُ وَالَّذِينَ يَمْكُرُونَ السَّيِّئَاتِ لَهُمْ عَذَابٌ شَدِيدٌ وَمَكْرُ أُوْلَئِكَ هُوَ يَبُورُ 927{فاطر/10}.

One should remember that all of these good and virtuous qawl, words, or utterances are with the Fadl[928] and Rahmah[929] of Allah ☝ as mentioned:

يُثَبِّتُ اللَّهُ الَّذِينَ آمَنُواْ بِالْقَوْلِ الثَّابِتِ فِي الْحَيَاةِ الدُّنْيَا وَفِي الآخِرَةِ وَيُضِلُّ اللَّهُ الظَّالِمِينَ وَيَفْعَلُ اللَّهُ مَا يَشَاءُ 930{إبراهيم/27}.

.الحمدالله عدد خلقه و زنت عرشه و مداد كلمات 931

Similarly, a bad uttered word (kalimah) or group of words (qawl) becomes the reality that can lead to the displeasure of Allah ☝ as mentioned in this ayah of discussion. It becomes a reality- a reality that could lead the person to an accountability and to a bad outcome if the person does not ask tawbah from Allah ☝.

As also mentioned in وَلَوْلَا إِذْ سَمِعْتُمُوهُ قُلْتُم مَّا يَكُونُ لَنَا أَن نَّتَكَلَّمَ بِهَذَا سُبْحَانَكَ هَذَا بُهْتَانٌ عَظِيمٌ 932{النور/16}, the words carrying lies, slandering, and backbiting can include these meanings. Yet, the person should not carry them and

---

927. Whoever desires honor [through power]—then to Allah belongs all honor. To Him ascends good speech, and righteous work raises it. But they who plot evil deeds will have a severe punishment, and the plotting of those—it will perish.
928. Favor.
929. Mercy.
930. Allah keeps firm those who believe, with the firm word, in worldly life and in the Hereafter. And Allah sends astray the wrongdoers. And Allah does what He wills.
931. Praise be to god, the number of his creation and weighed his throne and words of words.
932. And why, when you heard it, did you not say, "It is not for us to speak of this. Exalted are You, [O Allah]; this is a great slander"?

should immediately stay at the opposite side of these lies as mentioned
933سُبْحَانَكَ هَذَا بُهْتَانٌ عَظِيمٌ.

So, one should not really take lying or bad words lightly because
they really reflect the inner disposition of the person as mentioned in
the hadith، 934آية المنافق ثلاث ، إذا حدث كذب ، وإذا وعد أخلف
[وإذا اوتمن خان] [7] [4]. This hadith can also differentiate and detail
these types. In another hadith, Rasulullah ﷺ said another trait as
mentioned 935أَرْبَعٌ مَنْ كُنَّ فِيهِ كَانَ مُنَافِقًا خَالِصًا ، وَمَنْ كَانَتْ فِيهِ خَصْلَةٌ مِنْهُنَّ كَانَتْ
فِيهِ خَصْلَةٌ مِنَ النِّفَاقِ حَتَّى يَدَعَهَا : إِذَا اوْتُمِنَ خَانَ ، وَإِذَا حَدَّثَ كَذَبَ ، وَإِذَا عَاهَدَ غَدَرَ ، وَإِذَا
خَاصَمَ فَجَرَ] [7].

In other perspectives, these utterances can become realities like the
trees that we see in our everyday life as mentioned in the Qurān:

أَلَمْ تَرَ كَيْفَ ضَرَبَ اللّهُ مَثَلاً كَلِمَةً طَيِّبَةً كَشَجَرَةٍ طَيِّبَةٍ أَصْلُهَا ثَابِتٌ وَفَرْعُهَا فِي السَّمَاء
936{إبراهيم/24}

تُؤْتِي أُكُلَهَا كُلَّ حِينٍ بِإِذْنِ رَبِّهَا وَيَضْرِبُ اللّهُ الأَمْثَالَ لِلنَّاسِ لَعَلَّهُمْ يَتَذَكَّرُونَ
937{إبراهيم/25} وَمَثْلُ كَلِمَةٍ خَبِيثَةٍ كَشَجَرَةٍ خَبِيثَةٍ اجْتُثَّتْ مِن فَوْقِ الأَرْضِ مَا لَهَا مِن
قَرَارٍ 938{إبراهيم/26}

Therefore, in the Qurān, in Jannah, there are only good realities
formed from good utterances as mentioned لَّا يَسْمَعُونَ فِيهَا لَغْوًا وَلَا كِذَّابًا
939{النبأ/35}.

In all of the above renderings, the utterances of a person are not lost
but preserved. Therefore, ahlullah940 similar to praying to sunnah before
fardh, they prepare themselves before the required stimulation referred

---

933. Exalted are You, [O Allah]; this is a great slander"?
934. The signs of a munāfiq are three: When he talks, he lies; when he promises, he breaks his promise; and when he is trusted, he breaks the trust.
935. Whoever has all these four traits altogether in oneself, then this person is a definite munāfiq. Whoever has one of these traits, then this person carries one of the signs of nifāq until he or she leaves this trait. When he talks, he lies; when he promises he breaks his promise, when he is trusted he breaks the trust; and when he is in argument, he does not observe any limits.
936. Have you not considered how Allah presents an example, [making] a good word like a good tree, whose root is firmly fixed and its branches [high] in the sky?
937. It produces its fruit all the time, by permission of its Lord. And Allah presents examples for the people that perhaps they will be reminded.
938. And the example of a bad word is like a bad tree, uprooted from the surface of the earth, not having any stability.
939. The Day when man will remember that for which he strove.
940. The people of Allah ﷺ.

to as fardh through the optional rituals referred as sunnah. In other words, they try to control their thoughts similar to the sunnah, before they utter the words similar to the fardh. At the end, in fiqh, the person is responsible and accountable about their utterances not their thoughts. A person is responsible and accountable from fardh but not sunnahs. Yet, if one misses sunnah, then this person will likely miss their fardh. If one does not control their thoughts they will not be able to control their utterances, words, that come to our world of realities.

Therefore, if one analyzes, there are numerous sunnahs that one can follow compared to few fardh. Similarly, a person can have numerous thoughts during the day or hour. The person is expected to have less verbalized utterances as compared to his or her thoughts. One can analyze the life of Rasulullah ﷺ. Most of the time he saw was in silence. When he saw talked as the Jawamul Kalim, one could count the words but they had deep and layered meanings.

When the person controls these thoughts with constant husnu-thann[941] and goodness and virtue as instructed by Allah ﷻ and Rasulullah ﷺ, then the words that come from the person will be good, pure, and will penetrate the hearts and minds inshAllah.

One can correlate this discussion here with the concept of intention in fiqh. In other words, thoughts or ideas can become the intention of the person when the person substantiates them in their mind or heart. In other words, if there is a bad thought, the person can terminate it with "astagfirullah". But, if the person holds on to a bad thought, it is as if catching a bird as mentioned by Imam Ghazali about different thoughts [28]. Then this becomes the person's intention.

At this point, intention forms or leads the person to the action. Whether the person is successful or not in this action, the person is judged and accountable according to their intention in front of Allah ﷻ.

In legal rulings, a person who forms an intention of a good deed but cannot achieve it or do it still receives the reward of that action from Allah ﷻ due to their good intention. A person who had a bad intention but controlled himself or herself still gets a reward from Allah ﷻ because of the effort of holding back of themselves. A person who had a bad intention but was not able to put it into action can be punished due to their intention or not punished by Allah ﷻ due to the Mercy of Allah ﷻ

---

941. Good thoughts.

because the action did not become a reality of the visible world. A person who had a bad intention and executed an action will be accountable in front of Allah ﷻ.

If one considers the expression "Be" when mentioned for Allah ﷻ in the Qurān, for Allah ﷻ, we don't use the same vocabulary of differentiation of word, action, or being in reality. Allah ﷻ has the Mashiyyah[942] of Will. When there is the Mashiyyah of Allah ﷻ anything and everything can happen with the Divine Mashiyyah. When one analyzes the expression "Kun fa Yakun", the word "Kun" repeated before its existence and after its existence, can show us that the Mashiyyah of Allah is the essence in creation and existence.

The word "fa" can indicate especially in our human understanding the reasons and causalities. In other words, for different hikmahs, Allah ﷻ creates in our universe causality relationships through natural and social sciences. There is no need of this for Allah ﷻ. One of the hikmahs can be the servitude of causes as a curtain expected to be removed by humans. In other words, trials and tests and our existence require a lit bit of effort to see the Real Doer of everything, Allah ﷻ beyond these very thin-looking or transparent curtains. If there is none, everything will be obvious and there will not be a purpose or procedure of tests and trials for imān.

At another level, when these thin-looking or transparent curtains are removed, then in our language we call them miracles. In other words, there is no causality. There is no thin-looking curtain. In these cases, we get shocked. An example of fire not burning Ibrahim as is one example.

To give this simple and straightforward reality, one can see this for Isa as. There was no causality. There was no "fa". The direct Kun or "Be" was there. Therefore, one of the names of Isa as in the Qurān is "kalimullah", the word of Allah ﷻ. One reviews the ayahs of the Qurān around this word kalimah as:

يَا أَهْلَ الْكِتَابِ لاَ تَغْلُواْ فِي دِينِكُمْ وَلاَ تَقُولُواْ عَلَى اللّهِ إِلاَّ الْحَقِّ إِنَّمَا الْمَسِيحُ عِيسَى ابْنُ مَرْيَمَ رَسُولُ اللّهِ وَكَلِمَتُهُ أَلْقَاهَا إِلَى مَرْيَمَ وَرُوحٌ مِّنْهُ فَآمِنُواْ بِاللّهِ وَرُسُلِهِ وَلاَ تَقُولُواْ ثَلاَثَةٌ

---

942. Divine permission.

انتَهُواْ خَيْرًا لَّكُمْ إِنَّمَا اللّهُ إِلَهٌ وَاحِدٌ سُبْحَانَهُ أَن يَكُونَ لَهُ وَلَدٌ لَّهُ مَا فِي السَّمَاوَات وَمَا فِي الأَرْضِ وَكَفَى بِاللّهِ وَكِيلاً 943{النساء/171}

In the case of other creation, there is the "fa" causalities. In the case of Isa as or Adam as there is no "fa". Or in the case of Isa as there is the partial "fa" as his mother, Maryam rh. In the case of Adam as there is no "fa"

This is the same expression mentioned in the Bible. Yet, this is a miracle as we call it in our language among many other miracles shown to us by Allah ﷻ. Yet, people can turn any miracle into wrong interpretations. All miracles can be considered without "fa", without causalities as reminders for us that causalities are only thin-looking, transparent curtains and one should wake up when the time comes. Yet, a lot of people are sleeping. They attach themselves to these causalities, reasons, nature, or that which is popularly called "science." May Allah ﷻ protect us and guide us and end our life in this dunya as a true Muslim, Ameen.

In other words, everything is kalimullah representing the Mashiyyah944 of Allah ﷻ as mentioned وَإِذْ يَعِدُكُمُ اللّهُ إِحْدَى الطَّائِفَتِيْنِ أَنَّهَا لَكُمْ وَتَوَدُّونَ أَنَّ غَيْرَ ذَاتِ الشَّوْكَةِ تَكُونُ لَكُمْ وَيُرِيدُ اللّهُ أَن يُحِقَّ الْحَقَّ بِكَلِمَاتِهِ وَيَقْطَعَ دَابِرَ الْكَافِرِينَ 945{الأنفال/7}. Another example of this can be وَجَعَلَ كَلِمَةَ الَّذِينَ كَفَرُواْ السُّفْلَى وَكَلِمَةُ اللّهِ هِيَ الْعُلْيَا وَاللّهُ عَزِيزٌ حَكِيمٌ 946{التوبة/40}. In these cases, kalimah when attributed to Allah ﷻ is the Mashiyyah of Allah ﷻ and kalimah for humans is their verbalized utterances of their intention. The intentions of humans can be good or bad. Yet, Allah ﷻ's Mashiyyah is always good, virtuous, and high as mentioned وَكَلِمَةُ اللّهِ هِيَ الْعُلْيَا947. The people of kufr and nifāq have the bad, evil, and lowly intentions as mentioned كَلِمَةَ الَّذِينَ كَفَرُواْ السُّفْلَى948.

---

943. O People of the Scripture, do not commit excess in your religion or say about Allah except the truth. The Messiah, Jesus, the son of Mary, was but a messenger of Allah and His word which He directed to Mary and a soul [created at a command] from Him. So believe in Allah and His messengers. And do not say, "Three"; desist—it is better for you. Indeed, Allah is but one God. Exalted is He above having a son. To Him belongs whatever is in the heavens and whatever is on the earth. And sufficient is Allah as Disposer of affairs.

944. Divine permission.

945. [Remember, O believers],when Allah promised you one of the two groups—that it would be yours—and you wished that the unarmed one would be yours. But Allah intended to establish the truth by His words and to eliminate the disbelievers.

946. And made the word of those who disbelieved the lowest, while the word of Allah —that is the highest. And Allah is Exalted in Might and Wise.

947. While the word of Allah —that is the highest.

948. Word of those who disbelieved the lowest.

The meaning of Mashiyyah for kalimah with this rendering can also highlight and make it easier to understand the ayahs such as وَلَقَدْ آتَيْنَا مُوسَى الْكِتَابَ فَاخْتُلِفَ فِيهِ وَلَوْلَا كَلِمَةٌ سَبَقَتْ مِن رَّبِّكَ لَقُضِيَ بَيْنَهُمْ وَإِنَّهُمْ لَفِي شَكٍّ مِّنْهُ مُرِيبٍ {هود/110}949

Therefore, kalamullah of the Qurān shows us what Allah ﷻ wants from us, the Mashiyyah950 of Allah ﷻ. So, this is a big ni'mah, Alhamdulillah as also mentioned وَتَمَّتْ كَلِمَتُ رَبِّكَ صِدْقًا وَعَدْلاً لاَّ مُبَدِّلِ لِكَلِمَاتِهِ وَهُوَ السَّمِيعُ الْعَلِيمُ {الأنعام/115}951.

As a side rendering, the person can likely approach the Mashiyyah of Allah ﷻ with istikharah, or mashwarah952 as may be, one can interestingly analyze وَمَا تَفَرَّقُوا إِلَّا مِن بَعْدِ مَا جَاءهُمُ الْعِلْمُ بَغْيًا بَيْنَهُمْ وَلَوْلَا كَلِمَةٌ سَبَقَتْ مِن رَّبِّكَ إِلَى أَجَلٍ مُّسَمًّى لَّقُضِيَ بَيْنَهُمْ وَإِنَّ الَّذِينَ أُورِثُوا الْكِتَابَ مِن بَعْدِهِمْ لَفِي شَكٍّ مِّنْهُ مُرِيبٍ {الشورى/14}953 in Sûrah. If a person wants Allah ﷻ to talk to them, this person should read the Qurān. It is a big honor for us. Musa as received this honor at another level as mentioned وَلَمَّا جَاء مُوسَى لِمِيقَاتِنَا وَكَلَّمَهُ رَبُّهُ قَالَ رَبِّ أَرِنِي أَنظُرْ إِلَيْكَ قَالَ لَن تَرَانِي وَلَكِنِ انظُرْ إِلَى الْجَبَلِ فَإِنِ اسْتَقَرَّ مَكَانَهُ فَسَوْفَ تَرَانِي فَلَمَّا تَجَلَّى رَبُّهُ لِلْجَبَلِ جَعَلَهُ دَكًّا وَخَرَّ موسَى صَعِقًا فَلَمَّا أَفَاقَ قَالَ سُبْحَانَكَ تُبْتُ إِلَيْكَ وَأَنَا أَوَّلُ الْمُؤْمِنِينَ {الأعراف/143}954. As we read the Qurān and when Allah ﷻ is talking to us in the Qurān, we may get so excited as in the case of the above ayah mentioned for Musa as. We may want to be even closer to Allah ﷻ and due to our excitement ask from Allah ﷻ for that which is beyond our humanness as mentioned قَالَ لَن تَرَانِي وَلَكِنِ انظُرْ إِلَى الْجَبَلِ فَإِنِ اسْتَقَرَّ مَكَانَهُ فَسَوْفَ تَرَانِي فَلَمَّا تَجَلَّى رَبُّهُ لِلْجَبَلِ جَعَلَهُ دَكًّا وَخَرَّ موسَى صَعِقًا فَلَمَّا أَفَاقَ قَالَ سُبْحَانَكَ تُبْتُ إِلَيْكَ وَأَنَا أَوَّلُ الْمُؤْمِنِينَ {الأعراف/143}955. Yet, in these excitements,

---

949. And We had certainly given Moses the Scripture, but it came under disagreement. And if not for a word532 that preceded from your Lord, it would have been judged between them. And indeed they are, concerning it [i.e., the Qurān], in disquieting doubt.
950. Divine permission.
951. And the word of your Lord has been fulfilled in truth and in justice. None can alter His words, and He is the Hearing, the Knowing.
952. Group discussion.
953. And they have upon me a [claim due to] sin, so I fear that they will kill me."
954. And when Moses arrived at Our appointed time and his Lord spoke to him, he said, "My Lord, show me [Yourself] that I may look at You." [Allah] said, "You will not see Me, but look at the mountain; if it should remain in place, then you will see Me." But when his Lord appeared to the mountain, He rendered it level, and Moses fell unconscious. And when he awoke, he said, "Exalted are You! I have repented to You, and I am the first of the believers."
955. And when Moses arrived at Our appointed time and his Lord spoke to him, he said, "My Lord, show me [Yourself] that I may look at You." [Allah] said, "You will not see Me, but look at the mountain; if it should remain in place, then you will see Me." But when his Lord appeared to the mountain, He rendered it level, and Moses fell unconscious. And when he awoke, he said, "Exalted are You! I have repented to You, and I am the first of the believers."

as people of tasawwuf refer to it as sakr, we should always say سُبْحَانَكَ[956] تُبْتُ إِلَيْكَ وَأَنَا أَوَّلُ الْمُؤْمِنِينَ.

If we want to talk to Allah ﷻ, we make dua and pray salah, and perform other ibadahs as mentioned by Ali ra.

One of the ayahs where one may possibly analyze the Mashiyyah[957] of Allah ﷻ and the disposition of humans is mentioned in an intricate pattern mentioned is إِذْ جَعَلَ الَّذِينَ كَفَرُوا فِي قُلُوبِهِمُ الْحَمِيَّةَ حَمِيَّةَ الْجَاهِلِيَّةِ فَأَنزَلَ اللَّهُ سَكِينَتَهُ عَلَى رَسُولِهِ وَعَلَى الْمُؤْمِنِينَ وَأَلْزَمَهُمْ كَلِمَةَ التَّقْوَى وَكَانُوا أَحَقَّ بِهَا وَأَهْلَهَا وَكَانَ اللَّهُ بِكُلِّ شَيْءٍ عَلِيمًا[958] {الفتح/26}.

In this ayah one can analyze different perspectives.

Kufr and shirk stem from arrogance, vanity, negative judgment, jealousy, or other diseases of the heart as mentioned with the word الْحَمِيَّةَ[959]. This position of the heart can be in a lowly and ignorant stance due to lack of education, open-mindedness, and sticking to the customs, norms, culture, and social values blindly without any critical thinking and empathy for others as mentioned with the expression حَمِيَّةَ الْجَاهِلِيَّةِ[960].

On the other hand, imān requires the opposite stance. In other words, if one applies the word kalimah كَلِمَةَ to humans, it can have the meanings of intention. The place of intention is the heart and mind. As also interpreted in tafsir by Imam Maturudi [30], in this verse كَلِمَةَ[961] التَّقْوَى can signify the ikhlas. In other words, the true intention of a mumi'n is to have ikhlas, sincerity.

Ikhlas requires the opposite of kufr. It requires empathy, open-mindedness, humbleness, humility, and a judgment-free personality. The person with true humbleness and humility gives all the true due to Allah ﷻ. The person of kufr takes everything on himself or herself with arrogance.

Therefore, the person of imān gets sakinah فَأَنزَلَ اللَّهُ سَكِينَتَهُ عَلَى رَسُولِهِ[962] وَعَلَى الْمُؤْمِنِينَ. Here, فَ can indicate this causality, sababiyah. In other

---

956. "Exalted are You! I have repented to You, and I am the first of the believers."
957. Permission.
958. When those who disbelieved had put into their hearts chauvinism—the chauvinism of the time of ignorance. But Allah sent down His tranquility upon His Messenger and upon the believers and imposed upon them the word of righteousness, and they were more deserving of it and worthy of it. And ever is Allah, of all things, Knowing.
959. Chauvinism.
960. The chauvinism of the time of ignorance.
961. Word of righteousness.
962. So Allah ﷻ revealed his tranquility to his Messenger ﷺ and to the believers.

words, if the person maintains the state of heart with taqwa, ikhlas, then he or she will be always in the state of sakinah.

The expression of وَكَانُوا أَحَقَّ بِهَا وَأَهْلَهَا[963] can allude to the Mashiyyah of Allah ﷻ as well as the tiny free will of the person when one engages himself or herself with taqwa, ikhlas, and sincerity.

Everything happens at the level of heart and no one knows any person's true state of taqwa, ikhlas, and sincerity except Allah ﷻ as mentioned وَكَانَ اللَّهُ بِكُلِّ شَيْءٍ عَلِيمًا[964].

It is interpreted in tafsir of Ibn Kathir (rh) that the topics of this ayah is about the munāfiqeen [32].

اللهم اجعلنا من اهل كلمة التقوى[965]

[113]

وَلَوْلاَ فَضْلُ اللّهِ عَلَيْكَ وَرَحْمَتُهُ لَهَمَّت طَّائِفَةٌ مُّنْهُمْ أَن يُضِلُّوكَ وَمَا يُضِلُّونَ إِلاَّ أَنفُسَهُمْ وَمَا يَضُرُّونَكَ مِن شَيْءٍ وَأَنزَلَ اللّهُ عَلَيْكَ الْكِتَابَ وَالْحِكْمَةَ وَعَلَّمَكَ مَا لَمْ تَكُنْ تَعْلَمُ وَكَانَ فَضْلُ اللّهِ عَلَيْكَ عَظِيمًا[966] {النساء/113}

In everyone's lifespan, the expression {النساء/113}[967] وَكَانَ فَضْلُ اللهِ عَلَيْكَ عَظِيمًا is very critical to realize. If we really don't see this reality of the Fadl of Allah ﷻ individually, then those moments of awareness and heedlessness can be considered the worms of kufr coming and biting our imān. May Allah ﷻ protect us.

One of the biggest ni'mahs and Fadl of Allah ﷻ is mentioned as وَأَنزَلَ اللهُ عَلَيْكَ الْكِتَابَ وَالْحِكْمَةَ وَعَلَّمَكَ مَا لَمْ تَكُنْ تَعْلَمُ[968]. This is one of the biggest ni'mahs[969] and Fadl[970] of Allah ﷻ because they build our imān.

Imān is one's sweet and honey-based appreciative and grateful relationship with Allah ﷻ, Rabbul Alamin.

---

963. And they were more deserving of it and worthy of it.
964. And ever is Allah, of all things, Knowing.
965. O Allah, make us from among the people of piety.
966. And if it was not for the favor of Allah upon you, [O Muhammad], and His mercy, a group of them would have determined to mislead you. But they do not mislead except themselves, and they will not harm you at all. And Allah has revealed to you the Book and wisdom and has taught you that which you did not know. And ever has the favor of Allah upon you been great.
967. And ever has the favor of Allah upon you been great.
968. And Allah has revealed to you the Book and wisdom and has taught you that which you did not know.
969. Blessings.
970. Favor.

Any feelings of disgust can be related to one's unappreciative and ungrateful attitude toward Allah ﷻ, implicitly and explicitly. This is called kufr in terminology.

Any engagements of kufr can be similar to the worms attacking one's imān. If there is no imān in a person, then the person can be soaked in kufr. He or she may not even realize these disgusting, spiritual worms are present although this person can be considered to be drenched in a swamp of worms.

[171-175]

يَا أَهْلَ الْكِتَابِ لاَ تَغْلُواْ فِي دِينِكُمْ وَلاَ تَقُولُواْ عَلَى اللّهِ إِلاَّ الْحَقَّ إِنَّمَا الْمَسِيحُ عِيسَى ابْنُ مَرْيَمَ رَسُولُ اللّهِ وَكَلِمَتُهُ أَلْقَاهَا إِلَى مَرْيَمَ وَرُوحٌ مِّنْهُ فَآمِنُواْ بِاللّهِ وَرُسُلِهِ وَلاَ تَقُولُواْ ثَلاَثَةٌ انتَهُواْ خَيْرًا لَّكُمْ إِنَّمَا اللّهُ إِلَـهٌ وَاحِدٌ سُبْحَانَهُ أَن يَكُونَ لَهُ وَلَدٌ لَّهُ مَا فِي السَّمَاوَات وَمَا فِي الأَرْضِ وَكَفَى بِاللّهِ وَكِيلاً 971{النساء/171} لَّن يَسْتَنكِفَ الْمَسِيحُ أَن يَكُونَ عَبْداً لِلّهِ وَلاَ الْمَلآئِكَةُ الْمُقَرَّبُونَ وَمَن يَسْتَنكِفْ عَنْ عِبَادَتِهِ وَيَسْتَكْبِرْ فَسَيَحْشُرُهُمْ إِلَيهِ جَمِيعًا 972{النساء/172} فَأَمَّا الَّذِينَ آمَنُواْ وَعَمِلُواْ الصَّالِحَاتِ فَيُوَفِّيهِمْ أُجُورَهُمْ وَيَزيدُهُم مِّن فَضْلِهِ وَأَمَّا الَّذِينَ اسْتَنكَفُواْ وَاسْتَكْبَرُواْ فَيُعَذِّبُهُمْ عَذَابًا أَلُيمًا وَلاَ يَجِدُونَ لَهُم مِّن دُونِ اللّهِ وَلِيًّا وَلاَ نَصِيرًا 973{النساء/173} يَا أَيُّهَا النَّاسُ قَدْ جَاءكُم بُرْهَانٌ مِّن رَّبِّكُمْ وَأَنزَلْنَا إِلَيْكُمْ نُورًا مُّبِينًا 974{النساء/174} فَأَمَّا الَّذِينَ آمَنُواْ بِاللّهِ وَاعْتَصَمُواْ بِهِ فَسَيُدْخِلُهُمْ فِي رَحْمَةٍ مِّنْهُ وَفَضْلٍ وَيَهْدِيهِمْ إِلَيْهِ صِرَاطًا مُّسْتَقِيمًا 975{النساء/175}

---

971. O People of the Scripture, do not commit excess in your religion or say about Allah except the truth. The Messiah, Jesus, the son of Mary, was but a messenger of Allah and His word which He directed to Mary and a soul [created at a command] from Him. So believe in Allah and His messengers. And do not say, "Three"; desist—it is better for you. Indeed, Allah is but one God. Exalted is He above having a son. To Him belongs whatever is in the heavens and whatever is on the earth. And sufficient is Allah as Disposer of affairs.

972. Never would the Messiah disdain to be a servant of Allah, nor would the angels near [to Him]. And whoever disdains His worship and is arrogant—He will gather them to Himself all together.

973. And as for those who believed and did righteous deeds, He will give them in full their rewards and grant them extra from His bounty. But as for those who disdained and were arrogant, He will punish them with a painful punishment, and they will not find for themselves besides Allah any protector or helper.

974. O mankind, there has come to you a conclusive proof from your Lord, and We have sent down to you a clear light.

975. So those who believe in Allah and hold fast to Him—He will admit them to mercy from Himself and bounty and guide them to Himself on a straight path.

It is interesting to analyze the above ayah, especially the rendering of وَ لاَ تَقُولُواْ ثَلاَثَةٌ انتَهُواْ خَيْرًا لَّكُمْ إِنَّمَا اللهُ إِلَهٌ وَاحِدٌ سُبْحَانَهُ أَن يَكُونَ لَهُ وَلَدٌ لَّهُ مَا فِي السَّمَاوَاتِ وَمَا فِي الأَرْضِ وَكَفَى بِاللهِ وَكِيلاً 976{النساء/171} with لَّقَدْ كَفَرَ الَّذِينَ قَالُواْ إِنَّ اللهَ ثَالِثُ ثَلاَثَةٍ وَمَا مِنْ إِلَهٍ إِلاَّ إِلَهٌ وَاحِدٌ وَإِن لَّمْ يَنتَهُواْ عَمَّا يَقُولُونَ لَيَمَسَّنَّ الَّذِينَ كَفَرُواْ مِنْهُمْ عَذَابٌ أَلِيمٌ 977{المائدة/73}.

These two approaches to trinity can allude to the personal understanding of trinity among Christians. If the person believes in One Creator as God but may not possibly locate the notion of trinity then, the Qurān can display an advice as وَ لاَ تَقُولُواْ ثَلاَثَةٌ انتَهُواْ خَيْرًا لَّكُمْ إِنَّمَا اللهِ إِلَهٌ وَاحِدٌ سُبْحَانَهُ أَن يَكُونَ لَهُ وَلَدٌ لَّهُ مَا فِي السَّمَاوَاتِ وَمَا فِي الأَرْضِ وَكَفَى بِاللهِ وَكِيلاً 978{النساء/171}. This style may have a softer stance of advice to the ones who cannot locate themselves but showing the proper disposition of a Christian.

On the other hand, if the person falls into shirk with the disposition of shirk and leaves monotheism, there is a more direct, straightforward, and shocking effect with the style of لَّقَدْ كَفَرَ الَّذِينَ قَالُواْ إِنَّ اللهَ ثَالِثُ ثَلاَثَةٍ وَمَا مِنْ إِلَهٍ إِلاَّ إِلَهٌ وَاحِدٌ وَإِن لَّمْ يَنتَهُواْ عَمَّا يَقُولُونَ لَيَمَسَّنَّ الَّذِينَ كَفَرُواْ مِنْهُمْ عَذَابٌ أَلِيمٌ 979{المائدة/73}. الله اعلم 980.

In the end, we as humans don't know any person's real disposition of imān. The belief, imān is between the person and Allah . In other words, we don't have the means to judge people.

---

976. And do not say, "Three"; desist—it is better for you. Indeed, Allah is but one God. Exalted is He above having a son. To Him belongs whatever is in the heavens and whatever is on the earth. And sufficient is Allah as Disposer of affairs.

977. They have certainly disbelieved who say, "Allah is the third of three." And there is no god except one God. And if they do not desist from what they are saying, there will surely afflict the disbelievers among them a painful punishment.

978. And do not say, "Three"; desist—it is better for you. Indeed, Allah is but one God. Exalted is He above having a son. To Him belongs whatever is in the heavens and whatever is on the earth. And sufficient is Allah as Disposer of affairs.

979. They have certainly disbelieved who say, "Allah is the third of three." And there is no god except one God. And if they do not desist from what they are saying, there will surely afflict the disbelievers among them a painful punishment.

980. Allah knows best.

6

Surah Maidah

[23]

قَالَ رَجُلَانِ مِنَ الَّذِينَ يَخَافُونَ أَنْعَمَ اللّهُ عَلَيْهِمَا ادْخُلُواْ عَلَيْهِمُ الْبَابَ فَإِذَا دَخَلْتُمُوهُ فَإِنَّكُمْ
غَالِبُونَ وَعَلَى اللّهِ فَتَوَكَّلُواْ إِن كُنتُم مُّؤْمِنِينَ 981 {المائدة/23}

982قَالَ رَجُلَانِ مِنَ الَّذِينَ يَخَافُونَ أَنْعَمَ اللّهُ عَلَيْهِمَا In the above ayah, the expression
is important to analyze. When Allah ﷻ gives us so much n'imah, we
unfortunately don't recognize it.

One can realize the repetition of this expression 31 times " فَبِأَيِّ آلَاء
رَبِّكُمَا تُكَذِّبَانِ 983{الرحمن/13} " in the surah of Rahman. Yet, we don't realize
this constant benefit that we receive, required for our existence and
survival.

In this ayah, the people who recognize this are mentioned as 984يَخَافُونَ
أَنْعَمَ اللّهُ عَلَيْهِمَا. In other words, when Allah ﷻ gives the person so much,
the initial step is to recognize it. Then a person can have fear after this
recognition for different possible reasons.

The person does not want to displease Allah ﷻ after Allah ﷻ gives
him or her so much. The person has the fear of losing this n'imah if he or
she displeases Allah ﷻ. In this case, if the person has this genuine stance,
then that person can pray to Allah ﷻ for guidance in the way that pleases
Allah ﷻ. 985اللهم اجعلنا منهم. امين.

---

981. Said two men from those who feared [to disobey] upon whom Allah had bestowed favor,
"Enter upon them through the gate, for when you have entered it, you will be predominant.
And upon Allah rely, if you should be believers."
982. Said two men from those who feared [to disobey] upon whom Allah had bestowed favor.
983. So which of the favors of your lord do you deny.
984. those who feared [to disobey] upon whom Allah had bestowed favor
985. Oh Allah make us from among them.

9

Surah A'raf

[120-122]

{الأعراف/120}986 وَأُلْقِيَ السَّحَرَةُ سَاجِدِينَ

{الأعراف/122}988 رَبِّ مُوسَى وَهَارُونَ {الأعراف/121}987 قَالُواْ آمَنَّا بِرِبِّ الْعَالَمِينَ

{الشعراء/48}990 رَبِّ مُوسَى وَهَارُونَ {الشعراء/47}989 قَالُوا آمَنَّا بِرَبِّ الْعَالَمِينَ

Sometimes, we admire and follow someone without any question. This can be a good and pious teacher. With what we have seen in this person during his or her life, this can make the person just trust this person fully. This trust can come especially when the person can compare this trusted friend or teacher with others. For example, in a society, if there are people who are all in the habit of lying, cheating, not being reliable, having a vulgar attitude or using vulgar language, and if a person is so upset or even disgusted with these renderings in this society, then if the person finds a person with character traits of truthfulness, reliability, gentleness and honesty, then the person can follow this friend without much question. One can compare and have empathy about Abu Bakr siddiq ra when the Prophet saw told him about Islam, he immediately followed him without any question. In this case, Abu Bakr ra could not have known about the details of Islam. He did not question the Prophet saw. But, he knew that whatever Muhammad his prior friend, and now Rasulullah ﷺ tells him, Abubakr follows without any question because he trusted Rasulullah ﷺ from what he experienced in his life with the Prophet saw before the start of messengership, SubhanAllah!

Therefore, this level of Abu Bakr ra can be called siddiqiyah. Whatever the Prophet saw did, Abu Bakr ra followed and accepted without any question, even without a second's hesitation. One can think about the case of the Mi'raj when Abu Bakr ra said, "If the Prophet said

---

986. And the magicians fell down in prostration [to Allah].
987. They said, "We have believed in the Lord of the worlds,
988. The Lord of Moses and Aaron."
989. They said, "We have believed in the Lord of the worlds,
990. The Lord of Moses and Aaron."

he did it, I believed in it." SubhanAllah! In one perspective, Abu Bakr ra was chosen to spend all of his life with Rasullullah ﷺ before and after prophethood. Therefore, Abu Bakr ra knew the Prophet saw very well.

Similarly, one can ask why the prior magicians, now these fresh believers, mention رَبِّ مُوسَى وَهَارُونَ [991] but[992] they don't say بِربِّ الْعَالَمِينَ} {الأعراف/121}, wasn't this sufficient to say? This case was similar to the above case of Abu Bakr ra. The prior magicians were possibly disgusted with the norms of their society, etc. However, when they met and witnessed the true and genuine signs shown by Musa and Harun as given by Allah ﷻ, they immediately accepted. They did not know the details of this true imān or tawhid as presented by Musa and Harun as. Therefore, they mentioned رَبِّ مُوسَى وَهَارُونَ which meant, "We trust Musa and Harun, whatever and however it should be believed in Rabbul A'lamin, we believe in it because we don't know the details of this new and fresh imān that we choose now." [993] والله اعلم.

[129]

قَالُوٓاْ أُوذِينَا مِن قَبْلِ أَن تَأْتِيَنَا وَمِن بَعْدِ مَا جِئْتَنَا قَالَ عَسَىٰ رَبُّكُمْ أَن يُهْلِكَ عَدُوَّكُمْ
وَيَسْتَخْلِفَكُمْ فِي الأَرْضِ فَيَنظُرَ كَيْفَ تَعْمَلُونَ [994]{الأعراف/129}

Sometimes, or most of the time, we judge achievements according to our exposure to difficulties. The current problems, difficulties, and oppression of Muslims through different means in different places make us feel uneasy. This uneasiness and concern should be there as mentioned by Rasulullah ﷺ in that believers are similar to a body. When an organ or part of the body hurts, all of the body feels the pain [2] [15].

Yet, in our individual lives we are at all times accountable to Allah ﷻ whether the conditions are seemingly good or evil. In other words, if one assumes a time that Muslims are all in peace and they hold the position of power in the world, the expression وَيَسْتَخْلِفَكُمْ فِي الأَرْضِ فَيَنظُرَ

---

991. The lord of Moses and Aaron.
992. They said " We have believed in the lord of the worlds.
993. Allah knows best.
994. They said, "We have been harmed before you came to us and after you have come to us." He said, "Perhaps your Lord will destroy your enemy and grant you succession in the land and see how you will do."

{129/الأعراف}995 كَيْفَ تَعْمَلُونَ in this ayah can still indicate that we will still be accountable in front of Allah ﷻ individually with our responsibilities.

Allah ﷻ is al-Adl, Just. Our purpose and aim is to please Allah ﷻ in all conditions of this short lifespan. Sometimes, holding power, position, and wealth can cause the person to displease Allah ﷻ in his or her engagements. There are many incidents of this in Muslim history.

We are required to show this struggle that our aim is to please Allah ﷻ regardless of each condition as mentioned وَيَسْتَخْلِفَكُمْ فِي الأَرْضِ فَيَنظُرَ كَيْفَ {129/الأعراف}996 تَعْمَلُونَ. Yet, we should ask and pray to Allah ﷻ 'afw and 'afiyah with the duas of Rasulullah ﷺ, for easy and comfortable means of life as we are weak.

Surah Anfal

[27-29]

يَا أَيُّهَا الَّذِينَ آمَنُواْ لاَ تَخُونُواْ اللّهَ وَالرَّسُولَ وَتَخُونُواْ أَمَانَاتِكُمْ وَأَنتُمْ تَعْلَمُونَ 997{27/الأنفال} وَاعْلَمُواْ أَنَّمَا أَمْوَالُكُمْ وَأَوْلاَدُكُمْ فِتْنَةٌ وَأَنَّ اللّهَ عِندَهُ أَجْرٌ عَظِيمٌ 998{28/الأنفال} يَا أَيُّهَا الَّذِينَ آمَنُواْ إِن تَتَّقُواْ اللّهَ يَجْعَل لَّكُمْ فُرْقَاناً وَيُكَفِّرْ عَنكُمْ سَيِّئَاتِكُمْ وَيَغْفِرْ لَكُمْ وَاللّهُ ذُو الْفَضْلِ الْعَظِيمِ 999{29/الأنفال}

One asks the question: What is the ideal expected relationship of a parent with his or her children? Allah ﷻ mentions the word أَمَانَاتِكُمْ1000 then, the phrase أَمْوَالُكُمْ وَأَوْلادُكُ1001 follows. The same word أَمَانَاتِكُمْ is also used in different places such as in surah Ahzab with a meaning of free will or free choice as interpreted by the mufassirun.If we take these meanings, amanah1002 can mean the responsibility of or being in charge of our own selves with right decision making and choice in the ways that Allah ﷻ is pleased with us.

---

995. And grant you succession in the land and see how you will do."
996. And grant you succession in the land and see how you will do."
997. O you who have believed, do not betray Allah and the Messenger or betray your trusts while you know [the consequence].
998. And know that your properties and your children are but a trial and that Allah has with Him a great reward.
999. O you who have believed, if you fear Allah, He will grant you a criterion and will remove from you your misdeeds and forgive you. And Allah is the possessor of great bounty.
1000. Your trusts.
1001. Your properties and your children.
1002. Truth.

Similarly, other amanahs are given regarding wealth, children, and the role of the husband at home or in the family with the word qawwamah.

In all of these perspectives, the person may seem to own or have authority over these externally, yet once the person forgets this responsibility in its proper terms and rather claims ownership, then all of these engagements and responsibilities can become a fitnah فِتْنَةٌ[1003], trials and tests for the person as mentioned in this ayah and in other places. This responsibility is extremely difficult to fulfill in the proper and correct expected dispositions.

In another perspective, Allah ﷻ puts us in charge or gives us psudo-authority on earth, in the universe, and in our responsibilities. This is called pseudo because the Real Authority is Allah ﷻ. This pseudo-authority may be called khalifah in its technical sense as well.

If we analyze different relationships, why and how it is called pseudo-authority, and how it becomes fitnah, tests and trials, then some different notions can be revealed.

For example, in a child and parent relationship, a parent witnesses the child's growth from infancy to childhood to the teenage years. The parents go through different difficulties and they expect certain manners and gratitude for this upbringing. Yet, when it doesn't happen, then this relationship with the child becomes a fitnah, a test or trial, for the parent because there were expectations of the parent from their children and now they are not fulfilled. Depending on the magnitude of the fitnah, the child can be belligerent or rude or even disconnect themselves from their parents claiming that the parents did not do anything for them.

In this case, the ayahs always present the solution as يَا أَيُّهَا الَّذِينَ آمَنُواْ لاَ تَخُونُواْ اللَّهَ وَ الرَّسُولَ[1004] or يَا أَيُّهَا الَّذِينَ آمَنُواْ إِن تَتَّقُواْ اللَّهَ يَجْعَل لَّكُمْ فُرْقَاناً[1005]. This shows that the person should always establish a relationship with everything with the reference point to Allah ﷻ and Rasulullah ﷺ. If the person moves on from these trials or fitnahs by turning to Allah ﷻ, then Allah ﷻ can open the doors and change these depressive and complicated situations into the openings of victory.

On another perspective, the difficulties parents go through for their children is nothing compared to the creation of this child by Allah ﷻ. In

---

1003. A trial.
1004. O you who have believed, do not betray Allah and the Messenger.
1005. O you who have believed, if you fear Allah, He will grant you a criterion

other words, really, the parents do not contribute much to their growth but Allah ﷻ makes them grow. One can compare this concept of the pseudo-authority of humans as khalifah with the Real Authority by Allah ﷻ.

Yet, there are a lot of people on earth including us, who do not truly appreciate and show gratitude to Allah ﷻ. In this regard, Allah ﷻ still feeds people every day, gives health and existence although Allah ﷻ can terminate lives at any time.

Finally, one can see that everything on earth including social and family relationships, the universe, the earth, and our own egos are given to us in order to use them as a measuring stick to truly strive and struggle to appreciate, Allah ﷻ. The ayah[1006] و ما خلقت الجن و الانس الا ليعبدون is interpreted as[1007] ليعلمون [7 or الله اعلم, ليشعرون[1008]][1009].

<h1 style="text-align:center">10</h1>

Surah Tawbah

[25]

لَقَدْ نَصَرَكُمُ اللَّهُ فِي مَوَاطِنَ كَثِيرَةٍ وَيَوْمَ حُنَيْنٍ إِذْ أَعْجَبَتْكُمْ كَثْرَتُكُمْ فَلَمْ تُغْنِ عَنكُمْ شَيْئًا وَضَاقَتْ عَلَيْكُمُ الْأَرْضُ بِمَا رَحُبَتْ ثُمَّ وَلَّيْتُم مُّدْبِرِينَ [1010]{التوبة/25}

وَعَلَى الثَّلَاثَةِ الَّذِينَ خُلِّفُواْ حَتَّى إِذَا ضَاقَتْ عَلَيْهِمُ الأَرْضُ بِمَا رَحُبَتْ وَضَاقَتْ عَلَيْهِمْ أَنفُسُهُمْ وَظَنُّواْ أَن لاَّ مَلْجَأَ مِنَ اللّهِ إِلاَّ إِلَيْهِ ثُمَّ تَابَ عَلَيْهِمْ لِيَتُوبُواْ إِنَّ اللّهَ هُوَ التَّوَّابُ الرَّحِيمُ [1011]{التوبة/118}

One of the key expressions is وَضَاقَتْ عَلَيْكُمُ الأَرْضُ بِمَا رَحُبَتْ[1012]. It can be important to analyze the above ayahs and this expression within the

---

1006. I have not created man and jinn except that they worship me.
1007. That they may know.
1008. That they may understand.
1009. Allah knows best.
1010. Allah has already given you victory in many regions and [even] on the day of hunayn, when your great number pleased you, but it did not avail you at all, and the earth was confining for you with [i.e., in spite of] its vastness; then you turned back, fleeing.
1011. And [He also forgave] the three who were left alone [i.e., boycotted, and then regretted their error] to the point that the earth closed in on them in spite of its vastness and their souls confined [i.e., anguished] them and they were certain that there is no refuge from Allah except in Him. Then He turned to them so they could repent. Indeed, Allah is the Accepting of repentance, the Merciful.
1012. That the earth closed in on them in spite of its vastness.

context of the addressee. In both cases, the addressee is the people of imān. In this case, one's true imān can necessitate that one not consent to any type of engagements that are related to the displeasure of Allah ﷻ. As the sahabah embody the true imān, the expressions of وَضَاقَتْ[1013] عَلَيْكُمُ الأَرْضُ بِمَا رَحُبَتْ can be at the peak levels in their inner feelings of this expression. One can refer to this as conscience. Rasulullah ﷺ mentions that the true imān of a person reveals itself when the person perceives going back to kufr as similar to going back to Jahannam [15]. Any type of involvement related with the displeasure of Allah ﷻ can lead to kufr incrementally. Therefore, having this type of disgust or repulsion within oneself is a desired state of true imān in the engagements displeasing Allah ﷻ.

[46]

وَلَوْ أَرَادُواْ الْخُرُوجَ لأَعَدُّواْ لَهُ عُدَّةً وَلَكِن كَرِهَ اللَّهُ انبِعَاثَهُمْ فَثَبَّطَهُمْ وَقِيلَ اقْعُدُواْ مَعَ الْقَاعِدِينَ[1014] {التوبة/46}

The word كَرِهَ in the above ayah is used in a very rare usage in the Qurān when it is attributed to Allah ﷻ. There are other places in the Qurān where the word كَرِهَ is often attributed to people. If we look at the translations of the above ayah for example:

And if they had intended to go forth, they would have prepared for it [some] preparation. But Allah disliked their being sent, so He kept them back, and they were told, "Remain [behind] with those who remain" [1]

For, had they been [truly] desirous of setting out [with thee], they would surely have made some preparation therefore: but God was averse to their taking the field, and so He caused them to hold back when it was said, "[You may] stay at home with all [the others] who stay at home." [3]

In this case, one should analyze what it is that displeases Allah ﷻ. Accordingly, with the emphasis of this word كَرِهَ as it is rarely attributed to Allah ﷻ, one should avoid these renderings and not even get close to their boundaries, [1015]الله اعلم.

1013. That the earth closed in on them in spite of its vastness.
1014. And if they had intended to go forth, they would have prepared for it [some] preparation. But Allah disliked their being sent, so He kept them back, and they were told, "Remain [behind] with those who remain."
1015. Allah knows best.

[103]

خُذْ مِنْ أَمْوَالِهِمْ صَدَقَةً تُطَهِّرُهُمْ وَتُزَكِّيهِم بِهَا وَصَلِّ عَلَيْهِمْ إِنَّ صَلَاتَكَ سَكَنٌ لَّهُمْ وَاللهُ
سَمِيعٌ عَلِيمٌ 1016{التوبة/103}

This ayah can indicate that if one wants sakinah in one's life, one should recite Salawat for Rasulullah ﷺ more often. Then, Rasulullah ﷺ responds to each Salawat as mentioned with the expression[1017] صَلِّ عَلَيْهِمْ, as the response of Rasulullah ﷺ receiving our salam and Salawat as mentioned with[1018] إِنَّ صَلَاتَكَ will inshaAllah be a source of peace, calmness and tranquility as mentioned سَكَنٌ لَّهُمْ[1019].

One can review in the Qurān that especially when the addressee is directly, implicitly, or explicitly Rasulullah ﷺ that actually, the instruction informs us to be like Rasulullah ﷺ, to follow Rasulullah ﷺ, to keep the high esteem and respect of Rasulullah ﷺ, and to implement all teachings of belief, social life, and others as exemplified by Rasulullah ﷺ. Although one may not be able to follow the sunnah fully, they know and realize that the sunnah shows the perfect and utmost application of everything at their zenith levels. With this understanding one can take every ayah of the Qurān accordingly with personal relevance inshAllah.

For example, if we review the ayah يَا أَيُّهَا الَّذِينَ آمَنُوا لَا تَدْخُلُوا بُيُوتَ النَّبِيِّ إِلَّا أَن يُؤْذَنَ لَكُمْ إِلَى طَعَامٍ غَيْرَ نَاظِرِينَ إِنَاهُ وَلَكِنْ إِذَا دُعِيتُمْ فَادْخُلُوا فَإِذَا طَعِمْتُمْ فَانتَشِرُوا وَلَا مُسْتَأْنِسِينَ لِحَدِيثٍ إِنَّ ذَلِكُمْ كَانَ يُؤْذِي النَّبِيَّ فَيَسْتَحْيِي مِنكُمْ وَاللهُ لَا يَسْتَحْيِي مِنَ الْحَقِّ وَإِذَا سَأَلْتُمُوهُنَّ مَتَاعًا فَاسْأَلُوهُنَّ مِن وَرَاءِ حِجَابٍ ذَلِكُمْ أَطْهَرُ لِقُلُوبِكُمْ وَقُلُوبِهِنَّ وَمَا كَانَ لَكُمْ أَن تُؤْذُوا رَسُولَ اللهِ وَلَا أَن تَنكِحُوا أَزْوَاجَهُ مِن بَعْدِهِ أَبَدًا إِنَّ ذَلِكُمْ كَانَ عِندَ اللهِ عَظِيمًا 1020{الأحزاب/53} one can say, in this we learn the etiquette of being a guest. Yet, how

---

1016. Take, [O Muhammad], from their wealth a charity by which you purify them and cause them increase, and invoke [Allah's blessings] upon them. Indeed, your invocations are reassurance for them. And Allah is Hearing and Knowing.
1017. And invoke [Allah's blessings] upon them.
1018. Indeed, your invocations.
1019. Reassurance for them.
1020. O you who have believed, do not enter the houses of the Prophet except when you are permitted for a meal, without awaiting its readiness. But when you are invited, then enter; and when you have eaten, disperse without seeking to remain for conversation. Indeed, that [behavior] was troubling the Prophet, and he is shy of [dismissing] you. But Allah is not shy of the truth. And when you ask [his wives] for something, ask them from behind a partition. That is purer for your hearts and their hearts. And it is not [conceivable or lawful] for you to harm the Messenger of Allah or to marry his wives after him, ever. Indeed, that would be in the sight of Allah an enormity.

can the ayah relate to me when it mentions a specific high and noble character of Rasulullah ﷺ as[1021] إِنَّ ذَٰلِكُمْ كَانَ يُؤْذِي النَّبِيَّ فَيَسْتَحْيِي مِنكُمْ.

In this case, Allah ﷻ possibly shows the adab and etiquette of being a host like Rasulullah ﷺ. In other words, it can be difficult for the host when guests are engaged in conversations and they don't want to leave the house. Yet, it is still the highest and noblest host adab to be patient and not tell them to leave as Rasulullah ﷺ practiced,[1022] الله اعلم.

[119]

يَا أَيُّهَا الَّذِينَ آمَنُوا اتَّقُوا اللَّهَ وَكُونُوا مَعَ الصَّادِقِينَ[1023] {التوبة/119}

It is interesting to analyze the word كُونُوا in the above ayah. This word can entail the strong suggested dispositions of a person within a group as the siga of this word كُونُوا can include a group or jama'ah.

In other words, sometimes a person may not know what position to take in group affiliations, especially when the group is under attack with different types of true or false defamation cases. A person may not know what to do—if he or she should defend the group or leave the group or be neutral, especially with the normative interpretations of not being involved with fitnah, as suggested by the Prophet 2] ﷺ].

In this case, the expression مَعَ الصَّادِقِينَ[1024] can have different renderings. One of the cases suggests that

when the person is with a group implementing amr bilma'ruf[1025] and nahy ani'l munkar[1026] and have the genuine teachings of the Qurān and sunnah as mentioned again around the word كُونُوا[1027] as

يَا أَيُّهَا الَّذِينَ آمَنُوا كُونُوا أَنصَارَ اللَّهِ كَمَا قَالَ عِيسَى ابْنُ مَرْيَمَ لِلْحَوَارِيِّينَ مَنْ أَنصَارِي إِلَى اللَّهِ قَالَ الْحَوَارِيُّونَ نَحْنُ أَنصَارُ اللَّهِ فَآمَنَت طَّائِفَةٌ مِّن بَنِي إِسْرَائِيلَ وَكَفَرَت طَّائِفَةٌ فَأَيَّدْنَا الَّذِينَ مَعَ آمَنُوا عَلَى عَدُوِّهِمْ فَأَصْبَحُوا ظَاهِرِينَ[1028] {الصف/14} then, the expression[1029]

1021. Indeed, that [behavior] was troubling the Prophet, and he is shy of [dismissing] you.
1022. Allah knows best.
1023. O you who have believed, fear Allah and be with those who are true.
1024. With those who are true.
1025. Command the good.
1026. Forbid the evil.
1027. And be.
1028. O you who have believed, be supporters of Allah, as when Jesus, the son of Mary, said to the disciples, "Who are my supporters for Allah?" The disciples said, "We are supporters of Allah." And a faction of the Children of Israel believed and a faction disbelieved. So We supported those who believed against their enemy, and they became dominant.
1029. Those who are true.

الصَّادِقِينَ can require not to leave them when they are being oppressed or attacked.

In addition to the above required point, another important reason to be affiliated with a group is due to dispositions of justice- individual or social justice as mentioned with the word كُونُواْ in كُونُواْ آمَنُواْ الَّذِينَ أَيُّهَا يَا قَوَّامِينَ بِالْقِسْطِ شُهَدَاء لِلّهِ وَلَوْ عَلَى أَنفُسِكُمْ أَوِ الْوَالِدَيْنِ وَالأَقْرَبِينَ إِن يَكُنْ غَنِيًّا أَوْ فَقَيرًا فَاللّهُ أَوْلَى بِهِمَا فَلاَ تَتَّبِعُواْ الْهَوَى أَن تَعْدِلُواْ وَإِن تَلْوُواْ أَوْ تُعْرِضُواْ فَإِنَّ اللّهَ كَانَ بِمَا تَعْمَلُونَ خَبِيرًا {النساء/135}[1030]. This point is emphasized as لِلّهِ قَوَّامِينَ آمَنُواْ الَّذِينَ أَيُّهَا يَا. شُهَدَاء بِالْقِسْطِ وَلاَ يَجْرِمَنَّكُمْ شَنَآنُ قَوْمٍ عَلَى أَلاَّ تَعْدِلُواْ اعْدِلُواْ هُوَ أَقْرَبُ لِلتَّقْوَى وَاتَّقُواْ اللّهَ إِنَّ اللّهَ خَبِيرٌ بِمَا تَعْمَلُونَ[1031] {المائدة/8}.

One can realize some similar meanings with the word كُونُواْ[1032] in group affiliations in other parts of the Qurān in order to understand which group the person should be affiliated with and continue this affiliation with them. One can realize in group identities that one should not blindly follow the leader but rather follow the message that the group leader instructs. This key point is mentioned again around the word كُونُواْ as:مَا كَانَ لِبَشَرٍ أَن يُؤْتِيَهُ اللّهُ الْكِتَابَ وَالْحُكْمَ وَالنُّبُوَّةَ ثُمَّ يَقُولَ لِلنَّاسِ كُونُواْ عِبَادًا لِّي مِن دُونِ اللّهِ وَلَكِن كُونُواْ رَبَّانِيِّينَ بِمَا كُنتُمْ تُعَلِّمُونَ الْكِتَابَ وَبِمَا كُنتُمْ تَدْرُسُونَ[1033] {آل عمران/79}.

Surah Yunus

[57-58]

يَا أَيُّهَا النَّاسُ قَدْ جَاءتْكُم مَّوْعِظَةٌ مِّن رَّبِّكُمْ وَشِفَاء لِّمَا فِي الصُّدُورِ وَهُدًى وَرَحْمَةٌ لِّلْمُؤْمِنِينَ {يونس/57}[1034] قُلْ بِفَضْلِ اللّهِ وَبِرَحْمَتِهِ فَبِذَلِكَ فَلْيَفْرَحُواْ هُوَ خَيْرٌ مِّمَّا يَجْمَعُونَ {يونس/58}[1035]

1030. Those who take disbelievers as allies instead of the believers. Do they seek with them honor [through power]? But indeed, honor belongs to Allah entirely.
1031. O you who have believed, be persistently standing firm for Allah, witnesses in justice, and do not let the hatred of a people prevent you from being just. Be just; that is nearer to righteousness. And fear Allah; indeed, Allah is Acquainted with what you do.
1032. And.
1033. It is not for a human [prophet] that Allah should give him the Scripture and authority and prophethood and then he would say to the people, "Be servants to me rather than Allah," but [instead, he would say], "Be pious scholars of the Lord because of what you have taught of the Scripture and because of what you have studied."
1034. O mankind, there has come to you instruction from your Lord and healing for what is in the breasts and guidance and mercy for the believers.
1035. Say, "In the bounty of Allah and in His mercy—in that let them rejoice; it is better than what they accumulate."

From the above ayahs, one can understand the ni'mah of the Qurān and Rasulullah ﷺ in the teachings of the hadith and Sunnah. One can analyze the different effects of these ni'mahs on the person: وَشِفَاء لَّمَا فِي الصُّدُورِ:[1036] Our hearts are constantly changing. Accordingly, our position of our composure symbolized with the word chest, الصُّدُور, expanding can indicate tranquility, serenity, sakina, happiness, peacefulness, and calmness. The opposite of the chest contracting can indicate stress, fears, anxiety, and depression. The absence of the Qurān and Sunnah can put the person into the squeezing spiritual kufr states of dirt, filth, dying, drowning, and suffocating being engulfed in gloomy piles of darkness. Yet, the Qurān and teachings of the Rasulullah ﷺ are شِفَاء, cure, constantly bringing the person into the spiritual states and oceans of expansion into beautiful, aromatic, shining, cool, colorful, and sakina states of imān.

وَهُدًى:[1037] The pearls and diamond teachings of the Qurān and Sunnah constantly shows guidance.

[1038] وَرَحْمَةٌ: These teachings are blessing from Allah ﷻ. In these blessings, there are multifold of barakah.

Therefore, one should really be happy, content, delightful, comfortable, satisfied, and quenched with this huge and critical Fadl[1039] and Rahmah of Allah ﷻ as mentioned بِفَضْلِ اللهِ وَبِرَحْمَتِهِ فَبِذَلِكَ فَلْيَفْرَحُوا[1040]. If one really realizes this ni'mah[1041] of Allah ﷻ, this is better than anything and everything that one can own and have relationship with as mentioned هُوَ خَيْرٌ مِّمَّا يَجْمَعُونَ[1042].

[61]

وَمَا تَكُونُ فِي شَأْنٍ وَمَا تَتْلُو مِنْهُ مِن قُرْآنٍ وَلاَ تَعْمَلُونَ مِنْ عَمَلٍ إِلاَّ كُنَّا عَلَيْكُمْ شُهُودًا إِذْ تُفِيضُونَ فِيهِ وَمَا يَعْزُبُ عَن رَّبِّكَ مِن مِّثْقَالِ ذَرَّةٍ فِي الأَرْضِ وَلاَ فِي السَّمَاء وَلاَ أَصْغَرَ مِن ذَلِكَ وَلا أَكْبَرَ إِلاَّ فِي كِتَابٍ مُّبِينٍ[1043] {يونس/61}

1036. And healing for what is in the breasts.
1037. Guidance.
1038. Mercy.
1039. Favor.
1040. "In the bounty of Allah and in His mercy—in that let them rejoice.
1041. Blessings.
1042. It is better than what they accumulate.
1043. And, [O Muhammad], you are not [engaged] in any matter or recite any of the Qurān and you [people] do not do any deed except that We are witness over you when you are involved in it. And not absent from your Lord is any [part] of an atom's weight within the earth or within the heaven or [anything] smaller than that or greater but that it is in a clear register.

This is an ayah that shows the real position of the person with Allah ﷻ. Allah ﷻ is with us in all renderings. Assuming otherwise is a shirk. Our heedlessness makes us forget this reality. Yet, the people of Allah ﷻ adjust even their sitting position due to the embodiment of this reality in their lives. They are for sure certainly careful about what they say, where they look, what they hear, who they talk with, what they do, and even, what they think. Even in the positive, calming, and solacing journeys of engagements with the Qurān through recitation, tafakkur[1044], tadabbur[1045], and tathakkur[1046], one should not forget that Allah ﷻ is fully aware of all of these engagements through emotions, mind, heart, and different unnamed faculties of the rûh and qalb.

At one perspective, this ayah amplifies and encourages the person to be in these engagements because these uplifting engagements with the Qurān are not self-induced or artificial. Yet, Allah ﷻ and all other assigned agents such as malaika witness all of them.

In the realm of religious and spiritual experience and knowledge, there is also the dilemma of concerns that are especially pushed forward by Freudian and other self-induced psychological and philosophical impulses. In these romanticisms, they try to disconnect the genuine nature of one's relationship with Allah ﷻ and they try to promote terms that would define certain emotional and mental states.

Lastly, they wrongly correlate and assume by defining terms for these states that there is a disconnect between the person and Allah ﷻ. There is no causality from one to another. Unfortunately, a lot of people are trapped with these new and updated looms of temptations amplified by the nafs and shaytan. Simply, they don't realize that one can realize and define terms, but that does not mean that they don't still exist when one establishes relationship with Allah ﷻ.

This is the biggest difference between modern psychology and the intrinsic sciences of tasawwuf[1047]. Modern psychology defines these terms. Tasawwuf goes beyond by using, updating, and expanding these terms. Tasawwuf defines and uses these definitions to apply them within the teachings of the Qurān and the Sunnah.

The relevancy point of tasawwuf is much more than the mere psychology of a person. Tasawwuf from the core of Islam, the Qurān

---

1044. Contemplating.
1045. Think deeply.
1046. Reminded {of basic reality}.
1047. Islamic mysticism.

and hadith, shows applicability, relevance, and soothing immediate outcomes of sakina, hope, tranquility, and solace with Allah ﷻ in this life and in the afterlife.

Yet, the field of psychology induces immediate mind renderings with artificial self-sufficiency and artificial confidence leading to arrogance similar to a balloon filled with air. It looks big from outside but it does not have any weight. After all of these artificial renderings, if not properly used and appropriated, and when the person does not find relevance and true application in these teachings, then the person is instructed to take the next step which is solacing oneself with the approaches of psychiatry which is is forgetting everything, but treating all these growing sicknesses with medicine and substances. The prescribed substances through these fields and unprescribed substances available on the streets illegally are the outcomes of the same wrong renderings of our time.

Instead, if one takes the next step using all of these definitions towards a useful, relevant, genuine and more scientific approach to realities with teachings of the Qurān, then these efforts of psychologists and philosophers will be complete and complementary.

One should see the knowledge presented in the Qurān and hadith as a source of data. If there is a book, data, and knowledge that is very strongly announced, stated, and declared to be sent directly from the Creator and is still precise, accurate, exact, detailed, original, complete, and authentic as a manual of the person as mentioned, لَقَدْ أَنزَلْنَا إِلَيْكُمْ كِتَابًا {الأنبياء/10}[1048] فِيهِ ذِكْرُكُمْ أَفَلَا تَعْقِلُونَ, then leaving it behind, and ignoring its teachings is unscientific and illogical.

Yet, regardless of the politics of the church and state, the grassroots need with the promotion of wellness centers in America and in the West can show this unavoidable outcome.

1048. We have certainly sent down to you a Book [i.e., the Qurān] in which is your mention. Then will you not reason?

[85]

فَقَالُواْ عَلَى اللّهِ تَوَكَّلْنَا رَبَّنَا لاَ تَجْعَلْنَا فِتْنَةً لِّلْقَوْمِ الظَّالِمِينَ [1049] {يونس/85}

When the person is scared from people's fitnah and thulm[1050], then this dua is very critical to read and ask from Allah ﷻ as رَبَّنَا لَا تَجْعَلْنَا فِتْنَةً لِّلْقَوْمِ[1051] الظَّالِمِينَ.

12

Surah Hud

[11]

إلاَّ الَّذِينَ صَبَرُواْ وَعَمِلُواْ الصَّالِحَاتِ أُوْلَئِكَ لَهُم مَّغْفِرَةٌ وَأَجْرٌ كَبِيرٌ [1052] {هود/11}

One of the key words in surah Hud is sabr, patience. Yet, it is very difficult to achieve.

[45-46]

وَنَادَى نُوحٌ رَّبَّهُ فَقَالَ رَبِّ إِنَّ ابْنِي مِنْ أَهْلِي وَإِنَّ وَعْدَكَ الْحَقُّ وَأَنتَ أَحْكَمُ الْحَاكِمِينَ [1053] {هود/45}

قَالَ يَا نُوحُ إِنَّهُ لَيْسَ مِنْ أَهْلِكَ إِنَّهُ عَمَلٌ غَيْرُ صَالِحٍ فَلاَ تَسْأَلْنِ مَا لَيْسَ لَكَ بِهِ عِلْمٌ إِنِّي أَعِظُكَ أَنْ تَكُونَ مِنَ الْجَاهِلِينَ [1054] {هود/46}

It is interesting to analyze the above ayah around the word and notion of أَهْل. One can ask: What is the definition of ahil? Is it the blood relationship? This notion can mean the closest or intimate circle or family of a person with whom the person is working toward the same

---

1049. So they said, "Upon Allah do we rely. Our Lord, make us not [objects of] trial for the wrongdoing people.

1050. Oppression.

1051. Our Lord, make us not [objects of] trial for the wrongdoing people.

1052. Except for those who are patient and do righteous deeds; those will have forgiveness and great reward.

1053. And Noah called to his Lord and said, "My Lord, indeed my son is of my family; and indeed, Your promise is true; and You are the most just of judges!"

1054. He said, "O Noah, indeed he is not of your family; indeed, he is [one whose] work was other than righteous, so ask Me not for that about which you have no knowledge. Indeed, I advise you, lest you be among the ignorant."

goal of pleasing Allah ﷻ. In this perspective of the above ayah, although a person can have a child, if the child does not work with others to please Allah ﷻ then this child is excluded from the circle of ٱللّٰه اعلم [1055] أَهْل.

Surah Yusuf

[13-14 & 17]

قَالَ إِنِّي لَيَحْزُنُنِي أَن تَذْهَبُواْ بِهِ وَأَخَافُ أَن يَأْكُلَهُ الذِّئْبُ وَأَنتُمْ عَنْهُ غَافِلُونَ [1056] {يوسف/13}
قَالُواْ لَئِنْ أَكَلَهُ الذِّئْبُ وَنَحْنُ عُصْبَةٌ إِنَّا إِذًا لَّخَاسِرُونَ [1057] {يوسف/14}

قَالُواْ يَا أَبَانَا إِنَّا ذَهَبْنَا نَسْتَبِقُ وَتَرَكْنَا يُوسُفَ عِندَ مَتَاعِنَا فَأَكَلَهُ الذِّئْبُ وَمَا أَنتَ بِمُؤْمِنٍ لَّنَا وَلَوْ كُنَّا صَادِقِينَ [1058] {يوسف/17}

It is interesting to analyze the above ayahs around the key word [1059] الذِّئْبُ. One can drive multiple different points from this word.

One can be the modern approach of opportunistic theories in our time. Yaqub as as the father gives them a possible reason and the children use the same reason against their father as an opportunistic approach, ٱللّٰه اعلم, (Sûrah Yûsuf) [4]. They use the same argument against their father. In argumentation rules and etiquette, it is expected that one should have some respect and well-mannered discourse with one's teacher and parents. Sometimes, the person may not want to win the argument or debate because the other party is the parent or one's respected teacher. The person intentionally and purposefully lets the other person win it and lets the argument be over. This is not the case here.

In children and parent relationships, one should never give a possible excuse to a child that he or she can later use against the parent in a different context. In other words, a parent can sincerely give an example to teach the child. Yet, the children may use this example for his or her selfish benefit against the parent later although the parent

---

1055. Allah knows best.
1056. [Jacob] said, "Indeed, it saddens me that you should take him, and I fear that a wolf would eat him while you are of him unaware."
1057. They said, "If a wolf should eat him while we are a [strong] clan, indeed, we would then be losers."
1058. They said, "O our father, indeed we went racing each other and left Joseph with our possessions, and a wolf ate him. But you would not believe us, even if we were truthful."
1059. A wolf.

used this example in another context, but the children can misuse it. SubhanAllah, this may be experienced already by many Muslims.

[24]

وَلَقَدْ هَمَّتْ بِهِ وَهَمَّ بِهَا لَوْلَا أَن رَّأَى بُرْهَانَ رَبِّهِ كَذَلِكَ لِنَصْرِفَ عَنْهُ السُّوءَ وَالْفَحْشَاء إِنَّهُ مِنْ عِبَادِنَا الْمُخْلَصِينَ 1060{يوسف/24}

It is interesting to note that when a person is on the path of Allah ﷻ sincerely similar to the people of mukhlas as mentioned عِبَادِنَا الْمُخْلَصِينَ 1061, it is always possible that Allah ﷻ can stop and block some evils as mentioned السُّوءَ وَالْفَحْشَاء 1062 afflicting him or her. This can be done through different means as mentioned بُرْهَانَ رَبِّهِ 1063. The person may or may not understand the purpose of these means immediately. Yet, these means have a purpose and this purpose is to help this person and protect him or her from possible evil outcomes as mentioned لِنَصْرِفَ عَنْهُ 1064.

[62]

وَقَالَ لِفِتْيَانِهِ اجْعَلُواْ بِضَاعَتَهُمْ فِي رِحَالِهِمْ لَعَلَّهُمْ يَعْرِفُونَهَا إِذَا انقَلَبُواْ إِلَى أَهْلِهِمْ لَعَلَّهُمْ يَرْجِعُونَ 1065{يوسف/62}

One can review in the above one of the marketing strategies. To make the customer come back, the customer can realize that there is a "win-win" situation in this transaction.

[64-67]

قَالَ هَلْ آمَنُكُمْ عَلَيْهِ إِلاَّ كَمَا أَمِنتُكُمْ عَلَى أَخِيهِ مِن قَبْلُ فَاللّهُ خَيْرٌ حَافِظًا وَهُوَ أَرْحَمُ الرَّاحِمِينَ 1066{يوسف/64} وَلَمَّا فَتَحُواْ مَتَاعَهُمْ وَجَدُواْ بِضَاعَتَهُمْ رُدَّتْ إِلَيْهِمْ قَالُواْ يَا أَبَانَا

1060. And she certainly determined [to seduce him], and he would have inclined to her had he not seen the proof [i.e., sign] of his Lord. And thus [it was] that We should avert from him evil and immorality. Indeed, he was of Our chosen servants.
1061. Our chosen servants.
1062. Evil and immorality.
1063. The proof [i.e., sign] of his Lord.
1064. That We should avert from him.
1065. And [Joseph] said to his servants, "Put their merchandise into their saddlebags so they might recognize it when they have gone back to their people that perhaps they will [again] return."
1066. He said, "Should I entrust you with him except [under coercion] as I entrusted you with his brother before? But Allah is the best guardian, and He is the most merciful of the merciful."

مَا نَبْغِي هَذِهِ بِضَاعَتُنَا رُدَّتْ إِلَيْنَا وَنَمِيرُ أَهْلَنَا وَنَحْفَظُ أَخَانَا وَنَزْدَادُ كَيْلَ بَعِيرٍ ذَلِكَ كَيْلٌ يَسِيرٌ {يوسف/65} 1067 قَالَ لَنْ أُرْسِلَهُ مَعَكُمْ حَتَّى تُؤْتُونِ مَوْثِقًا مِّنَ اللهِ لَتَأْتُنَّنِي بِهِ إِلَّا أَن يُحَاطَ بِكُمْ فَلَمَّا آتَوْهُ مَوْثِقَهُمْ قَالَ اللهُ عَلَى مَا نَقُولُ وَكِيلٌ {يوسف/66} 1068 وَقَالَ يَا بَنِيَّ لَا تَدْخُلُواْ مِن بَابٍ وَاحِدٍ وَادْخُلُواْ مِنْ أَبْوَابٍ مُّتَفَرِّقَةٍ وَمَا أُغْنِي عَنكُم مِّنَ اللهِ مِن شَيْءٍ إِنِ الْحُكْمُ إِلاَّ لِلّهِ عَلَيْهِ تَوَكَّلْتُ وَعَلَيْهِ فَلْيَتَوَكَّلِ الْمُتَوَكِّلُونَ {يوسف/67} 1069

Then, this is the exact argument that the children make against Yaqub as as they mention قَالُواْ يَا أَبَانَا مَا نَبْغِي هَذِهِ بِضَاعَتُنَا رُدَّتْ إِلَيْنَا 1070.

Yet, if one analyzes the approach of Yaqub as in the beginning قَالَ 1071 هَلْ آمَنُكُمْ عَلَيْهِ إِلاَّ كَمَا أَمِنتُكُمْ عَلَى أَخِيهِ مِن قَبْلُ فَاللهُ خَيْرٌ حَافِظًا, Yaqub as mentions one of the Names of Allah ﷻ as فَاللهُ خَيْرٌ حَافِظًا 1072. Then, the children use the same argument with the same word when they mention وَنَحْفَظُ 1073 أَخَانَا. One can realize that the children used the same argument in the case of Yusuf as being eaten by a wolf. First, Yaqub as mentioned it and the children used it against their father.

In this process similar to a chess game, when the person makes their move with the projection of the other party then, there is the possibility of the person getting what they want.

If we take the above dialogue with the current approaches of decision or game theory [31], Yusuf as is above them with the basirah, hikmah 1074 that Yusuf as can project their action by putting their initial asset. This is using the basirah, hikmah, or game or decision theory strategies in a good way.

1067. And when they opened their baggage, they found their merchandise returned to them. They said, "O our father, what [more] could we desire? This is our merchandise returned to us. And we will obtain supplies [i.e., food] for our family and protect our brother and obtain an increase of a camel's load; that is an easy measurement."

1068. [Jacob] said, "Never will I send him with you until you give me a promise [i.e., oath] by Allah that you will bring him [back] to me, unless you should be surrounded [i.e., overcome by enemies]." And when they had given their promise, he said, "Allah, over what we say, is Witness."

1069. And he said, "O my sons, do not enter from one gate but enter from different gates; and I cannot avail you against [the decree of] Allah at all. The decision is only for Allah; upon Him I have relied, and upon Him let those who would rely [indeed] rely."

1070. They said, "O our father, what [more] could we desire? This is our merchandise returned to us.

1071. He said, "Should I entrust you with him except [under coercion] as I entrusted you with his brother before? But Allah is the best guardian.

1072. But Allah is the best guardian.

1073. And protect our brother.

1074. Wisdom.

On the other hand, Yaqub as can know the outcomes of these engagements as the Prophet of Allah ﷻ. Yet, as a show of respect to the external causes, signs, and reasons, Yaqub as prefers to be the embodiment of tawakkul, reliance, and patience, sabir. This case can be similar to the case of Uhud. Rasulullah ﷺ knew the result of the war and losses as the Prophet of Allah ﷻ. Yet, with a similar approach of establishing causality relations through mashwarah, or istisharah among humans, Rasulullah ﷺ executed the majority's opinion in joining the battle of Uhud,[1075] الله اعلم.

14

Surah Hijr

وَلَقَدْ جَعَلْنَا فِي السَّمَاء بُرُوجًا وَزَيَّنَّاهَا لِلنَّاظِرِينَ [1076]{الحجر/16}

Some of the key words that can be focused on in this ayah can be زَيَّنَّاهَا[1077] and لِلنَّاظِرِينَ[1078]. The first word زَيَّنَّاهَا can indicate the perfection, the beauty, the order, and the structure in all of the creation of Allah ﷻ. The second word لِلنَّاظِرِينَ can indicate the divine encouragement for humans and jinn to uncover, recognize, and appreciate all of the ni'mahs[1079] of Allah ﷻ.

The words seeing with ru'ya and looking with nazar can have differences. Nazar as mentioned in this ayah لِلنَّاظِرِينَ can indicate seeing with the efforts of thinking, recognizing, and appreciating.

This ayah can indicate the possibilities of observing the sky with the intention of fulfilling the encouragement in this ayah. This can be observing the sky at night or in the daytime with the intention of increasing one's iman about how Allah ﷻ created everything perfectly and beautifully as one of the Names of Allah ﷻ is Al-Jamal[1080].

In addition, the engagements as a profession in astronomy, physics, and space-related sciences can transform one's job-related engagements

---

1075. Allah knows best.
1076. And We have placed within the heaven great stars and have beautified it for the observers.
1077. Have beautified it.
1078. For the observers.
1079. Blessings.
1080. The Beautiful.

to a superior purpose of increasing one's imān in Allah ﷻ with one's intention of fulfilling the encouragement in this ayah. The similar case can be present with one's intention in other types of professions such as medicine.

Surah Nahl

[89]

وَيَوْمَ نَبْعَثُ فِي كُلِّ أُمَّةٍ شَهِيدًا عَلَيْهِم مِّنْ أَنفُسِهِمْ وَجِئْنَا بِكَ شَهِيدًا عَلَى هَؤُلَاء وَنَزَّلْنَا
عَلَيْكَ الْكِتَابَ تِبْيَانًا لِّكُلِّ شَيْءٍ وَهُدًى وَرَحْمَةً وَبُشْرَى لِلْمُسْلِمِينَ 1081 {النحل/89}

The sababi-nuzul[1082] of the above in its original, focused, and hass application can indicate Rasulullah ﷺ as mentioned جِئْنَا بِكَ شَهِيدًا[1083]. The rusul of other ummahs can be indicated with فِي كُلِّ أُمَّةٍ شَهِيدًا[1084].

In it's a'mm and general application, the testimony وَيَوْمَ نَبْعَثُ فِي كُلِّ[1085] أُمَّةٍ شَهِيدًا عَلَيْهِم مِّنْ أَنفُسِهِمْ can possibly indicate the teachers, shuyukh, and the ones who are being followed. In this perspective, teaching someone is good and encouraged especially in the matters of the original teachings of the Qurān and sunnah. Yet, if there are any problems and issues in these teachings and people follow the person, being in front of Allah ﷻ as a teacher and with these followers can be a very heart-stopping disposition, may Allah ﷻ protect us, Ameen.

In this perspective, the approaches of the tariqahs' proposal to authenticate their chain, silsilah, going back to Rasulullah ﷺ can be somehow comforting. At the same time, it can be risky. What if Rasulullah ﷺ does not accept this authenticity claim or being linked to his teachings? Both true declarations and false claims will all be finalized in Yawmul Qiyamah, may Allah ﷻ protect us, Ameen.

1081. And [mention] the Day when We will resurrect among every nation a witness over them from themselves [i.e., their prophet]. And We will bring you, [O Muhammad], as a witness over these [i.e., your nation]. And We have sent down to you the Book as clarification for all things and as guidance and mercy and good tidings for the Muslims.
1082. Reason of narration.
1083. And We will bring you, [O Muhammad], as a witness.
1084. Among every nation a witness.
1085. And [mention] the Day when We will resurrect among every nation a witness over them from themselves [i.e., their prophet].

In this perspective, one can possibly better understand the expression[1086] وَجِئْنَا بِكَ شَهِيدًا عَلَى هَؤُلَاء. There are small or big groups, silsalas, schools among Muslims as well as among ummahs prior to Rasulullah ﷺ including ummah of Musa as, Isa as, and all others mentioned and not mentioned in the Qurān. Yet, Rasulullah ﷺ is the controller, overseer, imam, and shahid[1087] of all [9]. This shows another high level of Rasulullah ﷺ. As we are again in full appreciation to Allah ﷻ that we are the direct followers of al-Imam, as-Shahid, Rasulullah ﷺ.

15

Surah Kahf

[28]

وَاصْبِرْ نَفْسَكَ مَعَ الَّذِينَ يَدْعُونَ رَبَّهُم بِالْغَدَاةِ وَالْعَشِيِّ يُرِيدُونَ وَجْهَهُ وَلَا تَعْدُ عَيْنَاكَ عَنْهُمْ تُرِيدُ زِينَةَ الْحَيَاةِ الدُّنْيَا وَلَا تُطِعْ مَنْ أَغْفَلْنَا قَلْبَهُ عَن ذِكْرِنَا وَاتَّبَعَ هَوَاهُ وَكَانَ أَمْرُهُ فُرُطًا[1088] {الكهف/28}

It is interesting to analyze the expression وَاصْبِرْ نَفْسَكَ[1089]. If one approaches this expression literally, one can realize the constant struggle of a person with one's own raw self, nafs. Yet, the nafs constantly asks evil, shahwat, bad thoughts or feelings. A person who is aware of all of these desires of nafs, with the grace of Allah ﷻ, can try to divert and guide these desires to the halal and virtuous engagements. However, it is very difficult because the nafs incessantly wants and seeks to be in the valleys of desires.

Therefore, وَاصْبِرْ نَفْسَكَ can show this very intimate yet very difficuly struggle.

At another level, Allah ﷻ teaches us to be together with the people who have this understanding of self-struggle and not be alone on this spiritual difficult journey as mentioned مَعَ الَّذِينَ يَدْعُونَ رَبَّهُم بِالْغَدَاةِ وَالْعَشِيِّ[1090].

1086. And We will bring you, [O Muhammad], as a witness over these [i.e., your nation].
1087. Witness.
1088. And keep yourself patient [by being] with those who call upon their Lord in the morning and the evening, seeking His countenance. And let not your eyes pass beyond them, desiring adornments of the worldly life, and do not obey one whose heart We have made heedless of Our remembrance and who follows his desire and whose affair is ever [in] neglect.
1089. And keep yourself patient.
1090. With those who call upon their Lord in the morning and the evening.

In the end, the people who are in struggle with their own selves aim to please Allah ﷻ يُرِيدُونَ وَجْهَهُ[1091].

The expression وَلَا تَعْدُ عَيْنَاكَ عَنْهُمْ[1092] can allude to the responsibility of teaching and helping others, or it can indicate the difficulty of being alone in full solitude in the betterment of one's self. Rasulullah ﷺ mentions that "the barakah of Allah ﷻ is with the jama'ah, in social solidarity [16]". Or, it can have both meanings[1093], الله اعلم.

16

Surah Kahf

[80-82]

وَأَمَّا الْغُلَامُ فَكَانَ أَبَوَاهُ مُؤْمِنَيْنِ فَخَشِينَا أَن يُرْهِقَهُمَا طُغْيَانًا وَكُفْرًا[1094] {الكهف/80}
فَأَرَدْنَا أَن يُبْدِلَهُمَا رَبُّهُمَا خَيْرًا مِّنْهُ زَكَاةً وَأَقْرَبَ رُحْمًا[1095] {الكهف/81} وَأَمَّا الْجِدَارُ
فَكَانَ لِغُلَامَيْنِ يَتِيمَيْنِ فِي الْمَدِينَةِ وَكَانَ تَحْتَهُ كَنزٌ لَّهُمَا وَكَانَ أَبُوهُمَا صَالِحًا فَأَرَادَ رَبُّكَ
أَنْ يَبْلُغَا أَشُدَّهُمَا وَيَسْتَخْرِجَا كَنزَهُمَا رَحْمَةً مِّن رَّبِّكَ وَمَا فَعَلْتُهُ عَنْ أَمْرِي ذَلِكَ تَأْوِيلُ مَا
لَمْ تَسْطِع عَّلَيْهِ صَبْرًا[1096] {الكهف/82}

When one analyzes the words in the above ayahs فَأَرَدْنَا[1097] and فَأَرَادَ[1098] رَبُّكَ, in the first case the angels or other possible means can work under the command of Allah ﷻ to execute the order of Allah ﷻ as mentioned with فَأَرَدْنَا. In the latter case, it is about taking care of orphans that Allah ﷻ directly attributes to the Zat, the Divine Self with the expression فَأَرَادَ رَبُّكَ. One can also relate to a similar rendering when the Prophet saw mentions that he will be so close to the person who takes care of the needs of an orphan and the Prophet saw points to two adjacent fingers

---

1091. Seeking His countenance.
1092. And let not your eyes pass beyond them.
1093. Allah knows best.
1094. And as for the boy, his parents were believers, and we feared that he would overburden them by transgression and disbelief.
1095. So we intended that their Lord should substitute for them one better than him in purity and nearer to mercy.
1096. And as for the wall, it belonged to two orphan boys in the city, and there was beneath it a treasure for them, and their father had been righteous. So your Lord intended that they reach maturity and extract their treasure, as a mercy from your Lord. And I did it not of my own accord. That is the interpretation of that about which you could not have patience."
1097. So we intended.
1098. So your Lord intended.

in order to indicate this closeness. One can see how the importance of taking care of an orphan is reflected in the wording of the ayah, اعلم الله[1099].

[109]

قُل لَّوْ كَانَ الْبَحْرُ مِدَادًا لِّكَلِمَاتِ رَبِّي لَنَفِدَ الْبَحْرُ قَبْلَ أَن تَنفَدَ كَلِمَاتُ رَبِّي وَلَوْ جِئْنَا بِمِثْلِهِ مَدَدًا[1100] {الكهف/109}

وَلَوْ أَنَّمَا فِي الْأَرْضِ مِن شَجَرَةٍ أَقْلَامٌ وَالْبَحْرُ يَمُدُّهُ This ayah with similar ayahs of مِن بَعْدِهِ سَبْعَةُ أَبْحُرٍ مَّا نَفِدَتْ كَلِمَاتُ اللَّهِ إِنَّ اللَّهَ عَزِيزٌ حَكِيمٌ[1101] {لقمان/27} can indicate different possibilities.

The scholars of religion should not be arrogant when they understand the Qurān and scriptures. Allah ﷻ can send scriptures, rolls, and tablets that could have Infinite quantity and quality of data explaining and detailing the Uluhuiyyah[1102] and Rububiyyah[1103] of Allah ﷻ as well as contents as presented in the Qurān and hadith and others.

Sometimes, after a writer starts, he or she may not stop writing due to the zeal and constant flowing ideas in his or her mind due to the Grace and Fadl[1104] of Allah ﷻ. Yet, Allah ﷻ mentions that Allah ﷻ is the One Who has the Real and Infinite knowledge.

On another note, these ayahs encourage people to constantly learn until they die. There is no limit in learning the ma'rifatullah[1105], the knowledge and experiences about Allah ﷻ as Allah is Al-Baqi[1106], without any limits.

1099. Allah knows best.
1100. Say, "If the sea were ink for [writing] the words of my Lord, the sea would be exhausted before the words of my Lord were exhausted, even if We brought the like of it as a supplement."
1101. And if whatever trees upon the earth were pens and the sea [was ink], replenished thereafter by seven [more] seas, the words of Allah would not be exhausted. Indeed, Allah is Exalted in Might and Wise.
1102. Realm pf power.
1103. Lordship.
1104. Favor.
1105. Knowledge of Allah ﷻ.
1106. The Everlasting; The Eternal.

17

Surah Hajj

وَمِنَ النَّاسِ مَن يُجَادِلُ فِي اللَّهِ بِغَيْرِ عِلْمٍ وَيَتَّبِعُ كُلَّ شَيْطَانٍ مَّرِيدٍ [1107]{الحج/3}

وَمِنَ النَّاسِ مَن يُجَادِلُ فِي اللَّهِ بِغَيْرِ عِلْمٍ وَلَا هُدًى وَلَا كِتَابٍ مُّنِيرٍ [1108]{الحج/8}

In the first case, there is a group of people who defend evil by merely following others without thinking as mentioned كُلَّ شَيْطَانٍ مَّرِيدٍ [1109]. In the other case, there is another group of people who defend evil by using demagogy but not critical thinking, any type of guidance, or scientific clear methods as mentioned[1110] وَلَا هُدًى وَلَا كِتَابٍ مُّنِيرٍ. In both cases, there is no critical thinking, or guidance but both are following their desires. The first are followers and the second are their leaders, [9] والله اعلم[1111].

[11]

وَمِنَ النَّاسِ مَن يَعْبُدُ اللَّهَ عَلَى حَرْفٍ فَإِنْ أَصَابَهُ خَيْرٌ اطْمَأَنَّ بِهِ وَإِنْ أَصَابَتْهُ فِتْنَةٌ انقَلَبَ عَلَى وَجْهِهِ خَسِرَ الدُّنْيَا وَالْآخِرَةَ ذَلِكَ هُوَ الْخُسْرَانُ الْمُبِينُ [1112]{الحج/11}

The above ayah can be first analyzed in its context of sabab-nuzul[1113]. As it was reported, there were people in Madinah who gained some sustenance with Islam but later, they somehow lost these bounties and turned away from the initial disposition of being a true Muslim [9].

Yet, this ayah can also shed lights for us about how we engage ourselves with the teachings of Islam. There is a very subtle and fine point between one's advancement of piety and practice in the religion and the amount of worldly gains. Sometimes, when this subtle point is

---

1107. And of the people is he who disputes about Allah without knowledge and follows every rebellious devil.
1108. And of the people is he who disputes about Allah without knowledge or guidance or an enlightening book [from Him],
1109. And follows every rebellious devil.
1110. Without knowledge or guidance or an enlightening book [from Him].
1111. Allah knows best.
1112. And of the people is he who worships Allah on an edge. If he is touched by good, he is reassured by it; but if he is struck by trial, he turns on his face [to the other direction]. He has lost [this] world and the Hereafter. That is what is the manifest loss.
1113. Reason for narration.

overlooked or missed, then the person can change his or her disposition, may Allah ﷻ protect us, Ameen

Surah Nûr

[41]

أَلَمْ تَرَ أَنَّ اللَّهَ يُسَبِّحُ لَهُ مَن فِي السَّمَاوَاتِ وَالْأَرْضِ وَالطَّيْرُ صَافَّاتٍ كُلٌّ قَدْ عَلِمَ صَلَاتَهُ وَتَسْبِيحَهُ وَاللَّهُ عَلِيمٌ بِمَا يَفْعَلُونَ[1114] {النور/41}

This ayah is very interesting especially if one analyzes around the declaration of كُلٌّ قَدْ عَلِمَ صَلَاتَهُ وَتَسْبِيحَهُ[1115]. This ayah is really important to analyze our position, purpose, and reality of existence within the creation of other beings, animals, plants, stars, galaxies, and every creation that is known or unknown to us.

According to Imam Razi [9], وَالطَّيْرُ[1116] is mentioned because they are between the السَّمَاوَاتِ وَالْأَرْضِ[1117]. According to Imam Baghawi [10], he narrates from Mujahid rhas والتسبيح لسائر الخلق[1119]، لصلاة لبني آدم[1118], that salah is especially given as a gift of remembrance of Allah ﷻ to humans and dhikr in the form of tasbih given to all other creation.

19

Surah Furqan

[32]

وَقَالَ الَّذِينَ كَفَرُوا لَوْلَا نُزِّلَ عَلَيْهِ الْقُرْآنُ جُمْلَةً وَاحِدَةً كَذَلِكَ لِنُثَبِّتَ بِهِ فُؤَادَكَ وَرَتَّلْنَاهُ تَرْتِيلًا[1120]{الفرقان/32}

1114. Do you not see that Allah is exalted by whomever is within the heavens and the earth and [by] the birds with wings spread [in flight]? Each [of them] has known his [means of] prayer and exalting [Him], and Allah is Knowing of what they do.
1115. Each [of them] has known his [means of] prayer and exalting [Him].
1116. [By] the birds.
1117. The heavens and the earth.
1118. To pray for the children of Adam.
1119. And praise the rest of creation.
1120. And those who disbelieve say, "Why was the Quran not revealed to him all at once?" Thus [it is] that We may strengthen thereby your heart. And We have spaced it distinctly.

Especially, we are in the area of everything being customized or individualized. One can think about customized drinks, individualized education plans, etc. Then, one can really realize another miracle of the Qurān- that the revelation was in pieces and individualized as the last scripture to be valid until the End of Days in accordance with the trends of time and people. With all of the other clear signs, this can make the person again say " اشهد ان لا اله الا الله و اشهد ان محمد رسول الله[1121] "

The ahlu-kitab can assert that since their scripture was revealed at once it can bear more authenticity. Although one can initially consider this miracle form of Tawrāh, each book and scripture can fill the need and target the audience of its time.

On another perspective, each case of the Qurān's individual ayahs being revealed to Rasulullah ﷺ can be similar to the full Tawrah being revealed at once. In other words, if previously there was a miraculous event of a one-time nuzūl of Tawrah, then there were numerous events of nuzūls of revelations to Rasulullah ﷺ. So, if we look at the quantity of the miraculous events at the encounter of the Qurān with the case of revelation, then one can realize that there are even more due to the process of the numerous piece-by-piece revelation, الله اعلم[1122].

One can review the word inzāl in the Qurān with different forms of its usage to allude to the fact of the process of piece-by-piece revelation.

[33]

وَلَا يَأْتُونَكَ بِمَثَلٍ إِلَّا جِئْنَاكَ بِالْحَقِّ وَأَحْسَنَ تَفْسِيرًا [1123] {الفرقان/33}

SubhanAllah, this ayah along with others in the Qurān, educates us of the need for the sweet uslub and style of teaching to others. In other words, when we are in the position of teaching our children, family members, and others, we sometimes tend to get angry and not be nice. Yet, the Qurān constantly addresses humans' minds, hearts, and all of the different faculties to repair and block any types of spiritual holes caused by temptations, evil thoughts, and the renderings of Shaytan and one's own nafs.

1121. I bear witness that there is no god except Allah ﷻ, and I bear witness that Muhammed ﷺ is the prophet of Allah ﷻ.
1122. Allah ﷻ knows best.
1123. And they do not come to you with an example [i.e., argument] except that We bring you the truth and the best explanation.

In this perspective, when one analyzes the above ayah, the ayah mentions the possible arguments that people can bring into the discourses of the religion. Yet, Allah ﷻ mentions that the examples and the logic that are presented in the Qurān are true, real, logical, consistent, rational, coherent, clear, and much better than theirs. A person of sound mind and heart can easily differentiate them.

[61-62]

تَبَارَكَ الَّذِي جَعَلَ فِي السَّمَاءِ بُرُوجًا وَجَعَلَ فِيهَا سِرَاجًا وَقَمَرًا مُنِيرًا 1124{الفرقان/61}
وَهُوَ الَّذِي جَعَلَ اللَّيْلَ وَالنَّهَارَ خِلْفَةً لِمَنْ أَرَادَ أَن يَذَّكَّرَ أَوْ أَرَادَ شُكُورًا 1125{الفرقان/62}

It is important to realize that change is a n'imah from Allah ﷻ. When a person observes this change in nature and in oneself with the correct tools of imān, then the person can constantly increase his or her connection and marifah of Allah ﷻ as mentioned with أَن يَذَّكَّرَ[1126]. Once the person realizes and recognizes this constant change as a ni'mah, then the person is expected to make shukr as mentioned شُكُورًا[1127] {الفرقان/62}.

One can analyze the above ayahs around the different types of light and how we benefit from them, and how the change of light in their intensity, color, and frequency can affect us. One can observe with different types of lights emitted or encountered from stars, the sun, and reflected from the moon as mentioned تَبَارَكَ الَّذِي جَعَلَ فِي السَّمَاءِ بُرُوجًا وَجَعَلَ فِيهَا سِرَاجًا وَقَمَرًا مُنِيرًا[1128] {الفرقان/61}.

One can analyze change of type and intensity of light with the change of day and night as mentioned وَهُوَ الَّذِي جَعَلَ اللَّيْلَ وَالنَّهَارَ خِلْفَةً[1129].

On the other hand, one can analyze today's light industry detailing all of these for our daily applications as soft light, white light, day light, blue light, or yellow light. There are studies showing the effect of different types of light with their intensity and color affecting human psychology and physiology [5]. One can also analyze why or how our spiritual

---

1124. Blessed is He who has placed in the sky great stars and placed therein a [burning] lamp and luminous moon.
1125. And it is He who has made the night and the day in succession for whoever desires to remember or desires gratitude.
1126. To remember.
1127. Gratitude.
1128. Blessed is He who has placed in the sky great stars and placed therein a [burning] lamp and luminous moon.
1129. And it is He who has made the night and the day in succession.

faculties are affected by different types of light with their intensity causing brightness, gloominess, darkness, and other possibilities.

In this sense this change of light in the day or night with other factors are all ni'mah[1130] from Allah ﷻ as mentioned also in:

قُلْ أَرَأَيْتُمْ إِن جَعَلَ اللَّهُ عَلَيْكُمُ اللَّيْلَ سَرْمَدًا إِلَى يَوْمِ الْقِيَامَةِ مَنْ إِلَهٌ غَيْرُ اللَّهِ يَأْتِيكُم بِضِيَاءٍ أَفَلَا تَسْمَعُونَ {القصص/71}[1131] قُلْ أَرَأَيْتُمْ إِن جَعَلَ اللَّهُ عَلَيْكُمُ النَّهَارَ سَرْمَدًا إِلَى يَوْمِ الْقِيَامَةِ مَنْ إِلَهٌ غَيْرُ اللَّهِ يَأْتِيكُم بِلَيْلٍ تَسْكُنُونَ فِيهِ أَفَلَا تُبْصِرُونَ {القصص/72}[1132] وَمِن رَّحْمَتِهِ جَعَلَ لَكُمُ اللَّيْلَ وَالنَّهَارَ لِتَسْكُنُوا فِيهِ وَلِتَبْتَغُوا مِن فَضْلِهِ وَلَعَلَّكُمْ تَشْكُرُونَ {القصص/73}[1133]

At this time, we have timetables for sunset and sunrise for all different places in the world. There are places in the world which have very limited sunlight at certain times of the year. One can survey the psychology of the people who appreciate the limited sunlight on those days. They may try to achieve what they need to at those times. The modern concept of daylight savings arrangement of global change of times alludes to this fact that the people try to use the sunlight and benefit from it. So, Allah ﷻ alludes to this global current practice of changing nights and daylight. In this regard, although it is very clear, a lot of people can take this for granted like other ni'mahs, bounties of Allah ﷻ and be in the category of non-appreciation. As mentioned in وَمِن رَّحْمَتِهِ جَعَلَ لَكُمُ اللَّيْلَ وَالنَّهَارَ لِتَسْكُنُوا فِيهِ وَلِتَبْتَغُوا مِن فَضْلِهِ وَلَعَلَّكُمْ تَشْكُرُونَ {القصص/73}[1134], these are all from the Rahmah and Fadl of Allah ﷻ that a person realizes it, appreciates it, and makes shukr as mentioned in وَلَعَلَّكُمْ تَشْكُرُونَ[1135].

Therefore, one should recognize all of these n'imahs from Allah ﷻ and constantly be in the state of shukur and hamd as mentioned لِّمَنْ أَرَادَ أَن يَذَّكَّرَ أَوْ أَرَادَ شُكُورًا {الفرقان/62}[1136].

1130. Blessings.
1131. Say, "Have you considered: if Allah should make for you the night continuous until the Day of Resurrection, what deity other than Allah could bring you light? Then will you not hear?"
1132. Say, "Have you considered: if Allah should make for you the day continuous until the Day of Resurrection, what deity other than Allah could bring you a night in which you may rest? Then will you not see?"
1133. And out of His mercy He made for you the night and the day that you may rest therein and [by day] seek from His bounty and [that] perhaps you will be grateful.
1134. And out of His mercy He made for you the night and the day that you may rest therein and [by day] seek from His bounty and [that] perhaps you will be grateful.
1135. And [that] perhaps you will be grateful.
1136. For whoever desires to remember or desires gratitude.

In all of the above ayahs, one of the common themes with a similar context is the necessary embodiment of shukr and hamd as mentioned شُكُورًا [1137]{الفرقان/62} and [1138]{القصص/73} وَلَعَلَّكُمْ تَشْكُرُونَ.

Surah Shuarah

[13-14]

وَيَضِيقُ صَدْرِي وَلَا يَنطَلِقُ لِسَانِي فَأَرْسِلْ إِلَى هَارُونَ [1139]{الشعراء/13} وَلَهُمْ عَلَيَّ ذَنبٌ فَأَخَافُ أَن يَقْتُلُونِ [1140]{الشعراء/14}

The true mumi'n does not feel comfortable if he or she is involved with a possibility of a sin. This person does not forget this engagement possibly all of his or her life. One can see the position of Musa as, although this was an accident and mistake on his part, he mentions that وَيَضِيقُ صَدْرِي [1141] وَلَا يَنطَلِقُ لِسَانِي and he does not forget about this as mentioned وَلَهُمْ [1142] عَلَيَّ ذَنب.

[15]

قَالَ كَلَّا فَاذْهَبَا بِآيَاتِنَا إِنَّا مَعَكُم مُّسْتَمِعُونَ [1143]{الشعراء/15}

Sometimes, we forget that Allah ﷻ sees and hears us. In other words, we are not alone as mentioned:
أَلَمْ تَرَ أَنَّ اللَّهَ يَعْلَمُ مَا فِي السَّمَاوَاتِ وَمَا فِي الْأَرْضِ مَا يَكُونُ مِن نَّجْوَى ثَلَاثَةٍ إِلَّا هُوَ رَابِعُهُمْ وَلَا خَمْسَةٍ إِلَّا هُوَ سَادِسُهُمْ وَلَا أَدْنَى مِن ذَلِكَ وَلَا أَكْثَرَ إِلَّا هُوَ مَعَهُمْ أَيْنَ مَا كَانُوا ثُمَّ يُنَبِّئُهُم بِمَا عَمِلُوا يَوْمَ الْقِيَامَةِ إِنَّ اللَّهَ بِكُلِّ شَيْءٍ عَلِيمٌ [1144]{المجادلة/7}

Yet, we forget this very important reality. Therefore, possibly, this important and critical reality is reminded to us in different styles and formats in the Qurãn. Why is this important? This is the essence of the religion and this can be called ihsãn [15].

1137. Gratitude.
1138. And [that] perhaps you will be grateful.
1139. And that my breast will tighten and my tongue will not be fluent, so send for Aaron.
1140. And they have upon me a [claim due to] sin, so I fear that they will kill me."
1141. And that my breast will tighten and my tongue will not be fluent.
1142. And they have upon me a [claim due to] sin.
1143. [Allah] said, "No. Go both of you with Our signs; indeed, We are with you, listening.
1144. Have you not considered that Allah knows what is in the heavens and what is on the earth? There is in no private conversation three but that He is the fourth of them, nor are there five but that He is the sixth of them—and no less than that and no more except that He is with them [in knowledge] wherever they are. Then He will inform them of what they did, on the Day of Resurrection. Indeed Allah is, of all things, Knowing.

When the person walks on the steps of this reality, then the person starts watching what he or she says, where he or she spends their time, why he or she engages with an action. Why? He or she knows that everything is being recorded. Or, at a true and higher level, Allah ﷻ sees and hears everything. With this reality, this life is limited. Soon, we will meet with Allah ﷻ to answer for all our renderings and engagements in life.

The notion of silence as observed in the life of Rasulullah ﷺ and his followers as awliya of Allah can be an outcome of this embodiment of ihsan. In other words, the person does not talk unless it is necessary. When they talk there is a stimuli, a reason, an intention to please Allah ﷻ. However, during the action of the talking engagement, they achieve the most difficult part of this action of talking: this is to only talk what is necessary. Then, to stop when they are done. Then, it is to go back to their natural state of silence, being in the state of ihsān. In other words, this is being in the state of constantly being seen, heard, watched, monitored by Allah ﷻ and by other beings such as angels, respectively.

This state in its application can give the person solace, sakina, tranquility, and cause the person to have the life of jannah on the grounds of the world.

Yet, nafs, shaytan, external distractions, and internal distractions are always there. It is important to ignore them and continue the peaceful states of being with Allah ﷻ as indicated with the word "a'fwfu":

يَا أَيُّهَا الَّذِينَ آمَنُوا إِنَّ مِنْ أَزْوَاجِكُمْ وَأَوْلَادِكُمْ عَدُوًّا لَكُمْ فَاحْذَرُوهُمْ وَإِنْ تَعْفُوا وَتَصْفَحُوا وَتَغْفِرُوا فَإِنَّ اللَّهَ غَفُورٌ رَحِيمٌ 1145{التَغابن/14}

This is very difficult. It can be given by Allah ﷻ if one desires to be with Allah ﷻ and if one takes Allah ﷻ as only the Khalil as Rasulullah ﷺ did.

Therefore, the silent moments of Rasulullah ﷺ, at the minimum, can be these moments of muraqaba and ihsan filled with sakina, solace, tranquility.

Assuming otherwise or forgetting or being heedless that Allah ﷻ hears, sees, and is aware can be a shirk according to its levels.

1145. O you who have believed, indeed, among your spouses and your children are enemies to you, so beware of them. But if you pardon and overlook and forgive—then indeed, Allah is Forgiving and Merciful.

The pain of chaos and disorder causes darkness and kufr. The sakina of being under structure, order, and control in the company of Allah ﷻ constantly causes the person to be in the state of sakina.

Therefore, ihsān is not the scary or uncomfortable state of being monitored at all times but it is the state of being in the company of the Beloved, Allah ﷻ and knowing and realizing it. This Friend does not leave the person anywhere, at any time, SubhanAllah. This is the Real Friend.

132

اللهم اجعلنا منهم. امين[1146]

وَاتَّقُوا الَّذِي أَمَدَّكُم بِمَا تَعْلَمُونَ [1147]{الشعراء/132}

The above is a very interesting ayah that really summarizes and focuses on one of the biggest wrong assumptions that we make as humans. Allah ﷻ gives a lot of ni'mahs, but we take them for granted as mentioned بِمَا تَعْلَمُونَ[1148]. In other words, knowing something or being in habitual engagement with something does not mean that the person should forget the daily needs and that we constantly are in need and enjoy ourselves with what we are given by Allah ﷻ, as also mentioned Baqawi [32] and Samarkandhi. The following ayahs explain this as أَمَدَّكُم بِأَنْعَامٍ وَبَنِينَ[1149] {الشعراء/133} وَجَنَّاتٍ وَعُيُونٍ [1150]{الشعراء/134}.

Surah Naml

[7-8]

إِذْ قَالَ مُوسَى لِأَهْلِهِ إِنِّي آنَسْتُ نَارًا سَآتِيكُم مِّنْهَا بِخَبَرٍ أَوْ آتِيكُم بِشِهَابٍ قَبَسٍ لَّعَلَّكُمْ تَصْطَلُونَ [1151]{النمل/7} فَلَمَّا جَاءهَا نُودِيَ أَن بُورِكَ مَن فِي النَّارِ وَمَنْ حَوْلَهَا وَسُبْحَانَ اللَّهِ رَبِّ الْعَالَمِينَ [1152]{النمل/8}

1146. Oh Allah make us from among them.
1147. And fear He who provided you with that which you know.
1148. With that which you know.
1149. Provided you with grazing livestock and children.
1150. And gardens and springs.
1151. [Mention] when Moses said to his family, "Indeed, I have perceived a fire. I will bring you from there information or will bring you a burning torch that you may warm yourselves."
1152. But when he came to it, he was called, "Blessed is whoever is at the fire and whoever is around it. And exalted is Allah, Lord of the worlds.

When one analyzes the above ayahs, the adab of tanzih is very critical as mentioned {8/النمل}[1153] وَسُبْحَانَ اللَّهِ رَبِّ الْعَالَمِينَ. In this case, the harf وَ can indicate this immediate urge to apply the adab of tanzîh[1154] in the mind and heart. This harf is not فَ which may indicate order or a little bit of delay. Or, the harf فَ can indicate causality and yet it is not used here. Because, humans are constantly involved in the engagements of wrong, misconceptions, and errors about the knowledge of the Transcendent Infinite Divine Reality, Allah ﷻ. These mistaken renderings can be normal as a human reality as long as the person embodies the adab of tanzîh.

In other words, these normalizations require the constant adab of tanzîh regardless of a possible apparent cause as in this case of the ayah. Therefore, the harf وَ can indicate this immediate, constant, and continuous urge and need to always keep the adab of tanzîh with the verbal divine phrases of سُبْحَانَ اللَّهِ رَبِّ الْعَالَمِينَ[1155] and at the same time, the heart and mind-related feelings, thoughts, and engagements of سُبْحَانَ اللَّهِ رَبِّ الْعَالَمِينَ.

If one reviews the testimony نُودِيَ أَن بُورِكَ مَن فِي النَّارِ وَمَنْ حَوْلَهَا[1156], there is the appearance of majhûl, passive form. As is interpreted in the tafasir, the majhûl can indicate the required respect for the shiar. Another possibility about the usage of majhûl can be to remind and instill in the person the required engagements of adab with Uluhiyyah.

[9]

فَلَمَّا جَاءَهَا نُودِيَ أَن بُورِكَ مَن فِي النَّارِ وَمَنْ حَوْلَهَا وَسُبْحَانَ اللَّهِ رَبِّ الْعَالَمِينَ {8/النمل}[1157] يَا مُوسَى إِنَّهُ أَنَا اللَّهُ الْعَزِيزُ الْحَكِيمُ[1158] {9/النمل}

To detail the apparent cause of adab of tanzih[1159] وَسُبْحَانَ اللَّهِ رَبِّ الْعَالَمِينَ in this ayah, the ayah states فَلَمَّا جَاءَهَا نُودِيَ أَن بُورِكَ مَن فِي النَّارِ وَمَنْ حَوْلَهَا وَسُبْحَانَ

1153. And exalted is Allah, Lord of the worlds.
1154. Dislike.
1155. And exalted is Allah, Lord of the worlds.
1156. He was called, "Blessed is whoever is at the fire and whoever is around it.
1157. But when he came to it, he was called, "Blessed is whoever is at the fire and whoever is around it. And exalted is Allah, Lord of the worlds.
1158. O Moses, indeed it is I—Allah, the Exalted in Might, the Wise."
1159. And exalted is Allah, Lord of the worlds.

اللَّهِ رَبِّ الْعَالَمِينَ {8/النمل}[1160] يَا مُوسَى إِنَّهُ أَنَا أللَّهُ الْعَزِيزُ الْحَكِيمُ [1161]{9/النمل}. If there is no adab of tanzîh, then the person could be stuck with the apparent and literal, and be without any adab of tanzîh and assume the ways of fire worshippers. Yet, it is interesting to note that the embodiment of adab of tanzîh as وَسُبْحَانَ اللَّهِ رَبِّ الْعَالَمِينَ is between two ayahs.

In other words, one can expect that the reason that the expression وَسُبْحَانَ اللَّهِ رَبِّ الْعَالَمِينَ is not mentioned after the occurrence of يَا مُوسَى وَسُبْحَانَ اللَّةَ رَبِّ الْعَالَمِينَ يَا مُوسَى إِنَّهُ أَنَا أللَّةُ as إِنَّهُ أَنَا اللَّهُ الْعَزِيزُ الْحَكِيمُ {9/النمل}[1162] الْعَزِيزُ الْحَكِيمُ. This could still be correct and we can still say it. However, there is a very critical teaching in the order. The adab of tanzîh وَسُبْحَانَ اللَّهِ رَبِّ الْعَالَمِينَ comes before the occurrence of apparent cause that would necessitate the adab of tanzîh to already be present beforehand . Allah ﷻ teaches that the person should always be prepared and ready in his or her mind and heart as a human with the adab of tanzîh before the things happen.

In other words, in preventative medicine, the person makes preparations before the diseases come. When they come, the body already has the antidote for this disease and it is prepared. Similarly, when the heart and mind are ready before the occurrence of cases that would definitely require tanzîh, then the person will not make the same mistakes and acquire diseases and kill themselves like the fire worshippers.

On another note, Allah ﷻ fulfills all of our needs as Al-Razzaq[1163], As-Samad[1164] and with other Divine Names and Attributes. Musa as is in need of fire because of different reasons أَوْ آتِيكُم بِشِهَابٍ قَبَسٍ لَّعَلَّكُمْ تَصْطَلُونَ. In this case, our prime needs can urge us to do things that may cause us to sometimes forget the Real Doer, Allah ﷻ although we could be a mu'min and Muslim. Yet, everything with simple causes in creation are created by Allah ﷻ. When Ibrahim as realized this about fire, Ibrahim as asked his need directly from Allah ﷻ without any angelic intervention.

In every humanly need engagement, the person should first turn to the Real Fulfiller of all Needs, Allah ﷻ. Then, Allah ﷻ can make the

---

1160. But when he came to it, he was called, "Blessed is whoever is at the fire and whoever is around it. And exalted is Allah, Lord of the worlds.
1161. O Moses, indeed it is I—Allah, the Exalted in Might, the Wise."
1162. O Moses, indeed it is I—Allah, the Exalted in Might, the Wise."
1163. The Sustainer.
1164. The Eternal.

simple means active and fulfill the need of the person. Sometimes, our needs are sent as reminders as a test through weakness, hunger, health, and fear by Allah ﷻ in order for us to turn fully to Allah ﷻ. In these cases, if we turn to the fake need fulfillers, then it is going to increase our pain and we will eventually die, may Allah ﷻ protect us, Ameen.

Sometimes, if the person does not remember this, their need can become their deity. In the literal sense, people worship fire, nature, the sun, stars, fish (Solomon Islands) because they see them as their sustenance and dependency. Yet, this is the result of people's wrong understanding when Allah ﷻ sends different signs, messages, and needs.

When the mailman constantly brings packets to someone, the person is expected to fully appreciate the sender. Then the person can appreciate partially, on another scale, the delivery person as well, although he or she is paid by the sender. Yet, it will be absurd and foolish if the person totally forgets the sender and gives more credit than is due to the delivery person similar to the case of Isa as with Christians.

Similarly, Allah ﷻ is the Real Sender of all bounties, ni'mahs and gifts every day to us. The Sun, the night, the day, the air, the water, the health, the children, the fire, the trees, the birds, and countless others are some of them. These come with the signs on them, labeled and stamped as "they are working under the Real Sender, Allah ﷻ."

The Prophets, messengers, and books are the representatives and documents sent directly by the Sender, solely and completely dedicated for the purpose of explaining this for humans.

Yet, with all of the different explanations, if the person is still being ungrateful and not recognizing it, then it presents a huge problem for the person.

On another analysis of the phrase إنَّهُ, the pronoun, dhamir is mentioned as " هذه الهاء هاء عِماد . وهو أسم لا يظهر . وقد فسّر " accoding to Farra' According to Zamahkshari [43] it is " يجوز أن يكون ضمير الشأن ", it وأن يكون راجعاً إلى ما دل عليه ما قبله ، يعني : أنّ مكلمك أنا ، واالله بيان لأنا . والعزيز is الحكيم

The possibilities of the prounon being shan or 'imad. Dhamir shan or the pronoun of shan can be used to give the azamah, honor and emphasis. Dhamir 'imad or the pronoun of 'imad can be used to specify and make the case khass, specific.

[24 → 60-63]

وَجَدتُّهَا وَقَوْمَهَا يَسْجُدُونَ لِلشَّمْسِ مِن دُونِ اللَّهِ وَزَيَّنَ لَهُمُ الشَّيْطَانُ أَعْمَالَهُمْ فَصَدَّهُمْ عَنِ السَّبِيلِ فَهُمْ لَا يَهْتَدُونَ 1165{النمل/24}

&

أَمَّنْ خَلَقَ السَّمَاوَاتِ وَالْأَرْضَ وَأَنزَلَ لَكُم مِّنَ السَّمَاء مَاء فَأَنبَتْنَا بِهِ حَدَائِقَ ذَاتَ بَهْجَةٍ مَّا كَانَ لَكُمْ أَن تُنبِتُوا شَجَرَهَا أَإِلَهٌ مَّعَ اللَّهِ بَلْ هُمْ قَوْمٌ يَعْدِلُونَ 1166{النمل/60} أَمَّن جَعَلَ الْأَرْضَ قَرَارًا وَجَعَلَ خِلَالَهَا أَنْهَارًا وَجَعَلَ لَهَا رَوَاسِيَ وَجَعَلَ بَيْنَ الْبَحْرَيْنِ حَاجِزًا أَإِلَهٌ مَّعَ اللَّهِ بَلْ أَكْثَرُهُمْ لَا يَعْلَمُونَ 1167{النمل/61} أَمَّن يُجِيبُ الْمُضْطَرَّ إِذَا دَعَاهُ وَيَكْشِفُ السُّوءَ وَيَجْعَلُكُمْ خُلَفَاء الْأَرْضِ أَإِلَهٌ مَّعَ اللَّهِ قَلِيلًا مَّا تَذَكَّرُونَ 1168{النمل/62} أَمَّن يَهْدِيكُمْ فِي ظُلُمَاتِ الْبَرِّ وَالْبَحْرِ وَمَن يُرْسِلُ الرِّيَاحَ بُشْرًا بَيْنَ يَدَيْ رَحْمَتِهِ أَإِلَهٌ مَّعَ اللَّهِ تَعَالَى اللَّهُ عَمَّا يُشْرِكُونَ 1169{النمل/63}

One of the styles found in the Qurān is that when there is a topic or case introduced, the same topic can be addressed again as the discussion and cases are built up. In its technical term of language, one can call this Baratul Istidlal. One can witness this in many places in the Qurān.

One of the possible occurrences of this is when there are people who do not have true tawhid but have shirk such as attributing to the sun the value of deity as mentioned in ayah 24. Then, there is an immediate response given to this wrong disposition in the following ayah as:

1165. I found her and her people prostrating to the sun instead of Allah, and Satan has made their deeds pleasing to them and averted them from [His] way, so they are not guided.

1166. [More precisely], is He [not best] who created the heavens and the earth and sent down for you rain from the sky, causing to grow thereby gardens of joyful beauty which you could not [otherwise] have grown the trees thereof? Is there a deity with Allah? [No], but they are a people who ascribe equals [to Him].

1167. Is He [not best] who made the earth a stable ground and placed within it rivers and made for it firmly set mountains and placed between the two seas a barrier? Is there a deity with Allah? [No], but most of them do not know.

1168. Is He [not best] who responds to the desperate one when he calls upon Him and removes evil and makes you inheritors of the earth? Is there a deity with Allah? Little do you remember.

1169. Is He [not best] who guides you through the darknesses of the land and sea and who sends the winds as good tidings before His mercy? Is there a deity with Allah? High is Allah above whatever they associate with Him.

أَلَّا يَسْجُدُوا لِلَّهِ الَّذِي يُخْرِجُ الْخَبْءَ فِي السَّمَاوَاتِ وَالْأَرْضِ وَيَعْلَمُ مَا تُخْفُونَ وَمَا تُعْلِنُونَ
{النمل/25}1170 اللَّهُ لَا إِلَهَ إِلَّا هُوَ رَبُّ الْعَرْشِ الْعَظِيمِ 1171{النمل/26}

Then, more details can come addressing the same issue as presented in the same surah with the ayahs 60-63, اعلم الله. One of the main goals of the Qurān is to establish true tawhid [13]. To address this issue, there are many cases presented along with their problems and solutions.

In historical occurrences and today, it is interesting to note that most of the people know Allah ﷻ and they somehow accept Allah ﷻ. The problem is due to ascribing to other this relationship with Allah ﷻ. Non-Muslims can do this explicitly. Muslims don't do this openly as the open declaration of shahadah eliminates this, but they may do it unknowingly or in hidden dispositions. The Prophet ﷺ mentions that he was afraid for Muslims in later generations, not about the explicit shirk but the implicit one [1].

[40]

قَالَ الَّذِي عِندَهُ عِلْمٌ مِّنَ الْكِتَابِ أَنَا آتِيكَ بِهِ قَبْلَ أَن يَرْتَدَّ إِلَيْكَ طَرْفُكَ فَلَمَّا رَآهُ مُسْتَقِرًّا
عِندَهُ قَالَ هَذَا مِن فَضْلِ رَبِّي لِيَبْلُوَنِي أَأَشْكُرُ أَمْ أَكْفُرُ وَمَن شَكَرَ فَإِنَّمَا يَشْكُرُ لِنَفْسِهِ وَمَن
كَفَرَ فَإِنَّ رَبِّي غَنِيٌّ كَرِيمٌ 1172{النمل/40}

It is very important to recognize the bounties of Allah ﷻ and make shukr and not ignore it. The attitude of ignoring is mentioned with the word كَفَرَ1173. The opposite of kufr in this sense is أَشْكُرُ1174. The disposition of أَشْكُرُ includes both the iman and appreciation and gratitude. One of the duas of the Prophet saw is "alhamdulillahi allazi kafana wa awana waarwana ghayra makfiyyi wa la makfur, laka al hamd, rabbana ghayra makfiyyi wa la muwadda'i wa la mustagniyan a'nhu" [1]. This dua can be mentioned regarding any bounties such as food and others. The critical

---

1170. [And] so they do not prostrate to Allah, who brings forth what is hidden within the heavens and the earth and knows what you conceal and what you declare.
1171. Allah—there is no deity except Him, Lord of the Great Throne."
1172. Said one who had knowledge from the Scripture, "I will bring it to you before your glance returns to you." And when [Solomon] saw it placed before him, he said, "This is from the favor of my Lord to test me whether I will be grateful or ungrateful. And whoever is grateful—his gratitude is only for [the benefit of] himself. And whoever is ungrateful—then indeed, my Lord is Free of need and Generous."
1173. Ungrateful.
1174. Grateful.

words in this dua and this ayah state that kufr is presented as not having the recognition of making shukr and hamd to Allah ﷻ.

[41-44]

قَالَ نَكِّرُوا لَهَا عَرْشَهَا نَنظُرْ أَتَهْتَدِي أَمْ تَكُونُ مِنَ الَّذِينَ لَا يَهْتَدُونَ {النمل/41}1175 فَلَمَّا جَاءتْ قِيلَ أَهَكَذَا عَرْشُكِ قَالَتْ كَأَنَّهُ هُوَ وَأُوتِينَا الْعِلْمَ مِن قَبْلِهَا وَكُنَّا مُسْلِمِينَ 1176{النمل/42} وَصَدَّهَا مَا كَانَت تَّعْبُدُ مِن دُونِ اللَّهِ إِنَّهَا كَانَتْ مِن قَوْمٍ كَافِرِينَ 1177{النمل/43} قِيلَ لَهَا ادْخُلِي الصَّرْحَ فَلَمَّا رَأَتْهُ حَسِبَتْهُ لُجَّةً وَكَشَفَتْ عَن سَاقَيْهَا قَالَ إِنَّهُ صَرْحٌ مُّمَرَّدٌ مِّن قَوَارِيرَ قَالَتْ رَبِّ إِنِّي ظَلَمْتُ نَفْسِي وَأَسْلَمْتُ مَعَ سُلَيْمَانَ لِلَّهِ رَبِّ الْعَالَمِينَ 1178{النمل/44}

One can analyze the method of tabligh in the above ayahs. The free choice or free will is not taken from the person as mentioned نَنظُرْ1179 أَتَهْتَدِي أَمْ تَكُونُ مِنَ الَّذِينَ لَا يَهْتَدُونَ. In other words, some ingredients and tools of guidance are shown to the person, and at the end it may or may not work, and Allah ﷻ knows it. Then, the previous years of misguidance are explained as وَصَدَّهَا مَا كَانَت تَّعْبُدُ مِن دُونِ اللَّهِ1180 that when a person is attached to something, elevating it above Allah ﷻ then, this becomes a hindrance in recognizing the true tawhid. The other is one's group belonging or identity as mentioned إِنَّهَا كَانَتْ مِن قَوْمٍ كَافِرِينَ1181.

In another case of magicians as فَأُلْقِيَ السَّحَرَةُ سَاجِدِينَ {الشعراء/46}1182 shows قَالُوا آمَنَّا بِرَبِّ الْعَالَمِينَ {الشعراء/47}1183 رَبِّ مُوسَى وَهَارُونَ {الشعراء/48}1184 changing positions after seeing miracles. In the first case, Sulayman as puts some ingredients for Balqis to convince her for her guidance. In the

---

1175. He said, "Disguise for her her throne; we will see whether she will be guided [to truth] or will be of those who is not guided."
1176. So when she arrived, it was said [to her], "Is your throne like this?" She said, "[It is] as though it was it." [Solomon said], "And we were given knowledge before her, and we have been Muslims [in submission to Allah].
1177. And that which she was worshipping other than Allah had averted her [from submission to Him]. Indeed, she was from a disbelieving people."
1178. She was told, "Enter the palace." But when she saw it, she thought it was a body of water and uncovered her shins [to wade through]. He said, "Indeed, it is a palace [whose floor is] made smooth with glass." She said, "My Lord, indeed I have wronged myself, and I submit with Solomon to Allah, Lord of the worlds."
1179. We will see whether she will be guided [to truth] or will be of those who is not guided."
1180. And that which she was worshipping other than Allah had averted her [from submission to Him].
1181. Indeed, she was from a disbelieving people."
1182. So the magicians fell down in prostration [to Allah].
1183. They said, "We have believed in the Lord of the worlds.
1184. The Lord of Moses and Aaron."

latter case, Allah ﷻ guides the magicians through miracles. Surprisingly even, Musa as may not have expected this result, [1185]اعلمالله.

At another angle if one compares the two cases as:

and [1186]{النمل/44} قَالَتْ رَبِّ إِنِّي ظَلَمْتُ نَفْسِي وَأَسْلَمْتُ مَعَ سُلَيْمَانَ لِلَّهِ رَبِّ الْعَالَمِينَ

قَالُوا آمَنَّا بِرَبِّ الْعَالَمِينَ [1187]{الشعراء/47} رَبِّ مُوسَى وَهَارُونَ [1188]{الشعراء/48},

one can realize that in both cases the names of the people to be followed are mentioned. In other words, وَأَسْلَمْتُ مَعَ سُلَيْمَانَ لِلَّهِ رَبِّ الْعَالَمِينَ [1189]{النمل/44} and رَبِّ مُوسَى وَهَارُونَ {الشعراء/48}. One can ask, why they need to mention the names of the Prophets. Wasn't it sufficient if they just said "آمَنَّا بِرَبِّ الْعَالَمِينَ [1190]" ? The possible answer for this is that in both cases they don't know the details of tawhid. The true tawhid requires the true marifah of Allah ﷻ. Therefore, they mention that they believe in Allah ﷻ and they believe however it is expected to believe similar to Musa as, Harun as, and Sulayman as with all the true attributes and sifah of Allah ﷻ. This approach can also be witnessed in, for example:

أَمْ كُنتُمْ شُهَدَاءَ إِذْ حَضَرَ يَعْقُوبَ الْمَوْتُ إِذْ قَالَ لِبَنِيهِ مَا تَعْبُدُونَ مِن بَعْدِي قَالُوا نَعْبُدُ إِلَهَكَ وَإِلَهَ آبَائِكَ إِبْرَاهِيمَ وَإِسْمَاعِيلَ وَإِسْحَاقَ إِلَهًا وَاحِدًا وَنَحْنُ لَهُ مُسْلِمُونَ [1191]{البقرة/133}

The true tawhid of Allah ﷻ requires not making explicit or implicit shirk. This builds up with the authentic knowledge, practice, humbleness and ikhlās.

From another perspective, one can compare the above two cases in which Balqis rh says وَأَسْلَمْتُ[1192] and magicians say آمَنَّا[1193]. This can show the difference between a worldly means of dawah with Islām in the case of Balqis rh and the supernatural events of miracles leading to imān compared to the case of magicians. There is the Divine miracles as the Divine Intervention taking the person vertically skipping the وَأَسْلَمْتُ[1194]

1185. Allah knows best.
1186. She said, "My Lord, indeed I have wronged myself, and I submit with Solomon to Allah, Lord of the worlds."
1187. They said, "We have believed in the Lord of the worlds."
1188. The Lord of Moses and Aaron."
1189. And I submit with Solomon to Allah, Lord of the worlds."
1190. We have believed in the Lord of the worlds.
1191. Or were you witnesses when death approached Jacob, when he said to his sons, "What will you worship after me?" They said, "We will worship your God and the God of your fathers, Abraham and Ishmael and Isaac—one God. And we are Muslims [in submission] to Him."
1192. And I submit.
1193. We have believed.
1194. And I submit.

part and directly being in imān as mentioned with اٰمَنَّا. This staging from islam to imān mentioned in قَالَتِ الْأَعْرَابُ اٰمَنَّا قُل لَّمْ تُؤْمِنُوا وَلَكِن قُولُوا أَسْلَمْنَا وَلَمَّا يَدْخُلِ الْإِيمَانُ فِي قُلُوبِكُمْ وَإِن تُطِيعُوا اللَّهَ وَرَسُولَهُ لَا يَلِتْكُم مِّنْ أَعْمَالِكُمْ شَيْئًا إِنَّ اللَّهَ غَفُورٌ رَّحِيمٌ {الحجرات/14}[1195]. This staging is also mentioned in hadith Jibril (as) [7].

On another note, one can analyze the expression[1196] قِيلَ لَهَا ادْخُلِي الصَّرْحَ. When one is interacting with the other gender, expected etiquettes of being nice, kind, and as popularized with the word "being a gentlemen" can be witnessed. Especially, in the engagements of dawah, kindness and good character can be as important as delivering the message. There are a lot of women who became Muslim and married Muslim men. They have experienced Islam with full, logical, and perfect teachings. Yet, they went through difficulties due to unkind treatment from their husbands and had divorces. Then, their Muslim identities became shattered due to representations of Islam in their close experiences with Muslims.

[66 & 82]

بَلِ ادَّارَكَ عِلْمُهُمْ فِي الْاٰخِرَةِ بَلْ هُمْ فِي شَكٍّ مِّنْهَا بَلْ هُم مِّنْهَا عَمُونَ {النمل/66}[1197]

وَإِذَا وَقَعَ الْقَوْلُ عَلَيْهِمْ أَخْرَجْنَا لَهُمْ دَابَّةً مِّنَ الْأَرْضِ تُكَلِّمُهُمْ أَنَّ النَّاسَ كَانُوا بِآيَاتِنَا لَا يُوقِنُونَ {النمل/82}[1198]

The curtain over yaqin[1199] بَلْ هُمْ فِي لَا يُوقِنُونَ {النمل/82} is due to shakk[1200], شَكٍّ مِّنْهَا بَلْ هُم مِّنْهَا عَمُونَ {النمل/66}. As mentioned in the very beginning of the Qurān, وَبِالْاٰخِرَةِ هُمْ يُوقِنُونَ {البقرة/4}, the expected trait of a believer is having certainty about the afterlife. One of the ways to remove skepticism is to use comparison and contrast in order to go to the levels of certainty beyond the curtain of skepticism.

1195. The bedouins say, "We have believed." Say, "You have not [yet] believed; but say [instead], 'We have submitted,' for faith has not yet entered your hearts. And if you obey Allah and His Messenger, He will not deprive you from your deeds of anything. Indeed, Allah is Forgiving and Merciful."

1196. We have believed in the Lord of the worlds.

1197. Rather, their knowledge is arrested concerning the Hereafter. Rather, they are in doubt about it. Rather, they are, concerning it, blind.

1198. And when the word [i.e., decree] befalls them, We will bring forth for them a creature from the earth speaking to them, [saying] that the people were, of Our verses, not certain [in faith].

1199. Not certain [in faith].

1200. Rather, they are in doubt about it. Rather, they are, concerning it, blind.

There are different mental and emotional faculties in a human. One of them is doubt or skepticism. With the coordination of the external elements such as Shaytan and internal elements of nafs, sometimes this notion of doubt can put a curtain on a very clear and explicit reality. In that perspective, the Qurān presents examples to remove the possible skeptical subterranean dispositions in a person's mind and heart that block the very obvious realities.

After all of these obvious signs and examples, if the person is persistent in a skeptical disposition, then the person can put himself or herself in a very destructive self-denial position that can hurt the person immediately in this world and in the afterlife. The popular phenomena of philosophers finding themselves in cognitive and spiritual dead ends in their lives and being emotionally, mentally, and psychologically disturbed even committing suicide, are due to not being able make the jump from skeptical holes to certainty peak dispositions.

Therefore, once the person goes beyond the veil of skepticism, then he or she should be fully confident and say and embody, "I am a thousand percent certain that I will meet with Allah ﷻ. If the concealmeant of the unseen is removed from me, my yaqin, certainty will not change because I am at that level now." اللهم اجعلنا منهم، امين[1201]

[76-86]

إِنَّ هَذَا الْقُرْآنَ يَقُصُّ عَلَى بَنِي إِسْرَائِيلَ أَكْثَرَ الَّذِي هُمْ فِيهِ يَخْتَلِفُونَ [1202] {النمل/76}

وَإِنَّهُ لَهُدًى وَرَحْمَةٌ لِّلْمُؤْمِنِينَ [1203] {النمل/77} إِنَّ رَبَّكَ يَقْضِي بَيْنَهُم بِحُكْمِهِ وَهُوَ الْعَزِيزُ الْعَلِيمُ [1204] {النمل/78} فَتَوَكَّلْ عَلَى اللَّهِ إِنَّكَ عَلَى الْحَقِّ الْمُبِينِ [1205] {النمل/79} إِنَّكَ لَا تُسْمِعُ الْمَوْتَى وَلَا تُسْمِعُ الصُّمَّ الدُّعَاءَ إِذَا وَلَّوْا مُدْبِرِينَ [1206] {النمل/80} وَمَا أَنتَ بِهَادِي الْعُمْيِ عَن ضَلَالَتِهِمْ إِن تُسْمِعُ إِلَّا مَن يُؤْمِنُ بِآيَاتِنَا فَهُم مُّسْلِمُونَ [1207] {النمل/81} وَإِذَا وَقَعَ الْقَوْلُ عَلَيْهِمْ أَخْرَجْنَا لَهُمْ دَابَّةً مِّنَ الْأَرْضِ تُكَلِّمُهُمْ أَنَّ النَّاسَ كَانُوا بِآيَاتِنَا لَا

1201. Oh Allah, make us from among them.
1202. Indeed, this Qurān relates to the Children of Israel most of that over which they disagree.
1203. And indeed, it is guidance and mercy for the believers.
1204. Indeed, your Lord will judge between them by His [wise] judgement. And He is the Exalted in Might, the Knowing.
1205. So rely upon Allah; indeed, you are upon the clear truth.
1206. Indeed, you will not make the dead hear, nor will you make the deaf hear the call when they have turned their backs retreating.
1207. And you cannot guide the blind away from their error. You will only make hear those who believe in Our verses so they are Muslims [i.e., submitting to Allah].

يُوقِنُونَ 1208{النمل/82} وَيَوْمَ نَحْشُرُ مِن كُلِّ أُمَّةٍ فَوْجًا مِّمَّن يُكَذِّبُ بِآيَاتِنَا فَهُمْ يُوزَعُونَ 1209{النمل/83} حَتَّى إِذَا جَاؤُوا قَالَ أَكَذَّبْتُم بِآيَاتِي وَلَمْ تُحِيطُوا بِهَا عِلْمًا أَمَّاذَا كُنتُمْ تَعْمَلُونَ 1210{النمل/84} وَوَقَعَ الْقَوْلُ عَلَيْهِم بِمَا ظَلَمُوا فَهُمْ لَا يَنطِقُونَ 1211{النمل/85} أَلَمْ يَرَوْا أَنَّا جَعَلْنَا اللَّيْلَ لِيَسْكُنُوا فِيهِ وَالنَّهَارَ مُبْصِرًا إِنَّ فِي ذَلِكَ لَآيَاتٍ لِّقَوْمٍ يُؤْمِنُونَ 1212{النمل/86}

When one analyzes the ayah with dabbah along with the other key words of عِلْمًا1214, يُوقِنُونَ1213, مُسْلِمُونَ, one can possibly think that the truth of the message will be so widespread through this dabbah maybe through different broadcasting, internet, courses, or other means, that people will find it logical. Yet, due to not being humble and submitting themselves, they will not follow it as mentioned[1215] إِلاَّ مَن يُؤْمِنُ بِآيَاتِنَا فَهُم مُسْلِمُونَ{النمل/81}, اللّه اعلم [1216]. Possibly, at these times, banu israil will see clearly about the complementary and the reality role of the Qurān and Islam as mentioned in[1217] إِنَّ هَذَا الْقُرْآنَ يَقُصُّ عَلَى بَنِي إِسْرَائِيلَ أَكْثَرَ الَّذِي هُم فِيهِ يَخْتَلِفُونَ {النمل/76}.

[1218]وَإِذَا وَقَعَ الْقَوْلُ عَلَيْهِمْ أَخْرَجْنَا لَهُمْ دَابَّةً مِّنَ الْأَرْضِ When one analyzes this ayah and others in the discussions of eschatology, one should first have the purpose, intention, and goal of studying about it before involving and indulging oneself in it.

The topics of eschatology can bring fear, uneasiness, anxiety, disturbance, and distraction for the common people and children if they are not first contextualized for a person. Therefore, I don't think

---

1208. And when the word [i.e., decree] befalls them, We will bring forth for them a creature from the earth speaking to them, [saying] that the people were, of Our verses, not certain [in faith].

1209. And [warn of] the Day when We will gather from every nation a company of those who deny Our signs, and they will be [driven] in rows.

1210. Until, when they arrive [at the place of Judgement], He will say, "Did you deny My signs while you encompassed them not in knowledge, or what [was it that] you were doing?"

1211. And the decree will befall them for the wrong they did, and they will not [be able to] speak.

1212. Do they not see that We made the night that they may rest therein and the day giving sight? Indeed in that are signs for a people who believe.

1213. Not certain {in faith}.

1214. Knowledge.

1215. You will only make hear those who believe in Our verses so they are Muslims [i.e., submitting to Allah].

1216. Allah ﷻ knows best.

1217. Indeed, this Qurān relates to the Children of Israel most of that over which they disagree.

1218. And when the word [i.e., decree] befalls them, We will bring forth for them a creature from the earth.

that these topics should be freely chatted about without any monitoring, and explanations. There should be discussions with people in order to extrapolate their assumed instilled meanings after these talks or lectures about eschatology.

This disposition of purpose about eschatology is suggested by Rasulullah ﷺ when a person asked about the anticipated time of the End of Times, then Rasulullah ﷺ directed him to a purpose by saying, "What did you prepare for it?" [2]When people talk about the unknown events of the future, there should be a purpose and goal. It should not be similar to the discussion of popular media events.

One of the intentions can be to normalize the occurrences of these events as Rasulullah ﷺ explained for us.

Another can be to set goals of preparation according to the objectives that Rasulullah ﷺ set for us.

Another can be to use these as means to communicate with other groups in interfaith relations about eschatology. When they realize we have similar expectations such as about Isa as, this can be an avenue for them to realize our commonalities. When the essence and structure of the original teachings of the religion from Allah ﷻ are lost in scriptures and religious teachings, then the unknowns, predictions, mystical and eschatological teachings become main points of discussion to motivate the masses.

However, this is not the main point of a religion. The biggest problem here is that the purpose of the religion is to live in the present by making spiritual investments through good work and 'ibadah with ikhlas for the life in this world and primarily after death. An individual who cannot help himself or herself spiritually cannot help others. During or after personal spiritual care, one can help others with their social, spiritual, and other problems.

Another reason that people can become involved with knowledge about eschatology is to help others and to minimize social problems. Using religious teachings and expectations to increase chaos, individual and social problems contradicts the basics premises of any religion. Allah ﷻ, God, Adonai, or Elohim, however we refer to Our Creator with beautiful names, will not be pleased with us by using religious teachings for destruction and to increase chaos in our short lifespan. Yes, our life is short. We will meet our Creator soon. Regardless of their religious, ethnic, identity, or group affiliations, everyone will experience accountability in front of the Creator of all universes, galaxies, and people. This accountability will entail not only the actions but also the motivating intentions.

Yet, if there are people or trends who involve themselves with these fasād, evil engagements, one should remember that everyone will be accountable in front of Allah ﷻ individually. The Qurān in different ayahs depicts the enormously disappointing frustrations of people in front of Allah when people will expect benefits from their group affiliations as they used to do in the world.

May Allah ﷻ protect us from being the cause of destruction to ourselves and others, Ameen.

20

Surah Qasas

[32]

اسْلُكْ يَدَكَ فِي جَيْبِكَ تَخْرُجْ بَيْضَاء مِنْ غَيْرِ سُوءٍ وَاضْمُمْ إِلَيْكَ جَنَاحَكَ مِنَ الرَّهْبِ فَذَانِكَ بُرْهَانَانِ مِن رَّبِّكَ إِلَى فِرْعَوْنَ وَمَلَئِهِ إِنَّهُمْ كَانُوا قَوْمًا فَاسِقِينَ [1219] {القصص/32}

It is interesting to note that in the expression وَاضْمُمْ إِلَيْكَ جَنَاحَكَ مِنَ الرَّهْبِ [1220], Musa as opens his arms as a sign of fear. To eliminate the fear, he is instructed to hold his arms close to his body. It is interesting to note that the adrenaline gland, which excretes the hormones for fear, is located where the arms are touching the body. As a way of calming down these glands, one can hold one's arms in a tight situation, especially during the times of fear and anxiety, الله اعلم[1221].

1219. Insert your hand into the opening of your garment; it will come out white, without disease. And draw in your arm close to you [as prevention] from fear, for those are two proofs from your Lord to Pharaoh and his establishment. Indeed, they have been a people defiantly disobedient."
1220. And draw in your arm close to you [as prevention] from fear.
1221. Allah ﷻ knows best.

[44-46]

وَمَا كُنتَ بِجَانِبِ الْغَرْبِيِّ إِذْ قَضَيْنَا إِلَى مُوسَى الْأَمْرَ وَمَا كُنتَ مِنَ الشَّاهِدِينَ
[القصص/44]1222 وَلَكِنَّا أَنشَأْنَا قُرُونًا فَتَطَاوَلَ عَلَيْهِمُ الْعُمُرُ وَمَا كُنتَ ثَاوِيًا فِي أَهْلِ
مَدْيَنَ تَتْلُو عَلَيْهِمْ آيَاتِنَا وَلَكِنَّا كُنَّا مُرْسِلِينَ 1223 {القصص/45} وَمَا كُنتَ بِجَانِبِ الطُّورِ
إِذْ نَادَيْنَا وَلَكِن رَّحْمَةً مِّن رَّبِّكَ لِتُنذِرَ قَوْمًا مَّا أَتَاهُم مِّن نَّذِيرٍ مِّن قَبْلِكَ لَعَلَّهُمْ يَتَذَكَّرُونَ
{القصص/46}1224

If one analyzes the above ayahs, there is the repetition of the phrase "وَمَا
كُنتَ". By just analyzing these ayahs, one can increase one's knowledge
about Rabbul Alamin, Allah ﷻ as Our Creator and one can realize
that we are humans, as the creation of Allah ﷻ. These ayahs, similar
to others, show us that Transcendent Reality, Allah ﷻ causes us to
understand our reality by giving examples through our language and
revealing our limitations to us so that we understand our humanness.
In our memories, one can recall and recollect the words humbleness
and humility with the word humanness. It is as if the true notion of
humanness comes with humbleness and humility.

In this regard, yes, Rasulullah ﷺ was special, chosen but yet, he ﷺ
was also a human. The expressions وَمَا كُنتَ1225 repeatedly telling us that
our Beloved Prophet ﷺ was human but chosen by Allah ﷻ. Rasulullah ﷺ
was the embodiment of humility and humbleness with the embodiment
of gratitude and gratefulness to Allah ﷻ essentially, and the to the
creation as the reflection of this essential. Even, the Qurān mentions
about Rasulullah ﷺ as: وَمَا أَرْسَلْنَاكَ إِلَّا رَحْمَةً لِّلْعَالَمِينَ {الأنبياء/107}. The Qurān
specifically mentions the high status of Rasulullah ﷺ embodying this
role model for all creation.

If Rasulullah ﷺ was human at the summit of humanity and human
history, then it is very important and easy to normalize our humanity.

After this, the next step is that we need to actualize all of the ayahs
of the Qurān on ourselves as if the Qurān is revealed to us directly. As

---

1222. And you, [O Muhammad], were not on the western side [of the mount] when We
revealed to Moses the command, and you were not among the witnesses [to that].
1223. But We produced [many] generations [after Moses], and prolonged was their duration.
And you were not a resident among the people of Madyan, reciting to them Our verses, but
We were senders [of this message].
1224. And you were not at the side of the mount when We called [Moses] but [were sent] as
a mercy from your Lord to warn a people to whom no warner had come before you that they
might be reminded.
1225. And you were not.

suggested by some, it may help to embody the meanings and experiences, and emotions instilled by the Qurān in different circumstances. For example, let us assume a person traveling on a highway at night is passing next to the mountains. There is no town or human residence close to this place. Only this person in the middle of night, passing near a huge mountain and then, reading this ayah [1226] وَمَا كُنتَ بِجَانِبِ الطُّورِ إِذْ نَادَيْنَا or وَمَا كُنتَ بِجَانِبِ الْغَرْبِيِّ إِذْ قَضَيْنَا إِلَى مُوسَى الْأَمْرَ وَمَا كُنتَ مِنَ الشَّاهِدِينَ [1227]{القصص/44}. It can be easier at this time to embody one's limitations, happenings in the past, loneliness except refuge in Allah ﷻ and other realities that can combine with the circumstances.

Therefore, the Qurān's revelation in pieces establishes more robust and a stronger embodiment through different circumstances, cases, contexts, times, and places. Therefore, this type of sabab nuzul is another Fadl[1228] and Rahmah[1229] to our ummah from Allah ﷻ. It can have a more amplified effect on humans. Humans are expected to appreciate more when they embody a reality, individualize and personalize it. Yes, the amplified effect of an individualized approach to the Qurān by revelation in pieces is there. Therefore, the Qurān emphasizes this reality and ni'mah[1230] from Allah ﷻ in the verb form with Anzalna[1231] and Nazalna[1232].

وَقَالَ الَّذِينَ كَفَرُوا لَوْلَا نُزِّلَ عَلَيْهِ الْقُرْآنُ جُمْلَةً وَاحِدَةً كَذَلِكَ لِنُثَبِّتَ بِهِ فُؤَادَكَ وَرَتَّلْنَاهُ تَرْتِيلًا [1233]{الفرقان/32}

Especially, we are in the area of everything being customized or individualized. One can think about customized drinks, individualized education plans, etc. Then, one can really realize another miracle of the Qurān- that the revelation was in pieces and individualized. With all

---

1226. And you were not at the side of the mount when We called [Moses].
1227. And you, [O Muhammad], were not on the western side [of the mount] when We revealed to Moses the command, and you were not among the witnesses [to that].
1228. Favor.
1229. Mercy.
1230. Blessings.
1231. We have sent down.
1232. And we sent down.
1233. And those who disbelieve say, "Why was the Qurān not revealed to him all at once?" Thus [it is] that We may strengthen thereby your heart. And We have spaced it distinctly.

other clear signs, this can make the person again say "اشهد ان لا اله الا الله و
"اشهد ان محمد رسول الله[1234]

The ahlu-kitab can argue that since their scripture was revealed at once it can bear more authenticity. Although one can initially consider this miracle form of Tawrah, yet each book and scripture can fill the need and target the audience of its time.

On another perspective, each case of the Qurān's ayahs being revealed to Rasullah ﷺ can be similar to the full tawrah being revealed at once. In other words, if previously there was a miraculous event of a one-time nuzûl of tawrah then, there were numerous events of nuzuls of revalations to Rasulullah ﷺ. So, if we look at the quantity, miraculous events in the encounter of the Qurān can be even more [1235]الله اعلم.

[52-54]

الَّذِينَ آتَيْنَاهُمُ الْكِتَابَ مِن قَبْلِهِ هُم بِهِ يُؤْمِنُونَ [1236]{القصص/52} وَإِذَا يُتْلَى عَلَيْهِمْ قَالُوا آمَنَّا بِهِ إِنَّهُ الْحَقُّ مِن رَّبِّنَا إِنَّا كُنَّا مِن قَبْلِهِ مُسْلِمِينَ [1237]{القصص/53} أُولَئِكَ يُؤْتَوْنَ أَجْرَهُم مَّرَّتَيْنِ بِمَا صَبَرُوا وَيَدْرَؤُونَ بِالْحَسَنَةِ السَّيِّئَةَ وَمِمَّا رَزَقْنَاهُمْ يُنفِقُونَ [1238]{القصص/54}

It is interesting to witness in this ayah the exact responses of ahlu-kitab today. When the person is genuinely exchanging ideas with ahlu-kitab, the confirmation statements such as "Yes, we believe the same, for in the Bible, there is a verse that teaches the same" can be heard and witnessed from them often as mentioned in the ayah وَإِذَا يُتْلَى عَلَيْهِمْ قَالُوا آمَنَّا بِهِ إِنَّهُ الْحَقُّ مِن رَّبِّنَا إِنَّا كُنَّا مِن قَبْلِهِ مُسْلِمِينَ[1239]{القصص/53}.

In this perspective, imān is real and not an identity tag classified by people. It is a disposition of heart and mind only truly known by Allah ﷻ. If one accepts and empathizes with this notion, then our roles of interaction with ahlu-kitab can transform to other dimensions.

1234. I bear witness that there is no god except Allah ﷻ, and I bear witness that Muhammed ﷺ is the messenger of Allah ﷺ.
1235. Allah ﷻ knows best.
1236. Those to whom We gave the Scripture before it—they are believers in it.
1237. And when it is recited to them, they say, "We have believed in it; indeed, it is the truth from our Lord. Indeed we were, [even] before it, Muslims [i.e., submitting to Allah]."
1238. Those will be given their reward twice for what they patiently endured and [because] they avert evil through good, and from what We have provided them they spend.
1239. And when it is recited to them, they say, "We have believed in it; indeed, it is the truth from our Lord. Indeed we were, [even] before it, Muslims [i.e., submitting to Allah]."

[76]

إِنَّ قَارُونَ كَانَ مِن قَوْمِ مُوسَى فَبَغَى عَلَيْهِمْ وَآتَيْنَاهُ مِنَ الْكُنُوزِ مَا إِنَّ مَفَاتِحَهُ لَتَنُوءُ بِالْعُصْبَةِ أُولِي الْقُوَّةِ إِذْ قَالَ لَهُ قَوْمُهُ لَا تَفْرَحْ إِنَّ اللَّهَ لَا يُحِبُّ الْفَرِحِينَ 1240 {القصص/76}

The expression إِنَّ اللَّهَ لَا يُحِبُّ الْفَرِحِينَ[1241] can show the ideal disposition of a person in one's inner stability of heart, emotions, and feelings. The state of one's alertness, wakefulness, and awareness is very important and critical. Especially, the inner feelings of joy, satisfaction, and happiness accompanied by arrogance can be in the category of الْفَرِحِينَ.

[78]

قَالَ إِنَّمَا أُوتِيتُهُ عَلَى عِلْمٍ عِندِي أَوَلَمْ يَعْلَمْ أَنَّ اللَّهَ قَدْ أَهْلَكَ مِن قَبْلِهِ مِنَ الْقُرُونِ مَنْ هُوَ أَشَدُّ مِنْهُ قُوَّةً وَأَكْثَرُ جَمْعًا وَلَا يُسْأَلُ عَن ذُنُوبِهِمُ الْمُجْرِمُونَ 1242 {القصص/78}

Positive uncertainty on the path is the motivating factor to help the person. When the person does not know his or her true relationship with Allah ﷻ until he or she dies, this keeps the person moving on the path. When the person claims something in spiritual and worldly bounties, then at that time the person loses. This ayah is one of the prime examples of this case. One of the prime and emphasized expressions is in إِنَّمَا أُوتِيتُهُ عَلَى عِلْمٍ عِندِي[1243]. This is unfortunately representative of most of our realities in life.

People can be hard workers in order to achieve a goal, to be promoted in their job, and to receive different titles, recognition, and monetary boost. Yet, when the person إِنَّمَا أُوتِيتُهُ عَلَى عِلْمٍ عِندِي, then the person is in loss in reality. All the power and skills of working, understanding, living, and others are given by Allah ﷻ. Therefore, saying "Alhamdulillah" is the key. Alhamdulillah is the verbal utterance of the expected inner disposition of the person to give all of the due credit, real appreciation,

---

1240. Indeed, Qârûn was from the people of Moses, but he tyrannized them. And We gave him of treasures whose keys would burden a band of strong men; thereupon his people said to him, "Do not exult. Indeed, Allah does not like the exultant.

1241. Indeed, Allah does not like the exultant.

1242. He said, "I was only given it because of knowledge I have." Did he not know that Allah had destroyed before him of generations those who were greater than him in power and greater in accumulation [of wealth]? But the criminals, about their sins, will not be asked.

1243. I was only given it because of knowledge I have.

gratitude, thankfulness, and gratefulness to Allah ﷻ. When someone claims a virtue, then he or she loses it.

Moving positively and with hope until one dies, yet knowing that any type of spiritual security or safety can knock down the person is one of the key elements in practice, الله اعلم[1244].

[81]

فَخَسَفْنَا بِهِ وَبِدَارِهِ الْأَرْضَ فَمَا كَانَ لَهُ مِن فِئَةٍ يَنصُرُونَهُ مِن دُونِ اللَّهِ وَمَا كَانَ مِنَ الْمُنتَصِرِينَ[1245] {القصص/81}

وَلَمْ تَكُن لَّهُ فِئَةٌ يَنصُرُونَهُ مِن دُونِ اللَّهِ وَمَا كَانَ مُنتَصِرًا[1246] {الكهف/43} هُنَالِكَ الْوَلَايَةُ لِلَّهِ الْحَقِّ هُوَ خَيْرٌ ثَوَابًا وَخَيْرٌ عُقْبًا[1247] {الكهف/44}

فَمَا اسْتَطَاعُوا مِن قِيَامٍ وَمَا كَانُوا مُنتَصِرِينَ[1248] {الذاريات/45}

One of the key words in the above ayahs is[1249] الْمُنتَصِرِينَ. The ayahs reveal the importance of understanding and embodying the notion that there is no one who can help the person except Allah ﷻ.

When there is a problem, we tend to seek people's help. Then, most or all of the time, the problem gets worse and we get into depressive states. Then, over time, as a ni'mah[1250] from Allah ﷻ, we start forgetting the magnitude of the initial effects of this problem, as al-insan means 'the one who forgets'. Then, the effect of this problem fades. On the other hand, if the person takes another route when the problem happens, that is, to run to Allah ﷻ to solve, to beg, and to cry, then the person can transform this evil-seeming incident into a very fruitful opportunity. One can really have an opportunity to use and make an advantage out of this evil-seeming incident. Yet, there are very few who use this approach. Today's increasing number of mental clinics can be proof

---

1244. Allah ﷻ knows best.
1245. And We caused the earth to swallow him and his home. And there was for him no company to aid him other than Allah, nor was he of those who [could] defend themselves.
1246. And there was for him no company to aid him other than Allah, nor could he defend himself.
1247. There the authority is [completely] for Allah, the Truth. He is best in reward and best in outcome.
1248. And they were unable to arise, nor could they defend themselves.
1249. To defend themselves.
1250. Blessings.

of this although there is need for them for the ones who don't know how to transform these evil-seeming incidents into an opportunity of a mental and heart boost which would cause the person to become self-dependent, confident, and strong by reliance on Allah ﷻ. Rather, the person becomes dependent on the medicine, these clinics, and humans.

The real friend, waliyy, is always Allah ﷻ. It is expected that the person should realize this at all times: at the end, during and before all trials, losses, gains, in good health, and regarding wealth as mentioned هُنَالِكَ الْوَلَايَةُ لِلَّهِ الْحَقِّ هُوَ خَيْرٌ ثَوَابًا وَخَيْرٌ عُقْبًا[1251].

[86]

كُنتَ تَرْجُو أَن يُلْقَى إِلَيْكَ الْكِتَابُ إِلَّا رَحْمَةً مِّن رَّبِّكَ فَلَا تَكُونَنَّ ظَهِيرًا لِّلْكَافِرِينَ[1252] {القصص/86}

قَالَ رَبِّ بِمَا أَنْعَمْتَ عَلَيَّ فَلَنْ أَكُونَ ظَهِيرًا لِّلْمُجْرِمِينَ[1253] {القصص/17}

وَيَعْبُدُونَ مِن دُونِ اللَّهِ مَا لَا يَنفَعُهُمْ وَلَا يَضُرُّهُمْ وَكَانَ الْكَافِرُ عَلَى رَبِّهِ ظَهِيرًا[1254] {الفرقان/55}

قُل لَّئِنِ اجْتَمَعَتِ الإِنسُ وَالْجِنُّ عَلَى أَن يَأْتُواْ بِمِثْلِ هَذَا الْقُرْآنِ لاَ يَأْتُونَ بِمِثْلِهِ وَلَوْ كَانَ بَعْضُهُمْ لِبَعْضٍ ظَهِيرًا[1255] {الإسراء/88}

When we analyze the above verses around the word ظَهِيرًا[1256], it is interesting to realize that it has a negative meaning. The common meaning of this word in the above ayahs can be supporting one another in the engagements of lies, fabrications, oppression, falsehood, injustice, unfairness, and ungratefulness.

1251. There the authority is [completely] for Allah, the Truth. He is best in reward and best in outcome.
1252. And you were not expecting that the Book would be conveyed to you, but [it is] a mercy from your Lord. So do not be an assistant to the disbelievers.
1253. He said, "My Lord, for the favor You bestowed upon me, I will never be an assistant to the criminals."
1254. But they worship rather than Allah that which does not benefit them or harm them, and the disbeliever is ever, against his Lord, an assistant [to Satan].
1255. Say, "If mankind and the jinn gathered in order to produce the like of this Qurān, they could not produce the like of it, even if they were to each other assistants."
1256. Assistance.

A Muslim can possibly be in this wrong disposition without realizing it. Therefore, this possibility is mentioned and believers are warned against it as فَلَا تَكُونَنَّ ظَهِيرًا لِّلْكَافِرِينَ[1257] {القصص/86}.

An example of this is mentioned in the case of Musa as. Musa as knows the possibility of these engagements in life which displease Allah ☀. Therefore, he asks for protection so as not to be in this disposition as mentioned فَلَنْ أَكُونَ ظَهِيرًا لِّلْمُجْرِمِينَ[1258] {القصص/17}.

On the other hand, the support of kafir or munāfiq to each other is obvious in wrong engagements. They explicitly do this as mentioned وَكَانَ الْكَافِرُ عَلَى رَبِّهِ ظَهِيرًا[1259] {الفرقان/55}.

Then, Allah ☀ mentions and challenges them even if they support each other strongly and openly in their wrong and false engagements as mentioned وَلَوْ كَانَ بَعْضُهُمْ لِبَعْضٍ ظَهِيرًا[1260] {الإسراء/88}, they will not be able to disprove, invalidate, and undermine this clear and strong truth of the Qurān as mentioned[1261] قُل لَّئِنِ اجْتَمَعَتِ الإِنسُ وَالْجِنُّ عَلَى أَن يَأْتُوا بِمِثْلِ هَذَا الْقُرْآنِ لاَ يَأْتُونَ بِمِثْلِهِ.

Surah Ankabut

[22]

وَمَا أَنتُم بِمُعْجِزِينَ فِي الْأَرْضِ وَلَا فِي السَّمَاء وَمَا لَكُم مِّن دُونِ اللَّهِ مِن وَلِيٍّ وَلَا نَصِيرٍ[1262] {العنكبوت/22}

It is interesting to note and review the legal definitions of waliy, وَلِيّ, in fiqh. The word وَلِيّ in the Qurān comes in many times with the word نَصِير[1263]:

أَلَمْ تَعْلَمْ أَنَّ اللَّهَ لَهُ مُلْكُ السَّمَاوَاتِ وَالْأَرْضِ وَمَا لَكُم مِّن دُونِ اللَّهِ مِن وَلِيٍّ وَلاَ نَصِيرٍ[1264] {البقرة/107}

1257. So do not be an assistant to the disbelievers.
1258. I will never be an assistant to the criminals."
1259. And the disbeliever is ever, against his Lord, an assistant [to Satan].
1260. They could not produce the like of it, even if they were to each other assistants."
1261. Say, "If mankind and the jinn gathered in order to produce the like of this Qurān, they could not produce the like of it,
1262. And you will not cause failure [to Allah] upon the earth or in the heaven. And you have not other than Allah any protector or any helper.
1263. Helper/assistant.
1264. Do you not know that to Allah belongs the dominion of the heavens and the earth and [that] you have not besides Allah any protector or any helper?

قُلْ مَن ذَا الَّذِي يَعْصِمُكُم مِّنَ اللَّهِ إِنْ أَرَادَ بِكُمْ سُوءًا أَوْ أَرَادَ بِكُمْ رَحْمَةً وَلَا يَجِدُونَ لَهُم مِّن دُونِ اللَّهِ وَلِيًّا وَلَا نَصِيرًا 1265{الأحزاب/17}

خَالِدِينَ فِيهَا أَبَدًا لَّا يَجِدُونَ وَلِيًّا وَلَا نَصِيرًا 1266{الأحزاب/65}

وَلَوْ شَاء اللَّهُ لَجَعَلَهُمْ أُمَّةً وَاحِدَةً وَلَكِن يُدْخِلُ مَن يَشَاءُ فِي رَحْمَتِهِ وَالظَّالِمُونَ مَا لَهُم مِّن وَلِيٍّ وَلَا نَصِيرٍ 1267{الشورى/8}

وَمَا أَنتُم بِمُعْجِزِينَ فِي الْأَرْضِ وَمَا لَكُم مِّن دُونِ اللَّهِ مِن وَلِيٍّ وَلَا نَصِيرٍ 1268{الشورى/31}

وَلَوْ قَاتَلَكُمُ الَّذِينَ كَفَرُوا لَوَلَّوُا الْأَدْبَارَ ثُمَّ لَا يَجِدُونَ وَلِيًّا وَلَا نَصِيرًا 1269{الفتح/22}

In this perspective, one of the features of a good waliyy is to protect the person and to always think and consider the best interest of the person. In its truest sense, there is no true waliy other than Allah ﷻ as mentioned وَمَا لَكُم مِّن دُونِ اللَّهَ مِن وَلِيٍّ وَلَا نَصِير 1270. When the person understands this, most of his or her problems can be solved inshAllah. The Qurān repeats this very critical notion to inscribe this critical essence into the person's heart and mind.

[48-49]

وَمَا كُنتَ تَتْلُو مِن قَبْلِهِ مِن كِتَابٍ وَلَا تَخُطُّهُ بِيَمِينِكَ إِذًا لَّارْتَابَ الْمُبْطِلُونَ 1271{العنكبوت/48} بَلْ هُوَ آيَاتٌ بَيِّنَاتٌ فِي صُدُورِ الَّذِينَ أُوتُوا الْعِلْمَ وَمَا يَجْحَدُ بِآيَاتِنَا إِلَّا الظَّالِمُونَ 1272{العنكبوت/49}

These ayahs in another perspective can signify the importance of reading, writing, and acquiring knowledge.

1265. Say, "Who is it that can protect you from Allah if He intends for you an ill or intends for you a mercy?" And they will not find for themselves besides Allah any protector or any helper.
1266. Abiding therein forever, they will not find a protector or a helper.
1267. And if Allah willed, He could have made them [of] one religion, but He admits whom He wills into His mercy. And the wrongdoers have not any protector or helper.
1268. And you will not cause failure [to Allah] upon the earth. And you have not besides Allah any protector or helper.
1269. And if those [Makkans] who disbelieve had fought you, they would have turned their backs [in flight]. Then they would not find a protector or a helper.
1270. And you have not besides Allah any protector or helper.
1271. And you did not recite before it any scripture, nor did you inscribe one with your right hand. Then [i.e., otherwise] the falsifiers would have had [cause for] doubt.
1272. Rather, it [i.e., the Qurān] is distinct verses [preserved] within the breasts of those who have been given knowledge. And none reject Our verses except the wrongdoers.

21

Surah Luqman

[12-19]

وَلَقَدْ آتَيْنَا لُقْمَانَ الْحِكْمَةَ أَنِ اشْكُرْ لِلَّهِ وَمَن يَشْكُرْ فَإِنَّمَا يَشْكُرُ لِنَفْسِهِ وَمَن كَفَرَ فَإِنَّ اللَّهَ
غَنِيٌّ حَمِيدٌ 1273 {لقمان/12} وَإِذْ قَالَ لُقْمَانُ لِابْنِهِ وَهُوَ يَعِظُهُ يَا بُنَيَّ لَا تُشْرِكْ بِاللَّهِ إِنَّ
الشِّرْكَ لَظُلْمٌ عَظِيمٌ 1274 {لقمان/13} وَوَصَّيْنَا الْإِنسَانَ بِوَالِدَيْهِ حَمَلَتْهُ أُمُّهُ وَهْنًا عَلَى وَهْنٍ
وَفِصَالُهُ فِي عَامَيْنِ أَنِ اشْكُرْ لِي وَلِوَالِدَيْكَ إِلَيَّ الْمَصِيرُ 1275 {لقمان/14} وَإِن جَاهَدَاكَ
عَلَى أَن تُشْرِكَ بِي مَا لَيْسَ لَكَ بِهِ عِلْمٌ فَلَا تُطِعْهُمَا وَصَاحِبْهُمَا فِي الدُّنْيَا مَعْرُوفًا وَاتَّبِعْ
سَبِيلَ مَنْ أَنَابَ إِلَيَّ ثُمَّ إِلَيَّ مَرْجِعُكُمْ فَأُنَبِّئُكُم بِمَا كُنتُمْ تَعْمَلُونَ 1276 {لقمان/15} يَا بُنَيَّ
إِنَّهَا إِن تَكُ مِثْقَالَ حَبَّةٍ مِّنْ خَرْدَلٍ فَتَكُن فِي صَخْرَةٍ أَوْ فِي السَّمَاوَاتِ أَوْ فِي الْأَرْضِ
يَأْتِ بِهَا اللَّهُ إِنَّ اللَّهَ لَطِيفٌ خَبِيرٌ 1277 {لقمان/16} يَا بُنَيَّ أَقِمِ الصَّلَاةَ وَأْمُرْ بِالْمَعْرُوفِ
وَانْهَ عَنِ الْمُنكَرِ وَاصْبِرْ عَلَى مَا أَصَابَكَ إِنَّ ذَلِكَ مِنْ عَزْمِ الْأُمُورِ 1278 {لقمان/17}
وَلَا تُصَعِّرْ خَدَّكَ لِلنَّاسِ وَلَا تَمْشِ فِي الْأَرْضِ مَرَحًا إِنَّ اللَّهَ لَا يُحِبُّ كُلَّ مُخْتَالٍ فَخُورٍ
1279 {لقمان/18} وَاقْصِدْ فِي مَشْيِكَ وَاغْضُضْ مِن صَوْتِكَ إِنَّ أَنكَرَ الْأَصْوَاتِ لَصَوْتُ
الْحَمِيرِ 1280 {لقمان/19}

1273. And We had certainly given Luqmān wisdom [and said], "Be grateful to Allah." And whoever is grateful is grateful for [the benefit of] himself. And whoever denies [His favor]—then indeed, Allah is Free of need and Praiseworthy.
1274. And [mention, O Muhammad], when Luqmān said to his son while he was instructing him, "O my son, do not associate [anything] with Allah. Indeed, association [with Him] is great injustice."
1275. And We have enjoined upon man [care] for his parents. His mother carried him, [increasing her] in weakness upon weakness, and his weaning is in two years. Be grateful to Me and to your parents; to Me is the [final] destination.
1276. But if they endeavor to make you associate with Me that of which you have no knowledge, do not obey them but accompany them in [this] world with appropriate kindness and follow the way of those who turn back to Me [in repentance]. Then to Me will be your return, and I will inform you about what you used to do.
1277. [And Luqmān said], "O my son, indeed if it [i.e., a wrong] should be the weight of a mustard seed and should be within a rock or [anywhere] in the heavens or in the earth, Allah will bring it forth. Indeed, Allah is Subtle and Acquainted.
1278. O my son, establish prayer, enjoin what is right, forbid what is wrong, and be patient over what befalls you. Indeed, [all] that is of the matters [requiring] resolve.
1279. And do not turn your cheek [in contempt] toward people and do not walk through the earth exultantly. Indeed, Allah does not like everyone self-deluded and boastful.
1280. And be moderate in your pace and lower your voice; indeed, the most disagreeable of sounds is the voice of donkeys."

One of the notions about hikmah[1281] is in its implementation when a person is given authority. When a person has authority and power over others, then the notion of hikmah becomes very critical.

One of the manifestations of this power is in family life. When there is a power or authority such as that of parents, they are expected to implement this authority with hikmah.

The implementation of authority can be open to a lot of abuses, destructions, run-aways, rebellions, uproars, and anger on the subjects if there is no hikmah.

Especially in the closed circuits of physical spaces called houses or norms dictated by the culture, these abuses can be difficult to detect, know, and eventually help alleviate.

One of these cases is the relationship between the children and parents. Adults or parents can have the means to abuse children mentally, emotionally, and physically. Yet, in these cases, it can be difficult for a child to speak up and address their concerns, especially when and if these cases are done in constant upbringing of children at homes or houses in parent/adult and child relationships. In other words, abuse or maltreatment can be more difficult publicly and with stronger individuals of character and age ascompared to private venues such as homes and weak individuals such as children.

Therefore, this surah is very critical to analyze to highlight these perspectives.

One of the critical points of this surah is that unsupervised and private authority requires hikmah with the weakest, the children. Authority and power are not given to a person to abuse but to establish structure and order so that one can encounter and be in the worlds of hikmah. In this type of society, family, and education, the students or learners discover the realities in their self-struggle with relevance. Instead of implementing something due to the fear of the authority or power in the short-term, the hikmah builds in them the character traits of self-confidence, strength, and the true imãn in their relationship with Allah ﷻ.

Now if one can analyze the below ayahs in the highlights of hikmah, how Luqman as implements as a parent, one can really realize this long-term investment in the choice of words and style:

1281. Wisdom.

يَا بُنَيَّ إِنَّهَا إِن تَكُ مِثْقَالَ حَبَّةٍ مِّنْ خَرْدَلٍ فَتَكُن فِي صَخْرَةٍ أَوْ فِي السَّمَاوَاتِ أَوْ فِي الْأَرْضِ يَأْتِ بِهَا اللَّهُ إِنَّ اللَّهَ لَطِيفٌ خَبِيرٌ 1282 {لقمان/16} يَا بُنَيَّ أَقِمِ الصَّلَاةَ وَأْمُرْ بِالْمَعْرُوفِ وَانْهَ عَنِ الْمُنكَرِ وَاصْبِرْ عَلَى مَا أَصَابَكَ إِنَّ ذَلِكَ مِنْ عَزْمِ الْأُمُورِ 1283 {لقمان/17} وَلَا تُصَعِّرْ خَدَّكَ لِلنَّاسِ وَلَا تَمْشِ فِي الْأَرْضِ مَرَحًا إِنَّ اللَّهَ لَا يُحِبُّ كُلَّ مُخْتَالٍ فَخُورٍ 1284 {لقمان/18} وَاقْصِدْ فِي مَشْيِكَ وَاغْضُضْ مِن صَوْتِكَ إِنَّ أَنكَرَ الْأَصْوَاتِ لَصَوْتُ الْحَمِيرِ 1285 {لقمان/19}

The word choice يَا بُنَيَّ can allude to this softness, gentleness, and kindness in teaching instead of yelling, hitting, or being mean to the child as the holder of authority. Yet, the authority can engage in those acts, but the real authority as described in the Qurān does not abuse, but rather aims to get the highest results in child education and in all human relations.

The teaching إِنَّهَا إِن تَكُ مِثْقَالَ حَبَّةٍ مِّنْ خَرْدَلٍ فَتَكُن فِي صَخْرَةٍ أَوْ فِي السَّمَاوَاتِ أَوْ فِي الْأَرْضِ يَأْتِ بِهَا اللَّهُ إِنَّ اللَّهَ لَطِيفٌ خَبِيرٌ 1286 {لقمان/16} instills the child or any person with the All-Knowing, All- Wise, Higher, Just, Fair, Kind, Gentle, and Loving Authority, Allah ﷻ. The reference point of the child or person is not an immediate weak human authority that can incline injustice or abuse but their true accountability is with the Highest Fair Just Gentle Loving Authority of Allah ﷻ. In this sense, this implements in the individual or a child a very critical principle of the decision-making process about their own selves as well as in their authority of others. This is that ultimately there is a just and fair accountability for all human engagements beyond the weak, unjust, and unfair accountabilities of humans.

The teachings يَا بُنَيَّ أَقِمِ الصَّلَاةَ وَأْمُرْ بِالْمَعْرُوفِ وَانْهَ عَنِ الْمُنكَرِ وَاصْبِرْ عَلَى مَا أَصَابَكَ إِنَّ ذَلِكَ مِنْ عَزْمِ الْأُمُورِ 1287 {لقمان/17} can practically show how to

---

1282. [And Luqmān said], "O my son, indeed if it [i.e., a wrong] should be the weight of a mustard seed and should be within a rock or [anywhere] in the heavens or in the earth, Allah will bring it forth. Indeed, Allah is Subtle and Acquainted.

1283. O my son, establish prayer, enjoin what is right, forbid what is wrong, and be patient over what befalls you. Indeed, [all] that is of the matters [requiring] resolve.

1284. And do not turn your cheek [in contempt] toward people and do not walk through the earth exultantly. Indeed, Allah does not like everyone self-deluded and boastful.

1285. And be moderate in your pace and lower your voice; indeed, the most disagreeable of sounds is the voice of donkeys."

1286. Indeed if it [i.e., a wrong] should be the weight of a mustard seed and should be within a rock or [anywhere] in the heavens or in the earth, Allah will bring it forth. Indeed, Allah is Subtle and Acquainted.

1287. O my son, establish prayer, enjoin what is right, forbid what is wrong, and be patient over what befalls you. Indeed, [all] that is of the matters [requiring] resolve.

substantiate this trait of decision making with hikmah and build this person up with strong character traits of fairness, patience, and justice. One of the key ways to embody these positive traits is by establishing five daily prayers, salah. At the same time, in social problems, family problems, or individual problems, the person should always look for the virtuous, the good, and try to stop evil, abuse, and injustice. Sometimes, change can come over time and the person should wait with patience.

The teachings وَلَا تُصَعِّرْ خَدَّكَ لِلنَّاسِ وَلَا تَمْشِ فِي الْأَرْضِ مَرَحًا إِنَّ اللَّهَ لَا يُحِبُّ كُلَّ مُخْتَالٍ فَخُورٍ {لقمان/18} 1288 وَاقْصِدْ فِي مَشْيِكَ وَاغْضُضْ مِن صَوْتِكَ إِنَّ أَنكَرَ الْأَصْوَاتِ لَصَوْتُ الْحَمِيرِ 1289 {لقمان/19} detail more about where people seem to be alienated from each other and from Allah ﷻ. This happens when people show the signs of arrogance in their attitudes and actions. Sometimes the person may not even mean to seem arrogant, so the person should always try to empathize with others such as in the ways of communication, tone of voice, and gestures in order to not abuse and offend them. Yet, being gentle, kind, and soft are the character traits. Allah ﷻ has created different animals so that we can take lessons from them. In some cases, we can try to emulate them such as being inspired by birds and then constructing planes and advancing in aviation. Or, by looking at some animals such as donkeys and taking an example from their loud and disturbing screams so that we do not emulate them in the intensity, tone, and harshness of our voices.

In all of the above discourses, the small scale authority of humans that we are sharing with others means that are we are constantly in the position of decision making and we are accountable in this decision making. This is the real goal and purpose of our life as

إِنَّا عَرَضْنَا الْأَمَانَةَ عَلَى السَّمَاوَاتِ وَالْأَرْضِ وَالْجِبَالِ فَأَبَيْنَ أَن يَحْمِلْنَهَا وَأَشْفَقْنَ مِنْهَا وَحَمَلَهَا الْإِنسَانُ إِنَّهُ كَانَ ظَلُومًا جَهُولًا 1290 {الأحزاب/72}

1288. And do not turn your cheek [in contempt] toward people and do not walk through the earth exultantly. Indeed, Allah does not like everyone self-deluded and boastful.

1289. And be moderate in your pace and lower your voice; indeed, the most disagreeable of sounds is the voice of donkeys."

1290. Indeed, We offered the Trust to the heavens and the earth and the mountains, and they declined to bear it and feared it; but man [undertook to] bear it. Indeed, he was unjust and ignorant.

The amānah[1291] as mentioned here can be our authority. Some may call this term khalifah. Our authority is over our own self. Our authority is over our nafs, heart, mind, and body. Our authority is also over others as parents, teachers, social, and professional positions of decision making.

In these roles of decision making, the only way to eliminate abuse and oppression is by embodying hikmah. The hikmah is, as agreed upon by the ulama, the Sunnah of Rasulullah ﷺ. One can analyze how Rasulullah ﷺ treated women, children, other fellows, animals, and even objects. Then, one can look at today's civilized notions of equality, justice, fairness, and prevention of abuse cases. A human, Rasulullah ﷺ, instructed by Allah ﷻ embodies the hikmah.

It is a different discussion if Muslims today or in the past thoroughly implement hikmah. As long as Muslims implement the true teachings of Rasulullah ﷺ, then they can approximate the true teachings of hikmah beyond their own cultural, identity, gender, and social blocks and barriers.

The oppression and abuse will oppress others. Each oppression against others will also oppress our own selves eventually. It is interesting to note that in Surah Ahzab where the critical verse of amanah is mentioned immediately follows Surah Luqman where one of the main themes is hikmah. Nothing in the Qurān is haphazard or random. Every letter, even dots on the letters, have a deep purpose.

To balance the above perspectives the subjects or children in this case should also realize their role in regard to their parents as mentioned

وَوَصَّيْنَا الْإِنسَانَ بِوَالِدَيْهِ حَمَلَتْهُ أُمُّهُ وَهْنًا عَلَى وَهْنٍ وَفِصَالُهُ فِي عَامَيْنِ أَنِ اشْكُرْ لِي وَلِوَالِدَيْكَ إِلَيَّ الْمَصِيرُ {لقمان/14}[1292] وَإِن جَاهَدَاكَ عَلَى أَن تُشْرِكَ بِي مَا لَيْسَ لَكَ بِهِ عِلْمٌ فَلَا تُطِعْهُمَا وَصَاحِبْهُمَا فِي الدُّنْيَا مَعْرُوفًا وَاتَّبِعْ سَبِيلَ مَنْ أَنَابَ إِلَيَّ ثُمَّ إِلَيَّ مَرْجِعُكُمْ فَأُنَبِّئُكُم بِمَا كُنتُمْ تَعْمَلُونَ[1293] {لقمان/15}

1291. Trust.
1292. And We have enjoined upon man [care] for his parents. His mother carried him, [increasing her] in weakness upon weakness, and his weaning is in two years. Be grateful to Me and to your parents; to Me is the [final] destination.
1293. But if they endeavor to make you associate with Me that of which you have no knowledge, do not obey them but accompany them in [this] world with appropriate kindness and follow the way of those who turn back to Me [in repentance]. Then to Me will be your return, and I will inform you about what you used to do.

It is interesting to note that the word وَوَصَّيْنَا الْإِنسَانَ[1294] is used. When Allah ﷻ makes wasiyyah[1295], this can possibly show that it becomes an unchanging rule or principle across generations of people. The word الْإِنسَانَ[1296] can show that this principle is for all humans. In this regard, one can now realize this unchanging principle across different religions and times and history and that there has been always an established teaching of respecting the parents, loving and appreciating them.

It is interesting to realize the word choice حَمَلَتْهُ أُمُّهُ[1297], that the mother carries the child but does not create the child. The mother is a vehicle to deliver the child who is created by Allah ﷻ. Yet, being this vehicle and making this favor on the child especially in this case as mentioned حَمَلَتْهُ أُمُّهُ وَهْنًا عَلَى وَهْنٍ وَفِصَالُهُ فِي عَامَيْنِ[1298].

Yet, the person should know the Real Creator, Allah ﷻ as mentioned أَنِ اشْكُرْ لِي[1299] because ultimately the person will go back to the Real Creator, Allah ﷻ as mentioned إِلَيَّ الْمَصِيرُ[1300]. Yet, it is also very critical as instructed and ordered by Allah ﷻ to be appreciative to the parents as mentioned وَلِوَالِدَيْكَ[1301]. Therefore, it is really difficult to please Allah ﷻ unless the child has a positive, pleasing relationship with the parents and respects, appreciates, and pleases them.

وَإِن جَاهَدَاكَ There can always be exceptions to this rule as mentioned عَلَى أَن تُشْرِكَ بِي مَا لَيْسَ لَكَ بِهِ عِلْمٌ فَلَا تُطِعْهُمَا وَصَاحِبْهُمَا فِي الدُّنْيَا مَعْرُوفًا وَاتَّبِعْ سَبِيلَ مَنْ أَنَابَ إِلَيَّ ثُمَّ إِلَيَّ مَرْجِعُكُمْ فَأُنَبِّئُكُم بِمَا كُنتُمْ تَعْمَلُونَ[1302] {لقمان/15}. This rule is if the parents urge the child to make shirk. Then, the person should not follow or listen to them. Yet, even in this case, the good and gentle manners toward them is still required as mentioned وَصَاحِبْهُمَا فِي الدُّنْيَا مَعْرُوفًا[1303]. They deserve good, nice, and gentle treatment because they were the

---

1294. And We have enjoined upon man {care}.
1295. Enjoined.
1296. Man.
1297. His mother carried him.
1298. His mother carried him, [increasing her] in weakness upon weakness, and his weaning is in two years.
1299. Be grateful to Me.
1300. To Me is the [final] destination.
1301. And to your parents.
1302. But if they endeavor to make you associate with Me that of which you have no knowledge, do not obey them but accompany them in [this] world with appropriate kindness and follow the way of those who turn back to Me [in repentance]. Then to Me will be your return, and I will inform you about what you used to do.
1303. Accompany them in [this] world with appropriate kindness.

vehicle of existence for this person's life. Therefore, the person should appreciate and still treat them with kindness, gentleness, and softness.

On a side note, one of the titles of Rasulullah ﷺ is ummi. In its word meaning, Rasulullah ﷺ makes us born like a mother in order to understand our true meaning, goal, and purpose in life. In this regard, Rasulullah ﷺ is a critical vital element for our spiritual existence in order to please Allah ﷻ. Similarly, it is really difficult to please Allah ﷻ unless the person has a positive, pleasing relationship with Rasulullah ﷺ, and they respect and appreciate Rasulullah ﷺ, and the sunnah and follow them as much as one can.

In this regard, one can understand why the order of rights due in Islamic jurisprudence is Allah ﷻ, then Rasulullah ﷺ and then the parents. One cannot know Allah ﷻ in the way that is authentic unless one knows Rasulullah ﷺ. One cannot know the true rights of one's parents unless one knows Rasulullah ﷺ. Therefore, true appreciation and imān require loving and preferring Allah ﷻ and Rasulullah ﷺ over our own selves and preferences. In simpler other words, true imān requires that we love Allah and Rasulullah ﷺ more than our own selves. Yet, this requirement may not be expected as the requirement of imān for the love of parents. Yet, it is critical and paramount to appreciate and please them in order to please Allah ﷻ and follow the teachings of Rasulullah ﷺ.

With a similar discussion and on a side note, one can understand, why mothers are expected to have more rights than a father in Islamic jurisprudence. Mothers serve more as the main vehicle in the delivery of a child for the creation of Allah ﷻ as

mentioned حَمَلَتْهُ أُمُّهُ وَهْنًا عَلَى وَهْنٍ وَفِصَالُهُ فِي عَامَيْنِ[1304]. The case of Maryam as serving as the main vehicle in the delivery of a child, Isa as, for the creation of Allah ﷻ can also possibly prove this point. Fathers cannot deliver a child.

On the other hand, the creation of Adam as without any vehicle of mother or father shows the direct creation of the first human being without any means or vehicles by Allah ﷻ. In that sense, the creation of Adam as can allude to the Uluhiyyah[1305] of Allah ﷻ as mentioned فَإِذَا

1304. His mother carried him, [increasing her] in weakness upon weakness, and his weaning is in two years.
1305. Realm of power.

سَوَّيْتُهُ وَنَفَخْتُ فِيهِ مِن رُّوحِي فَقَعُوا لَهُ سَاجِدِينَ 1306{الحجر/29}. The emphasis in the sign of Mutakallim as in سَوَّيْتُهُ1307, and وَنَفَخْتُ فِيهِ مِن رُّوحِي1308 can allude to this notion.

The creation of Isa as can allude to the Rububiyyah1309 of Allah ﷻ that Allah ﷻ showed the direct manifestation of Rububiyyah without any father as mentioned مَا قُلْتُ لَهُمْ إِلَّا مَا أَمَرْتَنِي بِهِ أَنِ اعْبُدُوا اللَّهَ رَبِّي وَرَبَّكُمْ وَكُنتُ عَلَيْهِمْ شَهِيدًا مَّا دُمْتُ فِيهِمْ فَلَمَّا تَوَفَّيْتَنِي كُنتَ أَنتَ الرَّقِيبَ عَلَيْهِمْ وَأَنتَ عَلَى كُلِّ شَيْءٍ شَهِيدٌ {المائدة/117}1310. The expression رَبِّي وَرَبَّكُمْ1311 can allude to this stance.

The creation of Rasulullah ﷺ can allude to the ubudiyyah to Allah ﷻ as the main, essence and goal of all creation as mentioned وَمَا خَلَقْتُ الْجِنَّ وَالْإِنسَ إِلَّا لِيَعْبُدُونِ 1312{الذاريات/56}

and سُبْحَانَ الَّذِي أَسْرَىٰ بِعَبْدِهِ لَيْلًا مِّنَ الْمَسْجِدِ الْحَرَامِ إِلَى الْمَسْجِدِ الْأَقْصَى الَّذِي بَارَكْنَا حَوْلَهُ لِنُرِيَهُ مِنْ آيَاتِنَا إِنَّهُ هُوَ السَّمِيعُ الْبَصِيرُ1313{الإسراء/1}. The word بِعَبْدِهِ1314 can allude to Rasulullah ﷺ as the epitome and real essence and fruit of all in all of the creation tree.

Fathers are expected to deliver other responsibilities later in life for the child. One can remember the hadith of Rasululah ﷺ as repeating three times the right of the mother over the father [15].If Allah ﷻ instructs us to be so very grateful, kind, loving, and gentle to our parents as they are our means and vehicle of our physical existence, and we are instructed to be so very grateful and loving to Rasulullah ﷺ by following the sunnah as much as we can and by showing our gratitude and appreciation with constant salawats to Rasulullah ﷺ as he saw is our means and critical sole element of our spiritual existence of ihsan, imān, and Islam, how about Allah ﷻ, the Real Giver without any vehicles?

1306. And when I have proportioned him and breathed into him of My [created] soul, then fall down to him in prostration."
1307. I have proportioned him.
1308. And breathed into him of My [created] soul.
1309. Lordship.
1310. I said not to them except what You commanded me—to worship Allah, my Lord and your Lord. And I was a witness over them as long as I was among them; but when You took me up, You were the Observer over them, and You are, over all things, Witness.
1311. My Lord and your Lord.
1312. And I did not create the jinn and mankind except to worship Me.
1313. Exalted is He who took His Servant [i.e.,Prophet Muhammad (ﷺ)] by night from al-Masjid al-harām to al-Masjid al-Aqsā, whose surroundings We have blessed, to show him of Our signs. Indeed, He is the Hearing, the Seeing.
1314. His Servant.

Therefore, the main and core of all of them are وَإِذْ قَالَ لُقْمَانُ لِاِبْنِهِ وَهُوَ يَعِظُهُ يَا بُنَيَّ لَا تُشْرِكْ بِاللَّهِ إِنَّ الشِّرْكَ لَظُلْمٌ عَظِيمٌ {لقمان/13}[1315] as mentioned in the very beginning. All of the above discussions start with this main teaching. Then, we try to locate everything within this perspective. Yes, recognizing the Real Giver, Allah ﷻ, and recognizing the deliverers of our spiritual and physical means as a show of respect to Allah ﷻ is key.

22

Surah Ahzab

[53]

يَا أَيُّهَا الَّذِينَ آمَنُوا لَا تَدْخُلُوا بُيُوتَ النَّبِيِّ إِلَّا أَن يُؤْذَنَ لَكُمْ إِلَى طَعَامٍ غَيْرَ نَاظِرِينَ إِنَاهُ وَلَكِنْ إِذَا دُعِيتُمْ فَادْخُلُوا فَإِذَا طَعِمْتُمْ فَانتَشِرُوا وَلَا مُسْتَأْنِسِينَ لِحَدِيثٍ إِنَّ ذَلِكُمْ كَانَ يُؤْذِي النَّبِيَّ فَيَسْتَحْيِي مِنكُمْ وَاللَّهُ لَا يَسْتَحْيِي مِنَ الْحَقِّ وَإِذَا سَأَلْتُمُوهُنَّ مَتَاعًا فَاسْأَلُوهُنَّ مِن وَرَاءِ حِجَابٍ ذَلِكُمْ أَطْهَرُ لِقُلُوبِكُمْ وَقُلُوبِهِنَّ وَمَا كَانَ لَكُمْ أَن تُؤْذُوا رَسُولَ اللَّهِ وَلَا أَن تَنكِحُوا أَزْوَاجَهُ مِن بَعْدِهِ أَبَدًا إِنَّ ذَلِكُمْ كَانَ عِندَ اللَّهِ عَظِيمًا [1316]{الأحزاب/53}

One can review the Qurān especially when the addressee is directly, implicitly or explicitly Rasulullah ﷺ that actually, the instruction informs us to be like Rasulullah ﷺ, to follow Rasulullah ﷺ, to keep the high esteem and respect of Rasulullah ﷺ, and to implement all teachings of belief, social life and others as exemplified by Rasulullah ﷺ. Although one may not be able to fully follow the sunnah, yet one knows and realizes that the sunnah shows the perfect and utmost application of everything at their zenith levels. With this understanding one can take every ayah of the Qurān accordingly with personal relevance inshAllah.

1315. And [mention, O Muhammad], when Luqmān said to his son while he was instructing him, "O my son, do not associate [anything] with Allah. Indeed, association [with Him] is great injustice."

1316. O you who have believed, do not enter the houses of the Prophet except when you are permitted for a meal, without awaiting its readiness. But when you are invited, then enter; and when you have eaten, disperse without seeking to remain for conversation. Indeed, that [behavior] was troubling the Prophet, and he is shy of [dismissing] you. But Allah is not shy of the truth. And when you ask [his wives] for something, ask them from behind a partition. That is purer for your hearts and their hearts. And it is not [conceivable or lawful] for you to harm the Messenger of Allah or to marry his wives after him, ever. Indeed, that would be in the sight of Allah an enormity.

For example, if we review the ayah يَا أَيُّهَا الَّذِينَ آمَنُوا لَا تَدْخُلُوا بُيُوتَ النَّبِيِّ إِلَّا أَن يُؤْذَنَ لَكُمْ إِلَى طَعَامٍ غَيْرَ نَاظِرِينَ إِنَاهُ وَلَكِنْ إِذَا دُعِيتُمْ فَادْخُلُوا فَإِذَا طَعِمْتُمْ فَانتَشِرُوا وَلَا مُسْتَأْنِسِينَ لِحَدِيثٍ إِنَّ ذَلِكُمْ كَانَ يُؤْذِي النَّبِيَّ فَيَسْتَحْيِي مِنكُمْ وَاللَّهُ لَا يَسْتَحْيِي مِنَ الْحَقِّ وَإِذَا سَأَلْتُمُوهُنَّ مَتَاعًا فَاسْأَلُوهُنَّ مِن وَرَاء حِجَابٍ ذَلِكُمْ أَطْهَرُ لِقُلُوبِكُمْ وَقُلُوبِهِنَّ وَمَا كَانَ لَكُمْ أَن تُؤْذُوا رَسُولَ اللَّهِ وَلَا أَن تَنكِحُوا أَزْوَاجَهُ مِن بَعْدِهِ أَبَدًا إِنَّ ذَلِكُمْ كَانَ عِندَ اللَّهِ عَظِيمًا {الأحزاب/53}, one can say, in this we learn the etiquette of being a guest. How can the ayah can relate to me for relevance when it mentions a specific high and noble character of Rasulullah ﷺ as: ١٣١٧إِنَّ ذَلِكُمْ كَانَ يُؤْذِي النَّبِيَّ فَيَسْتَحْيِي مِنكُمْ.

In this case, Allah ﷻ possibly shows the adab and etiquette of being a host like Rasulullah ﷺ. In other words, although it can be difficult for the host when guests are engaged in conversations and and don't want to leave the house, it is still the highest and noblest host adab to be patient and not tell them to leave as Rasulullah ﷺ practiced, ١٣١٨الله اعلم.

[60]

لَئِن لَّمْ يَنتَهِ الْمُنَافِقُونَ وَالَّذِينَ فِي قُلُوبِهِم مَّرَضٌ وَالْمُرْجِفُونَ فِي الْمَدِينَةِ لَنُغْرِيَنَّكَ بِهِمْ ثُمَّ لَا يُجَاوِرُونَكَ فِيهَا إِلَّا قَلِيلًا ١٣١٩{الأحزاب/60}

It is interesting to realize the word يُجَاوِرُونَكَ ١٣٢٠is used besides other possibilities. This can show the importance of having appreciation of the presence of the Prophet saw and possibly the pious salaf, awliya and of following the footsteps of the Prophet saw in one's life. In other words, a ni'mah or a blessing is taken away from people if they don't appreciate it. In this case, Rasulullah ﷺ is the biggest ni'mah. If they don't appreciate the Prophet saw, then this ni'mah would be taken away as mentioned in this ayah. Similarly, the people of knowledge, I'lm, and the people of I'badah, are ni'mah in a household or in a community. If the people don't appreciate them, then Allah ﷻ can take them away due to the people's ungrateful attitude towards them, الله اعلم.

1317. Indeed, that [behavior] was troubling the Prophet, and he is shy of [dismissing] you.
1318. Allah ﷻ knows best.
1319. If the hypocrites and those in whose hearts is disease and those who spread rumors in al-Madînah do not cease, We will surely incite you against them; then they will not remain your neighbors therein except for a little,
1320. Remain your neighbors.

[69]

يَا أَيُّهَا الَّذِينَ آمَنُوا لَا تَكُونُوا كَالَّذِينَ آذَوْا مُوسَى فَبَرَّأَهُ اللَّهُ مِمَّا قَالُوا وَكَانَ عِندَ اللَّهِ وَجِيهًا {الأحزاب/69}[1321]

This is again another distinction between the followers of Rasulullah ﷺ and the followers of other prophets alayhisallatu wasallam. The sahaba were very keen on Rasulullah ﷺ. They did not want anyone to even approach him with a bad look or intention toward Rasulullah ﷺ. Rasulullah ﷺ was the most precious being for them. They truly embodied loving and putting Allah ﷻ and Rasulullah ﷺ first in their list of life engagements.

Whereas, one can see the other followers as mentioned in the Qurãn as:

يَا أَيُّهَا الَّذِينَ آمَنُوا لَا تَكُونُوا كَالَّذِينَ آذَوْا مُوسَى فَبَرَّأَهُ اللَّهُ مِمَّا قَالُوا وَكَانَ عِندَ اللَّهِ وَجِيهًا {الأحزاب/69}[1322]

One of the reasons that Musa as can be an ulul a'zm messenger can be due to the disrespectful behavior that he was exposed to by his own people. When others disrespect you it may hurt you, but when the people around you such as your students or children disrespect you, that may hurt you even more.

Therefore, Musa as showed immense patience and one can remember these patience-related renderings with Yaqub with his own children. Patience is an avenue to raise one's level.

It is very interesting to note that in the same surah of Ahzab that same notion of a'za is mentioned before the above ayah for Musa as as:

يَا أَيُّهَا الَّذِينَ آمَنُوا لَا تَدْخُلُوا بُيُوتَ النَّبِيِّ إِلَّا أَن يُؤْذَنَ لَكُمْ إِلَى طَعَامٍ غَيْرَ نَاظِرِينَ إِنَاهُ وَلَكِنْ إِذَا دُعِيتُمْ فَادْخُلُوا فَإِذَا طَعِمْتُمْ فَانتَشِرُوا وَلَا مُسْتَأْنِسِينَ لِحَدِيثٍ إِنَّ ذَلِكُمْ كَانَ يُؤْذِي النَّبِيَّ فَيَسْتَحْيِي مِنكُمْ وَاللَّهُ لَا يَسْتَحْيِي مِنَ الْحَقِّ وَإِذَا سَأَلْتُمُوهُنَّ مَتَاعًا فَاسْأَلُوهُنَّ مِن وَرَاءِ حِجَابٍ ذَلِكُمْ أَطْهَرُ

1321. O you who have believed, be not like those who abused Moses; then Allah cleared him of what they said. And he, in the sight of Allah, was distinguished.
1322. O you who have believed, be not like those who abused Moses; then Allah cleared him of what they said. And he, in the sight of Allah, was distinguished.

لِقُلُوبِكُمْ وَقُلُوبِهِنَّ وَمَا كَانَ لَكُمْ أَن تُؤْذُوا رَسُولَ اللَّهِ وَلَا أَن تَنكِحُوا أَزْوَاجَهُ مِن بَعْدِهِ أَبَدًا إِنَّ ذَٰلِكُمْ كَانَ عِندَ اللَّهِ عَظِيمًا 1323 {الأحزاب/53}

Again the case of sahabah with this word of a'za can be due to not knowing the proper etiquette as mentioned in this ayah. The case of a'za with Musa as can be a case of knowing the etiquette but still not applying or insisting upon it[1324], اعلم الله. Therefore, Allah ﷺ mentions يَا أَيُّهَا الَّذِينَ آمَنُوا لَا تَكُونُوا كَالَّذِينَ آذَوْا مُوسَىٰ 1325 to the sahabah and to all of us.

Surah Saba

[1, 6, 5, 16, 54]

Each surah of the Qurān can address one primary disease of the current time. When one reviews this surah, this surah especially addresses the discourses of people approaching the true religion of Allah ﷺ with skepticism as mentioned إِنَّهُمْ كَانُوا فِي شَكٍّ مُّرِيبٍ 1326 {سبأ/54}, questioning, and arrogance as mentioned فَقَالُوا رَبَّنَا بَاعِدْ بَيْنَ أَسْفَارِنَا وَظَلَمُوا أَنفُسَهُمْ 1327. In other words, there may be people who at one point follow these teachings. There may be people who follow them and then change over time. This surah explains how Allah ﷺ stops sending the flowing ni'mah to them due to their ungrateful attitudes and their implicit arrogance as mentioned in the case of the people of Saba as mentioned فَأَعْرَضُوا فَأَرْسَلْنَا عَلَيْهِمْ سَيْلَ الْعَرِمِ وَبَدَّلْنَاهُم بِجَنَّتَيْهِمْ جَنَّتَيْنِ ذَوَاتَىْ أُكُلٍ خَمْطٍ وَأَثْلٍ وَشَيْءٍ مِّن سِدْرٍ قَلِيلٍ 1328 {سبأ/16}.

In this Surah, another interesting point is mentioned to actualize and classify people with today's academic approaches of critical thinking and knowledge. If people are only learning to argue or to disagree, this is

---

1323. O you who have believed, do not enter the houses of the Prophet except when you are permitted for a meal, without awaiting its readiness. But when you are invited, then enter; and when you have eaten, disperse without seeking to remain for conversation. Indeed, that [behavior] was troubling the Prophet, and he is shy of [dismissing] you. But Allah is not shy of the truth. And when you ask [his wives] for something, ask them from behind a partition. That is purer for your hearts and their hearts. And it is not [conceivable or lawful] for you to harm the Messenger of Allah or to marry his wives after him, ever. Indeed, that would be in the sight of Allah an enormity.

1324. Allah ﷺ knows best.

1325. O you who have believed, be not like those who abused Moses.

1326. Indeed, they were in disquieting doubt [i.e., denial].

1327. Our Lord, lengthen the distance between our journeys," and wronged themselves.

1328. But they turned away [refusing], so We sent upon them the flood of the dam, and We replaced their two [fields of] gardens with gardens of bitter fruit, tamarisks and something of sparse lote trees.

a destructive character trait even though they may be called professors or even distinguished professors as recognized by their universities. The ayah 1329﴿سبأ/5﴾ وَالَّذِينَ سَعَوْا فِي آيَاتِنَا مُعَاجِزِينَ أُوْلَئِكَ لَهُمْ عَذَابٌ مِّن رِّجْزٍ أَلِيمٌ can allude to this approach.

On the other hand, the people who have the intention of learning the genuine knowledge, but not using it as a means to argue are encouraged to further their studies and they are the real scholars as mentioned وَيَرَى الَّذِينَ أُوتُوا الْعِلْمَ الَّذِي أُنزِلَ إِلَيْكَ مِن رَّبِّكَ هُوَ الْحَقَّ وَيَهْدِي إِلَى صِرَاطِ الْعَزِيزِ الْحَمِيدِ 1330﴿سبأ/6﴾.

Therefore, this surah teaches that starting in the beginning one must be grateful to Allah ﷻ all of the time as mentioned مَا لَهُ الَّذِي لِلَّهِ الْحَمْدُ فِي السَّمَاوَاتِ وَمَا فِي الْأَرْضِ وَلَهُ الْحَمْدُ فِي الْآخِرَةِ وَهُوَ الْحَكِيمُ الْخَبِيرُ 1331﴿سبأ/1﴾.

Surah Fatir

[27-28]

أَلَمْ تَرَ أَنَّ اللَّهَ أَنزَلَ مِنَ السَّمَاء مَاء فَأَخْرَجْنَا بِهِ ثَمَرَاتٍ مُّخْتَلِفًا أَلْوَانُهَا وَمِنَ الْجِبَالِ جُدَدٌ بِيضٌ وَحُمْرٌ مُّخْتَلِفٌ أَلْوَانُهَا وَغَرَابِيبُ سُودٌ 1332﴿فاطر/27﴾ وَمِنَ النَّاسِ وَالدَّوَابِّ وَالْأَنْعَامِ مُخْتَلِفٌ أَلْوَانُهُ كَذَلِكَ إِنَّمَا يَخْشَى اللَّهَ مِنْ عِبَادِهِ الْعُلَمَاء إِنَّ اللَّهَ عَزِيزٌ غَفُورٌ 1333﴿فاطر/28﴾

يَا أَيُّهَا النَّاسُ إِنَّا خَلَقْنَاكُم مِّن ذَكَرٍ وَأُنثَى وَجَعَلْنَاكُمْ شُعُوبًا وَقَبَائِلَ لِتَعَارَفُوا إِنَّ أَكْرَمَكُمْ عِندَ اللَّهِ أَتْقَاكُمْ إِنَّ اللَّهَ عَلِيمٌ خَبِيرٌ 1334﴿الحجرات/13﴾

1329. But those who strive against Our verses [seeking] to cause failure—for them will be a painful punishment of foul nature.

1330. And those who have been given knowledge see that what is revealed to you from your Lord is the truth, and it guides to the path of the Exalted in Might, the Praiseworthy.

1331. [All] praise is [due] to Allah, to whom belongs whatever is in the heavens and whatever is in the earth, and to Him belongs [all] praise in the Hereafter. And He is the Wise, the Acquainted.

1332. Do you not see that Allah sends down rain from the sky, and We produce thereby fruits of varying colors? And in the mountains are tracts, white and red of varying shades and [some] extremely black.

1333. And among people and moving creatures and grazing livestock are various colors similarly. Only those fear Allah, from among His servants, who have knowledge. Indeed, Allah is Exalted in Might and Forgiving.

1334. O mankind, indeed We have created you from male and female and made you peoples and tribes that you may know one another. Indeed, the most noble of you in the sight of Allah is the most righteous of you. Indeed, Allah is Knowing and Acquainted.

It is very interesting to note in the above ayahs that Allah ﷻ mentions the colorful creation in nature as mentioned [1335]مُخْتَلِفًا أَلْوَانُهَا وَمِنَ الْجِبَالِ جُدَدٌ بِيضٌ وَحُمْرٌ مُخْتَلِفٌ أَلْوَانُهَا وَغَرَابِيبُ سُودٌ. Then, within this context, the colorful appearance of humans and animals are mentioned [1336]وَمِنَ النَّاسِ وَالدَّوَابِّ وَالْأَنْعَامِ مُخْتَلِفٌ أَلْوَانُهُ. Yet, it may be difficult for some to understand this diversity except the ones who have genuine and sincere knowledge as mentioned [1337]إِنَّمَا يَخْشَى اللَّهَ مِنْ عِبَادِهِ الْعُلَمَاء. The real purpose of this diversity is mentioned as[1338] لِتَعَارَفُوا in other words, to know, enjoy and celebrate this diversity, the diverse creation of Allah ﷻ. Yet, the noblest person for Allah ﷻ as mentioned in إِنَّ أَكْرَمَكُمْ عِنْدَ اللَّهِ is the person who has taqwa. Taqwa can be God consciousness, and the consciousness of accountability for all life renderings. For the elect, taqwa can mean even the accountability for one's thoughts.

[29]

إِنَّ الَّذِينَ يَتْلُونَ كِتَابَ اللَّهِ وَأَقَامُوا الصَّلَاةَ وَأَنْفَقُوا مِمَّا رَزَقْنَاهُمْ سِرًّا وَعَلَانِيَةً يَرْجُونَ تِجَارَةً لَّن تَبُورَ [1339]{فاطر/29}

أُولَئِكَ الَّذِينَ اشْتَرَوُا الضَّلَالَةَ بِالْهُدَى فَمَا رَبِحَت تِّجَارَتُهُمْ وَمَا كَانُوا مُهْتَدِينَ [1340]{البقرة/16}

It is interesting to analyze the above ayahs and other related parts of the Qurãn around the word to include the concept of business terms mentioned as تِجَارَةً[1341].

To illustrate this, a stock exchange is a market in which securities are bought and sold [12]. In this market, a bull market is the case of buying at stock at a lower price and selling it at a higher price at a later time. In this analogy, our existence is given to us at a very low price or

---

1335. We produce thereby fruits of varying colors? And in the mountains are tracts, white and red of varying shades and [some] extremely black.
1336. And among people and moving creatures and grazing livestock are various colors similarly.
1337. Only those fear Allah, from among His servants, who have knowledge.
1338. To know one another.
1339. Indeed, those who recite the Book of Allah and establish prayer and spend [in His cause] out of what We have provided them, secretly and publicly, [can] expect a transaction [i.e., profit] that will never perish—
1340. Those are the ones who have purchased error [in exchange] for guidance, so their transaction has brought no profit, nor were they guided.
1341. Transaction.

for free. Allah ﷻ buys the person's efforts for example as mentioned in the ayah يَتْلُونَ كِتَابَ اللَّهِ وَأَقَامُوا الصَّلَاةَ وَأَنفَقُوا مِمَّا رَزَقْنَاهُمْ سِرًّا وَعَلَانِيَةً [1342] for a high and no risk price mentioned as تِجَارَةً لَّن تَبُورَ [1343]. The opposite case is represented with اشْتَرَوُاْ الضَّلَالَةَ بِالْهُدَى فَمَا رَبِحَت تِّجَارَتُهُم [1344].

Another perspective in business engagements is that business entrepreneurs choose markets, societies, or governments where there is stability and security so that their businesses have the opportunity to grow, stabilize, and become established. It may not be wise to invest in a market where there is social chaos, instability, and insecurity. This can be called gambling as compared to good business practice. There can be a gain, but it is not predictable and it does not follow logic in the science of business.

As a side note, this is the difference between gambling and business. Gambling is based on chance and randomness. Business is based on logic, structure, and order. Gambling assumes darkness, unpredictability, chaos, and oppression. Business is based on reason, logic, fairness, ethics, security, and deterministic approaches or forecasting.

In a bigger picture, Allah ﷻ creates the entire universe with structure, stability, and order. Allah ﷻ maintains this order and security. As we think about earth in the context of space, it is very likely that meteors, bursting stars, and other effects in outer space could terminate the earth. Yet, Allah ﷻ maintains all of the order. Therefore, we refer to Allah ﷻ as Rabbul Alamin.

Then, as a default due to the Rahmah[1345] and Fadl[1346] of Allah ﷻ, the person is born and created by Allah ﷻ in a secure and safe business market to make his or her investment. This investment is as mentioned يَتْلُونَ كِتَابَ اللَّهِ وَأَقَامُوا الصَّلَاةَ وَأَنفَقُوا مِمَّا رَزَقْنَاهُمْ سِرًّا وَعَلَانِيَةً يَرْجُونَ تِجَارَةً لَّن تَبُورَ [1347]. Alhamdullilah, our job is not to establish or choose the place for our investments. Galaxies, stars, planets, earth and all of the creation serves

---

1342. Indeed, those who recite the Book of Allah and establish prayer and spend [in His cause] out of what We have provided them, secretly and publicly.

1343. A transaction [i.e., profit] that will never perish.

1344. The ones who have purchased error [in exchange] for guidance, so their transaction has brought no profit.

1345. Mercy.

1346. Favor.

1347. Those who recite the Book of Allah and establish prayer and spend [in His cause] out of what We have provided them, secretly and publicly, [can] expect a transaction [i.e., profit] that will never perish.

as our place of business transactions. They are already a secure and stable market, structure, or like a government established and maintained by Allah ﷻ. Now our part is to do our business either with the result of gain or loss, may Allah ﷻ protect us.

A business needs a secure market to invest in and to grow with safety. Allah ﷻ protects the universe so that we can do our business and grow.

23

Surah Saffat

[10]

إِلَّا مَنْ خَطِفَ الْخَطْفَةَ فَأَتْبَعَهُ شِهَابٌ ثَاقِبٌ 1348 {الصافات/10}

The above ayah is in the context of the shayatin/jinn trying to hear things related with the ʿalam of malakut[1349]. In this case, the phrase إِلَّا[1350] مَنْ خَطِفَ الْخَطْفَةَ can indicate the multifold of ibtilah or tests/trials for both jinn and humans. In other words, if Allah ﷻ wanted it to be so, with the Divine Mashiyyah[1351], they wouldn't be able to even approach the close proximity of the ʿalam of malakut. Yet, a limited enablement can be present in the perspectives of ibtilah, tests. It can be an ibtila, test/trial, for them who are trying to do something that they are prohibited to do. It can be an ibtilah for humans when these jinn bring what they hear with added false information to humans and they follow it as well,[1352] الله اعلم. On a side note, there is the case among the scholars that the interactions of jinn with the human realm and ʿalam of malakut has been limited by the nubbuwah of Rasulullah ﷺ.

1348. Except one who snatches [some words] by theft, but they are pursued by a burning flame, piercing [in brightness].
1349. World of angels.
1350. Except one who snatches [some words] by theft.
1351. Permission.
1352. Allah ﷻ knows best.

24

Surah Zumar

[42]

اللَّهُ يَتَوَفَّى الْأَنفُسَ حِينَ مَوْتِهَا وَالَّتِي لَمْ تَمُتْ فِي مَنَامِهَا فَيُمْسِكُ الَّتِي قَضَى عَلَيْهَا الْمَوْتَ وَيُرْسِلُ الْأُخْرَى إِلَى أَجَلٍ مُّسَمًّى إِنَّ فِي ذَلِكَ لَآيَاتٍ لِّقَوْمٍ يَتَفَكَّرُونَ [1353]{الزمر/42}

Death is one of the most intimidating phenomenon for the majority of humans. If one wants to know about the essence of death, this is one of the ayahs that indicate some highlights about death. The statement اللهُ[1354] يَتَوَفَّى الْأَنفُسَ حِينَ مَوْتِهَا وَالَّتِي لَمْ تَمُتْ فِي مَنَامِهَا can show that we are trained to die every day in our sleeps. In other words, our sleeping is similar to death. As the Prophet saw teaches us the dua for example: أَلْحَمْدُ لِلَّهِ[1355] [34] [22] اللَّهُمَّ بِكَ أَصْبَحْنَا وَبِكَ أَمْسَيْنَا وَبِكَ نَحْيَا وَبِكَ[1356]. or [35] [نَمُوتُ وَإِلَيْكَ النُّشُورُ]. Sometimes, waking up in a mood of agitation and sometimes waking up in a state of peace can symbolize different types of waking up from our graves as mentioned in Surah Yasin:

قَالُوا يَا وَيْلَنَا مَن بَعَثَنَا مِن مَّرْقَدِنَا هَذَا مَا وَعَدَ الرَّحْمَنُ وَصَدَقَ الْمُرْسَلُونَ [1357]{يس/52}

1353. Allah takes the souls at the time of their death, and those that do not die [He takes] during their sleep. Then He keeps those for which He has decreed death and releases the others for a specified term. Indeed in that are signs for a people who give thought.

1354. Allah takes the souls at the time of their death, and those that do not die [He takes] during their sleep.

1355. Praise be to god, who sent me peace altogether.

1356. O Allah, we enter the morning by you and we enter the evening by you. We live by you and we die by you and to you is gathering.

1357. They will say, "O woe to us! Who has raised us up from our sleeping place?" [The reply will be], "This is what the Most Merciful had promised, and the messengers told the truth."

25

Surah Jasiyah

[6-8]

{تِلْكَ آيَاتُ اللّهِ نَتْلُوهَا عَلَيْكَ بِالْحَقِّ فَبِأَيِّ حَدِيثٍ بَعْدَ اللّهِ وَآيَاتِهِ يُؤْمِنُونَ 1358 {الجاثية/6}
وَيْلٌ لِّكُلِّ أَفَّاكٍ أَثِيمٍ 1359 {الجاثية/7} يَسْمَعُ آيَاتِ اللّهِ تُتْلَى عَلَيْهِ ثُمَّ يُصِرُّ مُسْتَكْبِرًا كَأَن لَّمْ
يَسْمَعْهَا فَبَشِّرْهُ بِعَذَابٍ أَلِيمٍ 1360 {الجاثية/8}

It is interesting to analyze the above ayahs with the renderings of critical thinking, realities, and objective knowledge. Allah ﷻ mentioned that the knowledge presented and given by Allah ﷻ is the absolute truth as mentioned in تِلْكَ آيَاتُ اللّهِ نَتْلُوهَا عَلَيْكَ بِالْحَقِّ فَبِأَيِّ حَدِيثٍ بَعْدَ اللّهِ وَآيَاتِهِ يُؤْمِنُونَ[1361]. Yet, some can still engage in demagogy and try to show the opposite as mentioned with the word أَفَّاكٍ[1362]. This word is interesting. When there is the opposite case or direction of something, then this word أَفَّاكٍ can be used. In the contextual meanings, this word is translated as lie or slander because it is the opposite of a reality. The case of ifk with Aisha radiyallahu anha can be example of this. Then, the inner disposition of these people is explained further with يَسْمَعُ آيَاتِ اللّهِ تُتْلَى عَلَيْهِ ثُمَّ يُصِرُّ[1363] مُسْتَكْبِرًا كَأَن لَّمْ يَسْمَعْهَا. The realities are explained to them as mentioned with يَسْمَعُ آيَاتِ اللّهِ تُتْلَى عَلَيْهِ[1364] even though they want to make things upside down as mentioned with أَفَّاكٍ, and they want to continue with arrogance and blindness of stubbornness as mentioned يُصِرُّ مُسْتَكْبِرًا كَأَن لَّمْ يَسْمَعْهَا[1365]. It is interesting to note that the word يُصِرُّ[1366] is used in Arabic when donkeys look down and walk blindly and stubbornly without realizing where they are going.

1358. These are the verses of Allah which We recite to you in truth. Then in what statement after Allah and His verses will they believe?

1359. Woe to every sinful liar.

1360. Who hears the verses of Allah recited to him, then persists arrogantly as if he had not heard them. So give him tidings of a painful punishment.

1361. These are the verses of Allah which We recite to you in truth. Then in what statement after Allah and His verses will they believe?

1362. Sinful {person}.

1363. Who hears the verses of Allah recited to him, then persists arrogantly as if he had not heard them.

1364. Who hears the verses of Allah recited to him.

1365. Then persists arrogantly as if he had not heard them.

1366. Persists.

[24]

قُل لِّلَّذِينَ آمَنُوا يَغْفِرُوا لِلَّذِينَ لا يَرْجُونَ أَيَّامَ اللَّهِ لِيَجْزِيَ قَوْمًا بِما كَانُوا يَكْسِبُونَ
{الجاثية/14}1367

When one reviews the sabab nuzul of this ayah, in one narration, in the case of a nuzul of an ayah, one of the people from ahlu kitab mentions something very inappropriate and something not respectful about Allah ﷻ. When Omar ra hears this disrespectful attitude, he gets very upset and angry. Then, this ayah was revealed (Tafsir Sa'labi from Ibn Abbas ra) [36].

This can really give a lot of light to our interactions with non-Muslims about what we consider sacred and when they may not show respect towards those sacred things. The cartoon crisis and others can be some examples of these.

Here, Allah ﷻ mentions the very important point لا يَرْجُونَ أَيَّامَ[1368] اللَّهِ. This can mean that it is important for us as Muslims to understand and evaluate them from their own reference point and accordingly, one can still get upset and feel sad but we may need to move on as mentioned قُل لِّلَّذِينَ آمَنُوا يَغْفِرُوا[1369]. When one thinks about the time of Rasulullah ﷺ, there were a lot of sahabah who had previously given a very hard time to Rasulullah ﷺ and possibly, they were in similar dispositions as above. Yet, Rasulullah ﷺ implemented this teaching of قُل لِّلَّذِينَ آمَنُوا يَغْفِرُوا, and most of them became Muslim.

1367. Say, [O Muhammad], to those who have believed that they [should] forgive those who expect not the days of Allah [i.e., of His retribution] so that He may recompense a people for what they used to earn.
1368. Who expect not the days of Allah [i.e., of His retribution].
1369. Say, [O Muhammad], to those who have believed that they [should] forgive.

26

Surah Qaf

[22]

لَقَدْ كُنتَ فِي غَفْلَةٍ مِّنْ هَذَا فَكَشَفْنَا عَنكَ غِطَاءكَ فَبَصَرُكَ الْيَوْمَ حَدِيدٌ [1370]{ق/22}

In the ākhirah, the person has the certainty of seeing and understanding as mentioned in[1371] فَبَصَرُكَ الْيَوْمَ حَدِيد. This can be a case in this dunya for some people as well. Allah ﷻ can remove the veils of some individuals close to Allah ﷻ up to a degree in this dunya before they die as well, الله[1372] اعلم. Another case is presented as صُمٌّ بُكْمٌ عُمْيٌ فَهُمْ لاَ يَرْجِعُونَ [1373]{البقرة/18}. If they used their ability of seeing and take heed of what they see, have imān, and maintain this imān as mentioned with عُمْيٌ[1374], then they would not be munāfiq, الله اعلم.

27

Surah Rahman

[1-13]

الرَّحْمَنُ [1375]{الرحمن/1} عَلَّمَ الْقُرْآنَ [1376]{الرحمن/2} خَلَقَ الإِنسَانَ [1377]{الرحمن/3} عَلَّمَهُ الْبَيَانَ [1378]{الرحمن/4} الشَّمْسُ وَالْقَمَرُ بِحُسْبَانٍ [1379]{الرحمن/5} وَالنَّجْمُ وَالشَّجَرُ يَسْجُدَانِ [1380]{الرحمن/6} وَالسَّمَاء رَفَعَهَا وَوَضَعَ الْمِيزَانَ [1381]{الرحمن/7} أَلَّا تَطْغَوْا فِي الْمِيزَانِ [1382]{الرحمن/8} وَأَقِيمُوا الْوَزْنَ بِالْقِسْطِ وَلَا تُخْسِرُوا الْمِيزَانَ

1370. [It will be said], "You were certainly in unmindfulness of this, and We have removed from you your cover, so your sight, this Day, is sharp."
1371. So your sight, this Day, is sharp."
1372. Allah ﷻ knows best.
1373. Deaf, dumb and blind—so they will not return [to the right path].
1374. Blind.
1375. The most Merciful.
1376. Taught the Qurān.
1377. Created man.
1378. {And} taught him eloquence.
1379. The sun and the moon [move] by precise calculations.
1380. And the stars and the trees prostrate.
1381. And the heaven He raised and imposed the balance.
1382. That you not transgress within the balance.

{الرحمن/9} 1383 وَالْأَرْضَ وَضَعَهَا لِلْأَنَامِ 1384 {الرحمن/10} فِيهَا فَاكِهَةٌ وَالنَّخْلُ ذَاتُ الْأَكْمَامِ 1385 {الرحمن/11} وَالْحَبُّ ذُو الْعَصْفِ وَالرَّيْحَانُ 1386 {الرحمن/12} فَبِأَيِّ آلَاءِ رَبِّكُمَا تُكَذِّبَانِ 1387 {الرحمن/13}

In the descriptions of the ayahs of the Qurān, Allah ﷻ mentions different benefits of this perfection and the balance of this structure and order with the Rububiyah[1388] of Allah ﷻ.

Yes, as we talk constantly and incessantly about this structure and order in the universe, one can ask: Why it is important? Or, why it is important for me? The answer is very clear, yet we sometimes assume it or oversee it without clearly stating and locating our own selves with the answer.

If one asks, "Why is the structure and order in the universe important for me?" Then, the answer is, "Because I benefit from all of the structure and order. If there is no structure or order, everything is chaos. Everything is in destruction. There is no existence and there is no me. I don't exist. For me to exist, live, and maintain, I need a body, anatomical systems in my body such as a respiratory system, nervous system, circulatory system, excretion system, and others. I need an external environment or setting, a residence, earth, and universe to place my body in so that I can exist and live. If there is no structure and order in my body, then my existence in a perfect environment or earth may not mean much because I need to first maintain my body. Conversely, if I have a perfect body, then chaos in my external setting such as earth may not mean much because I may not exist due to the chaos."

In simpler terms, the person is in need of a perfect structure and order in order to exist and live. In other words, the person benefits fully from the perfection and structure in their own creation and in the universe. This is all from the Rububiyyah[1389] of Allah ﷻ.

In order to allude that humans constantly benefit from this structure and system of order, one can analyze the below ayahs in Surah Rahman:

1383. And establish weight in justice and do not make deficient the balance.
1384. And the earth He laid {out} for the creatures.
1385. Therein is fruit and palm trees having sheaths [of dates].
1386. And grain having husks and scented plants.
1387. So which of the favors of your lord would you deny.
1388. Lordship.
1389. Lordship.

الرَّحْمَنُ {الرحمن/1} عَلَّمَ الْقُرْآنَ {الرحمن/2} خَلَقَ الْإِنسَانَ {الرحمن/3} عَلَّمَهُ الْبَيَانَ {الرحمن/4} الشَّمْسُ وَالْقَمَرُ بِحُسْبَانٍ {الرحمن/5} وَالنَّجْمُ وَالشَّجَرُ يَسْجُدَانِ {الرحمن/6} وَالسَّمَاء رَفَعَهَا وَوَضَعَ الْمِيزَانَ {الرحمن/7} أَلَّا تَطْغَوْا فِي الْمِيزَانِ {الرحمن/8} وَأَقِيمُوا الْوَزْنَ بِالْقِسْطِ وَلَا تُخْسِرُوا الْمِيزَانَ {الرحمن/9} وَالْأَرْضَ وَضَعَهَا لِلْأَنَامِ {الرحمن/10} فِيهَا فَاكِهَةٌ وَالنَّخْلُ ذَاتُ الْأَكْمَامِ {الرحمن/11} وَالْحَبُّ ذُو الْعَصْفِ وَالرَّيْحَانُ {الرحمن/12} فَبِأَيِّ آلَاء رَبِّكُمَا تُكَذِّبَانِ {الرحمن/13}

One can realize 31 times the repetition of this expression " فَبِأَيِّ آلَاء رَبِّكُمَا تُكَذِّبَانِ {الرحمن/13} " in this surah. This teaching method can instill in the person the realization of this benefit that the person receives incessantly from the structure and order that Allah ﷻ created. In other words, this ayah constantly asks the person, "If you benefit from this structure, order, and ni'mahs[1390], then why do you deny?"

If one analyzes this repeated ayah, "Rabb" is used for Allah ﷻ to emphasize the Rububiyyah of Allah ﷻ. Yet, we don't realize this constant benefit we receive that is required for our existence and survival. We don't realize the benefit in this structure and order established by our Rabb, Allah ﷻ.

One can possibly realize why we need to say alhamdulillah at least 33 times after each prayer minimally five times each day.

28

Surah Mumtahina

[1]

If one reviews the surahs in this juz, Surah Mumtahina starts with يَا أَيُّهَا الَّذِينَ آمَنُوا لَا تَتَّخِذُوا عَدُوِّي وَعَدُوَّكُمْ أَوْلِيَاء تُلْقُونَ إِلَيْهِم بِالْمَوَدَّةِ وَقَدْ كَفَرُوا بِمَا جَاءكُم مِّنَ الْحَقِّ يُخْرِجُونَ الرَّسُولَ وَإِيَّاكُمْ أَن تُؤْمِنُوا بِاللَّهِ رَبِّكُمْ إِن كُنتُمْ خَرَجْتُمْ جِهَادًا فِي سَبِيلِي وَابْتِغَاء مَرْضَاتِي تُسِرُّونَ إِلَيْهِم بِالْمَوَدَّةِ وَأَنَا أَعْلَمُ بِمَا أَخْفَيْتُمْ وَمَا أَعْلَنتُمْ وَمَن يَفْعَلْهُ مِنكُمْ فَقَدْ ضَلَّ سَوَاء السَّبِيلِ [1391] {الممتحنة/1}. This ayah in the beginning of this Surah addresses

---

1390. Blessings.
1391. O you who have believed, do not take My enemies and your enemies as allies, extending to them affection while they have disbelieved in what came to you of the truth, having driven out the Prophet and yourselves [only] because you believe in Allah, your Lord. If you have come out for jihād [i.e., fighting or striving] in My cause and seeking means to My approval, [take them not as friends]. You confide to them affection [i.e., instruction], but I am most knowing of what you have concealed and what you have declared. And whoever does it among you has certainly strayed from the soundness of the way.

the believers about how to deal with different groups who are expected to appreciate and believe in the true teachings sent by Allah ﷻ through the Qurãn and Rasulullah ﷺ. These can be Christians, Jews, and munãfiqeen. Then, the following Surahs- Saff, Jumuah and Munãfiq- focus on each case respectively in detail with their issues.

Surah Saff

[6-8]

Surah Saff focuses on the case of Christians. For example,

وَإِذْ قَالَ عِيسَى ابْنُ مَرْيَمَ يَا بَنِي إِسْرَائِيلَ إِنِّي رَسُولُ اللَّهِ إِلَيْكُم مُّصَدِّقًا لِّمَا بَيْنَ يَدَيَّ مِنَ التَّوْرَاةِ وَمُبَشِّرًا بِرَسُولٍ يَأْتِي مِن بَعْدِي اسْمُهُ أَحْمَدُ فَلَمَّا جَاءهُم بِالْبَيِّنَاتِ قَالُوا هَذَا سِحْرٌ مُّبِينٌ {6/الصف}1392 وَمَنْ أَظْلَمُ مِمَّنِ افْتَرَى عَلَى اللَّهِ الْكَذِبَ وَهُوَ يُدْعَى إِلَى الْإِسْلَامِ وَاللَّهُ لَا يَهْدِي الْقَوْمَ الظَّالِمِينَ {7/الصف}1393 يُرِيدُونَ لِيُطْفِئُوا نُورَ اللَّهِ بِأَفْوَاهِهِمْ وَاللَّهُ مُتِمُّ نُورِهِ وَلَوْ كَرِهَ الْكَافِرُونَ {8/الصف}1394

These above ayahs are very critical. When one reviews the current Christian books, there are a lot of explicit mentionings of the Prophet saw referred to before by Isa as. For example, in United Methodist hymns that Christians constantly read, as in John: v. 14-15 where Jesus says, "My friend will come and teach similar teachings after me" [37]. One should review the original wordings. As one reviews the Christian theology, there are a lot of similarities with Islam which indicate these similar teachings indicated in their book by Isa as. Yet, although there are a lot of similarities, if a person puts urine in milk, they can't drink it. Similarly, in one's relationship with Allah ﷻ one cannot lie against Allah ﷻ and follow a false teaching as mentioned وَمَنْ أَظْلَمُ مِمَّنِ افْتَرَى عَلَى

1392. And [mention] when Jesus, the son of Mary, said, "O Children of Israel, indeed I am the messenger of Allah to you confirming what came before me of the Torah and bringing good tidings of a messenger to come after me, whose name is Ahmad." But when he came to them with clear evidences, they said, "This is obvious magic."

1393. And who is more unjust than one who invents about Allah untruth while he is being invited to Islām. And Allah does not guide the wrongdoing people.

1394. They want to extinguish the light of Allah with their mouths, but Allah will perfect His light, although the disbelievers dislike it.

اللَّهِ الْكَذِبَ وَهُوَ يُدْعَى إِلَى الْإِسْلَامِ وَاللَّهُ لَا يَهْدِي الْقَوْمَ الظَّالِمِينَ 1395 {الصف/7}. This lying or slandering in the matters of religion and tawhid can be worse then the above case of milk with that impurity.

There is a lot of effort today among different religious groups from ahlu kitab to conform these teachings to the contemporary spurting of inconsistent teachings about virtue, ethics, and morality. When one reviews these efforts through attending different Christian services and analyzing scholarship, they sound or look very modern and possible and plausible in their efforts of engaging their community. After a while, one can realize the real problem of the huge deviation in the original teachings of Isa as and other noble prophets. This change happened incrementally over time. Maybe it did not occur with fully evil intentions. Today, unfortunately, this deviation from the original teachings seems to be increasing. This can mean that with these modernizing (in reality, changing and altering) efforts of the original teachings- the authentic teachings in these scriptures of ahlu-kitab- may seem to fade away and can be totally lost. In other words, if there are some original teachings left today in these scriptures, they can also be lost with constant altering and adapting efforts. Yet, Allah ﷻ mentions that يُرِيدُونَ لِيُطْفِئُوا نُورَ اللَّهِ بِأَفْوَاهِهِمْ وَاللَّهُ مُتِمُّ نُورِهِ وَلَوْ كَرِهَ الْكَافِرُونَ 1396 {الصف/8} the revelation from Allah ﷻ will not disappear and people will not be able to make it disappear through alteration. The fading away will not happen but Allah ﷻ will complete the true and original teachings of this revival through the Qurān and the Prophet ﷺ.

Surah Jum'a

[5-7]

مَثَلُ الَّذِينَ حُمِّلُوا التَّوْرَاةَ ثُمَّ لَمْ يَحْمِلُوهَا كَمَثَلِ الْحِمَارِ يَحْمِلُ أَسْفَارًا بِئْسَ مَثَلُ الْقَوْمِ الَّذِينَ كَذَّبُوا بِآيَاتِ اللَّهِ وَاللَّهُ لَا يَهْدِي الْقَوْمَ الظَّالِمِينَ 1397 {الجمعة/5} قُلْ يَا أَيُّهَا الَّذِينَ هَادُوا إِن

1395. And who is more unjust than one who invents about Allah untruth while he is being invited to Islam. And Allah does not guide the wrongdoing people.

1396. They want to extinguish the light of Allah with their mouths, but Allah will perfect His light, although the disbelievers dislike it.

1397. The example of those who were entrusted with the Torah and then did not take it on is like that of a donkey who carries volumes [of books]. Wretched is the example of the people who deny the signs of Allah. And Allah does not guide the wrongdoing people.

زَعَمْتُمْ أَنَّكُمْ أَوْلِيَاء لِلَّهِ مِن دُونِ النَّاسِ فَتَمَنَّوُا الْمَوْتَ إِن كُنتُمْ صَادِقِينَ [1398] {الجمعة/6}
وَلَا يَتَمَنَّوْنَهُ أَبَدًا بِمَا قَدَّمَتْ أَيْدِيهِمْ وَاللَّهُ عَلِيمٌ بِالظَّالِمِينَ [1399] {الجمعة/7}

This surah takes the case of Jews after Surah Saff takes the case of Christians. One can review the religious scholarship especially among Muslims, Jews, and Christians. There are a lot of writings, critical analysis, and thinking. Yet, the ayahs [1400]مَثَلُ الَّذِينَ حُمِّلُوا التَّوْرَاةَ ثُمَّ لَمْ يَحْمِلُوهَا كَمَثَلِ الْحِمَارِ يَحْمِلُ أَسْفَارً allude to the fact that mere scholarship without practice and application in one's own life- I mean the scholar's or intellectual's life- will not have much value if the person does not benefit himself or herself with this acquired knowledge.

The above mistake or wrong rendering can be a practice among the ahlu-kitab, yet at the same time one can find groups among Muslims who identify themselves as Muslim yet go through very complicated analysis of the Qurān due to intellectual, academic, or motivational motives, yet they don't take heed or benefit their own selves. One should remember that the true effect of these sacred teachings with guidance is given by Allah ﷻ when the person shows the correct attitude of humbleness and humility with a respect to the salaf, predecessors, and canonized teachings at the same time, الله اعلم.

Surah Munāfiqun

As the continuation of the above surahs, one of the main themes of this surah is munāfiqeen as the name of the surah is given with this title. In this case, munāfiqeen can be composed of different groups. The categorization of munāfiqeen can be considered as the bottom of each group. In other words, they can have affiliation with ahlu-kitab or not. Yet, they have certain characteristics in common.

1398. Say, "O you who are Jews, if you claim that you are allies of Allah, excluding the [other] people, then wish for death, if you should be truthful."
1399. But they will not wish for it, ever, because of what their hands have put forth. And Allah is Knowing of the wrongdoers.
1400. The example of those who were entrusted with the Torah and then did not take it on is like that of a donkey who carries volumes [of books].

29

Surah Mulk

[1-4]

تَبَارَكَ الَّذِي بِيَدِهِ الْمُلْكُ وَهُوَ عَلَى كُلِّ شَيْءٍ قَدِيرٌ {الملك/1}1401 الَّذِي خَلَقَ الْمَوْتَ وَالْحَيَاةَ لِيَبْلُوَكُمْ أَيُّكُمْ أَحْسَنُ عَمَلًا وَهُوَ الْعَزِيزُ الْغَفُورُ 1402 {الملك/2} الَّذِي خَلَقَ سَبْعَ سَمَاوَاتٍ طِبَاقًا مَّا تَرَى فِي خَلْقِ الرَّحْمَنِ مِن تَفَاوُتٍ فَارْجِعِ الْبَصَرَ هَلْ تَرَى مِن فُطُورٍ 1403 {الملك/3} ثُمَّ ارْجِعِ الْبَصَرَ كَرَّتَيْنِ يَنقَلِبْ إِلَيْكَ الْبَصَرُ خَاسِئاً وَهُوَ حَسِيرٌ 1404 {الملك/4}

If one reviews the above ayahs and the similar ayahs such as أَأَنتُمْ أَشَدُّ خَلْقًا أَمِ السَّمَاء بَنَاهَا 1405 {النازعات/27}, one can realize fully again and again the 'Azamah[1406] of Allah ﷻ and our weakness or nothingness. In our current scientific terminologies related with astrophysics or astronomy, just the terms or quantities to express what is happening in space are a few simple and obvious examples of the 'Azamah of Allah ﷻ besides many cases. For example, instead of expressing the distance or time in meters, feet, hours, or days, the terminologies change to light years. A light year is defined as [5] "a unit of astronomical distance equivalent to the distance that light travels in one year, which is 9.4607×10^{12} km (nearly 6 trillion miles)." Then, when there are entities like galaxies and their related events, the quantity expressions are a billion light years or more.

If we look at quantities related with other parameters such as temperature, here the case for the sun is: [5] "The sun is a star of a type known as a G2 dwarf, a sphere of hydrogen and helium 870,000 miles (1.4 million km) in diameter that obtains its energy from nuclear fusion reactions in its interior, where the temperature is about 15 million°C. The surface is a little under 6,000°C." The human nomenclature of referring to the sun as "G2 dwarf" means that the sun is "a star of

---

1401. Blessed is He in whose hand is dominion, and He is over all things competent

1402. [He] who created death and life to test you [as to] which of you is best in deed—and He is the Exalted in Might, the Forgiving.

1403. [And] who created seven heavens in layers. You do not see in the creation of the Most Merciful any inconsistency. So return [your] vision [to the sky]; do you see any breaks?

1404. Then return [your] vision twice again. [Your] vision will return to you humbled while it is fatigued.

1405. Are you a more difficult creation or is the heaven? He [i.e., Allah] constructed it.

1406. Power.

relatively small size and low luminosity and temperature, including the majority of main sequence stars [5]." These are all a few examples of the macroscopic world that we try to understand with our terminologies.

In all of these mind-exploding cases, the 'Azamah[1407] of Allah ☬ is very clear and one can say تَبَارَكَ الَّذِي بِيَدِهِ الْمُلْكُ[1408]. At least to get a feeling of this 'azamah, there is an encouragement to understand the fields of science such as astronomy or astrophysics as mentioned in الَّذِي خَلَقَ[1409] سَبْعَ سَمَاوَاتٍ طِبَاقًا مَّا تَرَى فِي خَلْقِ الرَّحْمَنِ مِن تَفَاوُتٍ فَارْجِعِ الْبَصَرَ هَلْ تَرَى مِن فُطُورٍ. Yet, Allah ☬ mentions that in all of these renderings, when a person tries to understand them, they will have disabling, incapacitating, and debilitating effects on the person due to the 'Azam of Allah ☬ as mentioned ثُمَّ ارْجِعِ الْبَصَرَ كَرَّتَيْنِ يَنقَلِبْ إِلَيْكَ الْبَصَرُ خَاسِئًا وَهُوَ حَسِيرٌ[1410] {4/الملك}.

The word خَاسِئًا[1411] can indicate this effect if the person has the ability to observe and learn. Yet, to transform this effect of خَاسِئًا into the embodiment of خَاشِعًا[1412] as mentioned in لَوْ أَنزَلْنَا هَذَا الْقُرْآنَ عَلَى جَبَلٍ لَّرَأَيْتَهُ خَاشِعًا مُّتَصَدِّعًا مِّنْ خَشْيَةِ اللَّهِ وَتِلْكَ الْأَمْثَالُ نَضْرِبُهَا لِلنَّاسِ لَعَلَّهُمْ يَتَفَكَّرُونَ[1413] {21/الحشر}, one should accept these realities and submit to Allah ☬ fully. A scientist or a distinguished professor in these fields knowing them but still not accepting them can be considered lower than an inert mountain because even they know this and submit to Allah ☬ as mentioned in جَبَلٍ لَّرَأَيْتَهُ[1414] خَاشِعًا مُّتَصَدِّعًا مِّنْ خَشْيَةِ اللَّهِ.

After these engagements, one can try to realize some teachings of the ayah أَأَنتُمْ أَشَدُّ خَلْقًا أَمِ السَّمَاء بَنَاهَا[1415] {27/النازعات}.

1407. Power.

1408. Blessed is He in whose hand is dominion,

1409. [And] who created seven heavens in layers. You do not see in the creation of the Most Merciful any inconsistency. So return [your] vision [to the sky]; do you see any breaks?

1410. Then return [your] vision twice again. [Your] vision will return to you humbled while it is fatigued.

1411. Humbled.

1412. Fear.

1413. If We had sent down this Qurān upon a mountain, you would have seen it humbled and splitting from fear of Allah. And these examples We present to the people that perhaps they will give thought.

1414. A mountain, you would have seen it humbled and splitting from fear of Allah.

1415. Are you a more difficult creation or is the heaven? He [i.e., Allah] constructed it.

[15]

هُوَ الَّذِي جَعَلَ لَكُمُ الْأَرْضَ ذَلُولًا فَامْشُوا فِي مَنَاكِبِهَا وَكُلُوا مِن رِّزْقِهِ وَإِلَيْهِ النُّشُورُ
{الملك/15}[1416]

This ayah is super interesting and amazing. When one reviews the words in the scientific knowledge of approximately ~1500 years ago, the ayah may have meaning. Yet, when one analyzes this ayah today, it has an amazing opening.

The earth is moving with a few types of rotations. One way is around its own axis. The other way is around the sun. Yet with all of these constant, complex, and fast rotations and spins, we don't feel any of them. We walk on the earth as if the earth is staying still or flat as the earlier people interpreted in their scientific knowledge.

Today, physics and astronomy explain that the earth is experiencing fast, complex movement and rotations. Yet, there is a very delicate system of physics behind these motions that makes us still and stationary as explained by Newton. In this case, science explains the question of how.

At a higher level, this explanation of "how" inspires us to think the question about of "why" and then "who." In other words, the natural and social sciences with their established disciplines of explaining the "how" as the means serves to answer the next higher question of purpose, meaning, and goal with the question of "why" and "who."

In this regard, when one analyzes this ayah هُوَ الَّذِي جَعَلَ لَكُمُ الْأَرْضَ {الملك/15} [1417] وَإِلَيْهِ النُّشُورُ ذَلُولًا فَامْشُوا فِي مَنَاكِبِهَا وَكُلُوا مِن رِّزْقِهِ, then, the ayah mentions that, هُوَ [1418], Allah ﷻ is the One Who establishes this structure of the perfect balance and structure so that the person can witness the Rububiyyah of Allah ﷻ as the Care-Taker, Care-Giver, Sustainer and Upholder as mentioned with جَعَلَ لَكُمُ الْأَرْضَ ذَلُولًا فَامْشُوا فِي مَنَاكِبِهَا وَكُلُوا[1419] مِن رِّزْقِهِ. It is normally impossible but Allah ﷻ shows the possible and the miracle of this structure, systems, and order through the "means" of laws of physics, natural and social sciences.

1416. It is He who made the earth tame for you—so walk among its slopes and eat of His provision—and to Him is the resurrection.
1417. It is He who made the earth tame for you—so walk among its slopes and eat of His provision—and to Him is the resurrection.
1418. He.
1419. Made the earth tame for you—so walk among its slopes and eat of His provision.

Yet, this recognition is the purpose and goal and there is an accountability for this Rububiyyah[1420] of Allah ﷻ as mentioned وَإِلَيْهِ[1421] النُّشُورُ.

In other words, when science explains the 'how' in the universe as the means created and structured by Allah ﷻ, then, the person needs to take the next step of 'why' and 'who'. When the person knows and embodies this reality, 'ibadah or worship as the form of embodiment of appreciating Allah ﷻ, thanking Allah ﷻ and showing gratitude to Allah ﷻ becomes so natural, compulsive, and instinctive due to adoration, respect, and love.

Therefore, in Arabic language, the word 'Abd really means to adore something and then to follow and submit yourself. It is a wrong rendering in the translations when translated as "slave or worshipper especially when these words have some negative connotations in the Western world as the source of oppression.

[3-5]

مِّنَ اللهِ ذِي الْمَعَارِجِ [1422]{المعارج/3} تَعْرُجُ الْمَلَائِكَةُ وَالرُّوحُ إِلَيْهِ فِي يَوْمٍ كَانَ مِقْدَارُهُ خَمْسِينَ أَلْفَ سَنَةٍ [1423]{المعارج/4} فَاصْبِرْ صَبْرًا جَمِيلًا [1424]{المعارج/5}

Meeting with Allah ﷻ requires struggle, preparation, and cleansing oneself from the spiritual diseases. This takes time and patience. Although we don't know its true quality and quantity, but even archangels go through some type of process and preparation before they meet with Allah ﷻ as mentioned تَعْرُجُ الْمَلَائِكَةُ وَالرُّوحُ إِلَيْهِ فِي يَوْمٍ كَانَ مِقْدَارُهُ[1425] خَمْسِينَ أَلْفَ سَنَةٍ.

When a person wakes up in the morning after a nice sleep, he or she has energy and full focus about the important achievements of the day. The person is fully awake and fully focused. In this case, it is interesting to note that Musa as asks to meet with magicians in front of all of the public at the time of duha, the most focused and efficient time of the day,

---

1420. Lordship.
1421. And to Him is the resurrection.
1422. [It is] from Allah, owner of the ways of ascent.
1423. The angels and the Spirit [i.e., Gabriel] will ascend to Him during a Day the extent of which is fifty thousand years.
1424. So be patient with gracious patience.
1425. The angels and the Spirit [i.e., Gabriel] will ascend to Him during a Day the extent of which is fifty thousand years.

.قَالَ مَوْعِدُكُمْ يَوْمُ الزِّينَةِ وَأَن يُحْشَرَ النَّاسُ ضُحًى 1426 {طه/59} So that
people do not think that what they witnessed as miracles from Musa as
were illusions and so that they don't claim that they were sleepy at that
time.

Humans' preparation before they meet with Allah ﷻ can be the life
of barzah—a long, nice sleep or some prior preparations can make this
person ready before meeting with Allah ﷻ.

In the case of people who want to really meet with Allah ﷻ, they
may be eager to meet with Allah ﷻ but the person should have patience
as mentioned فَاصْبِرْ صَبْرًا جَمِيلًا1427.

Conversely, there may be others, but they may not be eager to meet
and be accountable as mentioned قَالُوا يَا وَيْلَنَا مَن بَعَثَنَا مِن مَّرْقَدِنَا هَذَا مَا وَعَدَ
الرَّحْمَنُ وَصَدَقَ الْمُرْسَلُونَ 1428{يس/52}

There can be people like shuhada, whom as soon as they die, they
may meet with Allah ﷻ. This can be due to their readiness in life in the
struggle of Allah ﷻ and dying in this state as a shahid.

There are many ways as mentioned مِّنَ اللَّهَ ذِي الْمَعَارِجِ 1429 to meet with
Allah ﷻ. Yet, Allah ﷻ is far from any type of boundaries, or human
thoughts as mentioned لَيْسَ كَمِثْلِهِ شَيْءٌ وَهُوَ السَّمِيعُ الْبَصِيرُ 1430{الشورى/11} فِيهِ.
These are the limits of language and humanness. If a person knows their
limit, then they don't pass their limits of adab. Similarly, one should have
adab in all of the ayahs and especially ayahs related with Allah ﷻ.

[10]

وَلَا يَسْأَلُ حَمِيمٌ حَمِيمًا1431 {المعارج/10}

One can analyze the word حَمِيمٌ1432 in the Qurān. As mentioned, [9]
قال ابن عباس الحميم القريب الذي يعصب له ، وعدم السؤال إنما كان لاشتغال كل أحد
بنفسه, this word can mean person's intimate friend. This intimate friend
cannot even ask the situation of their friend on that Day that everyone

---

1426. [Moses] said, "Your appointment is on the day of the festival when the people assemble
at mid-morning."
1427. So be patient with gracious patience.
1428. They will say, "O woe to us! Who has raised us up from our sleeping place?" [The reply
will be], "This is what the Most Merciful had promised, and the messengers told the truth."
1429. [It is] from Allah, owner of the ways of ascent.
1430. There is nothing like unto Him, and He is the Hearing, the Seeing.
1431. And no friend will ask [anything of] a friend.
1432. Friend.

is concerned about themselves. The similar meanings of this word can be found in different parts of the Qurān for example as:

وَلَا صَدِيقٍ حَمِيمٍ 1433{الشعراء/101}

وَأَنذِرْهُمْ يَوْمَ الْآزِفَةِ إِذِ الْقُلُوبُ لَدَى الْحَنَاجِرِ كَاظِمِينَ مَا لِلظَّالِمِينَ مِنْ حَمِيمٍ وَلَا شَفِيعٍ يُطَاعُ 1434{غافر/18}

وَلَا تَسْتَوِي الْحَسَنَةُ وَلَا السَّيِّئَةُ ادْفَعْ بِالَّتِي هِيَ أَحْسَنُ فَإِذَا الَّذِي بَيْنَكَ وَبَيْنَهُ عَدَاوَةٌ كَأَنَّهُ وَلِيٌّ حَمِيمٌ 1435{فصلت/34}

This word can also have different meanings as it is mentioned differently in the Qurān with the meaning of سخُن الذي يتطَايَر من غليانه as mentioned in the tafsir of tha'labi [36]. This meaning can be embedded for example:

كَغَلْيِ الْحَمِيمِ 1436{الدخان/46} خُذُوهُ فَاعْتِلُوهُ إِلَى سَوَاءِ الْجَحِيمِ 1437{الدخان/47} ثُمَّ صُبُّوا فَوْقَ رَأْسِهِ مِنْ عَذَابِ الْحَمِيمِ 1438{الدخان/48}

وَأَصْحَابُ الشِّمَالِ مَا أَصْحَابُ الشِّمَالِ 1439{الواقعة/41} فِي سَمُومٍ وَحَمِيمٍ 1440{الواقعة/42}

In this case, these types of punishments can be with this person constantly like an intimate friend, الله اعلم, may Allah ☾ protect all of us, Ameen.

1433. And not a devoted friend.
1434. And warn them, [O Muhammad], of the Approaching Day, when hearts are at the throats, filled [with distress]. For the wrongdoers there will be no devoted friend and no intercessor [who is] obeyed.
1435. And not equal are the good deed and the bad. Repel [evil] by that [deed] which is better; and thereupon, the one whom between you and him is enmity [will become] as though he was a devoted friend.
1436. Like the boiling of scalding water.
1437. [It will be commanded], "Seize him and drag him into the midst of the Hellfire.
1438. Then pour over his head from the torment of scalding water."
1439. And the companions of the left—what are the companions of the left?
1440. [They will be] in scorching fire and scalding water.

Surah Muzzammil

[5-7]¹⁴⁴¹

إِنَّا سَنُلْقِي عَلَيْكَ قَوْلًا ثَقِيلًا {المزمل/5} إِنَّ نَاشِئَةَ اللَّيْلِ هِيَ أَشَدُّ وَطْءًا وَأَقْوَمُ قِيلًا {المزمل/6} إِنَّ لَكَ فِي النَّهَارِ سَبْحًا طَوِيلًا {المزمل/7} وَاذْكُرِ اسْمَ رَبِّكَ وَتَبَتَّلْ إِلَيْهِ تَبْتِيلًا {المزمل/8}

Above is an interesting set of ayahs, for the ones who are involved with the spiritual care of others. Allah ﷻ is directly telling the Prophet Muhammad to take care of himself in his relationship with Allah ﷻ. The amount of work can overwhelm the person as mentioned قَوْلًا ثَقِيلًا¹⁴⁴², a heavy message meaning the responsibility of relating the message to others. Yet, this type of work necessitates charging oneself especially at nights in solitude with Allah ﷻ. The verse continues and mentions that in the daytime, there are a lot of engagements and preoccupation of the person with other things. Therefore, one should turn with the dhikr, remembrance of Allah, and turn to Allah with full focus before helping others.

Surah Al-Insan

[19]

وَيَطُوفُ عَلَيْهِمْ وِلْدَانٌ مُّخَلَّدُونَ إِذَا رَأَيْتَهُمْ حَسِبْتَهُمْ لُؤْلُؤًا مَّنثُورًا¹⁴⁴³ {الإنسان/19}

In the above ayah, the word وِلْدَانٌ¹⁴⁴⁴ is important to contextualize. When a person has a few children at different stages of developmental changes, he or she can realize in the growth of their children, that there can be an age at which their children are at the peak in terms of their sweetness, purity, naturalness, sincerity, and innate traits. The parents during these years especially enjoy spending time with their children.

1441. In The Name of God, The Most Gracious, The Dispenser of Grace: (5) Behold, We shall bestow upon thee a weighty message (6)[and,]verily,the hours of night the mind most strongly and speak with the clearest voice, (7)whereas by day a long chain of doings is thy portion. (8) But [whether by night or by day,] remember thy Sustainer's name, and devote thyself unto Him with utter devotion.
1442. A weighty message.
1443. There will circulate among them young boys made eternal. When you see them, you would think them [as beautiful as] scattered pearls.
1444. Young boys.

After the child loses these traits of sweetness and challenges the parents with disrespect, attitude, and arrogance, the person misses the old days when the children were so sweet, natural, and sincere. Some parents may wish in those difficult times and years with their children that the children stayed as sweet as they used to be and did not grow. These years can be around the toddler years for some people. In this case, the word وِلْدَانٌ can indicate this unchanged sweet interaction of the children with the person in the ākhirah, in the Jannah, اللهم اجعلنا منهم. امين[1445].

The same الْوِلْدَان who can be a source of happiness in this dunya and in the ākhirah, can be in much agitation due to the heaviness and seriousness of the Day of Judgment or the Day of Qiyamah, as mentioned فَكَيْفَ تَتَّقُونَ إِن كَفَرْتُمْ يَوْمًا يَجْعَلُ الْوِلْدَانَ شِيبًا [1446]{المزمل/17}, May Allah ﷻ protect us, Ameen.

30

Surah Bayyinah

[5]

وَمَا أُمِرُوا إِلَّا لِيَعْبُدُوا اللَّهَ مُخْلِصِينَ لَهُ الدِّينَ حُنَفَاءَ وَيُقِيمُوا الصَّلَاةَ وَيُؤْتُوا الزَّكَاةَ وَذَلِكَ دِينُ الْقَيِّمَةِ [1447]{البينة/5}

In this regard of the above ayah, the essence of oneness in I'badah is reminded with the expression[1448] لِيَعْبُدُوا اللَّهَ مُخْلِصِينَ لَهُ الدِّينَ حُنَفَاءَ opposite to its problematic approaches of multiplicity as implied by trinity. Although the concepts of prayers, and charity can be there in Christianity and other people of book, the required plug-in or updates are essential to have tawhid as mentioned لِيَعْبُدُوا اللَّهَ مُخْلِصِينَ لَهُ الدِّينَ حُنَفَاءَ وَيُقِيمُوا الصَّلَاةَ[1449] وَيُؤْتُوا الزَّكَاةَ.

1445. Oh Allah ﷻ, make us from amongst them.
1446. Then how can you fear, if you disbelieve, a Day that will make the children white-haired?
1447. And they were not commanded except to worship Allah, [being] sincere to Him in religion, inclining to truth, and to establish prayer and to give zakāh. And that is the correct religion.
1448. To worship Allah, [being] sincere to Him in religion, inclining to truth.
1449. To worship Allah, [being] sincere to Him in religion, inclining to truth, and to establish prayer and to give zakāh.

In this regard, the expression دِينُ الْقَيِّمَةِ[1450] can allude to this unchanging teaching of Allah ﷻ since the beginning of the creation for all humans through all of the prophets, messengers, and scriptures as sent by Allah ﷻ. The word الْقَيِّمَةِ[1451] can indicate this continuity in this unchanging teaching. Therefore, if one wants to identify similarities and commonalities among the religions, tawhid is the one that can establish this commonality as mentioned here إِلَّا لِيَعْبُدُوا اللَّهَ مُخْلِصِينَ لَهُ الدِّينَ حُنَفَاء[1452] or as mentioned in: قُلْ يَا أَهْلَ الْكِتَابِ تَعَالَوْاْ إِلَى كَلَمَةٍ سَوَاء بَيْنَنَا وَبَيْنَكُمْ أَلاَّ نَعْبُدَ إِلاَّ اللَّهَ وَلاَ نُشْرِكَ بِهِ شَيْئًا وَلاَ يَتَّخِذَ بَعْضُنَا بَعْضاً أَرْبَاباً مِّن دُونِ اللَّهِ فَإِن تَوَلَّوْاْ فَقُولُواْ اشْهَدُواْ بِأَنَّا مُسْلِمُونَ {آل عمران/64}[1453].

Therefore, today's language of religious engagement used by different institutionalized religions such as Judaism, Christianity, Islam, Buddhism, Hinduism and non-institutionalized religions such as spirituality, mysticism, and others can come together in a similar shared language of tawhid through different tools experienced in dedication, open-mindedness, devotion and practice. In this regard, they can have a similar and common language about the One and Unique Creator, Allah ﷻ as God, Elohim, Adonai, the One, and with other beautiful and perfect Names and Attributes of Allah ﷻ.

In this regard, tawhid has been the only unification or string theory for the true and genuine reality that can unify us and minimize our conflicts.

1450. Correct religion.
1451. Correct.
1452. Except to worship Allah, [being] sincere to Him in religion, inclining to truth.
1453. Say, "O People of the Scripture, come to a word that is equitable between us and you—that we will not worship except Allah and not associate anything with Him and not take one another as lords instead of Allah." But if they turn away, then say, "Bear witness that we are Muslims [submitting to Him]."

Surah Mau'n[1454]

أَرَأَيْتَ الَّذِي يُكَذِّبُ بِالدِّينِ {الماعون/1} فَذَلِكَ الَّذِي يَدُعُّ الْيَتِيمَ {الماعون/2} وَلَا يَحُضُّ عَلَى طَعَامِ الْمِسْكِينِ {الماعون/3} فَوَيْلٌ لِّلْمُصَلِّينَ {الماعون/4} الَّذِينَ هُمْ عَن صَلَاتِهِمْ سَاهُونَ {الماعون/5} الَّذِينَ هُمْ يُرَاؤُونَ {الماعون/6} وَيَمْنَعُونَ الْمَاعُونَ {الماعون/7}

One of the approaches to reading and benefitting from the Qurān is that if one wants or doesn't want something to happen, the person can read the words, expressions, ayahs, or surahs related with it. For example, in this case, if a person wants to concentrate on their Salah, then they can read this surah with the intention of not being heedless as one is praying their salah. The two ayahs فَوَيْلٌ لِّلْمُصَلِّينَ {الماعون/4} [1455] الَّذِينَ هُمْ عَن صَلَاتِهِمْ سَاهُونَ {الماعون/5} [1456] can especially allude to this, Allahu A'lam.

Surah Nasr

Everyone can be on a mission in the world in one's life. As Ibn Abbas ra was asked about the meaning of this surah [7], he mentioned that this surah indicated the approaching demise of Rasulullah ﷺ because the Rasulullah ﷺ's mission was over. Similarly, all of us can have a mission. When we seem to fulfill it inshAllah, we can say, "Oh Allah, we want to meet with You," as the Prophet ﷺ said, "Mala'ul a'la."

Similar to the previous discussion above, it is a common practice to read this surah due to its theme for any openings, success, or achievement-related engagements, الله اعلم.

1454. Have you seen the one who denies the Recompense?
For that is the one that drives away the orphan.
And does not encourage the feeding of the poor.
So woe to those who pray.
[But] who are heedless of their prayer.
Those who make show [of their deeds].
And withhold [simple] assistance.
So woe to those who pray.
[But] who are heedless of their prayer.
1455. So woe to those who pray.
1456. [But] who are heedless of their prayer.

Surah Masad

تَبَّتْ يَدَا أَبِي لَهَبٍ وَتَبَّ 1457{المسد/1} مَا أَغْنَى عَنْهُ مَالُهُ وَمَا كَسَبَ 1458{المسد/2}
سَيَصْلَى نَارًا ذَاتَ لَهَبٍ 1459{المسد/3} وَامْرَأَتُهُ حَمَّالَةَ الْحَطَبِ 1460{المسد/4} فِي جِيدِهَا
حَبْلٌ مِّن مَّسَدٍ 1461{المسد/5}

One can ask the hikmah that out of all people with their engagement of evil-doing to Rasulullah ﷺ: Why is only his uncle mentioned as a separate surah covering this topic? This surah could have been about Abu Jahil. Or, it could have mentioned others similar to Abu Lahab, but when we don't realize our position in our reference to our position, then the fall can be more deadly than to others.

Shaytan did not realize his position while being with angels and interacting and witnessing the Divine breezes, and his spiritual fall was the highest as mentioned: فَسَجَدَ الْمَلَائِكَةُ كُلُّهُمْ أَجْمَعُونَ 1462{ص/73} إِلَّا إِبْلِيسَ اسْتَكْبَرَ
وَكَانَ مِنَ الْكَافِرِينَ 1463{ص/74} قَالَ يَا إِبْلِيسُ مَا مَنَعَكَ أَن تَسْجُدَ لِمَا خَلَقْتُ بِيَدَيَّ أَسْتَكْبَرْتَ أَمْ
كُنتَ مِنَ الْعَالِينَ 1464{ص/75} قَالَ أَنَا خَيْرٌ مِّنْهُ خَلَقْتَنِي مِن نَّارٍ وَخَلَقْتَهُ مِن طِينٍ 1465{ص/76}
قَالَ فَاخْرُجْ مِنْهَا فَإِنَّكَ رَجِيمٌ 1466{ص/77} وَإِنَّ عَلَيْكَ لَعْنَتِي إِلَى يَوْمِ الدِّينِ 1467{ص/78}

Nuh's as wife and son did not realize their position in reference to one of the ulul azm Prophets of Allah ﷻ, although they witnessed the piety and virtue in their close time spent with Nuh as. Then they had a steep spiritual fall and this fall has been repeatedly mentioned in the Qurān. This was a cause of a very steep fall for them, yet it was a trial and test to increase the level of this prophet as.

When Lut's as wife did not realize her position in reference to one of the prophets of Allah ﷻ, although she witnessed the piety and virtue in her close time spent with Lut as, then she had a steep spiritual fall and her fall is repeatedly mentioned in the Qurān. This was a cause of

---

1457. May the hands of Abu Lahab be ruined, and ruined is he.
1458. His wealth will not avail him or that which he gained.
1459. He will [enter to] burn in a fire of [blazing] flames.
1460. And his wife [as well]- the carrier of firewood.
1461. Around her neck is a rope of [twisted] fiber.
1462. So the angels prostrated—all of them entirely.
1463. Except Iblees; he was arrogant and became among the disbelievers.
1464. [Allah] said, "O Iblees, what prevented you from prostrating to that which I created with My hands? Were you arrogant [then], or were you [already] among the haughty?"
1465. He said, "I am better than him. You created me from fire and created him from clay."
1466. [Allah] said, "Then get out of it [i.e., Paradise], for indeed, you are expelled.
1467. And indeed, upon you is My curse until the Day of Recompense."

a very steep fall for her, yet it was a trial and test to increase the level of this prophet as.

These are mentioned as

ضَرَبَ اللَّهُ مَثَلًا لِّلَّذِينَ كَفَرُوا امْرَأَةَ نُوحٍ وَامْرَأَةَ لُوطٍ كَانَتَا تَحْتَ عَبْدَيْنِ مِنْ عِبَادِنَا صَالِحَيْنِ فَخَانَتَاهُمَا فَلَمْ يُغْنِيَا عَنْهُمَا مِنَ اللَّهِ شَيْئًا وَقِيلَ ادْخُلَا النَّارَ مَعَ الدَّاخِلِينَ 1468 {التحريم/10}

قَالَ يَا نُوحُ إِنَّهُ لَيْسَ مِنْ أَهْلِكَ إِنَّهُ عَمَلٌ غَيْرُ صَالِحٍ فَلَا تَسْأَلْنِ مَا لَيْسَ لَكَ بِهِ عِلْمٌ إِنِّي أَعِظُكَ أَنْ تَكُونَ مِنَ الْجَاهِلِينَ 1469 {هود/46}

When Abu Lahab did not realize his position in reference to Rasulullah ﷺ, as he witnessed the upbringing of Rasulullah ﷺ, he saw and witnessed everything, then his fall was mentioned in the Qurān as a separate surah. The miracles, clarity, and obviousness of these miracles was much clearer for Rasulullah ﷺ as compared to others. Yet, when Abu Lahab did not accept this and he followed the group identity dynamics due to arrogance, then his case was mentioned as a separate surah.

This was the cause of a very spiritual steep fall for all of them, yet it was a trial and test to increase the level of these prophets of Allah ﷺ and especially with close family members. When the tests and trials come from others, it can be very difficult. Yet, when these trials are present from close kin and family members, their effect of difficulty can be much higher.

In this regard, Rasulullah ﷺ went through the trials and difficulties of all the prophets and in a much more extensive quantity and quality.

On another level, the people who are holding certain levels and positions in their religiosity as role models for others, their family members can fall steeper spiritually than others, May Allah ﷺ protect us. After everything they witness, sometimes they still follow others. Yet, this can be another trial and test to increase the level of these friends of Allah ﷺ (awliyaullah).

1468. Allah presents an example of those who disbelieved: the wife of Noah and the wife of Lot. They were under two of Our righteous servants but betrayed them, so they [i.e., those prophets] did not avail them from Allah at all, and it was said, "Enter the Fire with those who enter."
1469. He said, "O Noah, indeed he is not of your family; indeed, he is [one whose] work was other than righteous, so ask Me not for that about which you have no knowledge. Indeed, I advise you, lest you be among the ignorant."

BIBLIOGRAPHY

1. Vahide, S. *The Collection of Light* . s.l.: ihlas nur publication, 2001.
2. Sirhindi, Ahmad. *Maktubat Imam Rabbani Shaykh Ahmad Sirhindi Faruqi*. s.l.: Maktabah Mujaddidiyah (www.maktabah.org), 2008.
3. Al-Bukhari, M. *The translation of the meanings of Sahih Al-Bukhari*. s.l.: Kazi Publications, 1986.
4. Demirci, Muhsin. *Tefsir Tarihi (History of Exegesis of Quran)*. Istanbul: ifav, 2010. pp. 34–38.
5. As-Suyuti, Jalal ad-Din. *Gateway to the Qur'anic Sciences*. s.l.: Turath Publishing, 2017.
6. Kumek, Y. *The Noble Quran: Selected Passages From Al-Quran Al-Kareem With Interpreted Meanings*. Buffalo, New York: Medina House Publishing, 2020.
7. Kumek, Yunus J. *Practical Mysticism: Sufi Journeys of Heart and Mind*. Dubuque: Kendall Hunt, 2018.
8. Razi, M. *Mafatih al-Ghayb known as al-Tafsir al-Kabir*. Cairo: Dar Ibya al-Kutub al-Bahiyya, 1172.
9. Muslim, A. *Sahih Muslim (translated by Siddiqui, A.)*. s.l.: Peace Vision, 1972.
10. Al-Ghazali, M. *Ihya 'Ulum al-Din* . s.l.: Dar al-Fikr, 2004.
11. Kasir, Ibn. *Tafsir al-Qur'an al-Azim*. Beirut: Dar al-Ilm, 1982.
12. Bukhari, Muhammad Ibn Ismail. *Moral Teachings of Islam: Prophetic Traditions from Al-Adab Al-mufrad*. s.l.: Rowman Altamira, 2003.
13. Taftazani, At. *Sharhu Taftazani*. p. 69.
14. Aristotle. *Aristotle's Metaphysics*.
15. Kumek, Yunus. *Revealing Pearls and Diamonds: Selected Duas of Rasulullah saw*. s.l.: Medina House Publishing, 2019.
16. Arabi, Ibn. *Al Futuhat Al Makkiya*. s.l.: Dar Al-Kotob Al-Ilmiyah.
17. Raymond D. Berendt, Edith L. R. Corliss, Morris S. Ojalvo. *Quieting A Practical Guide to Noise Control*. s.l.: University Press of the Pacific, 2000. pp. 1–2.

18. Dawud, Abu (Sulaiman bin Ash'ath). *Sunan Abu Dawud.* riyadh: Darussalam, 2008.

19. Laney, Marti Olsen. *The Introvert Advantage: How to Thrive in an Extrovert World.* s.l.: Workman Publishing Company, 2002. p. 41.

20. Majah, Ibn. *Sunan Ibn Majah.* s.l.: Darus-Salam, 2007.

21. G., Muhammad F. *Ijaz of the Quran .* s.l.: Nile, 2008.

22. Oxford, University Press. Oxford Dictionaries. [Online] 2016. [Cited: 2016.] http://www.oxforddictionaries.com/us/definition/american_english/say.

23. Hanbal, Ahmad B. *Musnad Imam Ahmad Ibn Hanbal.* s.l.: Dar-Us-Salam Publications, 2012.

24. Shafi, Muhammad. *Ma'ariful Qur'an.* s.l.: maktaba-e Darul-Uloom, 2005. pp. 129–131. Vol. 1.

25. Al-Marghinani, Burhan Uddin Abu Al-Hasan Ali Ibn Abu Bakr Ibn Abdul Jaleel Ar-Rashidani. *Al Hidayah Sharh Bidayat Al-Mubtadi.* Beirut, Lebanon: Dar Al Hadith.

26. Al-Wahidi, Imam Ali Ibn Ahmad. *Alwajizu fi tafsiriil kitabil Aziz.* s.l.: Darul Qalam & Dar Shamia.

27. Tirmizi, M. *Jami At-Tirmizi.* s.l.: Dar-us-Salam, 2007.

28. Al-Hakim. *Mustadrak.* p. 1/612.

29. Hibban, Ibn. *As-Sahih.* pp. 4/612, 6/411.

30. Bolelli, Nusraddin. *Balagatul Arabiyya.* s.l.: ifav, 2009.

31. Ibrahim Kalin, John L. Esposito. *Islamophobia The Challenge of Pluralism in the 21st Century.* s.l.: Oxford University Press, USA, 2011. p. 192.

32. Maturidi, Abu Mansur Al. *Ta'wilat Ahl As Sunnah.* s.l.: Dar al Kotob al ilmiyyah,.

33. Oxford, University Press. Oxford Dictionaries. [Online] 2016. [Cited: 2016.] http://www.oxforddictionaries.com/us/definition/american_english/.

34. Thalabi, Abu Ishaq. *Al-Kashaf wal bayab.* Beirut: DKI, 2004.

35. Mojaddedi, Jawid. *The Wiley Blackwell Companion to the Qur'an.* s.l.: Wiley, 2017. p. 120.

36. AbdulFadl, Muhammad. *Lectures on Quran.* 2019.

37. Baghawi, Husayn. *Tafsir al-Baghawi al-musamma Ma'alim al-tanzil.* Bayrut: Dar al-Ma'rifah, 1987.

38. Ehrman, Bart D. *Misquoting Jesus The Story Behind Who Changed the Bible and Why.* s.l.: HarperOne, 2009.

39. Janney, Rebecca Price. *Then Comes Marriage? A Cultural History of the American Family.* s.l.: Moody Publishers, 2010. p. 108.
40. Rebeca Mejía-Arauz, Barbara Rogoff. *Children Learn by Observing and Contributing to Family and Community Endeavors: A Cultural Paradigm.* s.l.: Elsevier Science, 2015. p. 54.
41. Cox, R.R. *Schutz's Theory of Relevance: A Phenomenological Critique.* s.l.: Springer Netherlands, 2012.
42. O., Dr. Meggie. *LBGT issue from the Perspective of a ObGyn Specialist.* [interv.] Y. Kumek. March 17, 2016.
43. Zamakhshari, Abu Kassim. *Tafsir al-Kashaf.* Beirut: DKI, .
44. 'Imadi, Abu Al-Su'Ud Muhammad Ibn Muhammad Ibn Mus. *Tafsir abi al-su'ud, aw, irshad al-'aql al-salim ila mazaya al-qur'an al-karim.* s.l.: Turath For Solutions, 2013.
45. al-Ghazali, Abu Hamid. *The Quran and Its Exegesis (translation by Helmut Gatie).* s.l.: Oxford: Oneworld, 1996.
46. *Psychology and Light: The Effects of Light on Mental Functions.* Muensterberg, Hugo. 1916, Scientific American, Vol. 82, p. 406.
47. Shaykh Muhammad Nazim Adil Al-Haqqani, Shaykh Muhammad Hisham Kabbani. *Muhammad, the Messenger of Islam His Life & Prophecy.* s.l.: Islamic Supreme Council of America, 2002. p. 141.
48. Nasafi, I. *Tafsirul Nasafi.*
49. Ma'lūf, Luwīs. *Al Munjid Arabic Dictionary.* s.l.: Dar Al mashriq, 2000.
50. Shushmaruk, Peter. *Magnetic Universe.* s.l.: Lulu.com. p. 62.
51. Hauck, Dennis William. *The Complete Idiot's Guide to Alchemy.* s.l.: Alpha Books, 2008. p. 201.
52. Bizony, Piers. *How to Build Your Own Spaceship The Science of Personal Space Travel.* 2009. p. chapter 3.
53. *Surah Abasa.* Yener, M. s.l.: New Hope.
54. Pinna, Simon de. *Chemical Reactions.* s.l.: Gareth Stevens Pub. p. 32.

AUTHOR BIO

Dr. Kumek had classical training in Islamic sciences from the respected Shuyûqh/Teachers of Turkey, India, Egypt, Yemen, Somalia, Morocco, Sudan, and the United States. He stayed and studied classical Islamic sciences in Egypt and Turkey as well.

In his Western training, education and teaching experience, Dr. Kumek has acted as the religious studies coordinator at State University of New York (SUNY) Buffalo State and taught undergraduate and graduate courses in religious studies at SUNY at Buffalo State, Niagara University, Daemen College and Harvard Divinity School. Dr. Kumek also pursued doctorate degree in physics at SUNY at Buffalo published academic papers in the areas of quantum physics and medical physics. Then, he decided to engage with the world of social sciences through social anthropology, education, and cultural anthropology in his doctorate studies and subsequently, spent a few years as a research associate in the anthropology department of the same university and subsequently, completed a postdoctoral fellowship at Harvard Divinity school. Some of his book titles include sociology through religion, religious literacy through ethnography, selected passages from the Qurãn, selected passages from the Hadith (titled as Rasulullah ﷺ) and selected prayers of the Prophet Muhammad ﷺ (titled as Pearls and Diamonds). Dr. M. Yunus Kumek is currently teaching on Muslim Ministry and Spiritual Care at Harvard Divinity School.

ACKNOWLEDGMENTS

I would like to thank all my unnamed teachers, friends, and students for their input, ideas, suggestions, help, and support during and before the preparation of this book.

I would like to thank Dr. David Banks, faculty of the Department of Anthropology, State University of New York (SUNY), Sister Toni Hajdaj, Sister Umm Aisha, Dr. AbdulAhad, Br. Ali Rifat and His wife Sister Yildiz at-Turki, Sheikh Dr. Omar of Maryland al-Hindi, Sheikh Tamer of Buffalo, and Sheikh Ali of Hartford Seminary, Sisters Asya Hamad, Amina Osman, and Fatima Samrodia of Darul-Ulum Madania of Buffalo, Mufti Hussain Memon of Darul-Ulum Canada and Imam Khalil Qadri of Islamic Center of Niagara Frontier (ISNF) for all their editing, suggestions and comments.

I want to also thank the team of Medina House Publishing in all their preparations and efforts at all stages of this book especially Br. Murat, Br. Khalid (Halit), Br. Mehmet (Matt) and Sister Karen.

Lastly, I would like to thank all of my family members for their patience with me during the preparation of this book.

We ask Allah ﷻ to accept all our efforts with the Divine Karam, Fadl, and Grace but not with our faulty and limited efforts deeming rejection. اللَّهُمَّ صلِّ عَلى سَيِّدِناَ وَ حَبِيْبَنَا وَ مَوْلَانَا مُحَمَّد.

Index

www.ingramcontent.com/pod-product-compliance
Lightning Source LLC
Chambersburg PA
CBHW031043110426
42740CB00048B/819